THE
ORGANIZATION
OF THE
ENGLISH CUSTOMS SYSTEM
1696–1786

THE ORGANIZATION OF THE ENGLISH CUSTOMS SYSTEM
1696 - 1786

BY

ELIZABETH EVELYNOLA HOON

With a new introduction by
Rupert C. Jarvis

AUGUSTUS M. KELLEY PUBLISHERS
Clifton, New Jersey 07012

7153 4182 0

THIS BOOK WAS ORIGINALLY PUBLISHED IN THE
UNITED STATES OF AMERICA BY D. APPLETON-CENTURY
COMPANY INCORPORATED, SUPPORTED BY A FUND CONTRIBUTED
TO THE AMERICAN HISTORICAL ASSOCIATION BY THE
CARNEGIE CORPORATION OF NEW YORK

© NEW INTRODUCTION BY
RUPERT C. JARVIS 1968

Published in the U. S. A. by
AUGUSTUS M. KELLEY, PUBLISHERS
Clifton, New Jersey

PRINTED IN GREAT BRITAIN BY
LATIMER TREND & COMPANY LIMITED WHITSTABLE
FOR DAVID & CHARLES (PUBLISHERS) LIMITED
SOUTH DEVON HOUSE RAILWAY STATION
NEWTON ABBOT DEVON

TO MY MOTHER AND FATHER

CRITICAL HISTORICAL INTRODUCTION

THIS WORK sets out to be primarily a full analytical description of the British customs organization in the eighteenth century: a detailed account of a particular historical phase of an elaborate and ancient fiscal administration. Deliberately divorced from the broader questions of economic, fiscal and mercantile policy, it is a study in eighteenth-century institutional history. The author makes it clear in the first sentence of her preface that initially she had set out on an altogether more modest exercise, an account of customs abuses in the tobacco trade in the first third of the century and their effect upon Virginia and Maryland. Early in the course of this study, however, she realised that she would be seriously handicapped by the lack of any published work providing a detailed description of the very complex customs service. She therefore decided to furnish such a guide.

Before long Dr Hoon became aware of the magnitude of her task. She found that almost all the headquarter records of the eighteenth-century customs service had been destroyed in the fire in the London Custom House in 1814. In the absence of the unified integral comprehensive records of the central administration, her whole work therefore had to be pieced together from scattered sources of which the following are the most important: firstly, the various communications (where they survive) sent out by the Board of Customs, such as letters and orders to the various outposts and the copies of the reports, returns, petitions and other missives in the opposite direction; secondly, the documents sent by the board to the Treasury, and office copies and other documents standing in the Treasury files and minutes, received from or sent to the customs, or otherwise relating to customs business; thirdly, other documents (fewer in number and less important) which by the vagaries of archival history are now preserved in the British Museum or other similar collections;

fourthly, the various (printed) reports of the different commissions, most particularly the cited parliamentary papers; and fifthly, the contemporary handbooks of official procedure produced for, and mostly also by, the various officials in the ports (see page xi).

It is a tribute to Dr Hoon's keen analytical mind that such a precise, detailed yet unified study could be completed from such generally unpromising and fragmentary material. Although one may occasionally feel that the work never quite succeeds in entirely throwing off its original limitation of theme, sometimes seeming to lay undue emphasis on the customs abuses, nevertheless the completed study so thoroughly fulfilled its declared purpose that in its detailed descriptive factual aspects the author's work will surely never need to be done again. The work immediately and deservedly became the standard in this field.

Because of the very limitations Dr Hoon set herself, to describe administration without discussing policy, the work may require a little supplementary background in order to correct an imbalance here and there. One could question, for example:

1. The adequacy of the brief sketch of the medieval organization from which (it is held) so much of the eighteenth-century customs organization and accountancy more or less directly derived.

2. The preoccupation with abuses, wherever they can be found—particularly as regards the system of patent posts, patronage and fees—which derives from the narrower perspective and sharper focus of the earlier study.

3. The emphasis upon the inextricable complexity of customs accountancy, without any adequate reference to the historical circumstances that could reasonably be held to make that complexity more easily understandable.

4. The choice of the precise, but somewhat arbitrary, limits of the study, 1696–1786, and the confident assertion that these dates do in fact delimit a natural or clearly-defined historical period.

5. The somewhat too easy assertion[1] of a basic inflexibility of administration throughout the whole period, and the confident assumption of comparatively little alteration, of a posi-

tively static outlook, in the organization throughout the century.

Without the least derogation of Dr Hoon's most capable work, some additional remarks might appropriately be offered under each of these topics.

1. The Medieval Period

The inadequacy of the brief sketch of the department's medieval background and foundation derives from Dr Hoon's thesis that one of the principal factors constraining the eighteenth-century administration, rendering it inflexible and inefficient—one of the main 'abuses' in the original thesis—was the precise form of the organization, its method of staffing, and its pattern of accountancy, which was a mere legacy from medieval times. To grasp the full significance, therefore, of the relationship of the medieval customs system to that of the eighteenth century, it is necessary to trace the organization 'from its beginnings'. These Dr Hoon finds in the twenty-sixth year of Edward I in the *nova custuma* of 1275 (later known as the *antiqua custuma*) when '*custodes custumae* were appointed in certain specified ports to take direct charge for the crown of the collection of the customs'.

It seems more convincing, however, to find the first evidence of a centrally-administered customs system in the earlier administrative and fiscal experiments of the reign of John. The Winchester assize of customs of 1203–4 was certainly the earliest completely national customs in this country. It was all of a piece with John's other measures regarding administration, taxation and trade, for example his reorganization of the chancery, his rationalisation of the Cornish tin mines, and his reconstruction of the royal navy.[2] This deliberate effort on the part of the crown to replace a much older system that had lapsed into localism was part of an even wider fiscal policy to develop not only the taxation from trade, but the revenues from land, and indeed the yield of the royal demesne also. Since the new customs duty of one-fifteenth *ad valorem* was chargeable only upon overseas trade (whether import or export), certain coastwise traffic—

although not itself liable to customs duty—had to be brought under official control in order to prevent foreign (dutiable) trade being coloured as coastwise and free. The administration of this duty, its assessment, collection and account, remained always (so far as is known) in the hands of the crown, and was never infeudated or granted out, either to any of the lords or to the harbour-towns. Its administrative machine seems, like Minerva, to have been born fully grown. In every port-town half a dozen or so of the wisest and most substantial men, learned in the law *(sex vel septem vel plures de sapientioribus et legalioribus et ditioribus et valentioribus hominibus portus)* were 'picked out' to keep the assize.

Not only was the Winchester assize of 5 John the foundation of all medieval customs administration, it also contained all the characteristic elements of the modern assessing and accounting system (page xiv). In the result, all sea-borne trade, both foreign and coastwise, was properly recorded, with a sufficient description of the goods, the date of shipment, and the name of the merchant concerned. Particulars of coastwise shipments were required to be enrolled, the merchandise valued, the bonds taken from the shippers, to secure that any goods cleared coastwise from a port were in fact landed at some other place within the realm. Transactions in the foreign trade were required to be enrolled, the merchandise valued, the *quindecima* assessed and the duty collected in cash. The duty was to be paid to the local collectors or bailiffs, who were to keep the proceeds under lock and key (in *una salva arca* under *tres claves vel quatuor*) until returned to the 'head collectors' *(donec radatur capitalibus custodibus per cirographa contra baillivos)*. Other more direct officers of the crown were appointed as comptrollers to keep a counter-roll *(rotulos contra eos facient)*, an independent record of all moneys received, but not themselves to receive any. The particular significance of this form of organization was that the sea-ports which were for this purpose taken out of the body of the shire, without the intervention of the sheriff, accounted direct to the Exchequer.

The text of the basic document, enrolled as a letter patent,[3] was republished by N. S. B. Gras in 1918.[4] In dating the origin of the medieval English customs in the year 26 Edward I,

Dr Hoon preferred the authority of Crouch's *Complete Guide to the Officers . . . of the Outports* (1732) and the *First Report* of the Board of Customs (1857) (considered below). Henry Crouch, a clerk in the comptroller's office in the London Custom House, published *A Complete View of the British Customs* in 1724, intended primarily for the merchant public, which was sufficiently successful to justify *Part 2* in 1728.[5] In 1732 he produced his *Complete Guide to the Officers* for the general use of the custom-house officials. Notwithstanding that the Board of Customs refused their *imprimatur* to his projected *Complete Guide to Collectors*,[6] Crouch may be regarded as an efficient, capable and keen official, generally reliable on the law, practice and procedure of his own time.[7] Although he gives a number of statutory references for the medieval origin of such posts as the collector, the comptroller and the searcher, he was not anything of a medieval scholar and is not, therefore, in the medieval field, a citable authority.

Nor is the Board of Customs *First Report*—in contrast to that of the Inland Revenue—any more reliable. After the postmaster-general had decided in 1854 to present an annual report to Parliament, Trevelyan at the Treasury suggested in 1856 that both the Customs and the Inland Revenue might do the same. The *First Report* of the General Post Office was prefaced by an interesting account of the origin and growth of the British Post Office, in preparing which recourse had to be had to 'various historical notices' within the department, and 'where any doubt existed, care had been taken to verify the statements by reference to original sources'.[8] In 1857 both the Customs and the Inland Revenue produced a *First Report*, professedly based upon that of the Post Office. The *First Report* of the Inland Revenue, with its seventy-nine appendices and elaborate tables 'contained much information not readily available elsewhere'[9] regarding both the administration and the yield of earlier taxes, going back to the time after the Restoration when the excises were taken out of farm. This *Report* went quickly out of print so the Board re-issued it in 1870.[10] The aim was 'to produce a book of reference rather than anything in the nature of an essay or review, and to furnish facts from which others may draw inferences, rather than offer our opinions upon the subjects of which we have treated'. The Customs *First Report*, however, upon the authority of which Dr Hoon so frequently relies, is of a different calibre. In purporting to deal with the pre-Conquest and later medieval period, it displays no sign of medieval scholarship and, although it continues to appear in the cited bibliographies, a student should treat it with critical caution.

2. THE ABUSES OF PATENT AND PATRONAGE

The concern with abuses derives, as already suggested, at least in part from the earlier thesis; the principal targets for attack were to be the systems of patent and patronage. Although Dr Hoon has specifically stated that she has aimed to describe the organization, and not to study the policy which it was instituted to administer, the impression may be left that whatever is medieval is, on that account, an abuse. The medieval origins of these systems should be considered before examination of the administrative evolution of the customs organization of the eighteenth century, which inherited a medieval ramshackle concern and transmitted to the nineteenth century at least the makings of a modern civil-service department.

This is not the context in which to argue that patronage was not by any means peculiar to the eighteenth-century customs; that it belonged to the social evolution from the vertical property-servitude relationships essential to feudalism, to the horizontal contractual relationships characteristic of modern society. In medieval times, before a consciousness of public responsibility had displaced the identification of office with property, 'a government post' might be occupied as a sort of property (held by a tenure somewhat analogous to a kind of serjeanty). Sir William Holdsworth, for example, instances the posts held in the common-law courts and chancery, and many of the tenures by serjeanty,[11] as evidence of the widespread nature of this common conception of 'office' during the medieval period. This notion of office, not only as a piece of personal property but also as a saleable commodity, was general in all the great European countries at the time. No distinction had yet developed between offices and property. Feudalism was both a system of land tenure and a method of government.

At a time when there was already a highly-developed law and doctrine of property rights and services, there was as yet only a very rudimentary law of contract or doctrine of enforceable agreements. Therefore, when in medieval England the crown had an office to be filled, it did not enter into an agreement for a nominated person to perform the particular service. Instead, it granted by patent the right to the person to perform the particular duty, subject to certain conditions; one might be the patent right to receive fees. Because the various persons appointed to the offices originally instituted by the Winchester assize in 1203-4, or the *nova custuma* of 1275, were appointed by royal letter patent, these posts naturally fell into royal patronage. Thus, patents, patronage and fees tend to be thought of as a single complex. Although it has been argued that the sale of patent office, or the reversion of patent office, on a commercial basis (in the expectation of the fees) was not necessarily worse in its effect than the distribution of office by patronage,[12] yet it was by the exercise of the royal patronage in this respect and specifically in the customs, that the broader policy of the crown could be put into effect.[13]

The basic problem of staffing and accounting in the customs in the eighteenth century was much the same as in any other century from the thirteenth to the twentieth. Stated at its simplest it is this: if, in the village shop—in eighteenth-century England, medieval England or today—the assistant seriously ' fiddles the till ', there is an ultimate check in the state of the stock. If the goods are not on the shelf, the money should be in the till. If the goods are not on the shelf and the money is not in the till, there is evidence that something has gone unrecorded.

The customs had not the advantage of inhabiting such a simple world. If a particular consignment was not brought to duty, either on account of inefficiency or on account of corruption, there would, in the nature of the case, not only be no record of it, but there would be no trace of the fact that there was no record. A system of accountancy and control different from that of business was, therefore, essential. The basic principle was quite simple: the officer who is responsible to assess and charge the duty takes no part in the actual *receipt* of it (and therefore cannot 'fiddle' the cash); and the officer who *receives* and accounts the duty takes no part in assessing or charging it (and therefore cannot let the goods through without payment). Yet each side must be fully aware of the other, and an independent third agent must take an account of both. The basic document of 1203 referred to above required the duty to be paid by the receiving bailiff or officer to the head collector *per cirographa baillivos*. The comptroller was to keep an account of the duty upon the counter-roll, *but not himself to receive any*, and the duty received was to be kept in a safe *(in una salve arca)* under lock and key—three keys or perhaps four *(tres claves vel quatuor)*. In the 1275 scheme the keys were reduced to two, one for the collector and the other for the comptroller. Thus, nothing could be placed in the king's chest, nor taken from it without both sides of the service being involved.[14]

This system of accountancy and control 'by the counter-roll' *(per contrarotulum)* was a general medieval practice and was not by any means peculiar to the customs. There were counter-rolls in the Wardrobe[15] and the Exchequer[16] at least by the thirteenth century. Indeed, the Domesday Book itself was compiled by survey and counter-survey.

In every port there was a seal known as the cocket.[17] Indeed, more accurately it was not that the cocket was at the port; the port was where the cocket was. The very presence of the cocket constituted the harbour-town a 'port'.[18] This seal (or matrix) was in two halves, an upper and a lower. One half was in the custody of the collector and the other in the custody of the comptroller. No document could be sealed without both sides of the service being a party to it.[19] It was, for example, one of the developments of the interesting transitional period—the eighteenth century—that just as with the improvements of travel and communication the regional general-surveyors could be centralised and brought to London as surveyor-general,[20] so also with the development from simple physical things to the greater sophistication of accountancy, the comptrollers' functions could be centralised and the local comptrollers could be brought to London to be 'the accountant and comptroller general' of today.

When, therefore, the medieval exchequer put its own comptroller into a port, it was to keep a counter roll and thus be a check upon the collector, possibly the crown check upon the farmer's collector. Many historians writing since seem to have supposed that when the customs was taken out of farm, and the collector for the farmers became the collector for the crown, there was no longer any need for him to be checked, controlled or audited. Such a supposition fails to grasp the first principle of the system. Sometimes the customs staff themselves did not grasp its implications as in the port of Liverpool in 1723 and 1724,[21] when the Board had to spell it out to them. When a joint organization and methods investigation of the customs system was undertaken a few years ago, the overall efficiency of the service was attributed to the strict observance of this triangularity of the charging, receiving and auditing sides. It was explained to the 'outside' management experts that the practice was medieval.

During the transition period from medieval to modern times, a period of which the eighteenth century was such an important phase, the medieval material *things* (rolls and counter-rolls, pairs of keys, halves of the matrix and so forth) came to be translated into accountancy *processes*. Whilst this transition was in process, with its many administrative problems, the English customs also came to be the customs of Great Britain, and then (almost absent-mindedly, for there was no statutory or patent authority for it) the customs of the whole empire. During this period the whole nature and character of trade also was changing.

The administration was all the time saddled with a patronage system, exploited firstly by the crown and later by the politicians. The broader aspects of the exercise of patronage cannot be adequately dealt with here,[22] but it is interesting to compare the efficiency (or otherwise) of its sister service, the excise (the two were not amalgamated until 1909). The excises were the first instituted during Commonwealth times and, being parliamentary in origin, were initially free of any royal prerogative. Although *some* patents crept in with the Stuart Restoration, the excise retained a greater freedom from that handicap. In the meantime, the administration *qua* administration had to accept patronage as part of the given situation, and the various steps taken during the course of the eighteenth century by the commissioners of customs—themselves patronage officials—to extinguish it would make an interesting study.

One or two other aspects of the patronage system as it worked out in practice deserve comment. Its workings in the customs in the late seventeenth and the eighteenth centuries hold some indication of the growing religious and political toleration. Insofar as office still remained a form of property, if any holder of it could not, on account of religious conscience or political scruple, take the statutory oaths of office (that is, was not a conforming Anglican[23] or could not accept the Revolution settlement),[24] he would be, in effect, dispossessed of the benefits of his office. If, however, a more tolerant administration was broadly content that his office should be executed by deputy, all parties would be more or less satisfied, and the patentee was not thereby entirely 'deprived'. While the legislature was concentrating upon the religious conformity and political reliability of the staff, the administration was concentrating on efficiency. Many individual instances illustrate this, for patronage of itself did not assure *appointment* to office; it assured only *nomination*. Although any candidate for office stood little chance of appointment without a patronage nomination, such nomination did not necessarily lead to actual appointment—and this became more and more the case as the century wore on.

Who exactly were the patentees and what exactly they received from the crown was really a political and not an administrative issue. What is more important is the evolution, during the course of the century, in the conception of office. Generally speaking, any candidate for office having received a nomination from a patentee or other patron, had then to put himself 'under instruction' in his own time and at his own expense. The attitude seems to have been that the sum total of the departmental specialised knowledge was the property, not of the Board of Customs, but of the corporate body of officers. The local basic-grade officer would therefore instruct and the local supervisory-grade officer would examine. An *esprit* was developing. In a case in Liverpool in

1785, for example, a candidate for office was put under instruction as directed; at the end of six months fourteen officers, any one (or every one) of whom might have instructed him, together with four surveyors, any one of whom might have examined him, joined together to inform the Board in London that 'not withstanding the utmost attention they had given him' they not only found him unqualified, but reported that 'there is not the least prospect of him ever being competent to the duty and trust' of the post nominated.[25]

A great deal of what has been written about sinecures, patronage and fees in the public service in the seventeenth and eighteenth centuries, and particularly the eighteenth, is based on mere political pamphleteering. From record sources, however, it becomes clear that certification of competency grew to be a general practice. A nominated candidate was instructed in his own time at his own expense by his future colleagues, and was examined at his own cost by his future superior. Robert Burns is the best-known example. Nominated by Robert Graham of Fintry, a commissioner of excise, for a customs post, Robert Burns received instruction from the local officer at Tarbolton in Ayrshire. When he passed the examination, he was appointed to the post he desired in Dumfriesshire in 1789.

3. COMPLEX ACCOUNTANCY

Dr Hoon has much to say about the inextricable complexity of the revenue accounts and the fact that quite frequently as many as ten, eleven, twelve or even thirteen separate rates of duty, separately computed and separately accounted, might be legally chargeable on the selfsame package.[26] So complex was the eighteenth-century system of customs duties that merchants could not be expected to understand the liabilities of their own commodities, nor how to compute them. Importers would therefore employ the officers of the customs to make the 'entries' (or declarations) on their behalf and pay them a fee for so doing—a practice obviously open to abuse. Indeed, it has been suggested that some at least of the traffic was driven into illicit channels—smuggling—largely because of the inextricable complications of legal trade. In the present volume the complexity of the whole accounting system receives much emphasis, but—as is usual under this topic[27]—the real aim and origin of the system is never stated. Although, Dr Hoon did not set out to describe the policy being administered, one may well be left to assume from the account that the eighteenth-century customs institution was wantonly obscurantist.

The complications derived essentially and directly from the post-Revolution funding system. Too little attention has as yet been paid by the historian to the development of public credit between the Revolution and the mid-eighteenth century,[28] but there are reasons to believe that although the country had during the reigns of Charles II and James II fallen behind several of the continental powers in the organization of public credit—witness the shock of such crude expedients as the 'stop of the Exchequer' of 1672—it was by the rapid development of the English revenue, the organization of our national finances, and the establishment of public credit in the early eighteenth century that England, at least by the middle of the century, succeeded in overtaking her continental rivals. Before the introduction of the funding system, the timely repayment of any government loan, the due interest upon such loan, or any government annuity, was inevitably doubtful, depending on whether or not there chanced to be sufficient funds in hand at the right moment to meet the particular charge. As the growing volume of national expenditure, and particularly war expenditure, in the early 1690s could not be met out of revenue, a system of long-term borrowing as well as mere short-term borrowing was needed; the former gave rise to the conception of a 'national debt'. It was in order to establish public confidence in the national credit—a confidence in the national debt—that a funding system had to be devised and operated. The funding system offered to the investing public an absolute security, a certainty of timely repayment. This took the form of a statutory appropriation of the whole of the yield of stipulated items of taxation, the first charge upon which should be the 'service' of the particular debt. Various Acts of Parliament appropriated the yield of stipulated taxes strictly to the specified service: so that the whole of the appropriated moneys had to be distinguished throughout the entire course of the accounting procedure, both in the customs and in the exchequer. The broad effect was that the cost of the wars for more than a century—and from 1688 until 1815 England was at war much more often than she was at peace—could be met, not out of current revenue, but out of public loans.[29]

In a notable contribution to the administrative history of the eighteenth century, J. E. D. Binney has no hesitation in asserting that the successful working of this system 'ensured great advantages to the country, giving it unprecedented power and flexibility in the conduct of foreign policy and war'.[30] The system was, however, purchased at a cost, that of the admitted complexity of customs and exchequer accounting. The significance accorded to this complication in accountancy will depend upon the importance one attaches to the establishment of the national credit. One must note in any case the administrative problem of training a staff in the complexities of the accounting procedures absolutely required by the governing Acts of Parliament—given the then state of general literacy (and familiarity with the manipulation of figures) and the method of subordinate recruitment. The eventual consolidation of these separate funds, and hence the extinction of the consequent complications in departmental accountancy, could not be considered until the public confidence in the national credit had been firmly established. It is Pitt and the politicians who are usually awarded the credit (following presumably, the Board's *First Report*) for instituting the consolidated fund in 1787,[31] but it is particularly to be noted that the desirability of such consolidation was already being discussed in the customs *by the administration* by 1756,[32] and a definite plan was put forward departmentally to North in 1777[33]—a fact for which the Board in its *First Report*, presumably out of ignorance, took no credit.

4. THE PERIOD DELIMITED

Dr Hoon argues confidently for the years 1696 and 1786 as

the terminal dates of a definite historical period, although a number of other dates readily suggest themselves. It was in 1671, for example, that the English customs service was finally professionalised; it was in 1707 that the English system became the British. At the other end, the year 1776 (or 1783) marks the end of a 'special relationship' with the American territories. The plain truth is that if the dates 1696 and 1786 are not historical they are undoubtedly convenient. Certainly 1696 is the arbitrary date of the commencement of a very citable source of collected classified notes and extracts from the Board of Customs minutes and orders (associated with the name of Musgrave). A fire in 1715[34] destroyed not only Wren's custom house but also practically the whole of the post-1671 (or post-1643) records; hence the importance of Commissioner Musgrave's 'notes and extracts' chancing to date from 1696. The year 1786 is another convenient date on account of the publication of the *Thirteenth, Fourteenth and Fifteenth Reports of the Commission Appointed to Examine State and Take the Public Accounts*, which provide such a large amount of easily quotable material. It is on this account that Dr Hoon moves so much more easily in the latter half of the century than in the former. Perhaps on the whole the best dates would have been 1700–1800; a couple of noughts, being noncommittal and arbitrary, need no justification.

5. BASIC INFLEXIBILITY

The gradual development of the medieval physical elements in control in the customs organization rolls and counter rolls, keys, half-seals and so forth, into the more sophisticated methods of accountancy control has already been noted; and so has the gradual evolution of a *central* accounting control by the withdrawal (with gradually improving transport and communication facilities) of the local comptrollers and the eventual erection in London of the modern office of the Accountant and Comptroller General. The evolution of a central disciplinary control, which in its turn resulted in the development of a central office of expert technical information for the advice of the central administration has also been noted.[35]

Or, stating it in more modern terms, the development of the general-surveyors into the Surveyor-General, and later the Surveyor-General into the Chief Inspector and the Inspector-General of Waterguard. In fact two tendencies were at work: not only were the individual 'outports' becoming more controlled under the directions of the Board, but the Board of Customs and the Board of Excise were coming more and more under the central control of the Treasury.

Other changes also, of considerable significance, are discernible during the period. For example, the introduction and cultivation of a new statistical sense, and consequentially the compilation of systematised statistics relating to commodities, shipping and the balance of trade; the building up of a recognition of the headquarter establishment as the seat of authority, the source of authoritative pronouncement, and hence the 'only begetter' of the later 'codes' of instruction for the use and observation of the outport staff, leading to a general unification of the customs service throughout the ports; the introduction and the later perfection of the organization to 'register' merchant ships, the administrative procedure by which, and by which alone, any vessel becomes a British ship; the formation of policy out of administrative experience, sometimes with considerable constitutional significance, of which the best example is the 1765 change in the status of the Isle of Man; and the development of the much-maligned system of fees to make good what can only be called a deficiency in the public service brought about by not very closely related political issues.

We read much about the gradual decay and the eventual discontinuance during the eighteenth century of the system of account known as the exchequer port-books (dating from an administrative reform of Lord Treasurer Winchester in 1558). Those who loudly criticise the decay of this antiquated form of record do not always appreciate the purely statistical and truly modern form that replaced it. Professor Beloff has made the point that the late seventeenth century 'preoccupation with mathematics was an essential element in the novel governmental attitudes of the period'. William Petty in England (incidentally, a commissioner of excise) and Vauban in France, for example, 'began to turn to the possibility of using the statistical method for the study and regulation of society, for purposes more far-reaching and subtle than the simple enquiries into individual taxable capacity that inspired the Domesday Book and the other surveys of the Middle Ages'. Beloff speaks of Colbert's attention to the collection and analysis of statistics, and says it was during the period of his office ' that the regularity and continuity of the practice was first established '.[36]

In Commonwealth England, when the customs was first managed by a parliamentary commission, the need was already felt for more exact records of oversea trade, for customs accounts to record trade as well as taxation. At the Restoration, however, when the customs were put out to farm again, the crown could not very well require the farmers to compile the statistics of trade, apart from the revenue. It was only after the re-establishment of the commission in 1671 that such a course became possible. In 1696, at a time when interest in ' political arithmetic ' was beginning the English Board of Customs represented to the Treasury that if any ' distinct accompt of the Importation and Exportation of all commodities into and out of this Kingdom ' were required in order ' to make a balance of the trade between this kingdom and any part of the world ', it could not be accurately compiled.[37] In consequence the office of Inspector General of Imports and Exports was instituted in 1696 within the customs, to make up annual accounts.[38] Trade statistics in the sense in which we know them today could then be said to have been properly instituted.

For this reason, from the end of the seventeenth century the departmental records of the Inspector-General began to displace the older but continuing series of exchequer portbooks. The administration was even yet not fully ' out of court ', and this is an interesting example in administrative history of a new department not being vested (by its patent) with any authority over the more ancient court procedures within its own structure. Many of the anomalies and complications dealt with in this present volume derive from this. The departmental organization, therefore, busied itself with making good the basic ' want of method ' in the old, by devising a new procedure of its own, with its own accounts and own archive. Lacking any authority to kill the court procedure, the customs merely let it die. Hence while the newer statistical forms of record built up in accuracy and reliability, the older exchequer forms of record tended to falter and then to wither away.

Naturally, these redundant forms of exchequer record attracted contemporary criticism; for example, from the Commission to Examine, Take and State the Public Accounts in 1783,[39] and from the Select Committee in 1797. Eventually they were discontinued by Treasury order dated 14 March 1799. The oft-lamented gradual decay of the medieval accounting system within the English customs, and the eventual discontinuance of the exchequer port-book procedure, should therefore be reconsidered against the background of the introduction and the early perfection of the more modern departmental and statistical methods.

Another important development of the eighteenth century was the gradual, almost imperceptible, evolution of the Board of Commissioners as the fount and origin of all authority within the department. It has already been said that at the beginning of the period the corporate body of local basic-grade and supervisory officers considered that they owned the sum total of specialist knowledge. The earliest customs handbooks, digests of law, manuals of procedure, computations of total exigible rates and so on, were put out not by the Board but by the staff, by Henry Crouch, Samuel Baldwin, Charles Carkesse, Edward Burrow and others. As the century wore on, the Board became confident enough to warn their staff that these works had no real authority; by the end of the century they had established their now complete superiority. If not by 1800, then by 1812 the Board consolidated, printed and issued a work in two volumes consisting of their consolidated orders and letters, and forwarded a copy to every port 'for the governance of the staff'.

Another late-seventeenth and eighteenth-century development was the system of the registry of British merchant ships, a subject about which little has been said in this present work or elsewhere. Once 'registered' a vessel became a British ship, entitled to fly the British flag, subject to British jurisdiction, and qualified for the privileged colonial and coastwise trade. The definition in general, therefore, of a British ship and ultimately the identification, authentication and 'registration' of each and every British ship afloat, came to be fundamental to the operation of the Navigation Acts—which was itself essentially another customs matter. The official procedure involved examination in detail of the vessel's documentation, provision to the owners of legal documents of property title, and final determination of the vessel's nationality.[40] The English Board, to this end, during this particular period, had to organize a registry-general in London with competence over all the ports not only in England and Scotland (bearing in mind that during part of the period the English Board had technically no general competence over Scotland), but in all the colonies and in India, and also in the Isle of Man and the Channel Isles, where the constitutional situation was delicate and where in any case the Board had no fiscal jurisdiction. In addition to this central registry-general the English Board had to train 'registrars' in every port of registry, an entirely lay staff without any previous legal training or experience.[41]

The flexibility of the administration in the eighteenth century is also shown in its relation to the customs of the Isle of Man in the circumstance of that island's ambiguous constitutional status: in the early part of the century, a liberal toleration towards a local anomaly allied to a policy of mere containment; in about the middle of the century, a much sterner attitude towards a serious growing commercial racket; by 1765, a fundamental change in the whole constitutional position; and thereafter, a strict but fair policy which the Board particularly desired to make work. The fact that these points are missed in the work of a most careful overseas scholar is no criticism of such work, for almost certainly not one Englishman in ten thousand could describe the difference between the relation of the Isle of Man to the customs and the relation of the Isles of Scilly to the excise, as distinct from the relations of Orkney or Shetland with either. The Board of Commissioners of Customs, appointed by royal letter patent to manage the customs of the kingdom, in fact, lacked any authority to do so in the Isle of Man. The island was constitutionally 'part of the Crown but not of the Realm of England '. The king's writ—at least in matters fiscal—did not run there. The fiscal rights belonged with the lordship and were in private hands, earlier in the Stranges', Earls of Derby, but later in the Murrays', Earls (later Dukes) of Athol. They professed to be unable to dispose of it, even to the crown, by reason of the terms of the entail. In the result the independent fiscal rights of the island were extinguished by statutory purchase,[42] but the manner in which the customs reacted at various times to the unprecedented strains upon the service makes an interesting chapter in administrative history.

Another interesting development was in the matter of fees. Much has been written, a great deal of it from sources which although contemporary are little more than mere political propaganda. This is not the context in which to discuss the subject of fees in its broader aspects; but the ingenious method by which the administrators got round the difficulties on the omission—or the refusal—of Parliament to grant 'to the Crown' adequate funds to maintain the customs service is worth mention. Numerous duties had to be performed by the customs which were not fiscal by any definition. In a mercantilist England the navigation laws had to be administered, quarantine provisions imposed, the Greenland bounties superintended, public health safeguarded, shipping protected by registry provisions, lighthouse authorities assisted, the slave trade regulated, and a host of other services performed that had no identity with the customs duties narrowly conceived. Parliament passed numerous enactments requiring the superintendence by the customs service of many aspects of port and maritime life—but studiously refused to provide a civil list to maintain a service whose existence these enactments took for granted. If Parliament had no funds for this purpose, the crown had less. Without entering into the political reasons for this situation, it can be noted that other means had necessarily to be found. Much as in the seventeenth and eighteenth centuries the cost of maintaining the highways was, by a system of turnpikes, transferred from the parishes through which the roads chanced to pass to the traffic that used them, so by a skilful adaption of the medieval system of fees, the cost of the crown administration of a port was levied on the traffic passing through it.

This had a number of advantages. Not the least was the fact that the weight fell on those who benefited most. For example, it was an essential feature of the mercantilist system that the monopoly in colonial products was guaranteed to the merchants of this country. Tobacco, sugar and silk, for instance, could not legally be shipped from Virginia, the West Indies or India direct to Hamburg or Antwerp. They must be brought first to a home port. Upon such a transaction (in common with all others) the merchant concerned had to pay a certain fee, 1s 6d perhaps. It was little enough to pay for so considerable a privilege; but if the merchant body had not paid to keep their system going, the crown could not and Parliament would not have done so. One further advantage of this fee system—which is usually overlooked—was that it automatically attracted to a port the funds to employ additional (locally engaged) staff at the time when additional assistance was needed, and left no motive to the principal official to retain them after the need had passed.

It was not until 1812, when at last the cost of the customs service was charged fairly and squarely to Parliamentary funds, that reform finally came. Although the Board remains a prerogative body, created by royal letter patent, all officers of the Board, by being placed 'on the Parliamentary vote', became essentially responsible to Parliament through the Board. Officials, who during the previous century had been admitted by at least some form of qualifying examination, by the Trevelyan reform came to be admitted by competitive examination. To see this development in historical perspective one should consider it in comparison with other professions. During all this period appointments to HM ships, for example, were disposed of 'for affection, friendship or money'.[43] Appointments into the army were simpler—they were sold. In the last century a man who entered the customs by competitive examination could have bought a commission in the army for his grandson before these reforms got as far as the armed forces. In the established church the matters of patronage, fees and freeholds in appointments are still being discussed.

One important change relating to the customs records has

taken place since Dr Hoon undertook her research for this book. It has already been said that the absence of a surviving central archive necessarily implied reliance upon the surviving records of the various outports, located in Dr Hoon's day in the respective ports themselves. In the study of these records I have been privileged to visit every port, sub-port and 'creek' in the United Kingdom including the 'ancient and decayed' ports. Dr Hoon, however, had perforce (on account of their relative inaccessibility) to rely to some considerable extent upon certain extracts, selected and transcribed either by the late Henry Atton, the author of *The King's Customs*, or the late B. R. Leftwich, his successor in office. Since then, the Public Records Act of 1958 has provided for the centralising of all such Departmental records, and all the remaining outport records of this country, with the exception of the statutory shipping registry, have been centralised under the Public Record Office and re-classified into Public Record Office series.

This critical historical introduction ought not to be concluded without a clear expression of my keen appreciation of Dr Hoon's remarkable ability to grasp so completely and to re-state so clearly, not only the essential but also the incidental, facts of so complex an organization as that of the customs of the eighteenth century. She has long held in her debt those who study fiscal, administrative, maritime and colonial history, and indeed general history also.

Rupert C. Jarvis

[1] Another American scholar, Dr Stephen Baxter in *The development of the Treasury, 1660–1702* (London, 1957), p. 287 speaks of 'certain dangerous generalisations' and 'other "undoubtedly's"' of a dubious nature' with particular reference to pages 51, 58 and 203 below.

[2] For evidence of John's personal concern in this, see V. H. Galbraith, *Studies in the public records* (London, 1949), pp. 124–6.

[3] *Rotuli Litterarum patentium*, I, 42–3.

[4] *Early English customs system* (Harvard U.P., 1918), p. 53.

[5] Compare with the date given at p. 299, below.

[6] For a reference to a petition as to his loss in not being permitted to deliver the proposed book to his subscribers, see *Calendar of treasury books and papers, 1731–34*, p. 447.

[7] As to the note on Crouch at p. 299 below, detailed examination discloses errors; see, e.g. J. H. Andrews, 'To problems in the interpretation of the port books', in *Economic History Review*, 2nd series, IX (1956), 121.

[8] *Parliamentary Papers:* H. C. 1854–5 [1913], XX, 555.

[9] P.P. H.C. 1857 [2199] sess. 1 IV, 65.

[10] P.P. 1870 C[ommand] 82, 82–1, XX, 193–377.

[11] *History of English Law* (London, 1938), I, 246–52, 424–5.

[12] A. Harding, *A social history of English law* (Harmondsworth, 1966) p. 209.

[13] For an interesting study of the transfer, by means of patent and patronage, of the control of the customs of a port in the late fourteenth century from the hands of certain of the local burgesses (found to be 'tainted with scandal and corruption') to 'mixed teams drawn from the neighbouring country gentry of proved integrity and loyalty and from the professional civil service', see A. Steel, 'The collectors of the customs at Newcastle-upon-Tyne in the reign of Richard II', in J. C. Davies (ed), *Studies presented to Sir Hilary Jenkinson* (London, 1957), p. 413.

[14] Recently in a neighbouring village church, I saw a poor-box-cum-parish-chest, with a slot for contributions, and two padlocks. Anyone can put money in, but the rector cannot take any out except in the presence of a churchwarden, and the churchwardens cannot take any out except with the knowledge of the rector.

[15] T. F. T. Tout, *Chapters in the administrative history of medieval England*, VI (Manchester, 1933), p. 27.

[16] Colvin and Brown discuss the counter-roll in the emergence of the medieval office of the comptroller of works; R. A. Brown, H. M. Colvin and A. J. Taylor, *The history of the King's works*, I (London: HMSO 1963), pp. 169–70.

[17] 'Cocquet' and its variants derive from *quo quietus est*.

[18] R. C. Jarvis, 'The appointment of ports', *Economic History Review*, 2nd series, XI (1959), 460–1.

[19] When, for example, in the middle ages the customs of a port were assigned as a security for a crown loan (or the crown debts) one half of the seal was surrendered to the crown creditor(s).

[20] See p. xxi below.
[21] R. C. Jarvis, *Customs letter-books of the port of Liverpool, 1711–1813* (Manchester: Chetham Society, 1954), pp. 20 and 24.
[22] See, for example, G. E. Aylmer, *The king's servants* (London, 1961).
[23] 25 Car II, cap 2; 30 Car II, stat 2; and 1 Geo I, cap 55.
[24] 7–8 Will III, cap 27 and 1 Geo I, cap 55.
[25] Jarvis, *Customs letter-books*, pp. 130–1.
[26] Pages 25–7 and following pages.
[27] As a notable exception, see J. E. D. Binney, *British public finance and administration, 1774–92* (Oxford, 1958), pp. 104–16, for a lucid exposition of the whole system.
[28] For a stimulating work in this field, see P. G. M. Dickson, *The financial revolution in England: a study in the development of public credit, 1688–1756* (London, 1967).
[29] This was an important break into modern times. By arranging to pay the interest only on the debt, and 'sinking' the capital, wars could be waged leaving the debt to the future to pay.
[30] Binney, *British public finance*, p. 106.
[31] 27 Geo. III, cap 33.
[32] British Museum: Add MSS. 32864. f. 388, and below, p. 249.
[33] Binney, *British public finance*, p. 109.
[34] See *Daily Courant*, 15 January 1715. (The occurrence is usually misdated 1714.)
[35] pp. 113–15, below.
[36] *The age of absolutism* (London, 1963 ed.), p. 13.
[37] PRO: Treasury board papers, 15 July 1696 (T1/38, 302).
[38] Treasury minute book, 1695–6 (T29/8, 358–9).
[39] *Fourteenth Report*, III (1788), 103 and 563 ff.
[40] 26 Geo III, cap 60.
[41] For a fuller study of this problem, see R. Craig and R. C. Jarvis, *Liverpool Registry of Merchant Ships* (Manchester, 1967).
[42] 5 Geo III, cap 3 (see also PRO: Treasury papers, bun 434, nos. 302–6, and the relative Home Office papers). Although the departmental records usually refer to the 'proposed purchase' or 'late purchase' of the island (see p. 170), the island was not in fact purchased; it was only the fiscal rights that were acquired. Nor (see p. 170, n 3) was there ever 'British ownership' of the island, but only the resumption—or the assumption—of the fiscal rights. Nor can I agree with the remainder of that footnote, that 'more teas and brandies were smuggled on these coasts than when the government of the Isle of Man was in private hands'. The document cited is unmistakably clear that it was smuggling *from Ireland in 1778* that was greater than that in *1764 from the Isle of Man*.
See also R. C. Jarvis, 'Illicit trade with the Isle of Man, 1671–1765', *Transactions of the Lancashire & Cheshire Antiquarian Society*, LVIII (1948), 245–65.
[43] M. Lewis, *The navy in transition: a social history, 1814–1864* (London, 1965), pp. 99–100.

PREFACE

This study had its beginning in a survey of abuses in the British customs service from 1700 to 1733, as far as they affected the colonial tobacco industry and the consequent economic status of Virginia and Maryland. The results of that survey indicated the importance of continuing the investigation further into the eighteenth century. As the work advanced, it became apparent that the influence of the English customs service upon colonial commercial relations, colonial economic history, and the mercantile system as a whole could not be adequately interpreted without first reconstructing the organization of that service and delineating its position in the commercial program. No detailed account has been made of the nature of customs administration in the eighteenth century, at the very time when that administration had its greatest significance in the working of the mercantile system. I have undertaken this work with the hope of filling such a need. Furthermore, although the importance of eighteenth-century British commerce and finance has long been recognized, the nature of one of the most lucrative sources of revenue, the customs service, has never been examined. This book attempts to describe the elaborate organization which existed for the collection of a revenue that was used to meet the national debt and to finance the wars which helped Britain win her first empire. Finally, it is likely that at no other period have departments of government shaped more directly the course of events for Great Britain than in the eighteenth century; yet the field of eighteenth-century British institutional history has been relatively neglected. The aim of this book is to make clear the operation and influence of one of the most important of these departments—that dealing with the customs.

It has seemed wise to make this study primarily an analysis of an organization. This approach has been chosen, first, because there was comparatively little alteration in the institution throughout the eighteenth century; secondly, because in dealing with a subject of such scope I have thought it more helpful to present a cross-section of the system as a whole than to consider merely incidents in its history, though such incidents in as far as they determined policy or departmental organization have been carefully emphasized. It is to be hoped that this volume may be of service as a foundation for studies in the

PREFACE

fields of British economic policy, British administrative history and institutional organization, Anglo-colonial commercial relations, and colonial economic conditions. Accordingly I have outlined in detail the organization of the customs service, but have refrained from introducing deductions bearing on the broader relationships of the system. Interpretations growing out of this project may well be reserved for another volume.

In the preparation of this work I am deeply indebted to Professor C. M. Andrews of Yale University, at whose suggestion I began research in this country and continued it in England. To him I owe the training which prepared me for such a project, and to his valuable advice, drawn from a vast knowledge of British commercial interests, I am indebted for the plan of the undertaking in its earlier stages. To Professor A. P. Newton, Rhodes Professor of Imperial History in the University of London, I wish to express my gratitude for his helpful counsel throughout the course of my research. His insight into the complexities of the problems which arose in connection with the preparation of my data in final form was of crucial importance. I have also had the kind assistance of Mr. B. R. Leftwich, Librarian of the Custom House Library, whose understanding of the functioning of the customs system, particularly along practical lines, has shed light upon many a difficult problem. The Selections From Customs Outport Records, which Mr. Leftwich has compiled with great care, have been of inestimable service. I should also like to acknowledge my gratitude to Miss Agnes Roberts for the verification of certain references and for a critical reading of the manuscript, and to Mr. F. S. Pease, Jr. of Appleton-Century Company for his editorial work. I wish also to record my appreciation of the courtesies I received from the officials of the British Museum and the British Public Record Office, and from the Honorable Board of Customs Commissioners.

The preparation of this book was made possible in part by the award of the Piatt Memorial Fellowship of the American Association of University Women (1934–1935) and by the grant of a Yardley Foundation Fellowship of the New Jersey Federation of Women's Clubs (1933–1934). The publication of this volume has been financed by the American Historical Association, aided by a substantial grant from the University of London. To the officers of these several foundations I wish to express my deep gratitude.

ELIZABETH E. HOON

Staunton, Virginia

CONTENTS

CHAPTER		PAGE
I.	ADMINISTRATIVE PROBLEMS	1
II.	EXECUTIVE CONTROL	45
III.	THE CENTRAL OFFICE	92
IV.	THE ORGANIZATION OF THE PORT OF LONDON	122
V.	THE OUTPORTS	167
VI.	PERSONNEL	195
VII.	CUSTOMS PROCEDURE IN IMPORT, EXPORT, AND COASTWISE SHIPPING	243
VIII.	PROCEDURE IN SEIZURE CASES	270
	CONCLUSION	290
	TABLE OF ABBREVIATIONS USED IN FOOT-NOTE CITATIONS	292
	BIBLIOGRAPHY	293
	INDEX	303

CHAPTER I

Administrative Problems

The English customs system in the eighteenth century served two purposes: it constituted an integral part of the revenue system which returned vast sums into the Treasury, and it enforced trade policy upon which the protection and encouragement of industry and commerce depended. The revenue question confronted the government throughout the entire period; the imposition of increasingly high customs duties was determined by the exigencies of parliaments faced with the national debt and huge war loans. By the beginning of the eighteenth century extension of trade loomed large in the minds of statesmen and played an ever greater part in the mercantile policy of the day. Economic progress was judged by productive power in manufactures, by shipping, agricultural yield, and employment of labor; and a favorable balance of trade was valued to those ends.

Revenue and trade policy in the customs were often inseparable, though occasionally the collection of large sums of money was sacrificed to the commercial principle. Trade policy dictating the promotion of home industry and a favorable balance of trade was responsible for the encouragement of exports by the gradual abolition of export duties on manufactured articles, a reduction begun in the latter part of the seventeenth century and finally completed by Walpole. Restrictions and duties remained on the exportation of some English raw materials, however, the prohibition of the export of wool being a conspicuous instance of the operation of a commercial program for the benefit of home manufacturers. Trade policy further demanded at various times the prohibition of trade with France, either directly or by means of heavy duties, in order to secure the domestic market to home industry.[1] The part played by the customs system in the enforcement of the Acts of Trade indicates the influence both of fiscal and of trade policy upon the customs: proceeds of customs duties constituted an

[1] William C. Kennedy, *English Taxation 1640–1799, An Essay on Policy and Opinion* (London, 1913), esp. pp. 33–37, has proved very useful in indicating the influence of the two purposes of revenue and trade policy upon the customs.

important end of mercantile policy, even to the occasional sacrifice of the letter of the law, while the mechanism of customs collection offered a means of enforcing commercial restrictions.

It was in the majority of import duties that revenue and trade policy found common ground. The import of luxuries and manufactured articles which competed with British manufactures was discouraged by high rates, for they were believed to foster unnecessary consumption and to interfere with the productive activities of the state. At the same time, heavy duties on such articles furnished a lucrative source of revenue and concentrated welcome specie in the Exchequer. The importation of raw materials, on the other hand, was not discouraged; in fact it was regarded as being for the welfare of the nation, for such goods could be manufactured into products that could be exported at a much higher price than the material had cost, thus furthering both employment and shipping.[1] With respect to imports as a whole, however, trade policy and the need for revenue were together responsible for the imposition of high duties which persisted. Numerous branches of duties were imposed in the beginning of the period in the reigns of William III and Anne, and additional branches were created throughout the century, until by 1784 they numbered 100. Duties were enormously increased during the period, some of them many times over; but the gain to the Crown was not proportionately great. Though the eighteenth century saw a marked growth in revenue and commerce, it saw as well the loss of millions of pounds due to illicit trade provoked by the incidence of excessive duties, and the introduction of hopeless complexity into the customs organization. How much more revenue the British Exchequer might have realized had there been a different policy in regard to customs rates it is impossible to say; the time of Burke and Pitt and Adam Smith had not yet come.

The customs system, then, was the instrument for putting mercantile policy into effect at the British ports. It is the purpose of this study to describe the organization of that system as it existed throughout the eighteenth century for the collection of revenue. To state how far or in what degree the customs service fulfilled its dual purpose of revenue and trade policy is not here our concern, but rather to see what the system for achieving that purpose was like in itself. Hundreds of pages have been written on the commercial policy of England

---

[1] Br. Suviranta, *The Theory of the Balance of Trade in England, A Study in Mercantilism* (Helsingfors, 1923), Ch. V, has been of excellent assistance in this discussion.

ADMINISTRATIVE PROBLEMS

during the period, but the nature of the organization actually responsible for the working of the system at the British ports has been neglected. The present work aims at filling this gap in our knowledge.

The ninety years from 1696 to 1786 constitute the scope of investigation. During William's reign a national debt had been created which could be financed only through the growing wealth of the commercial classes. At the same time the merchants had been embarrassed by the war, and loud was their demand for government assistance to retrieve their fortunes. In 1696 trade received a new impetus and the organization of the mercantile system was finally completed. In that year was passed the last of the Navigation Acts which strengthened and consolidated the earlier Navigation Acts and completed the most important of the broad, statutory regulations governing colonial trade. Further, immediately before and after 1696, the imposition of numerous additional duties for revenue and protection defined the beginning of the elaborate system of rates which characterized eighteenth-century mercantilism. In the same year the Board of Trade and Plantations was established for the supervision of the country's trade interests. This body, though limited in powers, was of signal importance for the next eighty-six years because of its recommendations on commerce, manufactures, and colonial administration. To keep an account of the balance of trade, the office of Inspector-General of Imports and Exports was created in the same year. Finally, by 1696, a quarter of a century had elapsed since the customs system had been placed under the administration of a Board of Customs Commissioners. By that date the change from farming to commission had been effected and the broad outlines of the organization under which the customs system was to function for succeeding decades had taken shape. Thus the year 1696 marks at once the embarkation upon the mercantilism that is identified with the eighteenth century and represents the development of the organization which was to put it into effect.

During the next ninety years the customs mechanism operated in enforcement of the policy of high duties and commercial restrictions. By the end of the period the system of excessive customs duties which were notoriously evaded and the addition of hundreds of regulations governing their collection had reduced the customs service to a state of such confusion that only the sweeping reforms which had their modest beginnings in 1787 could have secured efficiency. In that year Pitt's Consolidation Act was passed, strongly supported by the recommendation of the Commissioners of Accounts who made the first exhaustive survey of the customs system. That act, which was the first of a series of customs reforms, consolidated the many branches of duties and greatly simplified the method of collection. Though there were afterwards many abuses, the Consolidation Act marked the end of the old and the beginning of the modern customs service. Therefore, since the year of its passage, 1787, may be taken to symbolize the downfall of the old eighteenth-century system, 1786 may be taken to represent the last year of the normal functioning of that system.

By 1786 the other aspect of the customs, its relation to the mercantile system, had also been altered. True, the Navigation Acts still remained on the statute books, but the enforcement of many of their provisions was yearly becoming more difficult. The loss of the American colonies in 1783 broke up the British commercial system, though that system would in any case have fallen of its own weight. By 1786, then, the old rigid mercantile order was giving way. Thus it becomes clear that the period between 1696 and 1786 constitutes a definite chapter in the history of the customs system, the importance of which warrants its careful study during these years.[1]

There was little systematic change in the general customs organization; it was largely static, and as a rule the description of different parts at fairly specific dates can be taken to apply to the whole. Since the system grew greatly in complexity but little in principle, it is impossible to speak of a marked development during the period. There was rather a multiplication of existing agencies than an alteration.

The construction of the eighteenth-century customs service can be interpreted only with reference to certain elements which were a part of the system that the Customs Board was called upon to administer, yet which the Commissioners were, for the most part, powerless to alter. Three problems touching organization confronted the Customs Board: the influence of the medieval customs organization upon that of the eighteenth century; the complex system of revenue which the Customs Commissioners had to enforce; and the extraneous duties performed by the customs officers. Singly or together, in many cases, these factors prescribed customs policy and defined the character of

---

[1] The following studies have been of particular value on the theory of mercantilism and the commercial system: *Cambridge History of the British Empire*, I, Ch. IX, pp. 268–299, C. M. Andrews, "The Acts of Trade"; *ibid.*, Ch. XX, pp. 561–602, J. F. Rees, "Mercantilism and the Colonies"; H. E. Egerton, *A Short History of British Colonial Policy* (London, 1910); W. Cunningham, *The Growth of English Industry and Commerce in Modern Times: The Mercantile System* (Cambridge, 1921).

ADMINISTRATIVE PROBLEMS

the Board's administration. Because the complexity of the eighteenth-century customs system was largely due to these considerations, this chapter will be confined to an examination of each in turn.

1. *The Influence of the Medieval Customs Organization upon the Eighteenth-Century Organization*

To appreciate the significance of the relationship of the medieval to the eighteenth-century organization, it is necessary to trace briefly the latter organization from its beginnings. In very early times no uniform system existed for the collection of the customs revenue. The duties were farmed in some instances to an enterprising merchant or courtier who received the right of collecting them in return for a specified annual sum, while in other cases the revenue was collected by officers appointed by the Crown or a local borough.

In 26 Edward I *custodes custumæ* were appointed in certain specified ports to take direct charge for the Crown of the collection of the customs. This was the beginning of the general institution of the office of customer, the most important of the Crown offices to be early established. Another official, the controller, was appointed coevally with the customer to act as a check upon him, while the searcher who supervised the import and export business, and the weigher and troneur apparently came into existence not long afterwards. These three principal Crown officers, the customer, controller, and searcher, were originally appointed by the King or by the Chancellor, Treasurer, King's Chamberlain, Barons of the Exchequer, and others, and their term of office was during pleasure only. The King retained possession of their patronage under the government of the Lord High Treasurer with the assent of the Council when necessary; but in the time of Henry VI it was so arranged that these customs offices could be created only by warrant sealed by the Treasurer and sent into the Chancery,[1] and from that time on such officers of the customs were under a more direct control of the Lord High Treasurer or the Lords

---

[1] *First Report of the Commissioners of Her Majesty's Custo s on the Customs* [Cd. 2186], p. 79, App. B, H.C. (1857), iii. For the history of these early offices, see *ibid.*, pp. 78–79; Henry Crouch, *A Complete Guide to the Officers of His Majesty's Customs in the Out-ports. Being Forms, Precedents, and Instructions for the Execution of every Branch of the Business of that Revenue* (London, 1732), pp. 2–4. Cf. *The Act of Tonnage & Poundage and Rates of Merchandise* (London, 1702), p. 698, "An Abridgment Of Several Statutes Now in Force and Use Relating to Her Majesty's Customs, which were made before the Act of Tonnage and Poundage, 12 Car. II."

of the Treasury when the Treasury was in commission. When originally appointed, the three patentees, the customer, controller, and searcher, had to take oath that they would remain resident in their ports and execute the office themselves without appointing substitutes.[1] Subsequent laws altered the requirement and gave rise to the system of deputies.

At times the administration of the customs system was transferred from these Crown officials to individuals who paid for the privilege of collecting the money. Throughout the medieval period and down to the Long Parliament, separate duties were often farmed, while in the time of James I most of the customs duties were amalgamated into the first great farm of the customs.[2] At such times officers of the farmers took over the collection of the duties, and their proceedings were checked by the Exchequer officials and the royal customs officers.[3] The Crown officer, the customer, who then no longer had charge of the collection of duties, remained, it appears, mainly for the purpose of returning into the Exchequer the accounts required of him and of directing the coast business in which the farmers had no concern.[4] The controller upon those occasions acted as a check on the collector, the farmer's officer who received the duties. The activities of the searcher became confined entirely to the export business.[5] Only occasionally, during the periods when the customs were out of farm, did the Crown officers have complete supervision of the collection.

Still another change came in 1643 when the Long Parliament turned out the farmers and regulated the collection of the revenue by means of a parliamentary committee whose members were appointed commissioners and collectors of the customs.[6] This form of administration was carried on by succeeding committees, in spite of an un-

---

[1] Crouch, *Complete Guide to Officers* (1732), pp. 2, 3–4.
[2] A. P. Newton, "The Establishment of the Great Farm of the English Customs," *Transactions of the Royal Historical Society*, Fourth Series, I (1918), 151. Frederick C. Dietz, *English Public Finance, 1558–1641* (New York, 1932), pp. 330–345.
[3] The Crown officers held a slightly different position under the great farm of James. See *ibid.*, p. 338.
[4] *The Reports of the Commissioners Appointed to Examine, Take, and State the Public Accounts of the Kingdom*, 1787, III, 170, "Fifteenth Report, Relative to the Payments to the Officers of the Customs at the Out Ports, and to other Charges of Management incurred on Account of the Customs Revenue for the Year 1784," 1786.
[5] See *ibid.*, III, 173–174.
[6] Ordinance 1642–3, Jan. 21, and Ordinance 1643, May 30. See *Acts and Ordinances of the Interregnum, 1642–1660*, edited by C. H. Firth and R. S. Rait (London, 1911), I, 163–164.

ADMINISTRATIVE PROBLEMS

successful attempt in 1657 to place the customs and excise in farm.¹ These committees, appointed by Parliament till 1660, and then by the King, continued to function until 1662, in which year those who had been serving as commissioners, together with one other person, became the lessees of a new farm.² The system of farming continued until 1671, when negotiations for a new farm broke down and the Board of Customs Commissioners was created.³

At this point the collector, originally the servant of the farmer, became a Crown officer. As the tenure of the various farms in the ports expired, collectors of the customs were appointed to all ports by the Board of Customs Commissioners, pursuant to Treasury warrant. The office of collector was thus gradually introduced and extended over the whole department, and to the collector was given complete responsibility for the collection of duties in a port and for the return of money and accounts into the customs office. With the controller, he had the general superintendence of the port as well. The old office of customer, the duties of which were transacted by deputy, was permitted to continue, however. This official still conducted the coast business and returned quarterly accounts of imports and exports, port books, and coast bonds into the Exchequer or customs office as the case might be; but his office had become unnecessary in executing these duties, some of which were entirely redundant.⁴

With respect to the coast transactions at an outport, though the customer actually conducted the business with the controller, the collector, by his examination and signature of coast documents which consisted of coast bonds and certificates, participated in the business and was held equally responsible with the other two officers.⁵ By 1784 the duties of the customers in the coast trade were either duplicated in

---

¹ C. H. Firth, *The Last Years of the Protectorate, 1656–1658* (London, 1909), II, 262–263.
² *Calendar of Treasury Books, 1660–1667*, XXXIX, 769; *Cobbett's Complete Collection of State Trials and Proceedings for High Treason and Other Crimes and Misdemeanors from the Earliest Period to the Present Time* (London, 1810), VI, 417–418.
³ P.R.O., Patent Roll, 23 Chas. II, Part 2, No. 1, Mem. 33, dorse–37, dorse, [1671], Sept. 27.
⁴ *Repts. of Comrs.*, 1787, III, 170, "Fifteenth Rept.," 1786. Cf. Samuel Forster, *A Digest of all the Laws Relating to the Customs, to Trade, and Navigation; with a short Historical Dissertation Concerning the Nature, Extent, and Method of Collection of the Ancient Revenue of the Crown* (London, 1727), pp. 355–356; *The Rules of the Water-side; or The General Practice of the Customs* (London, 1715), p. 91; Crouch, *Complete Guide to Officers* (1732), pp. 2, 4.
⁵ *Repts. of Comrs.*, 1787, III, 170–171, "Fifteenth Rept.," 1786.

the department of the collector or might easily have been executed there.[1]

The customer's duty, as a patent officer, of returning quarter books containing accounts of imports and exports to the customs office [2] appears to have become useless and generally disregarded by the customers. In the year 1784 only two patent customers sent in such quarter books, while from thirty-six ports neither patent customers nor their deputies submitted accounts. Twenty-eight of the thirty-five deputy customers who made returns of quarter books in 1784 were also the collectors at their respective ports; and if they submitted quarter books in both capacities, the accounts served no purpose as a check, since they were duplicates. Further, quarter books sent up by patent or deputy customers were disregarded in the customs office. The outport controller's books, returned quarterly from every port, were relied upon instead as a check on the collector; and the books of the customer were simply stored away in the central office without ever being examined.[3] As a duty remaining to the customer, the delivery of quarter books was totally useless.

An order of 7 Elizabeth requiring the annual return to the Queen's Remembrancer in the Exchequer of special parchment books,[4] known as port books, containing accounts of merchants' entries in and out, had become merely a relic. The customers had grown very irregular in their return of such books, while the accounts themselves claimed no attention in the Exchequer and only added confusion to the mass of useless records.[5] Even the appointment, in 1712, of a special cus-

[1] See *Repts. of Comrs.*, 1787, III, 172.
[2] Until after the Restoration the customer was an accountant of the Exchequer. In the reign of Charles II the office of the Controller-General of the Customs was established, and the customer thenceforth returned his accounts to that office. Forster, *Digest of Customs Laws* (1727), p. 356.
[3] *Repts. of Comrs.*, 1787, III, 171, "Fifteenth Rept., 1786."
[4] These parchment books, intended to detect and prevent frauds, were delivered in a tin box under the Exchequer seal to the several patent officers in London and the outports, and were required to be returned on oath. P.R.O., Treasury In-Letters, Treasury Board Papers, Bdl. 344, Nos. 5–8, "Touching the Port Books Sent by the Court of Exchequer to the Several Ports in England & Wales," a survey by Taylor [1751].
[5] *Repts. of Comrs.*, 1787, III, 171–172, "Fifteenth Rept.," 1786. In 1713, the Deputy Remembrancer of the Exchequer acquainted the Select Committee of the House of Lords that the port books were "in great confusion, not being looked into for a great while together"—that they were in the custody of the Usher of the Court of Exchequer but "he remembers not that they have been used." Nor at this time were the books found to be used by customs officers in the preparation of their accounts, though certain customs officials, probably mindful of the original value of these returns, were of opinion that "the Port books are of great consequence,

ADMINISTRATIVE PROBLEMS

toms officer for the examination of these registers [1] seems to have had little permanent effect upon their remittance and use. In 1751 an attempt was made to put an end to the return of port books, but Pelham, who was then Chancellor of the Exchequer, rejected the application and refused to alter the practice of the Court of Exchequer.[2] Six years later the Lords of the Treasury requested the Customs Department to advise them whether the books were annually delivered and whether they were of any use to the revenue. Wood, Secretary to the Customs Board, was informed by Edward Jackson, Inspector of the Exchequer Books in the Outports, "That they are constantly delivered every year out of the said Court, but that some of them have not been so regularly returned, and therefore he has given notice to the proper officers to return what are wanting immediately, and to be more punctual for the future." Wood concluded his report by observing, "Whether these Books are of any use to the Revenue, I cannot take upon me to say, although I see none they are of here; for as they are issued out of the Court of Exchequer by Virtue of an Order of that Court, and seem to have been calculated by, and for the use of, his Majestys Officers there, I presume they can best inform You of their Utility, and whether the purposes, for which they were originally intended, still subsist." [3] Though the Treasury deliberated again at this time on the subject of the port books,[4] no action appears to have been taken thereon; and in spite of the evident realization of the worthlessness of such records, their return remained a duty of the patent officers throughout the period.[5]

---

being the most correct accounts that are." Upon an address to the Queen that the port books be kept in order, the Queen's answer was returned that an able person had been appointed with a salary for that purpose. Historical Manuscripts Commission, *The Manuscripts of the House of Lords* (New Series), VIII, *1708–1710*, 29, 30.

[1] For Oxford's appointment of this officer by constitution, see P.R.O., Treasury Out-letters, Customs, XV, 423–425, 1712, June 24. Cf. *Calendar of Treasury Papers, 1708–1714*, p. 395, Lord Chief Baron Ward to Lord High Treasurer, 1712, June 14.

[2] P.R.O., Treasury Papers, Bdl. 344, No. 1, Taylor, Deputy Remembrancer, to Martin, 1757, Jan. 20. See also Taylor's representation to Martin on the port books [1751]. *Ibid.*, Bdl. 344, Nos. 5–8.

[3] *Ibid.*, Bdl. 344, No. 3, Wood to Martin, 1757, Feb. 1.

[4] *Ibid.*, Bdl. 344, No. 2, Taylor to Martin, 1757, Jan. 20.

[5] In a memorial of the Remembrancer of the Court of Exchequer to the Lords of the Treasury [1772 or 1773 in date], the cost of the delivery of these books to the London and outport patent officers for the preceding fifty years and more was represented as £491. 11s. 2d. per annum. *Ibid.*, Bdl. 498, No. 163, Lord Masham to Lords of Treas.

Moreover, the customer was not necessary for the delivery into the Exchequer of coast bonds, or bonds given by a merchant that he would land his coastwise goods at another British port. When taken by the customer, such bonds had to be approved by the collector and controller; and when the bonds were sent to the Exchequer by the customer, lists of them, examined and signed by the collector and other patent officers, also had to be sent to that office, to the Customs Board, and to the Solicitor for Coast Bonds in the Customs Department. It is obvious that the collector and controller could have transacted this business without the customer.[1]

From this short survey, it may be seen that the collector participated in practically all the few useful duties attributed nominally to the customer at the close of the century. What limited parts of the business the customer still conducted could easily have been taken over by the collector. The commissioners appointed to examine, take, and state the public accounts recommended in their "Fifteenth Report" (1786) that the collector's superintendence of the business at a port "should be rendered universal, and not be thus broken in upon by the Interference of the Customer, in useless Repetition of a Duty performed by, or to a Deprivation of that Business which ought to belong to the Collector."[2] The Commissioners concluded that however necessary to the customs the office of customer might have been in remote times, by 1786 it had ceased to be useful, and they declared it "wholly useless—ought, in Consistency, to have been suppressed upon the Change introduced into the Customs, by the Appointment of Collectors, subsequent to the Year 1671—and has been permitted to exist too long by above a Century."[3]

The old Crown offices of controller and searcher, on the other hand, remained useful in the functions performed by their deputies. The controller, it will be remembered, had originally been appointed as a check on the customer, who in early times had charge of the entire collection of the duties. In the eighteenth century he still held the same position as far as any service was left to the customer. When the collector supplanted the customer, however, in the chief superintendence of the port, it became necessary for the controller to act as a check on the collector, keeping similar books, examining and signing all accounts and despatches, and sharing with him the joint

[1] *Repts. of Comrs.*, 1787, III, 172, "Fifteenth Rept.," 1786.
[2] *Ibid.*, III, 172.
[3] *Ibid.*, III, 173.

ADMINISTRATIVE PROBLEMS

responsibility of the port. Consequently the office of controller was essential. That office, however, like that of the customer, was composed of two parts, one a sinecure, the holder of which transacted no business but drew the fees, and the other, the active part, in which a deputy did all the work. This old patent office, or sinecure, which had persisted from the time of its apparent creation under Edward I and the entire duty of which had long been done by deputy, served no useful purpose and should have been abolished.[1]

The other ancient Crown officer, the searcher, was likewise necessary to the customs business, though his duty had been greatly altered since the creation of the office. Originally he had been appointed to superintend the import, export, and coastwise business on the quays, but in time other officers known as land-waiters came to be appointed for the landing and examining of foreign goods imported, while coast-waiters attended to the unloading and shipping of goods carried coastwise; hence the searcher's functions became confined to the supervision of the export business.[2] He examined all good entered outwards to see that the quantity, quality, number, and weight agreed with the exporter's cocket and to detect fraud. When a drawback or refunding of duties was due on exported goods, he certified the actual shipping on the basis of which the money was paid. Like the patentee controller and the patentee customer, the patentee searcher was a sinecurist whose duties were all performed by deputy, and the patent part of the office should have been discontinued.[3]

Though in the time of Henry IV the old Crown officers of customer, controller, and searcher had been directed to be resident upon their offices,[4] as the ports grew in number adding to them member ports and creeks, these patentees found that they could not serve in person at all those places, and the practice of employing deputies began.[5] By 1 Elizabeth they were required to appoint at least one able and sufficient deputy or servant to reside in certain specified ports and in every port, creek, or road where a servant or any one of them had been continually resident for ten years [6]; and by a later act of 13

---

[1] *Repts. of Comrs.*, 1778, III, 173–174. On the controller, see Crouch, *Complete Guide to Officers* (1732), pp. 3, 4; see also *Rules of the Water-side* (1715), p. 91.

[2] Crouch, *Complete Guide to Officers* (1732), p. 3; *Repts. of Comrs.*, 1787, III, 174, "Fifteenth Rept.," 1786.

[3] *Ibid.*, III, 174.

[4] I Hen. IV, c. 13; 4 Hen. IV, c. 20; 13 Hen. IV, c. 5.

[5] *Repts. of Comrs.*, 1787, III, 177, "Fifteenth Rept.," 1786; *First Rept. of Comrs. of Cust. on Cust.* [Cd. 2186], p. 79, App. B., H.C. (1857), iii.

[6] 1 Eliz. c. 11, s. 8.

and 14 Charles II they were obliged to make provision for the transaction of their business, either by themselves or their deputies, whenever any member, creek, or place should be appointed by virtue of Exchequer commission.[1] In the eighteenth century these officers appointed their deputies at each of the member-ports and creeks under their jurisdiction and usually entrusted a deputy with the transaction of the business at the head-port. Crouch, writing in 1732, states that the customers "are scarce ever known to act themselves, unless where they are Collectors likewise; but in the smaller Ports do usually appoint the Collectors to be their Deputies, and in the larger Ports they have distinct Deputies; to whom they are obliged to allow at least twenty Pounds per Annum, or else to relinquish to them the whole Fees."[2] As for the controllers and searchers, he observes that it was the practice for them likewise to appoint deputies at the principal ports, "scarce any of them acting themselves." The controllers' deputies, in the smaller ports, were often the collectors' clerks, while the searchers' deputies were frequently the land-waiters; in the larger ports, however, it was usual for these officers to appoint deputies of their own.[3] By 1784 only ten patent officers at the outports acted in person; fifty-seven acted by deputy, and there were 299 deputies,[4] since one principal might appoint several deputies.[5] It was estimated

[1] 13 and 14 Chas. II, c. 11, s. 14. The searcher, however, rarely had a deputy at a creek, since foreign business was seldom transacted there. For the numbers of ports in the eighteenth century, see *infra,* Ch. V, p. 168.

[2] Crouch, *Complete Guide to Officers* (1732), p. 2. Even earlier in the period there was a like situation with respect to the customer. In 1708 (May 10) the Customs Board in a communication to Godolphin referred thus to the office of collector [customer] "wch office then [1674] (as in most parts now) was to be executed by Deputy, no constant attendance being necessary, the Patentees not having the Direccōn of any inferiour Officers nor Charged with the Receipt of money, wch is a matter of great hazard to the Collectors being to answer all Accidents of Remittances and other Losses to wch they are Subjected." P.R.O., Treas. Outletters, Cust., XV, 108.

[3] Crouch, *Complete Guide to Officers* (1732), pp. 3, 4.

[4] *Repts. of Comrs.*, 1787, III, 125, "Fifteenth Rept.," 1786. In the list of patent offices of 1784 are included several which in reality were held by constitution, though they formerly had been patent offices and were still so considered. At Bristol there were four patent king's-waiters in addition to the usual patentees common to all ports. In three head-ports the office of the customer was divided into two separate departments. Apart from the three principal patent places and the office of the Bristol king's-waiters, only one other outport post was executed by deputy in 1784—the coast-waiter for Sandwich. For a detailed account of the outport patent offices, see *ibid.,* III, 125, 585–587, App. No. 4.

[5] The customer of Plymouth in 1782 had substitutes in at least twelve different places. P.R.O., Chatham Papers, Bdl. 285, Musgrave to Shelburne, 1782, Dec. 10.

ADMINISTRATIVE PROBLEMS

in 1786 that, were the useless office of customer suppressed and the sinecure parts of the offices of controller and searcher discontinued, out of these 366 patent and deputy officers in the outports 157 unnecessary officers altogether might have been dispensed with.[1] The complexity introduced into the customs by the existence of so many worthless offices would have been bad enough if it had been confined to the inferior and unimportant posts of the establishment, but when it affected the business of two at least of the most important offices in the customs, it became a serious matter.[2]

Not only was there waste in the continuance of these useless departments, but the old Crown patent offices and the deputies to the customer laid a heavy expense on the public in salaries and fees. The principals received small salaries from the Crown by the terms of their patents, and in some cases they also had allowances on the customs establishment.[3] Emoluments of various kinds which accrued in the transaction of their business were granted to them by patent as well,[4] the fees constituting the most lucrative part of their remuneration.[5] Thus, to take an extreme case, at Chester the average annual remuneration of the customer for 1762–1764 was £78. 6s. 8d. in salary and £658. 2s. 10½d. in fees; for the patent controller, £20 in salary and £437. 0s. 6½d. in fees; and for the patent searcher, £3. 6s. 8d. in salary and £796. 13s. in fees.[6] The net expense of the office of customer at the outports in 1784 was £14,236. 15s. 9d.; that of the patent controllers and searchers who did not act and of the four patent king's-waiters in Bristol[7] was £8,879. 12s. 4½d., making an annual total of £23,116. 8s. 1½d.[8] The total charge to the public and to indi-

---

[1] *Repts. of Comrs.*, 1787, III, 180, "Fifteenth Rept.," 1786. On this page of the report the total number of patent and deputed outport officers in 1784 is given as 365.

[2] In London practically all the principal officers of the collection—the several customers, collectors, controllers, searchers, and surveyors—held their places by patent; and the chief executives in the Central Office were for the most part patentees as well. These officers were in a position similar to that of the outport patentees. See *infra*, Chs. III, IV.

[3] *Repts. of Comrs.*, 1787, III, 129-130, "Fifteenth Rept.," 1786.

[4] As indicated by the many Treasury fiants in the Treasury Out-letters, Customs.

[5] *Repts. of Comrs.*, 1787, III, 175-176, "Fifteenth Rept.," 1786.

[6] B.M., Additional Manuscripts, 8133, f. 6, "An Account of the Officers employed in the Revenue of the Customs in England with the Value of their Places, arising from Salaries, Fees and other Perquisites," Part I; see also P.R.O., Chatham Papers, Bdl. 285, Musgrave to Shelburne, 1782, Dec. 10.

[7] See *supra*, p. 12, n. 4.

[8] *Repts. of Comrs.*, 1787, III, 176, "Fifteenth Rept.," 1786.

viduals for the payment of all officers belonging to the outports was £146,977. 19s. 1½d.,[1] of which £23,116. 8s. 1½d., more than one sixth of the cost of the entire outport organization, was paid either for useless services or to sinecurists. This figure does not, however, accurately represent the expense of these offices, since the patentees allowed their deputies either a salary or fees for services really necessary in the case of the controller and the searcher.

These old offices not only made for complexity and expense: at times the interests of the revenue itself were sacrificed to them.[2] In the appointment and dismissal of deputies the patent officers had important privileges which sometimes conflicted with the administration of the Customs Commissioners. As the Treasury fiants[3] and an opinion of the Attorney-General[4] show, the principals had the power to appoint their deputies (subject, in most cases, to approval by the Treasury), together with the power to dismiss them.[5] The "Fifteenth Report" of the Commissioners of Accounts in 1786 indicates that no deputy appears to have been authorized to act upon the death, resignation, or removal of a patent officer, until a successor was appointed and the deputy was reappointed by the new principal.[6] At such times, however, the Customs Commissioners, empowered by the Treasury, undoubtedly directed the deputy to conduct the business.[7] When the

[1] *Repts. of Comrs.*, 1787, III, 153.

[2] *Ibid.*, III, 179; P.R.O., Chatham Papers, Bdl. 285, Musgrave to Shelburne, 1782, Dec. 10.

[3] The Treasury Out-letters, Customs, contain numerous instruments of appointment which required that deputies to the patent officers be first approved by the Lord High Treasurer or the Lords of the Treasury. E. g., *ibid.*, XVI, 195, 1714, Jan. 13.

[4] *Ibid.*, XV, 171, Cust. Comrs. to Godolphin, 1709, May 3.

[5] In the case of a London under-searcher in 1785 a customs solicitor gave his opinion that the patentee was legally vested with the right to dismiss his deputy. P.R.O., Treasury Papers, Bdl. 611, No. 104, Cust. Comrs. to Lords of Treas., 1785, Aug. 31.

[6] *Repts. of Comrs.*, 1787, III, 177, "Fifteenth Rept.," 1786.

[7] That such cases might have proved serious is shown by an extreme instance of the kind in 1775. In that year the office of the London Patent Collector-Inwards devolved to Sir Horatio Mann, Minister at Florence, who was unable to attend in London to take the oath of office immediately. The Customs Commissioners in much perplexity represented to the Lords of the Treasury that "as the Case is unprecedented, We are at a loss to know how and by whom the Collection is to be carried on during this Interval, and in what Manner and in whose Name, the Money so Collected is to be paid into the Hands of the Receiver General, in order to its being paid into the Exchequer.

"This being a matter of very great Importance, as well as peculiar Nicety and Difficulty in point of Law and prudence, We think it necessary to give Your Lordships this early Intimation of it, and pray to receive Your Lordship's Directions

ADMINISTRATIVE PROBLEMS 15

place of a deputy became vacant, his successor could not be appointed in regular and legal form save by a deputation from the patentee.[1] Thus it might happen that positions remained legally unfilled for some time while patent officers resided in other localities or could not be traced.[2] The danger that might arise to the revenue under such circumstances is evident in the case of Sir John Burgoyne, controller of the Port of Chester, who was in the West Indies in 1782. Respecting Burgoyne's absence, Sir William Musgrave, a Customs Commissioner, informed Shelburne that "as no Person can appoint his Deputies but himself, the Port of Beaumaris is now without a Comptroller for Want of his Deputation, And in Case his Substitute at Liverpoole should die, the Board would have no Comptroller upon the Collection of upwards of £200,000 Pr. Añn at that Port, and all the Accounts must stand still for several years 'till a fresh Deputation can be sent out & be return'd properly signed by him, to authorize some Person to officiate there."[3] As a matter of fact, Musgrave's fears were subsequently realized. The deputy controller at Liverpool did die, and the appointment of a new deputy by the patentee in the Indies required considerable time. This was represented by the Customs Commissioners to the Lords of the Treasury "who, to prevent this important Office from remaining vacant," issued a warrant to the Commissioners authorizing and requiring them to depute the person therein named to be deputy controller at Liverpool, upon his giving the same amount of security as was given by his predecessor.[4] Thus, when such cases arose in actual practice, the Lords of the Treasury unquestionably provided for a substitute to carry on the business and, as in the case of a London deputy king's-waiter, directed that he be permitted "to Act and Execute the said Office of Deputy King's Waiter as amply to all Intents and purposes as if he had been there-

---

herein." P.R.O., Treasury Papers, Bdl. 516, No. 248, Cust. Comrs. to Lords of Treas., 1775, Dec. 22.

[1] *Repts. of Comrs.*, 1787, III, 177, "Fifteenth Rept.," 1786.

[2] A report for 1784, relating to the patent officers at Hull, was returned in blank from that port to the Commissioners of Accounts, two of the patentees being in London and Dorchester respectively and the deputy to the third in Scotland. At several other ports similar conditions prevailed. The Board finally issued orders to the patent officers themselves but was unable to find all of them. *Ibid.*, III, 119–120.

[3] P.R.O., Chatham Papers, Bdl. 285, Musgrave to Shelburne, 1782, Dec. 10.

[4] *Repts. of Comrs.*, 1787, III, 177–178, "Fifteenth Rept.," 1786. Unfortunately the bond of the former deputy could not be found; consequently the amount of the security could not be ascertained. As a result, the appointment was again delayed and the Customs Commissioners were finally obliged to settle the penalty themselves.

unto appointed by the said Nichas Man [patentee]."[1] Such interference by patentees in the Board's administration, by putting the work of important offices in some respects outside the jurisdiction of the Customs Commissioners, seriously threatened the efficiency of the service.

Many deputies held several positions at one time, filling one or more offices on the establishment and acting as deputy to one or more patent officers. Deputy customers frequently served as collectors,[2] and a deputy searcher might be a tide-surveyor in a port.[3] Very often several offices were obviously incompatible, as when a deputy searcher acted also as deputy controller, which office was supposed to be his check. Furthermore, when a man held several offices, the duty in one or two inevitably had to suffer. The Board was well aware of the danger to the revenue from this practice, for instances are not wanting of an officer being obliged to choose in which of three capacities he would serve,[4] and of refusal by the Board to allow one man to hold two incongruous positions.[5]

[1] P.R.O., Treas. Out-Letters, Cust., XIX, 29, Lords of Treas. to Cust. Comrs., Collector-Inwards, and Principal Officers of London, 1726, June 4. The king's-waiters, engaged in the importation business at the waterside in the Port of London, were patent officers who executed their duty by deputy.

[2] E. g., Cust. Ho. Lib., Notes and Extracts from the Minutes and Orders issued by the Commissioners of the Customs for the Instruction and Government of their Officers, Presented to the Board of Customs by Sir William Musgrave, I, "Liverpoole," 1720, Aug. 3. This reference will henceforth be cited as "Extracts Board Minutes."

[3] E. g., P.R.O., Treas. Out-letters, Cust., XXIII, 309, West to Cust. Comrs., 1747, Mar. 7.

[4] E. g., Cust. Ho. Lib., Extracts Board Minutes, II, "Officers," 1712, May 16.

[5] The attitude of the Board in this connection is well defined in a case which arose in 1744. Upon receiving a letter from the Maldon collector informing them that one Jonas Maldon had been sworn into the employment of deputy controller and deputy searcher at Leigh, the Commissioners disapproved: "We esteem you very blameable for presuming to admit him into both the offices in direct breech of our resolution and directions signifyed to you in our order of the 2nd Aug. last with relation to Mr May, Deputy Comptroller. And it being incompatible with the service for any one person to execute both the Duties of Deputy Comptroller and Searcher, you are forth with to transmit us your answer why you admitted Jonas Maldon in breech of our said orders." (Cust. Ho. Lib., Selections from Customs Outport Records, compiled by B. R. Leftwich, (East Coast) 1923, p. 4, Maldon, Board to Collector, 1743-1762, 1744, Mar. 29.) In another case in 1786, upon a vacancy occurring in the office of patent customer and collector of Carlisle, the Customs Commissioners submitted to the Lords of the Treasury whether the collector should not be appointed by Treasury warrant "(in order to remedy the Inconveniences this Board had experienced, and the Injury the Revenue had suffered, by the Offices of the Customer and Collector being held by one and the same Person)." P.R.O., Treasury Papers, Bdl. 629, No. 90, Robinson to Rose,

ADMINISTRATIVE PROBLEMS

Sometimes deputies entirely unqualified for the customs business were appointed, with evil results. In 1782 Musgrave informed Shelburne that "many Patentees consider their Employments only as so many Farms, & let them out to Deputies very ill-qualified to serve the Publick, merely because they are the highest Bidders, & will send them the largest Rents; which compels such miserable Substitutes to be guilty of unreasonable Indulgences (to call them no worse) towards the Merchants, that they may extort from them unlawful Perquisites in return."[1] To give a single instance, we find John Wilson at Stockton on Tees writing to a patentee respecting the appointment of his deputy "wherein the recommendation of Mr. Hanson or of some one conversant in the Customs is extremely necessary for where a deputy is appointed who is an absolute stranger to the business of the Customs & consequently incapable of performing his duty, It not only derives a burthen on the other officers within doors but also a contempt on the office in general which was indeed Mr. Arundell's case with us."[2] Though the Customs Commissioners usually seem to have passed upon the qualifications of deputies to patent searchers and king's-waiters in London, and frequently upon those of the deputies to outport patentees, still many inefficient substitutes undoubtedly managed to hold office.

In some respects the system of payment of deputies threatened the security of the revenue. Deputies to the patent officers were paid by their principals either a specified allowance or a share of the fees, and occasionally they received a small salary on the customs establishment and a payment by incidents.[3] Allowances on the establishment appear principally to have been made when the remuneration from patentees was necessarily inconsiderable[4] or when new ports were set out and additional substitutes were necessary.[5] The sums which

---

1786, Apr. 6. In connection with this case, see also *ibid.*, Bdl. 626, No. 160, Stiles to Steele, 1786, Jan. 7.

[1] P.R.O., Chatham Papers, Bdl. 285, Musgrave to Shelburne, 1782, Dec. 10.

[2] Cust. Ho. Lib., Sel. from Cust. Outport Recds., Northern England, 1924, pp. 195–196, Stockton on Tees, Collector to Board, John Wilson to William Sharpe, 1756, May 25.

[3] E. g., see case of the deputy controller at Exeter. P.R.O., Treas. Out-letters, Cust., XXIV, 16, Cust. Comrs. to Lords of Treas., 1750, Nov. 28.

[4] E. g., *ibid.*, XVII, 93–94, Cust. Comrs. to Lords of Treas., 1718, Apr. 7; Treasury warrant, 1718, Apr. 18; Cust. Ho. Lib., Sel. from Cust. Outport Recds., South Coast, 1925, p. 41, Dartmouth, Board to Collector, 1732, July 11.

[5] The allowances to these deputies were inserted on the establishment to the credit of the patentees. E. g., see P.R.O., Treas. Out-letters, Cust., XVII, 178–179, Cust. Comrs. to Lords of Treas., 1719, May 14; Treasury warrant, 1719, June 9;

the principals allowed their deputies in the larger ports were small compared with the lucrative value of the patent employments, while in the smaller ports they were exceedingly meager.[1] In 1687 the Lord High Treasurer had regulated the allowances to deputy customers in the outports by ordering that the patentees should allow their respective deputies £20 per annum, unless the fees should fall short of the sum of £20, in which case the substitutes were to be allowed the value of the fees and no more. By a warrant of 1729–30 the patentees holding office at that date, and all future customers, controllers, and searchers, were subjected to like regulations in respect of allowances to their deputies; and both of these orders were confirmed by a warrant of 1761.[2] It is of some interest that deputies in the most important offices of the customs should legally be no better provided for by their principals after a lapse of seventy-four years, during which time a vast increase in commerce took place.[3] Though payments on the establishment and by incidents undoubtedly compensated somewhat for this, still such remuneration seems to have been kept down to a minimum, as may be illustrated by the case of the deputy controller at Exeter in 1750. Upon the establishment of a new deputy there, the Customs Commissioners informed the Lords of the Treasury that the former deputy had a total income of £60, consisting of an allowance of £10 on the establishment, £30 by incidents, and £20 by the principal, "which is more than is usually allowed to other Deputy Comptrollers"; and recommended that the new deputy be allowed no more than an additional £10 on the establishment, which, with the £20 from the patentee, would be sufficient in lieu of any allowance by incidents.[4] The method of payment between the patentee

---

XVII, 218, Cust. Comrs. to Lords of Treas., 1719, Sept. 9; Treasury warrant, 1719, Nov. 11.

[1] B.M., Add. MSS. 8133, "An Account of the Officers employed in the Revenue of the Customs in England with the Value of their Places, arising from Salaries Fees and other Perquisites."

[2] P.R.O., Treas. Out-letters, Cust., XXVI, 346, Treasury warrant, 1761, June 12; *Calendar of Treasury Books and Papers*, 1729–1730, p. 505, Treasury warrant, 1729–30, Jan. 27. The other warrant was dated 1687, Oct. 6.

[3] In 1782 Sir William Musgrave stated, with reference to the controller, that "this [remuneration] is really inadequate to the Service and ought to be encreased to £50 ℔ ann. at least." *Eighteenth Century Documents Relating to the Royal Forests, the Sheriffs, and Smuggling* [*University of Michigan Publications: History and Political Science*, VII], edited by Arthur Lyon Cross (New York, 1928), p. 251.

[4] P.R.O., Treas. Out-letters, Cust., XXIV, 16, Cust. Comrs. to Lords of Treas., 1750, Nov. 28; Treasury warrant, 1750, Dec. 11.

ADMINISTRATIVE PROBLEMS

and the deputy depended upon the terms of agreement between them, and those agreements varied from port to port.[1] Such an arrangement governing remuneration of deputies, together with the small allowances made, affected the personnel of such positions and must have encouraged inefficiency and corruption.

The Commissioners of Accounts, in summing up the powers of the patent officers in the appointment of their deputies, stated that a "Dominion of this Kind, vested in any Officer belonging to an Office such as the Customs, and in an Officer seldom bearing any Share in, ignorant of, and unconcerned about, the Duties of his Office; generally residing at a Distance from it; possibly absent from the Kingdom; seemed to us to offend against all good Order and sound principle; to make the Office subordinate to the Officer; and to lead to Consequences mischievous to the Revenue and dangerous for the Public." [2]

Though the system of patent offices was pernicious in that the privileges granted to such officers and the way in which they operated often proved detrimental to the service, it was to some extent kept within bounds by the supervision of the Customs Board. Authority over the patent officers was granted to the Customs Commissioners by their patent, which expressly stated that all officers of the customs appointed by letters patent, together with their deputies and all other officers, should obey such orders and directions as they should from time to time receive from the Commissioners.[3] Recognition of that authority was made in different connections throughout the period, receiving perhaps its most significant statement in an opinion of the Attorney-General in 1774.[4] But an instance in 1783 is of especial in-

---

[1] *Repts. of Comrs.,* 1787, III, 576, App. No. 2, "Fifteenth Rept.," 1786.
[2] *Ibid.,* III, 177.
[3] P.R.O., Patent Roll, 23 Chas. II, P. 2, No. 1, Mem. 35, dorse, [1671], Sept. 27. See *infra,* Ch. VI, p. 197, n. 3.
[4] See *infra,* Ch. II, p. 60, n., for the opinion. In this year the Commissioners signified to several of the Bench Officers disapproval of their conduct; but some of those officers "have of late adopted a most absurd Opinion that as they act under the immediate Appointment of their Principals who hold their Offices for Life or Years, that they are not amenable to this Board, nor subject to Our Orders and Controul, We are however with the Advice of His Majesty's Attorney General proceeding to take such measures as We are in hopes may prove effectual towards reducing them under the necessary Obedience and Subordination without which it will be impossible for Us to obey Your Lordships Commands according to Our Patent or even to furnish such Accounts or Information as may be required by the Houses of Parliament." P.R.O., Treasury Papers, Bdl. 507, No. 237, Cust. Comrs. to Lords of Treas., 1774, Aug. 25.

terest in its practical applications. In that year the Attorney-General gave his opinion relative to the Customs Commissioners' power to compel a London patent officer to see that his deputies should furnish accounts when called for and to obey all orders issued by the Board. Upon this statement of opinion, the Commissioners gave orders to the patent Bench Officers in the London Custom House that, in conformity with the fourteenth clause of the Commissioners' patent, they should observe such orders as they should receive from the Customs Commissioners for the time being or from any four of them, or the Board would without further notice cause such process at law to be commenced against the offenders for any disobedience of orders, as should be advised by the Attorney-General.[1]

The position of the Board of Customs Commissioners and the Lords of the Treasury in connection with the appointment of deputies is not too clear, but a few conclusions may be drawn. Though the power of appointment was vested in the patentees, by the latter part of the period the Lords of the Treasury had effected so active a participation in that patronage that it was stated "the Deputies to Patent Officers [are appointed] by the Principals, when the Treasury does not interfere; but the Person is more frequently recommended to the Commrs, and to the Patent Officers by a Letter from the Secretary of the Treasury."[2] In accord with this practice, though the Customs Commissioners had no authority in the actual appointment of deputies, they "procured" their appointment upon direction of the Lords of the Treasury[3] and retarded the appointment of deputies in some cases until the pleasure of the Lords had been signified.[4]

Throughout the period, the Customs Commissioners could "desire"

---

[1] Cust. Ho. Lib., Extracts Board Minutes, IV, 87–88, 1783, Jan. 28. Cf. P.R.O., Treasury Papers, Bdl. 584, Nos. 49–50, enclosure in No. 51, Stiles to Rose, 1783, Jan. 29. For an instance of earlier date, see Cust. Ho. Lib., Extracts Board Minutes, I, "Commissioners," 1724, July 3. Though these cases pertain to the London patent offices, they held for the outport patent places as well.

[2] P.R.O., Chatham Papers, Bdl. 231, manuscript booklet entitled, "The Business done in the Treasury by the Officers—distinguishing each Particular Branch."

[3] Numerous directions from the Lords of the Treasury to the Customs Commissioners bear evidence of this. See *infra,* Ch. VI, p. 200, n. 5. For reference to a refusal by a patentee to appoint the deputy named by the Treasury Board, see P.R.O., Treas. Out-letters, Cust., XXXIV, 343, Rose to Cust. Comrs., 1786, Feb. 20, and XXXIV, 350, Steele to Cust. Comrs., 1786, Mar. 20. For instance of a remonstrance by the Customs Board against the appointment of a deputy named by the Lords of the Treasury, see *infra,* Ch. II, p. 47, n. 4.

[4] See *infra,* Ch. VI, p. 200, n. 7; p. 201.

ADMINISTRATIVE PROBLEMS

or require patent officers to appoint deputies [1]; and in some cases they exercised a certain power of practical veto or approval in refusing them or admitting them into the service.[2] It seems to have been usual for the Customs Board to criticize the appointment of deputies to searchers and king's-waiters in London and frequently that of the outport deputies, though just what power was exerted over the deputies to the other patent officers in London is not so apparent.[3] One reference will illustrate the usual practice of the Customs Commissioners in connection with the appointment of deputies in the outports. John Margerum, patent controller at Ipswich, had dismissed Francis Pulham, deputy at the port of Harwich, and appointed Robert Stevens in his place. The Customs Commissioners informed Margerum that they very much disapproved of Stevens's character and therefore could not give their approbation to his appointment. To this Margerum replied that upon inquiry he could find no reason for revoking his deputation and that he had the same power as all other patent officers had, to appoint whom he pleased for his deputy providing he was properly qualified, and also to dismiss him when proper. The Customs Commissioners in a memorial on the case to the Lords of the Treasury observed, "That although it has been the Practice during the Course of many Years, for Patent Comptrollers to Appoint their own Deputies, yet, whenever it has appeared to this Board, that such Deputies were not qualified for their Employment, they have constantly refused to Accept of them—And that there has been several Instances of Patent Comptrollers having withdrawn their Deputations to such Persons, but not one Precedent of any Comptroller insisting upon the Appointing an Unqualified Person for his Deputy, after he had been objected to." The Customs Commissioners requested the Lords of the Treasury to signify their commands to

---

[1] E. g., Cust. Ho. Lib., Extracts Board Minutes, II, "Patent Officers," 1725, Feb. 9; Cust. Ho. Lib., Sel. from Cust. Outport Recds., West Coast, 1926, p. 122, Beaumaris, Board to Collector, 1723, Sept. 17.

[2] See for example Cust. Ho. Lib., Extracts Board Minutes, I, "Commissioners," 1752, Feb. 19; Sel. from Cust. Outport Recds. (South Coast) 1922, p. 116, Weymouth, Collector to Board, 1745–1750, 1749, Aug. 2. For an example of the reference of deputies of king's-waiters to the Customs Board, see P.R.O., Treas. Outletters, Cust., XV, 423, Oxford to Cust. Comrs., 1712, July 10. For instances of the Customs Board's presentments of deputies to the Treasury and Treasury warrant, see *ibid.*, XVI, 392, Treasury warrant, 1716, Oct. 2; XVI, 466, Cust. Comrs. to Lords of Treas., 1717, July 10; Treasury warrant, 1717, July 20.

[3] There are numerous instances of the Commissioners passing upon various London deputies, as contained in *ibid.*, XVI, 1712–1717.

Margerum, that he immediately recall his deputation to Stevens, and either act himself at Harwich or appoint some person properly qualified of whom the Customs Commissioners would approve.[1] The Treasury Board of course possessed and exercised the power of approval over deputies, as was specified in the creating of patent officers [2]; but the Customs Commissioners occasionally admitted deputies without such approval, as would appear from an instance in 1782 when a Treasury secretary directed the Customs Board "that in all future Cases of Vacancies of any Deputy Officers, You do agreable to the Directions in the Appointments of their Principals, not admit them to their Offices unless approved of by my Lords." [3]

Not only were the Commissioners apparently able to refuse a deputy in some cases, but they also were able to suspend a deputy [4] and to force his dismissal.[5] Furthermore, the consent of the Customs Board or that of the Lords of the Treasury was necessary for the dismissal of the deputy by the patentee, at least if the deputy received a salary from the Crown. For example, when the controller of Plymouth insisted upon the dismissal of one deputy and the appointment of another, "he was told by the Board that the Deputy being paid a Salary by the Crown, it was not in his Power to dismiss him without the

---

[1] P.R.O., Treasury Papers, Bdl. 325, No. 18, Cust. Comrs. to Lords of Treas., 1747, Mar. 27.

[2] For examples of Treasury approval of deputies to customers, searchers, and controllers, see P.R.O., Treas. Out-letters, Cust., XXXIII, 39, 41–44; Treasury warrants, 1782–1784. For a specific instance of the necessity of Treasury assent to an outport deputy controller, see *ibid.*, XVI, 195, Fiant, 1714, Jan. 13. For an indication of Treasury approval of a London deputy under-searcher, see P.R.O., Treasury Papers, Bdl. 609, No. 123, Form of appointment, 1784, Oct. In 1792, upon investigation of the practice on former occasions, it was found "to have been an invariable Rule to have the approbation of the Treasury on the appointment of the Deputy to the Chief Patent Searcher" in London. P.R.O., Chatham Papers, Bdl. 283, "Copy of the Boards order of the 31 Janry 1792 respecting the Deputy to the Chief Searcher, Po: London."

[3] P.R.O., Treas. Out-letters, Cust., XXXII, 86, Robinson to Cust. Comrs., 1782, Feb. 2. It is of interest to note, however, that Treasury approval—at least at the end of the period—did not automatically guarantee the admittance of the deputy by the Customs Board: in a case in 1792 the Commissioners declared that because of the inability and age of the deputy in question they could not admit his nomination," even though such nomination had met the approbation of the Lords of the Treasury." P.R.O., Chatham Papers, Bdl. 283, "Copy of the Boards order of the 31 Janry 1792 respecting the Deputy to the Chief Searcher, Po: London."

[4] *Repts. of Comrs.*, 1787, III, 399, App. No. 20, "Fourteenth Report, Relative to the Charges of Management of the Custom Duties in the Port of London for the Year 1784," 1785.

[5] E. g., P.R.O., Treas. Out-letters, Cust., XIX, 418, Ash to Lords of Treas. [1729].

ADMINISTRATIVE PROBLEMS

Consent of the Treasury or this Board; and as to any Complaint against his Deputy, the Commissioners had sent an Officer over to examine into them, and when an Answer comes he would have notice." [1]

Patent officers were to some extent held accountable for the behavior of their deputies and clerks, as was stated clearly by the Commissioners of Accounts in 1786: "The Patentee has always been considered as responsible for his Deputy." [2] Specific cases indicate that if a deputy refused to comply with Board orders, neglected his duty, or committed serious errors in its execution, the principal as well as the substitute could be held answerable. For example, in an instance in 1783 which involved the misconduct of the deputies of the Duke of Manchester, Patent Collector-Inwards in the Port of London, the Attorney-General was of opinion that "If this Subordinate Department hesitates any longer after application made to the Duke to do what is required by their Superiors the Commissioners it will be necessary to institute a proceeding by Scire facias to repeal a Patent the Duties of which are not performed, and which, in this Instance at least, appears to be a Clog upon the administration of so large a Branch of the Public Revenue—The Duke of Manchester is Answerable to the Publick for the Misconduct of his Deputies." [3] Two years later the salaries of certain Long Room patent officers in London were stopped because of delay in the accounts of their deputies; and the Commissioners declared that, whenever the accounts fell into such arrears, not only would they withhold payment of salaries until the work should be brought up to date, but they would also mulct the defaulter as he deserved. [4] In another instance proceedings in the Ex-

---

[1] Cust. Ho. Lib., Extracts Board Minutes, II, "Patent Officers," 1722, Jan. 9.

[2] From one instance it would appear that if the deputy had not been appointed by the patentee and the patentee further had had no voice in the appointment (as rarely happened), the principal could not be held responsible. *Repts. of Comrs.*, 1787, III, 178, "Fifteenth Rept.," 1786.

[3] P.R.O., Treasury Papers, Bdl. 584, No. 50, enclosure in No. 51, Stiles to Rose, 1783, Jan. 29. In a similar case the following year, upon a delay of the London Bench Officers in returning an account desired by the Treasury, Rose was commanded to acquaint the Customs Commissioners "that if a speedy Obedience is not now paid to the Directions before referred to as explained by my Letter to Your Secretary of Yesterday they [the Treasury Lords] will immediately direct Copies of the Patents of the offending Parties or their Principals to be laid before his Mˢ Attorney General that they may be informed whether such Interruptions to the publick Service may not be prevented in future." P.R.O., Treas. Out-letters, Cust., XXXIV, 275, Rose to Cust. Comrs., 1784, Dec. 10.

[4] Cust. Ho. Lib., Extracts Board Minutes, IV, 88, 89, 1785, Jan. 26, 29. For other examples of patentees' responsibility, see *ibid.*, I, "King's Waiters," 1721,

chequer and Queen's Bench were begun against an outport patent officer and his deputy because of some delinquency on the part of the deputy.[1] For failure or corruption in duty, the patent could be repealed by instituting proceedings by *scire facias*.[2]

Thus by insistence on the observance of their orders by the patent officers, and by their influence in the appointment or dismissal of deputies, the Customs Commissioners asserted their authority over the patent officers. On the other hand, the exercise by patent officers of the extensive powers of their position gave opportunity for the play of cross-purposes in administration and for the introduction of confusion into the system.

Such, then, was the general position of the old Crown offices in the eighteenth-century customs organization. The very existence of the useless office of customer and the sinecure parts of that of controller and searcher clogged administration. The salaries and fees of such offices were a needless expense, their cost to the public constituting a considerable proportion of the total upkeep of the outport offices. Though subordinate to the Customs Board, the patentees possessed certain power over their deputies in appointment, dismissal, and remuneration which permitted them extensive influence over the personnel of the offices, interfered with the actual functioning of the customs machinery under the direction of the Customs Commissioners, and conflicted with the best interests of the revenue. These anomalies in the system continued until the end of the eighteenth century,[3] though during the latter part of the period efforts were made to abolish them: in 1783 a bill for that purpose [4] was introduced in Parliament only to be defeated; in 1786 the Treasury announced its de-

---

Aug. 4; III, 35, 1769, Feb. 9. Occasionally, however, the principals were not deemed "culpable" for the neglect of their deputies. See *ibid.*, III, 277, 1759, May 30, 1770, Aug. 29.

[1] P.R.O., Treas. Out-letters, Cust., XVI, 147, Lowndes to Cust. Comrs., 1714, July 5.

[2] P.R.O., Treasury Papers, Bdl. 584, No. 50, enclosure in No. 51, Stiles to Rose, 1783, Jan. 29. For a specific example, see Cust. Ho. Lib., Extracts Board Minutes, II, "Patent Officers," 1746, Sept. 19.

[3] Final abolition was effected by act of Parliament, 38 Geo. III, c. 86, s. 1, 2, 3, 4.

[4] A copy of the printed bill is included in P.R.O., Chatham Papers, Bdl. 285, "A Bill for Vacating certain Grants. . . ." For the decision of the Treasury to introduce such a bill, see P.R.O., Treas. Out-letters, Cust., XXXIII, 390, Rose to Cust. Comrs., 1783, Jan. 30; and Cust. Ho. Lib., Extracts Board Minutes, V, 151, 1783, Jan. 31. In P.R.O., Chatham Papers, Bdl. 285, is a copy of the detailed account of customs patent offices, given by Musgrave to Shelburne, 1782, Dec. 10.

ADMINISTRATIVE PROBLEMS

cision to leave unfilled outport patent offices as they became vacant [1]; and in that same year the Commissioners of Accounts strongly recommended that "from the combined Considerations of Economy, Order, and Expedience," these patent offices should be abolished.[2]

Thus, during the eighteenth century two systems existed side by side in the customs: the outport patent officers persisted as relics of the medieval system, one of them, the customer, being entirely useless, and practically all of them transacting their duties by deputies; on the other hand, active officers of the customs who were either deputies or were appointed by Treasury warrant took actual charge of the collection of the revenue. The continuation of this system of outport patent offices was one of the sources of the complexity which characterized the organization of the eighteenth-century customs service.

2. *The Complex Revenue System*

The confused system of revenue laws which the customs establishment had to enforce complicated the problems of administration considerably. To appreciate the causes of intricacy in the scheme of duties, it is necessary to begin with a survey of those duties as settled by the Act of Tonnage and Poundage of 12 Charles II. The Book of Rates established by that act, which governed the assessment of customs duties, marks the first important attempt to consolidate all the customs laws regulating duties, and may be taken as the foundation of the system which persisted throughout the greater part of the eighteenth century.[3] By the Act of Tonnage and Poundage there were three duties payable on goods imported or exported: a tonnage duty, which was a definite rate levied on each tun of wine imported; a poundage duty, which amounted to a shilling in the pound on imports, according to the supposed value of the article as listed in the Book

---

[1] P.R.O., Treas. Out-letters, Cust., XXXIV, 352–353, Rose to Cust. Comrs., 1786, Apr. 12. For an example of a specific case, see *ibid.*, XXXIV, 408, Treasury warrant, 1786, Apr. 24.

[2] *Repts. of Comrs.*, 1787, III, 179, "Fifteenth Rept.," 1786. The draft of another bill in 1792, providing for the abolition of these offices, may be found in P.R.O., Chatham Papers, Bdl. 285, "Customs Bill 1792." In this bundle are numerous papers relating to the Bills of 1783 and 1792.

[3] 12 Chas. II, c. 4. See *Accounts and Papers*, XXXV, H.C. 366-I, p. 406 (1868–1869), "Public Income and Expenditure," Part II; *Repts. of Comrs.*, 1787, III, 285, App. No. 66, "Thirteenth Report, Relative to the Manner of Passing the Accounts of the Customs, in the Office of the Auditors of the Imprest," 1785. Earlier books of rates had been issued in 1558 and 1604.

of Rates or determined by the oath of the exporter; and the ancient duty on woollen cloth exported. Certainly calculation of such duties was simple enough—one duty for every article and that a fixed rate in the case of most commodities, specified according to their value in the Book of Rates. Even so there were slight complications in allowances of discounts for prompt payment of duty.[1]

Soon after the Great Statute of 12 Charles II, deviations from the system of tonnage and poundage took place and were the primary cause of the complexity of the eighteenth-century system.[2] As a greater revenue came to be needed and the old Book of Rates proved insufficient both as to the articles listed as dutiable and as to the value which determined their rate, many new duties were added and the old duties were greatly modified. Time and again customs laws were passed augmenting the revenue or altering the schedule of rates until they "early brought about a degree of intricacy and confusion which was the despair alike of those who had to pay and of those who had to receive these varying and complicated duties."[3] Even in the reign of Charles II, before the customs was put in commission, the laws relating to duties and regulation of trade had become so numerous and confused that according to the author of the *Index Vectigalium* (1670) they were "both difficult in the discovery and doubtful in the interpretation."[4] The first great increase in the classes of duties took place under William III. Anne's reign saw an even greater increase[5]; more branches of duties were imposed between 1702 and 1714 than had been levied during the preceding three reigns together.

To these divisions of duties, many others were added during the century, until by 1784 no less than 100 separate accounts of customs duties had been opened. While only sixty-eight of these 100 branches[6] were in force in 1784, the accounts of twenty-seven other heads still

---

[1] *Repts. of Comrs.*, 1787, III, 285, App. No. 66; cf. Crouch, *Complete Guide to Officers* (1732), p. iii.
[2] P.R.O., Treasury Papers, Bdl. 530, Nos. 250–251, Cust. Comrs. to Lords of Treas., 1777, Apr. 29; cf. copy in B.M., Add. MSS. 8133 C, ff. 13–14.
[3] *First Rept. of Comrs. of Cust. on Cust.* [Cd. 2186], p. 17, H.C. (1857), iii.
[4] *Ibid.*, p. 17.
[5] See *The History of our National Debts and Taxes from 1688 to 1751* (London, 1753), Part II, pp. 3–8; Part III, pp. 8–20.
[6] By a "branch" or "head" of duties is meant a separate duty placed on a particular article or class of articles. For example, a New Duty on Spice and Pictures, levied in William III's reign, and an Additional Duty on Spice and Pictures, exacted in Anne's reign, were each considered a distinct branch of duties, as was a subsidy or an additional 25 per cent rate on French goods.

ADMINISTRATIVE PROBLEMS

remained open and were returned every year by the Controller-General of the customs to the Auditor of the Imprest, and five other branches continued as Plantation Duties.¹

In some instances duties were placed on articles not originally listed in the Book of Rates; and in others they were exacted on enumerated commodities under the headings of new subsidies (5 per cent in the pound on the value of the goods),² one-third ³ and two-thirds subsidies,⁴ imposts,⁵ and additional duties upon particular goods—in some cases to the extent of fifteen different duties on one article.⁶ For example, if in 1784 a merchant were importing twenty reams of French Royal Paper (ten reams Atlas Fine and ten reams Super Royal Fine), he would have been obliged to pay duties under thirteen different heads—subsidies, imposts, and additional and specific duties falling on French goods and paper.⁷

Each of these branches of duties had to be kept separate in the customs accounts. Thus, if a merchant were paying the thirteen different duties on one shipment of paper, the amount of each duty was entered under its own heading on the merchant's warrant for landing the goods and in the officers' books; and the money received for each duty was likewise paid into the Exchequer separately under its own distinct branch. Each new duty when levied was appropriated to some specific service or fund, usually indicated by the act. In 1784, thirty-six branches of duties and one half of the branch known as customs were carried to their respective funds: the General Fund, the Aggregate Fund, South Sea Fund, and Sinking Fund; eight were unappropriated; and the remaining twenty-four with the other moiety of the customs branch were specified for certain services.⁸ While such

---

¹ *Repts. of Comrs.*, 1787, III, 29, "Thirteenth Rept.," 1785; *First Rept. of Comrs. of Cust. on Cust.* [Cd. 2186], pp. 67–68, App. A., H.C. (1857), iii.

² 9 and 10 Wm. III, c. 23, 1698; 21 Geo. II, c. 2, 1747; 32 Geo. II, c. 10, 1759. See *Accounts and Papers*, XXXV, H.C. 366–I, p. 406 (1868–1869), "Public Income and Expenditure," Part II; Stephen Dowell, *A History of Taxation and Taxes in England from the Earliest Times to the Year 1885* (London, 1888), II, 44, 59, 69, 118–119, 123, 137.

³ 2 and 3 Anne, c. 9, 1703.

⁴ 3 and 4 Anne, c. 5, 1704.

⁵ For general imposts, see 2 Wm. and Mary, c. 4, 1690; 4 and 5 Wm. and Mary, c. 5, 1692; 19 Geo. III, c. 25, 1779; 22 Geo. III, esp. c. 28, 39, 66, 1782.

⁶ *First Rept. of Comrs. of Cust. on Cust.* [Cd. 2186], p. 67, App. A., H.C. (1857), iii.

⁷ *Ibid.*, p. 18.

⁸ *Repts. of Comrs.*, 1787, III, 53, "Thirteenth Rept.," 1785. For some years before 1699, various fees, annuities, pensions, and other yearly payments were payable out of the customs revenue by virtue of dormant warrants. For example, in

28 ORGANIZATION OF THE ENGLISH CUSTOMS

appropriation continued, duties had to be kept separate in customs accounts and in those of the Exchequer so that their proceeds could be used for the purpose indicated by Parliament. Thus it was impossible to put an end to the distinction of duties in the customs accounts without first ending the appropriation of duties in the Exchequer.[1]

Not only did many separate heads of duties cause confusion in the system, but the different principles that many of them followed in calculations further complicated collection. Successive acts of Parliament imposed new rules of computation as they levied new duties; and as they increased rates upon the articles named in former acts, they prescribed new methods of assessment, until such varied and multiplied rules for finding the duties involved the accounts in the utmost intricacy.[2] Thus, duties might be based on the weight of the article or upon its value on oath, or upon the gross price at which the goods were publicly sold, or upon the number or measure of the commodity, or upon the aggregate of former duties[3]; and if a number of articles of different kinds were included in one bill of lading, as frequently happened, the assessor was obliged to resort to many different rules before he could calculate the duties under all their separate branches in one bill.[4] In 1785 it was necessary to use at least two rules of computation in almost every entry of goods liable to duty, and in many cases five rules were applied.[5] Furthermore, the duties were calculated to such minute fractions as to be irreducible to any current English coin. The Customs Board offered a staggering example of such complexity to the Lords of the Treasury in their recommendation of consolidation in 1777:

A Dozen Hammers imported are rated or Valued at, 4^{sh} and are to pay 9^d & $4/20^{ths}$ of a Penny and $4/5^{ths}$ of a 20th of a penny neat Duty for every Dozen—besides for every hundred weight of Iron contained in the Hammers $\genfrac{}{}{0pt}{}{s\ d}{4..8}$ and $5/20^{ths}$ of a Penny—Here Your Lordships see that *different*

1697–8 the customs cashier was empowered to pay the consul of Tripoli his salary of £380. (*Cal. Treas. Books*, Oct., 1697–Aug., 1698, p. 232, 1697–8, Jan. 27.) By warrant of 1699, Apr. 28, however, the Customs Commissioners were ordered to forbear making any further disbursements from dormant warrant other than for charges of management. P.R.O., Treas. Out-letters, Cust., XIV, 20.

[1] *Repts. of Comrs.*, 1787, III, 51, "Thirteenth Rept.," 1785.
[2] *Ibid.*, III, 21–22.
[3] *Ibid.*, III, 21, 286–287, App. No. 66.
[4] *Ibid.*, III, 21–22.
[5] *Ibid.*, III, 48. For example, five rules were employed in estimating the charges on unrated French ordinary painted paper, which paid fourteen duties. *Ibid.*, III, 48–49.

ADMINISTRATIVE PROBLEMS

Computations are to be raised from the supposed Value or Rate, the Number and Species of the Goods, and the weight of the Materials, in order to discover the Customs; and then that these Duties turn out in such Sums as can neither be well paid nor carried to account, especially if, as the Law now stands they are again to be sub divided into six Branches, and Entered in as many Columns under the Titles of the Old Subsidy, New Subsidy—⅓ Subsidy—⅔ Subsidy—Subsidy 1747 and Impost 1690, to which they are Subject.[1]

These duties had to do either with goods listed in the Book of Rates (as of 12 Charles II, c. 4, or of 11 George I, c. 7) or with goods charged with a specific tax. But there was a large number of articles, called the unrated goods, that were charged with *ad valorem* and discriminating duties, which occasioned much of the difficulty of computation. By an *ad valorem* duty is meant a tax on unrated goods levied according to the value of the article as declared by the oath of the importer, or, in the case of East India goods, upon their produce at sale. Calculation of the import duty on corn offers an instance of a different kind of *ad valorem* reckoning, whereby the market prices of middling English corn and grain in the various counties, as certified officially to the customs officers, determined the duty to be collected on any grain imported within such counties.[2]

Ad valorem rating was open to many abuses. Disputes arose between the merchants and the customs officers as to the value to be set upon such goods, and a certain amount of ill feeling entered into their relations.[3] Since the duty on practically all unrated goods, except East India goods, was dependent upon the oath of the importer, wide opportunity for fraud existed, while abuses in the computation of the duties on East India commodities, which duties were dependent upon sale prices, were notorious.[4] For instance, upon in-

[1] P.R.O., Treasury Papers, Bdl. 530, No. 253, Cust. Comrs. to Lords of Treas., 1777, Apr. 29.

[2] The price had to reach a certain level before foreign grain could be imported. See description of such procedure in computation of duties and its abuses, B.M., Add. MSS. 8133 B, ff. 91, 93, William Arnold [Cowes collector], "Observations on the Laws for Regulating the Importation and Exportation of Corn," in papers of Sir William Musgrave, "Revenue of Customs." See also reference to the Attorney-General's opinion confirming the practice of 1 James II, c. 19. P.R.O., Treas. Out-letters, Cust., XV, 253–254, Cust. Comrs. to Lord High Treasurer, 1709, Dec. 31. See also Cust. Ho. Lib., Letter Book, Wells, 1712 To 1730, p. 257, Carkesse to Gentlemen [Wells], 1728, Oct. 10.

[3] *First Rept. of Comrs. of Cust. on Cust.* [Cd. 2186], p. 23, H.C. (1857), iii.

[4] For one reference to unfortunate aspects of the methods of computing duties on unrated East India goods, see B.M., Add. MSS. 18903, ff. 162–163, Cust. Comrs. to Lords of Treas. [1717 ?]. See also ff. 179–186. During many years of

vestigation of a parliamentary committee into the method of computing duties on unrated East India goods, the Customs Commissioners in 1711 informed Oxford that they had observed by a vote of the House that "there has been a very great Loss to the Revenue of the Customes upon unrated East India Goods & other unrated Goods by the Method practiced in the Custome House in the Computing the Duties on the said unrated Goods," whereby there had been no more than £18. 8s. 9½d. per hundred received for the duties though there had been allowed for the same duties £52. 2s. 6d. It appeared that though an extra duty of 12 per cent on the goods had been levied, there had been no resulting addition to the revenue. Upon a subsequent report of the London patent officers to the Customs Board on the method, the Customs Commissioners offered their opinion that the values upon unrated goods (except from India), being ascertained "only upon the Oath of the Importer is a great Loss to the Revenue & puts Trade upon an unequall Foot. The Fair Merch^t who swears to the Full value of his Goods being not able to Trade with Those who are less conscientious in swearing." The Commissioners stated that in consequence they were making an addition to the Book of Rates by fixing the value on such goods not therein enumerated.[1] Upon this presentment the Attorney-General gave his opinion that "the making an Addiconall Book of Rates as proposed by the Com^{rs} of the Customs is the proper and only Method that can prevent the Losses that happen by ascertaining the Customs by the oath of The Importer." [2]

In 1725 Charles Carkesse completed the first general consolidation of duties since the passing of the Act of Tonnage and Poundage, and in that year, by 11 Geo. I, c. 7, an additional Book of Rates was issued relating to goods not listed in the original Book of Rates, or to goods that were charged with a specific duty. At the same time, some regulations calculated to prevent some of the abuses of *ad valorem* rating were made. Other books of rates were prepared in later years,

---

the period there were serious arrears in the payment of East India duties. Delays were unavoidable due to the time involved in adjustment of the prices of the goods and the arrangement of sales in order to assess the duties from them. See for example B.M., Add. MSS. 18903, f. 166, "Copy of the Patent Officers Report on the referred Mem^l [?] of the East India Comp^a," 1714, Feb. 7.

[1] For this account, see P.R.O., Treas. Out-letters, Cust., XV, 395–396, Cust. Comrs. to Lord High Treasurer, 1711, June 12.

[2] *Ibid.*, XV, 397, Northey's opinion, 1711, Aug. 24.

but succeeding alterations in the duties rendered them useless.[1] *Ad valorem* duties were continued, and even Pitt's Consolidation Act provided that some 300 of the 1,200 articles subject to duty should be charged *ad valorem*.[2]

If the computation of duties was difficult, the calculation of drawbacks upon reëxportation, which refunded the import duties paid, was even more so, for in some cases the drawback equaled the duties, while in others it amounted to only a fraction which varied on the different articles included in one entry.[3]

The multiplicity of methods by which the amounts of duties were determined was bad enough in the ordinary course of work; but when new taxes were added and seasonal rushes of business took place, customs accounts were retarded, additional customs officers had to be taken on as checks and clerks, further allowances had to be made to the customs officers for their extra labor, and the utmost complexity was introduced into the organization of the London staff and customs office in particular.[4] As for the outports, "The Collectors at the Out Ports by their frequent Applications to the Board, profess themselves ignorant. Errors in the Computations are daily; the Science difficult, possessed by few, and in Danger of being lost; and this in a Branch of the Revenue productive, improving, and essential to the Support and Credit of the Nation."[5] When "The Foreign Merchant may be frequently deterred from importing Goods, from his Ignorance of the Duties, and of the Legality of the Importation,"[6] there is no doubt as to the effect of such a system on the revenue.

Both at the beginning and at the end of the period, the numerous

[1] *Repts. of Comrs.*, 1787, III, 22, 50, "Thirteenth Rept.," 1785; cf. *First Rept. of Comrs. of Cust. on Cust.* [Cd. 2186], p. 67, App. A, H.C. (1857), iii. Of the various books of rates, the Customs Board observed in 1777 that the computations in the one compiled by Saxby (1757) had been brought to the greatest exactness and were continued to that time (1777) in a recent publication by Burrow. P.R.O., Treasury Papers, Bdl. 530, No. 251, Cust. Comrs. to Lords of Treas., 1777, Apr. 29.
[2] *First Rept. of Comrs. of Cust. on Cust.* [Cd. 2186], p. 68, App. A, H.C. (1857), iii. For the state of duties at the end of the century, see *Commons Reports*, 1803, XII, 60, "Fourth Report from the Select Committee on Finance, Collection of the Public Revenue, Customs," 1797.
[3] *Repts. of Comrs.*, 1787, III, 236, App. No. 23, "Thirteenth Rept.," 1785.
[4] The many communications which passed between the Treasury and Customs Boards, the nature of which is indicated in the Treasury Out-letters, Customs, bear evidence of this.
[5] *Repts. of Comrs.*, 1787, III, 48, "Thirteenth Rept.," 1785.
[6] *Ibid.*, III, 236, App. No. 23.

kinds of duties and the variety of their computation were the declared cause of the complexity of the revenue system. William Edgar, writing in 1713, observed that:

> The great difficulty that attends the knowledge of the Customs, especially the computation of the several Duties payable upon Importation or Exportation, arises chiefly from the many Branches of that Revenue, which are all to be kept seperate & distinct, for the uses & purposes to which they are respectively applicable; from the multiplicity of Statutes relative to the same;— and from the frequent alterations by subsequent, additional or explanatory Acts; or by repealing & sometimes again reviving Clauses in several of them, according to the exigencies & emergencies of the Nation, or as they were found to be good or bad in their consequences.[1]

And at the end of the period, the Commissioners of Accounts stated in their "Thirteenth Report":

> The Subject that has occurred to us, as the most important in this Inquiry, is the Intricacy and Perplexity that involve the Collection and Accounts of this Part of the Public Revenue. The Examination shews us, that the Number of Rules required in the Computation, and the Number of Branches under which the Accounts of these Duties are kept, are the principal Sources of this Evil.[2]

Besides the intricate principles of calculation, other causes added to the difficulty of computation. The amount of duties frequently varied according to the country from which the goods were imported: commodities of the East Indies, France, or the French Plantations were subject to much higher duties than merchandise from other places; and some goods were liable to higher duties unless imported in British ships and directly from the place of production.[3] Officers had to know their goods well in order not to be imposed upon by merchants passing off wares as articles of lower rating. The Customs Commissioners continually urged the customs officers to take good care that such goods be expertly examined. For example, in 1711, in order to prevent the outport officers being tricked by merchants passing French wines and brandy run from Scotland and other places under pretense of their being wines of other countries, the Board

---

[1] B.M., Harleian Manuscripts 4309, f. 3, William Edgar, "Vectigalium Systema or A Compleat View of that Part of the Revenue of Great Britain commonly called Customs." Edgar was Inspector-General of the ports in North Britain.

[2] *Repts. of Comrs.*, 1787, III, 47, "Thirteenth Rept.," 1785.

[3] *Ibid.*, III, 288, App. No. 66. For instance, drugs, rated by 12 Chas. II, c. 4, were subject to treble duties unless they conformed to this rule.

ADMINISTRATIVE PROBLEMS   33

ordered the customs officers to peruse the despatches carefully to see that they were not counterfeit; view and taste the wines; and if the officers were in doubt, to take the advice of the most skilled in the port or send samples to London that the Customs Commissioners might have the opinion of the Surveyor and Wine Taster; and in the case of brandies the officers were to consult the excise officers.[1] Occasionally merchants who dealt in the particular merchandise in question were called to assist customs officers in the identification of goods.[2] How to distinguish French from Silesia lawns, to tell English from French oysters, and to identify drugs were merely a few of the difficult problems that troubled the customs officers.[3] Well might the knowledge of goods chiefly have constituted "the greatest Mystery of the Water-side Business."[4]

Further, there were dozens of laws regulating imports or exports that had to do with the condition of the commodity, the size of the cask or hogshead in which it was imported, the tonnage of the ships which could bring it, allowances of draught (the deduction made for the turn of the scales), tare (the abatement permitted for the weight of the outside package that contained the goods), and damage, which were often a source of bewilderment to the officers.[5] Articles which were deserving of the drawback were subject to yet other rules, as were bounty commodities [6] such as tar and wheat, in which the quality of the material was taken into consideration. The customs acts levying duties and regulating their collection, passed prior to the accession of George III, numbered 800, and 1,300 more were added in the first fifty-three years of his reign. Of course these were not all in force at once, but the very necessity of determining which were effective and

---

[1] Cust. Ho. Lib., Letters to Dartmouth, 1675–6 To 1715, p. 265, Board to Collector and Principal Officers at Dartmouth, 1711, July 24.

[2] Henry Crouch, in his preface to *A Complete View of the British Customs* (London, 1727?), p. viii, states that officers could secure a knowledge of goods only by much practice and experience, and he advised that when an officer met with goods that he did not know well, he inform himself by consulting either "ancient & experienc'd Officers, or Persons dealing in those Commodities."

[3] See for examples: P.R.O., Treasury Papers, Bdl. 351, Nos. 101–102, Barrington to Lords of Treas., 1753, Apr. 16; Cust. Ho. Lib., Sel. from Cust. Outport Recds., South Coast, 1922, p. 161, Exeter, Collector to Board, 1771–1776, 1775, May 27; *Cal. Treas. Books and Papers*, 1742–1745, p. 465, Cust. Comrs. to Lords of Treas., 1743–4, Mar. 22.

[4] As declared by the author of *Rules of the Water-side* (1715), p. 123.

[5] See *The Statutes at Large* for these laws.

[6] See B.M., Add. MSS. 8133 C, f. 149, dated 1781, Nov. 6, for a list of commodities on which bounties were allowed and the acts which granted them.

which had lapsed only made the work of the customs officers more difficult.[1]

The merchant as well suffered from alterations in the law. Not infrequently he would find that what he had thought to be a perfectly legal cargo was seized because of the passing, perhaps unknown to him, of some law which restricted the importation of his particular commodity [2] or prohibited it.[3] The Lords of the Treasury and the Customs Board, however, accorded such cases sympathetic attention. Nevertheless, the ignorance of the merchants as to the many laws defining imports, allowances, discounts, and the like caused them much inconvenience and left them quite at the mercy of the customs officers.

In summing up the effect of such laws, a statement in *The History of Our National Debts and Taxes from 1688 to 1751* (1753), which refers to the situation at the end of the great increase of duties in Anne's reign, may be taken as typical of any period of the century:

> . . . from this short State of them [customs at the end of Anne's reign] we may see, what a Maze our Merchants must be in; but if we consider the many Exceptions, and Exceptions from Exceptions, the many Regulations, and Regulations of Regulations, for collecting those Customs, and for paying the Drawbacks upon Goods re-exported, we must conclude it impossible for any Merchant in this Country to be Master of his Business, if he be what we call a general Merchant; consequently he must trust to those honest Gentlemen called Custom-house Officers, both for the Duties he is to pay upon Importation, and the Drawbacks he is entitled to upon Exportation. Can we wonder at the Decay of our Commerce under such Circumstances? Should we not rather wonder that we have any left! [4]

At last the system became so full of confusion that in 1777 the Customs Board submitted a proposal to the Lords of the Treasury for the consolidation of the duties.[5] The Commissioners' observations on the benefits which would ensue from the establishment of net duties alone summarizes what were for the merchant, the customs organization, and the revenue the evils of the old system:

---

[1] *First Rept. of Comrs. of Cust. on Cust.* [Cd. 2186], p. 17, H.C. (1857), iii.

[2] E.g., see a case involving certain regulations in tobacco importation. P.R.O., Treas. Out-letters, Cust., XIV, 240 b, Treasury warrant, 1702, Feb. 15.

[3] See references to seizures of prohibited whalebone. *Ibid.*, XIII, 357, Treasury warrant, 1697, July 8, and elsewhere in this volume.

[4] *History of Our National Debts and Taxes* (1753), Part III, pp. 20–21.

[5] This proposal was submitted upon the request of the Lords of the Treasury. P.R.O., Treas. Out-letters, Cust., XXXI, 480, Robinson to Cust. Comrs., 1777, Mar. 3.

This alone will be of considerable benefit to Merchants and others concerned in Trade, because by this means they will be dispatched in infinitely less time than is now required to complete the Computations of the different Branches, and they or their Ordinary Clerks will be able to pass and Checque their Entries and other Transactions at the Custom House, without being at the expence either of keeping an Experienced Person on purpose for this business, or else of retaining some Officer of the Revenue as their Agent, who by this means is diverted from the due & proper Execution of his Duty and an improper, if not dangerous, connextion is formed between him and the Merchant contrary to Law;—It will thus be a saving not only to the Merchant, but to the Revenue in the Charges of Management by a discontinuance of such Officers as may be found unnecessary,—when they drop or are otherwise provided for; as also very considerably in the Article of Stationary;—Many Frauds and mistakes will also be prevented and more easily detected in the Computation of the Duties, Discounts, and Drawbacks;—the Collectors will consequently be able to settle their Cash Account with greater ease and accuracy, without being perpetually Embarrassed as they now are by trifleing subdivisions of the Total Duty when placed in wrong Columns; they will therefore have more leisure, and have it more in their power to Superintend the general business of their Ports, which is now either totally neglected or left to inferiors, while the principal Officer's whole time is thus unavoidably Employed in preparing and settling their complex Accounts— Lastly by thus rendering the business more easy and comprehensible, it is apprehended that the present Body of Merchants will not only extend their transactions more boldly, but others also will more readily engage in Mercantile transactions, whereby the National Trade and Revenue will be encreased.[1]

On the basis of this report, the Lords of the Treasury in 1781 directed the Customs Commissioners to lay before them a plan for the consolidation of the duties.[2] A committee was consequently appointed by the Customs Commissioners,[3] and a consolidation scheme was worked out. It was not until 1787 that the consolidation was finally effected.[4]

These numerous duties meant enormous increases in the amount of money levied. Five subsidies during the years between 1660 and 1759 raised duties upon the value of most goods from 5 per cent to 25 per

---

[1] P.R.O., Treasury Papers, Bdl. 530, Nos. 252–253, Cust. Comrs. to Lords of Treas., 1777, Apr. 29. For a copy of this report, see B.M., Add. MSS. 8133 C, ff. 13–24.
[2] P.R.O., Treas. Out-letters, Cust., XXXII, 478, Robinson to Cust. Comrs., 1781, Aug. 24.
[3] Cust. Ho. Lib., Extracts Board Minutes, IV, 296, 1781, Sept. 14, 28, Nov. 21; IV, 296–297, 1782, June 8. For further references to bills and papers in connection with the bill for Parliament, see *ibid.*, IV, 297–298.
[4] 27 Geo. III, c. 13.

cent [1]; while a large number of commodities paid further charges under imposts, and under additional acts which specified duties on particular articles. Taxes on the principal imports had become extremely burdensome; the tobacco duty, for instance, amounted in 1784 to five times the value of the commodity [2]; and the customs and excise duty on tea between 1759 and 1784 ranged from 65 per cent to 120 per cent *ad valorem*.[3]

High duties invariably produced notorious fraud and smuggling during the whole period, and as duties were so frequently levied, the system of collecting them became more confused and the service lent itself more and more to fraudulent practices. Illicit trade, in its turn, necessitated preventive measures which emphasized the negative side of customs administration. Precautions against smuggling occupied much of the attention not only of the Customs Commissioners, but also of the Lords of the Treasury and the Privy Council as well. Elaborate schemes for the guard of the coasts, which frequently included not only customs boats and riding officers, but bodies of soldiers and admiralty cruisers, were laid down from time to time following upon the levy of new high duties,[4] or upon a declaration of peace.[5] The administration was continually forced to cope with the problem of the insufficiency and ineffectiveness of the organization at the outports to deal with the nefarious trade. A complicated system of checks in the landing and shipping of goods and the calculation and collection of duties had to be employed to enforce the customs laws, and they resulted in the continuance of many offices the functions of which had become redundant. Violation of customs law was met with seizure and the prosecution of ship and cargo, matters which took up much of the time of the Customs Commissioners. They had

[1] Old subsidy of 1660, 12 Chas. II, c. 4; new subsidy of 1698, 9 and 10 Wm. III, c. 23; the one-third and two-thirds subsidies of 1703 and 1704, 2 and 3 Anne, c. 9, and 3 and 4 Anne, c. 5; the fourth subsidy of 1747, 21 Geo. II, c. 2; the fifth subsidy of 1759, 32 Geo. II, c. 10.

[2] *Parliamentary Papers*, XXXVI, *Reports*, VI, H.C. No. 59, p. 12 (1784), "Second Report from the Committee appointed to Enquire into the Illicit Practices used in Defrauding the Revenue."

[3] Leone Levi, *The History of British Commerce* (London, 1880), p. 52.

[4] As an instance of an extensive guard for the western coast during the high duties on French goods, proposed by the Customs Commissioners and warranted by the Lords of the Treasury, see P.R.O., Treas. Out-letters, Cust., XIII, 461–464, Treasury warrants, 1698, Sept. 27.

[5] E. g., see references to Treasury warrants reëstablishing customs smacks in 1713. *Ibid.*, XVI, 79–80, 1713, Dec. 31, and XVI, 118, 1713–4, Mar. 23.

ADMINISTRATIVE PROBLEMS

to direct compositions, make statements of opinion on seizure cases referred to them by the Lords of the Treasury, and give orders for sales of condemned goods; while new solicitors and other officers had to be added to the law department of the customs to cope with the increase in business due to the additional high duties and the evasion of them. Yet in spite of every attempt on the part of the customs administration to deal with this condition resulting from excessive duties, the revenue suffered heavy losses.

Thus did the intricate system of revenue which the Customs Department had to enforce necessarily complicate the problems of organization and administration: the numerous and high duties gave encouragement to fraud and smuggling which necessitated constant attention to preventive measures; the multiplicity of rules for estimating the duties, the many branches of duties and their appropriation, and the hundreds of regulations governing them confused the collection and accounts of the customs and required the institution of various checks in the business. The customs organization was vitally affected by the complex system of revenue that it had to operate.

3. *Extraneous Duties of the Customs Officers*

The working of the customs service in the eighteenth century was influenced by yet another element, the extraneous duties which the customs officers were obliged to perform. The collection of revenue, while it was the primary function of the customs organization, was only one of the many duties which devolved upon the department. The customs establishment was the logical instrument for enforcing trade laws and dealing with sundry matters relating to governmental interests in embargo, quarantine, protection of the coast in time of war, and the like. In addition there were many miscellaneous duties which fell to the lot of the officers. Even though the transaction of most of this business was justifiably entrusted to them, much of it lay totally outside the work of the department as a revenue-collecting machine; and an organization existing primarily for the receipt of money would necessarily be hampered by duties essentially foreign to its nature.

The enforcement of the Navigation Acts, particularly during the early part of the period, constituted no small part of the customs work and often gave the department much troublesome responsibility. Certain plantation commodities specified by law [1] were compelled to come to Britain, where they had to pay duty; and foreign goods, destined for the colonies, likewise had to pass through British ports as staples. It was not enough for a master merely to touch at the English port; he must unload the goods on to the quay and pay duty, even though the cargo might be reëxported with a drawback almost immediately.[2] The work of the officers was further complicated by the system of bonds and certificates ensuring the entry of certain cargoes at British or plantation ports. Goods had to be imported either in British bottoms or in ships of the country of origin and export, and customs officers were expected constantly to be on the watch for any violation of these regulations.[3] Problems arose in determining what ships were free.[4] Sometimes certificates from consuls or merchants in a foreign port were required to prove the source of goods upon entry inwards or their landing at a foreign port upon exportation. Decisions had to be made whether foreign manufactures from raw materials of certain countries were the product of the place from which the raw material came; and when foreign goods exported to Europe from a British port failed to find market and were returned to the port, proof had to be given that they had been legally imported in the first place.[5]

[1] To sugar, tobacco, cotton-wool, indigo, ginger, and dye-woods, specified in the Navigation Act, the act of 1764 added coffee, pimento, cocoa-nuts, pot and pearl ashes, whalefins, raw silk, hides, and skins, and restricted the shipping of lumber and iron to Britain.

[2] A very good instance of the requirement of such discharge in the case of log-wood may be found in an undated letter from the Board to Dartmouth, Cust. Ho. Lib., Letters to Dartmouth, 1675–6 to 1715, p. 188. A. B. Keith, *Constitutional History of the First British Empire* (Oxford, 1930), p. 69, notes that the requirement was often neglected but also frequently enforced.

[3] See, for example, the petition of several merchants of Warrington and Liverpool to the Lords of the Treasury, 1756, Aug. 30, in connection with a case which turned on a question of ships and the country of produce. P.R.O., Treasury Papers, Bdl. 368, No. 128.

[4] An interesting case in point was that of a ship which, originally English, was purchased by the French, and finally became the property of Sardinian subjects. (*Ibid.*, Bdl. 551, No. 122, Cust. Comrs. to Lords of Treas., 1779, Jan. 15.) Masters or captains of vessels, by 19 Geo. II, had even to report foreign-made sails on their vessels; for failure to do so they were liable to a penalty of £50. For example, see P.R.O., Treas. Out-letters, Cust., XXIV, 327, Cust. Comrs. to Lords of Treas., 1753, Nov. 16.

[5] See *First Rept. of Comrs. of Cust. on Cust.* [Cd. 2186], p. 23, H.C. (1857), iii.

ADMINISTRATIVE PROBLEMS

The rule that three fourths of the crew should be British caused endless difficulty. Because of death or the frequent desertion of men,[1] masters were often forced to take on foreigners in order to make the homeward voyage, and the number of British sailors consequently fell short of the required three fourths. Border-line cases in which the ship would perhaps be seized for being a fourth of a man short of the right quota often came up before the Customs Commissioners and the Lords of the Treasury.[2] The Treasury Out-letters, Customs, for the early years of the period, are full of cases turning on technical questions having to do with various aspects of the Navigation Acts which went to the Treasury and were reported upon by the Customs Comsioners. Much of the Board's time was given over to examination and statement of opinion on such cases.

A review of decisions in many instances reveals a keen balance of wisdom and sympathy. Careful to avoid establishing precedents, the Board seem to have kept the main purposes of trade and the welfare of the revenue, rather than the letter of the law, as their guiding principles. Decisions were tempered by the circumstances of the case; when a merchant was deserving of leniency because of ignorance or accident, and when duties were or could be paid which would amount to more than the King's part of the forfeiture entailed by condemnation, it might happen that the ship would be admitted to entry.[3] Again, the merchant might be "a very liberale Trader and pays great Customs, and as You have heard has otherwise well deserved of the Government," in which case his goods would very probably be discharged.[4] A report of the Customs Commissioners to the Lords of the Treasury wherein they offered their opinion that "such a Construccon of Law as might tend to the Forfeiture of the Shipps mencōned in that Rep^t however it might be justified by the lre [letter] of the Act of Navigacōn, Yet it seemed to them to be directly contrary to one maine purpose thereof, Viz^t The encouraging and increaseing of English Shipping," received favorable consideration by the Lords of the Treasury.[5]

---

[1] Desertions were frequent because of the poor fare and treatment that the crew received. P.R.O., Treas. Out-letters, Cust., XVI, 410, Cust. Comrs. to Lords of Treas., 1716, Nov. 16.
[2] E. g., *ibid.*, XIII, 423–424, Treasury warrant, 1698, Apr. 26.
[3] E. g., see *ibid.*, XIII, 292–293, Treasury warrant, 1696, Oct. 13.
[4] *Ibid.*, XIII, 272–273, Treasury warrant, 1696, July 31.
[5] *Ibid.*, XIII, 263–264, Treasury warrant, 1696, June 10.

For official information in connection with Britain's position in the carrying trade, collectors were obliged to keep accounts of the ships, their tonnage, their crews, whether they were British or foreign in original build, and other details. Vessels engaged in the plantation business had to be registered with the collectors, and a duplicate of the registration, together with these lists of ships, was transmitted to the officer who kept records of shipping in the customs office in London.[1]

The services of the Customs Department did not end with the collection of the customs revenue and the enforcement of the Navigation Acts; customs officers were obliged also to assist in the receipt of several duties which did not fall within their immediate province. Usually the outport collectors were appointed by the patentees of prisage and butlerage to levy and collect those allowances for them by either taking prisage in kind or making a composition for it and by receiving butlerage at the customary rate.[2] In Crouch's time at least it was usual for the Excise Commissioners to empower the outport customs collectors and surveyors to assist the excise port-gauger in the collection of the excise duty on imported liquors.[3] Although the Customs Department had no connection with the light-duties which were levied for the upkeep of the lighthouses, these were collected at some ports by the customs staff by virtue of authority from the Masters and Brethren of Trinity House[4]; and customs officers in other instances assisted the patentees of the several lighthouses or

---

[1] *Repts. of Comrs.*, 1787, III, 431, App. No. 51, "Fourteenth Rept.," 1785. See *infra*, Ch. III, pp. 117–118. Occasionally the officers were requested to send to London reports relating to local social and economic conditions—one of the most interesting of these, perhaps, being an account of persons emigrating to America and foreign countries from the various ports, with details concerning their employment, former residence, destination, and reasons for leaving Britain. P.R.O., Treas. Out-letters, Cust., XXX, 450, Robinson to Cust. Comrs., 1773, Dec. 9.

[2] Crouch, *Complete Guide to Officers* (1732), pp. 322–323. Prisage was the taking of wines for the King's use out of vessels, owned by English natives, which imported wines. Single prisage was reckoned at one tun in kind when the total quantity amounted to or exceeded ten tuns but was less than twenty. Butlerage was a two-shilling duty on every tun of wine (for which freight had to be paid) shipped into the realm by merchant strangers. The privilege of levying and collecting prisage and butlerage was granted by patent to certain persons, who frequently deputed the customs collectors to transact that business for them. See *ibid.*, pp. 321–323.

[3] *Ibid.*, p. 323; see also pp. 324, 326.

[4] P.R.O., Treasury Papers, Bdl. 332, No. 138, Cust. Comrs. to Lords of Treas., 1748, Sept. 13. E. g., see Cust. Ho. Lib., Sel. from Cust. Outport Recds., South Coast, 1922, p. 59, Poole, Collector to Board, 1758–1762, 1758, Mar. 20.

ADMINISTRATIVE PROBLEMS

their deputies for better receiving the duties due.[1] The sixpenny fee (deducted out of each seaman's wages every month) which masters had to pay for the support of Greenwich Hospital, was generally collected in the outports by the customs collectors, authorized by a deputation from the commissioners appointed by the Admiralty for the management of those duties.[2] The service proved a nuisance, for masters were continually trying to avoid payment. By regulations at various times the Customs Commissioners in such cases prohibited the clearing of the vessel [3]; directed that revenue officers remain on board [4] (at the master's expense); ordered that the masters' portages be stopped [5]; and resolved that no clearance inwards should be granted until receipts were produced that the duties were paid.[6]

Quarantine enforcement was also under the direction of the Customs Commissioners. By 1722 it constituted so large a part of the customs activity that the Lords of the Treasury granted the Customs Commissioners an additional allowance of £200 for the service, "being a very great Addition of Business and as you conceive no way relat^g to your Duty as Managers of the Custo^s."[7] When quarantine was placed on ships coming from any ports where the Plague was raging, or where they might have been exposed to infection, it was done by an Order in Council transmitted by the Lords of the Treasury to the Customs Board for execution.[8] Upon receipt of the order the Customs Commissioners informed the principal officers of the ports and issued their directions for the observance of the regulations. Super-

---

[1] See Cust. Ho. Lib., Extracts Board Minutes, I, "Collectors in the Out Ports," 1724, Oct. 10. For a specific case, see P.R.O., Treas. Out-letters, Cust., XV, 120, Treasury warrant, 1708, July 6; see also Cust. Comrs. to Lord High Treasurer, 1708, June 5.

[2] The money received under this head, together with the accounts of such sums, was remitted regularly from the outports and the Port of London to the office of the sixpenny duty in London. On the collection of the sixpenny duty, see Crouch, *Complete Guide to Officers* (1732), pp. 326–330. Cf. Charles M. Andrews, *Guide to the Materials for American History, to 1783, in the Public Record Office of Great Britain* (Washington, 1914), II, 61–63.

[3] See Cust. Ho. Lib., Extracts Board Minutes, III, 203, 1765, Dec. 4; 1766, Jan. 22.

[4] *Ibid.*, III, 203, 1766, Apr. 9, Sept. 19.

[5] *Ibid.*, III, 203, 1772, Nov. 11. A portage was an allowance to a master for the correct entry of his cargo.

[6] *Ibid.*, III, 204, 1775, Dec. 8.

[7] P.R.O., Treas. Out-letters, Cust., XVIII, 156–157, Treasury warrant, 1722, Dec. 19. Additional allowances were granted every year to officers employed in the execution of the quarantine service.

[8] For one reference see *ibid.*, XXIV, 181, Order of Council, 1752, June 30.

intended by these officers, the water guard in the ports saw that the ships performed quarantine at places specified by the customs officers and chief magistrates at the ports.[1] Goods were aired for a certain length of time, and the crew remained on board the ship until the expiration of quarantine.[2] Much of the Board's attention was taken up with business of this kind: the Commissioners attended the Council on matters of quarantine,[3] reported proceedings on enforcement from time to time,[4] and received Council orders for the discharge of specific ships.[5] The enforcement of the regulations caused the Customs Board much trouble, for quarantine was continually broken, sometimes by force.[6] Sympathy goes out to the Commissioners who lament in 1761 "the want of some far better Security against that Danger, than any Method, hitherto established in this Country" in execution of "the Burthensome, but important Service of Quarantine." [7]

The customs officers were responsible for the enforcement of embargo declared by Order in Council from time to time. They received embargo warrants (Treasury warrants issued pursuant to Orders in Council) which permitted certain ships to sail despite the embargo, in some instances on condition that they should furnish a complement of men for the navy. The Commissioners had to see that such orders were duly observed.[8]

[1] An Order in Council of 1709, Oct. 30, directed that when any difference arose between customs officers and the chief magistrates of the port touching places to be appointed for performance of quarantine by ships from the Baltic or for airing goods, the Customs Commissioners should appoint the proper places. (See P.R.O., Treas. Out-letters, Cust., XV, 210). In 1754, by Order of Council of Mar. 1, customs officers were empowered and required to appoint the places in the outports for the performance of quarantine by vessels not having infection on board. *Ibid.*, XXIV, 358.

[2] See *Repts. of Comrs.*, 1787, III, 366, App. No. 7, "Fourteenth Rept.," 1785, for a general survey of the quarantine service. The penalty for wilful breach of quarantine was very severe: the commander was prosecuted and, if convicted upon trial, suffered death. See reference, P.R.O., Treasury Papers, Bdl. 429, No. 295, Wood to Jenkinson, 1764, Oct. 3.

[3] Cust. Ho. Lib., Extracts Board Minutes, II, "Quarantain," 1720, Aug. 25; 1721, Apr. 26; 1729, Jan. 26.

[4] *Repts. of Comrs.*, 1787, III, 366, App. No. 7, "Fourteenth Rept.," 1785.

[5] E. g., P.R.O., Treas. Out-letters, Cust., XVII, 356, Order in Council, 1720, Feb. 10.

[6] P.R.O., Treasury Papers, Bdl. 403, No. 99, Cust. Comrs. to Lords of Treas., 1760, Apr. 2.

[7] *Ibid.*, Bdl. 408, No. 70, Cust. Comrs. to Lords of Treas., 1761, Feb. 7.

[8] The Treasury Out-letters, Customs, contain numerous instances of this. See *Cal. Treas. Books and Papers*, 1739–1741, p. 349. Cf. P.R.O., Chatham Papers, Bdl. 231, section headed "English Customs" in a manuscript booklet entitled "The

ADMINISTRATIVE PROBLEMS 43

Still other miscellaneous duties fell to the lot of the Customs Department. Early in the period it was enacted that officers should assist in procuring aid for ships that were in distress; and they were empowered to participate in settlement of salvage claims.[1] If goods were stranded, the officers, as Receivers of Wreck, were supposed to retrieve them for the owners.[2] Occasionally the customs staff in various ports was directed by warrant to aid the officers of prizes in securing in warehouses plundered goods that should arrive in the fleet.[3] In times of war the officers were called upon to guard the coast and to place their vessels under the orders of the Admiralty; they were required to inspect packet-boats, give information of the appearance of enemy ships, aid in carrying intelligence to and from the fleet, stop and search individuals, and assist in impressing seamen.[4]

Business done in the Treasury by the Officers—distinguishing each Particular Branch."

[1] Henry Atton and Henry Hurst Holland, *The King's Customs* (London, 1908), I, 165–166.

[2] As appears from a case in Cust. Ho. Lib., Sel. from Cust. Outport Recds., South Coast, 1922, p. 223, Penzance, Board to Collector, 1761–1769, 1768, May 10.

[3] As happened in 1702. P.R.O., Treas. Out-letters, Cust., XIV, 221, Treasury warrant, 1702, Nov. 6. On Apr. 29, 1702, the Customs Board represented to the Lords of the Treasury that with their other duties they could not undertake the management of prize ships and goods with which they found by a bill it was intended they should be burdened. *Cal. Treas. Papers*, 1702–1707, p. 10, Cust. Comrs. to Lords of Treas., 1702, Apr. 29. Cf. Hist. MSS. Com., *MSS. House of Lords* (New Series), V, *1702–1704*, 42–43.

[4] The State Papers Domestic, George II, for the years 1744 and 1745 contain illustrations of many of these requirements at the time of Prince Charlie's attempt. A section headed "English Customs" in a manuscript booklet entitled "The Business done in the Treasury by the Officers—distinguishing each Particular Branch" briefly indicates the nature of the customs service in time of hostilities. P.R.O., Chatham Papers, Bdl. 231. For a specific reference to Admiralty control of customs boats, see, for example, P.R.O., Treas. Out-letters, Cust., XXXII, 480, Robinson to Cust. Comrs., 1781, Sept. 3; XXXII, 414, Robinson to Cust. Comrs., 1779, Aug. 20. With respect to the examination of individuals, see for example *ibid.*, XXIII, 44, Scrope to Cust. Comrs., 1745, Dec. 4.

During the American Revolution, customs officers were further obliged to return elaborate reports relating to prizes, privateers, and ships arriving from and fitting out for America. They were directed to search all vessels clearing out for the American colonies and requested to coöperate with the Navy Board in unloading neutral ships brought into port with naval stores. In P.R.O., Treasury Papers, Bdl. 539 (1) are returns relating to prizes and privateers, 1778. Cf. *ibid.*, Bdl. 541. *Ibid.*, Bdl. 523, contains abstracts of reports on vessels shipping to and from America, 1775. With respect to the search of vessels, see *ibid.*, Bdl. 516, No. 369, Stanley to Robinson, 1775, Dec. 5; Nos. 258, 265, Howe to Robinson, 1775, Aug. 18. For reference to direction of coöperation with the Navy Board, see *ibid.*, Bdl. 551, No. 123, Stanley to Robinson, 1779, Jan. 26. Cf. No. 126, Cust. Comrs. to Lords of Treas., 1779, Jan. 23.

By this latter service, outport collectors were directed to receive such men as were sent for impress service to the port; pay the conductors of them twenty shillings for each fit man, and sixpence a mile for every mile they traveled not exceeding twenty miles; and keep the men at the rate of sixpence a day until they were called up.[1]

Such were the most important of a number of heterogeneous duties imposed upon the customs officers. Some of these duties were onerous and complicated and interfered directly with the more important service having to do with the collection of the revenue; though most of them fitted in as a part of the usual routine. In considering the nature of the department as a whole, however, it is well to remember that the collection of customs was only one of many functions, each having its own problems.

Any commentary on the customs service as it existed between the years 1696 and 1786 must take into account all its handicaps—the influence of the medieval customs traditions, the intricacy of the system under which the service labored, and the irrelevant functions it was often called upon to perform. Surely the chief responsibility for whatever deficiencies there were in the eighteenth-century customs service rests with the system rather than with its administrators.

[1] Cust. Ho. Lib., Sel. from Cust. Outport Recds., South Coast, 1922, p. 128, Weymouth, Board to Collector, 1733–1738, 1739, June 28. Cf. *Cal. Treas. Books and Papers,* 1739–1741, p. 33, Sir Charles Wager to [John Scrope], 1739, June 22. For references to this service at other times during the period, see P.R.O., Treasury Papers, Bdl. 369, No. 154, Cleveland to West, 1756, Mar. 25; Bdl. 475, Nos. 318–319, Stephens to Cooper, 1770, Oct. 31; *Cal. Treas. Papers,* 1697–1701-2, p. 161, Cust. Comrs. to Lords of Treas., 1698, May 16.

CHAPTER II

Executive Control

Ultimate responsibility for the effective carrying-out of fiscal and trade policy through the Customs Department rested with the Lords of the Treasury and the Commissioners of the Customs. The Treasury was vested with authority over the entire customs organization; more specifically it exercised control over the Board of Customs Commissioners. From very early times and more particularly from the reign of Henry VI, the customs establishment had been under the governance of the Lord High Treasurer [1]; but during the seventeenth and eighteenth centuries, at such times as the Treasury was put into commission [2] and after 1714, when the Treasury was permanently in commission, the Lords of the Treasury took over the control of the organization.

It was the business of the Treasury Board during the eighteenth century to decide all matters relating to the national revenue, "to give directions for the conduct of all Boards and persons entrusted with the receipt, management, or expenditure of the said Revenues; to sign all warrants for the necessary payments thereout, and generally to superintend every branch of revenue belonging to Your Majesty or the Public." [3] The Treasury, as the supreme authority in matters of revenue, determined the principles on which the Customs Board conducted its business and had immediate supervision of the customs establishment. It further constituted a board of appeal from the Board of Customs Commissioners, whose decision on petitions submitted by officers and merchants relating to customs affairs was not necessarily final.[4] Finally, the Treasury formed a connecting link between

---
[1] See 31 Hen. VI, c. 5; *First Rept. of Comrs. of Cust. on Cust.* [Cd. 2186], p. 79, App. B, H.C. (1857), iii.
[2] Sir Thomas L. Heath, *The Treasury* (London and New York, 1927), p. 33.
[3] *Ten Reports of the Commissioners Appointed by Act 25 Geo. III cap. 19, to enquire into the Fees, Gratuities, Perquisites, and Emoluments which are or have been lately received in the several Public Offices therein mentioned,* H.C. 309, p. 51 (1806), "Second Report," 1786, vii.
[4] *First Report from the Select Committee appointed to inquire into the Constitution and Management of the Customs; together with Minutes of Evidence*

the Customs Board and Parliament, the Council, and other departments of state.[1] It represented the interests of the customs in Parliament and also provided a channel of communication between the Customs Board and other branches of government. The Commissioners frequently applied to the Lords for requests to be made to the Council and directions relating to customs matters to be given to other state offices; and the Treasury Board in turn transmitted Council orders and communications from other departments to the Board of Customs. Thus the most obvious services rendered by the Lords of the Treasury to the administration of the customs system were their immediate superintendence of the Customs Commissioners, their work as a final authority in all matters relating to the customs, and their part as an intermediary between the customs and other departments of state.

By the patent which created the Board of Customs, the Commissioners were directed "to observe p'forme fullfill & keepe All & singular the Orders Rules Instruccons & direccons" given by the Lords of the Treasury or by the Lord High Treasurer and the Chancellor of the Exchequer when the Treasury was not in commission.[2] The Customs Board appear to have felt constrained to obey Treasury orders as such, even though they might consider individual orders of doubtful legality. For instance, in 1767, upon the Commissioners' expressing to the Treasury a wish to consult the proper Crown lawyers as to whether they were justified in acting upon a certain Treasury warrant, the Treasury insisted upon compliance with the direction. In a return communication the Customs Commissioners humbly informed the Lords that they had executed the act and bowed their will to My Lords: "it now becomes us to submit our Opinion to the Superior judgement of Your Lordships, to whom by the Constitution of this Board, we are Subordinate."[3] Nor, with the exception of the Privy Council and Parliament, would the Com-

---

and *Appendix*, H.C. 209, p. 101 (1851), Minutes of Evidence, xi. Though this statement was made in connection with the nineteenth-century organization, it held true in the eighteenth century.

[1] See *infra*.

[2] P.R.O., Patent Roll, 23 Chas. II, P. 2, No. 1, Mem. 35, dorse, [1671], Sept. 27.

[3] See P.R.O., Treasury Papers, Bdl. 459, Nos. 142–143, Cust. Comrs. to Lords of Treas., 1767, Aug. 26. For the papers on this case, see *ibid.*, Bdl. 459, Nos. 129–130, Cust. Comrs. to Lords of Treas., 1767, July 30; P.R.O., Treas. Out-letters, Cust., XXVIII, 53–56, Cooper to Cust. Comrs., 1767, Aug. 18. Cf. *First Rept. Sel. Com. on Cust.*, H.C. 209, p. 110 (1851), Minutes of Evidence, xi.

missioners own any other control,¹ while the Lords also appear to have been jealous of the relationship.² That the Customs Board did not, however, hesitate on occasion to differ from the Treasury and to question its policy is shown by their protests against a dangerous use of power ³ and in their occasional suspension of the execution of Treasury orders.⁴ Sometimes, though rarely, the Commissioners defended their proceedings in strong terms or insisted upon their powers as granted by their patent when they felt it to be necessary. In a case in 1782 the Customs Board stated that the Secretary was to represent to Mr. Burke "for their Lordships Information that this Board so far from declining, are always very ready to meet any Opportunity to justify their Conduct" and, with reference to their power of punishing customs officers, declared that it "is founded on the 4th Clause of the Commissioners Patent (a Copy whereof is to be enclosed) for their Lordships' Satisfaction." ⁵

[1] Several times the Commissioners hesitated to make certain reports to the Board of Trade and the Lords of the Admiralty, declaring that such reports should be given only with "the Directions of Parliament, the Lords of the Council, or this Board" [Treasury]. (P.R.O., Treas. Out-letters, Cust., XXXIV, 331, Steele to Cust. Comrs., 1785, Dec. 20. See *infra*, p. 86.) In one case the Commissioners did not feel that an opinion of the Attorney and Solicitor-General was sufficient authority for them to give more explicit directions to the Bench Officers for the clearance of certain vessels to New York in 1779. Without such direction, the Bench Officers in turn would not issue the clearances, a circumstance which provoked Eden to write Cooper: "In the midst of these official Niceties & Custom-House scruples, our Manufacturers are losing Employment, the Merchants are Disappointed, & the Supplies essential perhaps to the Existence of New York & its Dependencies are completely cut-off." P.R.O., Treasury Papers, Bdl. 549, No. 165, 1779, Feb. 22.

[2] See *infra,* p. 80, n.

[3] The irregularities in Treasury grants of leave of absence to officers directly affected the efficiency of the service and was a source of much irritation to the Customs Commissioners. (See *infra,* Ch. VI, pp. 225–227.) The Customs Board also was painfully aware of the limitation of its powers over officers appointed by constitution of the Treasury. See *infra,* Ch. VI, pp. 197–198, n.

[4] There are several instances, most of them having to do with the appointment of customs officers. For example, in a case in 1786 when the Treasury desired that one Morton be procured by the Customs Board as deputy controller of Southampton, the Commissioners acquainted the Lords, through their respective secretaries, that Morton was ignorant of the duties of the office, never having been in the customs service; and that because it was "materially requisite . . . that an able and *well qualified Person* . . . should be appointed to the Vacancy in question; . . . the Commissioners think it their duty to suspend carrying their Lordships Commands into execution, until they shall be favored with further directions upon this subject." P.R.O., Treasury Papers, Bdl. 637, Nos. 205–206, Stiles to Rose, 1786, Nov. 4.

[5] Cust. Ho. Lib., Extracts Board Minutes, IV, 196, 197, 1782, Apr. 26. There seems to have been considerable friction between the two Boards at this time.

It was the Treasury warrant that was chiefly the channel of authority between the Treasury and Customs Boards. By the system of warrants, the Lords of the Treasury delegated powers to the Customs Commissioners, authorizing them to take action in any particular customs case (such as the discharge of a seizure), to transact routine business for which Treasury direction was necessary (such as the quarterly payment of salaries), or to make use of a general power which they had not had before (such as that of removing established cruisers from one station to another).[1] By specific orders relating to all aspects of the service, the Lords secured the conformity of the Customs Board to their wishes and maintained close supervision over the operation of the system.

Both the Lords of the Treasury and the Customs Commissioners could determine customs policy, though the final decision always lay with the Treasury Board. That body was possessed of vast powers in this connection for it could remit forfeitures and penalties under the customs laws,[2] and, if its powers were similar to those of a cer-

---

In a case in the following year, Stiles acquainted Burke in explanation of certain proceedings: "Under all these precautions, the Commissioners flatter themselves, the Lords of the Treasury will be convinced, that this Board has not been wanting in the utmost diligence and attention, so far as depended upon themselves, for the Security, Economy and faithful and upright Management of this Revenue,— assuring their Lordships, that if they could have devised any better methods for that end, than what are now practiced, they would not have lost a moment's time, to have established the same,—as they can, with the greatest truth assert, that they will not yield to any of their Predecessors, in their daily Personal Attendance, and unremitting Zeal and labors for the Public Service, in all it's branches, within their department." (P.R.O., Treasury Papers, Bdl. 583, No. 376, 1783, Oct. 16.) In a letter from Stiles to Burke on the following day, with reference to still another case, the Commissioners defended themselves in considerable detail, concluding, "that no endeavours shall be wanting to facilitate the same [the return of certain accounts to the Treasury], so far as depends upon the Commissioners themselves, who are not conscious of any cause to be afraid of their Conduct being fully and impartially investigated." *Ibid.*, Bdl. 584, No. 58, 1783, Oct. 17.

[1] The volumes of Treasury Out-letters, Customs, contain copies of many such warrants.

[2] P.R.O., Treasury Papers, Bdl. 485, No. 21, wherein Mr. Webster begs the favor of Mr. Pratt "to receive the few precedents out of many, Where the Lords of Treasury, have remitted the Kings share of Goods & Penalties—the last of which is a Case exactly similar to Mr Websters, which was granted by the present Board without any Reference to the Com^rs of Customs," 1772, Aug. 13. (See appended list, No. 23. Cf. *Second Report from the Select Committee appointed to inquire into the Constitution and Management of the Customs; together with Minutes of Evidence and Appendix*, H.C. 604, p. 22 (1851), Part I, Minutes of Evidence, xi.) By an act of 4 Anne, the Treasury was given power to remit in-

EXECUTIVE CONTROL 49

tain nineteenth century board, as they appear to have been, the Lords had authority to relax the rigor of the law.[1] Every question which might involve the establishment of precedents or a modification of policy or the general welfare of the revenue had to come before the Treasury Board. From time to time the Lords requested the Commissioners to recommend measures to be taken and laws passed for improvement of the service; and if the Lords approved the proposals subsequently submitted to them, they requested the Commissioners to draft clauses into bills to be enacted as customs legislation.[2] Because of their concern with the broader aspects of administration the Lords played a considerable part in shaping the character of the service. Thus they recommended surveys of the ports [3] and inspection of officers,[4] and directed intensive investigations into smuggling.[5] Regu-

---

terest and cost on bonds in particular cases if it saw fit. P.R.O., Treas. Out-letters, Cust., XXIII, 561, Cust. Comrs. to Lords of Treas., 1748, Dec. 16.

[1] *First Rept. Sel. Com. on Cust.*, H.C. 209, pp. 109, 110 (1851), Minutes of Evidence, xi. In 1783 Lord North intervened with the Treasury in behalf of an individual whose effects were seized at Dover, "perhaps, according to Law, but if ever the Board of Treasury dispensed with the Law, from compassion or from conviction that the Case before them did not come within the intention of the Law, The present petitioner seems justly intitled to their interference & protection. I beg leave to recommend his case to the justice & humanity of the Board of Treasury." (P.R.O., Treasury Papers, Bdl. 587, No. 231, North to [Treasury Board secretary?], 1783, Nov. 15.) The Treasury, however, never dispensed with an Act of Parliament, as is put forcibly by Cooper to the Customs Board in a letter of April 7, 1769, "My Lords Cannot forbear to express some Surprize & concern that the Comm^{rs} should conceive it possible that from the Special circumstances of this or any other Case Their Lordships should think it proper to grant a Warr^t to dispense with an Act of Parliament." P.R.O., Treas. Out-letters, Cust., XXIX, 211.

[2] See, for example, P.R.O., Treasury Papers, Bdl. 380, Nos. 38, 41, Cust. Comrs. to Lords of Treas., 1758, Sept. 26, and enclosures.

[3] E. g., Cust. Ho. Lib., Extracts Board Minutes, I, "Commissioners," 1698, Sept. 22; 1699, Aug. 8; 1723, Apr. 30.

[4] E. g., P.R.O., Treasury Papers, Bdl. 636, No. 90, Stiles to Rose, 1786, Sept. 28.

[5] E. g., *ibid.*, Bdl. 429, No. 15, Cust. Comrs. to Lords of Treas., 1764, Sept. 5. See Nos. 1–5, 13, 17, 19–20. In illustration of the very active interest on the part of the Treasury in the enforcement of customs laws, part of a letter of Cooper to the Customs Board on October 16, 1766, may well be included. He states that the Lords of the Treasury, having considered the reports of collectors of several ports in western England from Plymouth to St. Ives, and observing how little proportion the brandies and wines legally entered bear to the consumption of those articles within the district, "Their Lordships have directed me, to write to you, upon this important Subject, and to signify to you, that it is their desire, that you would take this matter into your immediate deliberation, & to suggest to them whatever Remedies you think most proper & effectual to meet & to correct this grievance, whether it be by any change, to be made, in Numbers, Stations, or regulations of the Cutters, or by visitation, & inspection of the sev^l Ports, or by

lar accounts of the customs receipts and shipping, together with special accounts frequently ordered from time to time as occasion required, kept the Treasury informed as to the state of the revenue and the need for improvement in any division of the service. For the better enforcement of customs laws, the Treasury secured the assistance of various state departments and individuals.[1] While the Lords of the Treasury determined upon measures of importance which affected the system, it was not without the advice of the Customs Board, and the numerous papers submitted by the Treasury to the Commissioners clearly evince a dependence upon their judgment in policy.

Supervision by the Treasury Board was not confined to general matters of administration, for it included a surprising amount of customs routine. Since the Board of Customs proceeded under the authority of the Treasury, the Lords of the Treasury as a matter of course exercised a controlling power over every branch of the department which the Customs Commissioners directed. The appointment, numbers, salaries, and regulation of the customs staff were under the close supervision of the Treasury Board. Established officers were admitted to the service by instruments [2] originating with the Treasury; and deputies to patentees, as well as many inferior officers, frequently owed their selection to Treasury recommendation.[3] As the period wore on, the Lords increasingly manipulated the appointment machinery to the advantage of their own patronage.[4] The amount of

any other Measures, which you may think expedient, or which in your opinion, are found to be wanting in the administration or Collection of the Revenue of Customs; And their Lordships direct me to assure you, that they shall be willing & zealous on their Parts, to promote, & to give vigour & Execution, to any such effectual Plan." The Lords further desired that certain men, well-informed on the local conditions, attend the Customs Board "in order to give you all the Lights, & information, in their power, on this Matter." They also requested that further reports be returned from the western ports. "This is a matter upon which My Lords are more than ordinarily Sollicitous & as they mean to bring the State of it before Parliament in the next Session; Their Lordships are confident that the board of Customs, will lose no time in laying before the Treasury their information & Sentiments upon it." P.R.O., Treas. Out-letters, Cust., XXVIII, 126.

[1] See *infra*.
[2] By "instruments" are meant Treasury warrants, constitutions, and patents, all of which effected appointment. See *infra*, Ch. VI, pp. 195–198.
[3] See *supra*, Ch. I, p. 20; *infra*, Ch. VI, pp. 200–201.
[4] See *infra*, Ch. VI, pp. 168–204. With respect to Treasury participation in the patronage of the revenue departments during the eighteenth century, see Edward Hughes, *Studies in Administration and Finance, 1558–1825, with Special Reference to the History of Salt Taxation in England* (Manchester, 1934), esp. pp. 289, 291, 306–307, 308, 311–316.

EXECUTIVE CONTROL

established salaries constantly came under the review of the Treasury Lords whose warrant was necessary for payment of such sums and for increases, reductions, and other alterations. Rewards, as well, were bestowed by the Lords. Extensive control over officers' leave of absence was exercised by them, and numerous miscellaneous regulations affecting the officers' conduct had to receive the Treasury warrant.[1] Disbursements for the upkeep of the customs establishment were under the watchful eye of the Treasury Board, for the Customs Commissioners could not make payments beyond a certain fixed sum without a Treasury order.[2] Accounts were always being required and examined.

Because of their control over customs policy, personnel, and conditions of the service, the Lords of the Treasury had an active interest in general office business. They dealt with all kinds of petitions and representations submitted by merchants, private persons, customs officers, or the Customs Board, as the case might be. Such miscellaneous subjects as the following received their attention: admittance to entry of certain cargoes, remission of customs duties, compositions, orders for *noli prosequi* in seizures, delivery of bonds, release of merchants in debt or smugglers from jail, payment of shares of seizures, directions for delivery of goods of foreign ministers, investigations into complaints against customs officers, informations of frauds in the revenue and plans for their prevention, requests for rewards, positions, or promotions, and proposals for parliamentary legislation.[3]

---

[1] For discussion at greater length of the position of the Treasury in relation to the establishment, see *infra*, Ch. VI.

[2] This particular statement is given in connection with the nineteenth-century establishment, but it undoubtedly applied a century earlier. *First Rept. Sel. Com. on Cust.*, H.C. 209, p. 79 (1851), Minutes of Evidence, xi.

[3] As indicated by the material in the Treasury Papers and Treasury Out-letters, Customs. A section headed "English Customs" in a manuscript booklet entitled "The Business done in the Treasury by the Officers—distinguishing each Particular Branch" gives an excellent survey of the work of the Treasury in customs administration in 1782 or 1783. With respect to customs papers in the Treasury office, the writer states: "Various Petitions come before the Treasury Board on Custom house business; the Objects of which are principally for leave to compound Offences against the Custom Laws—for relief respecting Seizures—for Grants of the Kings Share of Seizures—for Indulgences respecting irregular importations, or exportations—or Petitions from Officers of the Customs for relief against supposed oppression in the Commissioners.—All of which are usually referred to the Board of the Customs for their report of the State of the Case, and their opinion what is fit to be done thereon: And the Board of Treasury upon receiving and considering these Reports, grant or reject the Prayer of the Petitioners— When granted it is commonly by Warrant, upon the Report itself." P.R.O., Chatham Papers, Bdl. 231.

52 ORGANIZATION OF THE ENGLISH CUSTOMS

The connection between the Treasury and Customs Boards in the administration of this system was maintained by the attendance of the Customs Commissioners on the Lords of the Treasury and by the scheme of petitions and papers. At times in the early part of the period the Commissioners called upon the Lords once a week [1]; but in 1718 the Treasury Board appointed the attendance of the Commissioners once a month "for the better dispatch of Business." [2] Such attendance was not regular throughout the period, however, and the Customs Commissioners met with the Lords less frequently or at extra times as well. Their presence was usually requested for consideration of memorials which they had submitted to the Treasury, or of problems that had been brought to the attention of the Lords by other government departments or by individuals. When special business was before the Treasury, as, for instance, consideration of the new tobacco act in 1751, the Customs Commissioners would meet with the Lords every few days, or as often as was necessary.[3]

The number of Commissioners who attended the Treasury varied. Sometimes all would be present; at other times, only a small number who had been appointed to report upon a particular investigation. Occasionally the Secretary alone called upon the Lords; two or three Commissioners were frequently present.[4] The year 1788 saw an important change in this practice. Two Commissioners were appointed as warrant chairmen [5] of the Customs Board, either one of whom, together with another Commissioner, had always to attend upon Parliament, the Council, and the Lords of the Treasury.[6] For that service an additional salary of £500 was allowed.[7] A Customs Board minute of 1791 simplified the method of selection of the Commissioner who should attend with one of the warrant chairmen from time to time.[8] These regulations would seem to indicate the transition to the

[1] Cust. Ho. Lib., Extracts Board Minutes, II, "Plantations," 1697; "Treasury," 1711, Mar. 18.
[2] *Ibid.*, I, "Commissioners," II, "Treasury," 1718, Mar. 28; cf. P.R.O., Treasury Minute Book, XXIV, Part I, 1, 1717, Mar. 22.
[3] Cust. Ho. Lib., Extracts Board Minutes, I, "Commissioners," 1751, Aug. 2, 6, 8 (with direction to see minutes of Sept. 17, 19), Dec. 4.
[4] As appears from entries under "Commissioners," *ibid.*, I, III, IV.
[5] Chairmen appointed by warrant of the Treasury Board.
[6] Cust. Ho. Lib., Extracts Board Minutes, IV, 207–208, 1788, Apr. 16. Possibly more than one other Commissioner attended with the warrant chairman. From the confused statement of this minute I am unable to say definitely that there was but the one Commissioner.
[7] *Ibid.*, IV, 206, 1788, Mar. 4.
[8] *Ibid.*, IV, 212, 1791, Jan. 5, in reconsideration of the minute of 1788, Apr. 16.

practice of the present day in which the permanent chairman acts as liaison officer between the Treasury and Customs Boards.

Frequently individual officers of the customs attended on the Treasury alone or with the Commissioners when their more specialized opinion was desired upon a particular case or project, or when the matter under consideration was the business of one of their departments.[1] At times, state officials or heads of other government departments, such as the Attorney-General or the Excise Commissioners, were present at the Treasury at the same time as the Customs Commissioners when the project under discussion involved a question of competence or of law, or when it required the coöperation of the two departments.[2] It is of interest to note, incidentally, that when the Customs and Excise Boards attended upon the Lords of the Treasury, the Customs Commissioners were called in first.[3] Private individuals, such as merchants and persons who brought complaints against the service or suggested plans for its improvement, were also summoned to the meetings of the Customs Commissioners and the Lords of the Treasury.[4]

The system of petitions and papers provided another link between the Customs and Treasury Boards. As has been indicated above, the Lords constantly received communications from state departments relating to customs and trade, as well as petitions and informations from merchants, officers, and private citizens, having to do with almost every subject imaginable connected with the customs. These papers the Treasury referred to the Customs Commissioners with

---

[1] E. g., see direction for the attendance of the customs solicitor (P.R.O., Treas. Out-letters, Cust., XXX, 410, Robinson to Cust. Comrs., 1772, May 27); see reference to the presence of the Auditors of the Imprest and Controller-General (*Cal. Treas. Books and Papers,* 1742–1745, p. 303, 1743, Aug. 3), or to the defense of a land-waiter on an irregularity (*Cal. Treas. Books,* Oct., 1697–Aug., 1698, p. 5, 1697, Oct. 12). It would seem that attendance of higher customs officers may have become something of a burden to the Lords. A Customs Board minute of 1790 directed that no officer except the Solicitor for London and the Western Ports, whose attendance at the Treasury was frequently and suddenly required, should presume to quit his duty to attend the Treasury or for any other reason without first apprising the Board if it was sitting at the time, or notifying the Secretary in a writing to be communicated to the Customs Commissioners. Cust. Ho. Lib., Extracts Board Minutes, V, 175, 1790, June 1.

[2] E. g., see attendance of the Attorney and Solicitor-General on the St. Sebastian Wine affair. *Cal. Treas. Books,* Oct., 1697–Aug., 1698, p. 77, 1698, Apr. 8.

[3] At least in the early part of the period. Cust. Ho. Lib., Extracts Board Minutes, I, "Commissioners," 1721, May 26.

[4] E. g., P.R.O., Treasury Minute Book, XIV, 148, 1703, Nov. 12; cf. *ibid.,* XXIV, Part II, 125, 1721, Jan. 11.

54 ORGANIZATION OF THE ENGLISH CUSTOMS

the usual endorsement, "The Right Honble the Lords Com^{rs} of his Maj^{ts} Treasury are pleased to Refer this Pet^n to the Com^{rs} of his Maj^{ts} Customs who are to consider the same and Report to their Lordships a State of the Pet^{rs} case together with their Opinion what is fit to be done therein."[1] Upon such a reference, the Customs Commissioners would consider the paper and refer it if necessary to the proper officers, whose opinions might enable the Board to decide more informedly upon the case. The documents would then be returned to the Lords of the Treasury, together with a brief report of the case and the Commissioners' judgment upon it. If the Lords were satisfied, they would order action in accordance with the Commissioners' recommendation.

The majority of Treasury papers sent to the Customs Board fall into two classes: communications containing directions or orders for a specified course of action and delegations of power in the form of warrants. There are numerous other papers as well, such as requests for information or reports, notifications that certain action had been or was to be taken, or recommendations on matters of policy. By means of memorials, representations, reports, and other communications having to do with the state of the revenue or with conditions in certain parts of the service, the Commissioners sought Treasury advice, assistance, or authorization as circumstances demanded.

On the whole, the relations between the Treasury and Customs Boards were harmonious. The Treasury Out-letters, Customs, show evidence that the Lords seldom departed from a recommendation of the Customs Commissioners, and upon occasion the Treasury Board thanked the Commissioners for their care of the revenue or signified approval of their proceedings.[2] As has been indicated, however, the

---

[1] P.R.O., Treas. Out-letters, Cust., XXVI, 11, Form of a reference, J. West, 1759, May 1. Similar endorsements may be found in the Treasury Papers. For a good account of the procedure of the Treasury on petitions at the beginning of the period, see *Cal. Treas. Papers,* 1556-7-1696, pp. xiv, xv.

[2] E. g., P.R.O., Treas. Out-letters, Cust., XXIV, 393, Hardinge to Cust. Comrs., 1754, Sept. 25. [Some of the Board having attended the Treasury with a memorial relating to certain customs officers in Bristol, the Lords of the Treasury] "have comanded me to return you their Thanks for that Attention to the Publick Service with which you have performed your Duty on this occasion. And my Lords are pleased to direct you to acquaint Mr Harnage and Mr Frewin with what Satisfaction their Lordships have received the Account you have given of their Conduct." The Lords desired that Frewin be recommended to them for a reward. For another case, see *ibid.,* XXVIII, 130, Cooper to Cust. Comrs., 1766, Dec. 17. [Upon considering your report of November 15th last] "My Lords Com^{rs} of his Maj^{ts} Treasury, have directed me to signify to you their entire

EXECUTIVE CONTROL

Commissioners jealously guarded their powers from Treasury encroachment.[1] At times they felt that the Treasury Board participated too actively in practical administration,[2] and they did not hesitate to disagree with Treasury policy when the good of the service made it necessary.[3] Neither were they slow to defend their own conduct.[4] Nevertheless, they deferred to the judgment of the Lords of the Treasury,[5] and on occasion apologized to them for some irregularity.[6] The Treasury at times overruled the Commissioners,[7] called them to account[8] or expressed disapproval of the Commissioners' attitude,[9]

---

approbation of the diligence dispatch & Ability with which you have considered & represented the great Variety of Material Points discussed in this Report."

[1] Regarding the Commissioners' power of dismissing officers, see *infra*, Ch. VI, pp. 210–211. With respect to their power of appointment to the London incidental tide-waiters' offices, see *infra*, Ch. VI, p. 201 (esp. n. 4). The Commissioners did not prevent a gradual Treasury usurpation of the patronage, nor, with few exceptions, did they make any serious effort to do so. On this subject, see *infra*, Ch. VI, pp. 198–204.

[2] See *infra*, Ch. VI, pp. 225–227.

[3] See *supra*, p. 47; *infra*, Ch. VI, p. 197, n. 3.

[4] See *supra*, p. 47.

[5] E. g., see *supra*, p. 46. Frequently the Commissioners concluded their recommendations or reports by submitting them to the "superior judgement" of their Lordships.

[6] See instance in Cust. Ho. Lib., Extracts Board Minutes, I, "Commissioners," 1752, Feb. 27, wherein the customs secretary was directed to wait on the Treasury and apologize for a delay in preparing accounts, occasioned by the neglect of the Bench Officers.

[7] For example, see a Treasury direction of reinstatement in the secretary's office of a clerk who had been dismissed by the Customs Commissioners. (P.R.O., Treas. Out-letters, Cust., XXIX, 491, Robinson to Cust. Comrs., 1771, Oct. 4.) In another case, upon the Customs Board's returning to the Treasury a Treasury warrant because the person appointed thereby was unqualified for the office, the Lords directed that the man be instructed and that as soon as he was qualified the Commissioners execute the warrant, which was "herewith returned" [to the Customs Board]. (*Ibid.*, XXXII, 441, Robinson to Cust. Comrs., 1780, Apr. 12.) There are various other instances during the period.

[8] In illustration, see a Treasury draft of Oct., 1780, to the Customs Commissioners, wherein they are directed to state to the Lords of the Treasury the ground and necessity upon which they have proceeded to appoint new officers upon incidents at Margate and to call on the patentees to appoint deputies there. P.R.O., Treasury Papers, Bdl. 559, No. 120.

[9] Such indication of disapproval generally took the polite but forceful form of "being surprised," the usual way of expressing displeasure to an important subordinate. In 1739, Dec. 5, Scrope informed the Commissioners that he was "commanded by their Lordships to signify to you their surprize that this affair [a report upon a draft bill], which is so very much pressed, meets with no greater despatch." (*Cal. Treas. Books and Papers, 1739–1741*, p. 67.) West wrote the Commissioners, 1752, Feb. 27, that the Lords "are very much Surprized that the Acco^{ts} called for by the H^o of Commons on Friday last have not yet been de-

and rebuked them for delayed [1] or unsatisfactory [2] reports; but such cases of disagreement were relatively few, and concurrence was the rule.

If the Treasury constituted the final authority in control of the customs system, the Customs Board was entrusted with the practical administration of that system. The Board of Customs Commissioners was created by patent in 1671.[3] Six Commissioners composed the first board, though the number was increased to seven two years later and varied between five and nine during the first hundred years of the history of the commission.[4] At the time of the union with Scotland, a distinct Board was established for Scotland with powers similar to those of the English commission.[5] These two boards functioned separately until 1723, when they were amalgamated under the title

---

livered." (P.R.O., Treas. Out-letters, Cust., XXIV, 130.) Cooper, 1769, Apr. 7, informed the Commissioners that their attitude on a certain matter "seems somewhat extraordinary to their Lordships," and that "My Lords Cannot forbear to express some Surprize & concern that the Comm^{rs} should conceive it possible that from the Special circumstances of this or any other Case Their Lordships should think it proper to grant a Warr^t to dispense with an Act of Parliament." (*Ibid.*, XXIX, 210, 211.) Burke was directed to acquaint the Commissioners that "My Lords had imagined that You in your general Superintendence were well and particularly informed from repeated enquiries, and frequent information of all the particulars [regarding smuggling] required by this board, & that it was on the inefficacy of your most vigorous exertions in consequence of such enquiries and informations that you had (passing by this board) applied yourselves to the Privy Council, but that finding not without surprize that this has not been the case, . . ." (*Ibid.*, XXXIII, 426–427, 1783, Oct. 9.) In a letter of 1786, Sept. 15, Rose told the Commissioners that "as many of the Proposed Regulations [for preventing frauds, which had been referred to them,] appeared to their Lordships to be extremely worthy of Attention their Lordships Command me to acq^t you they are much Surprised they have rec^d no Report thereon." (*Ibid.*, XXXIV, 371.) Though the Lords of the Treasury could be "extremely offended with the Conduct of those [Bench] Officers" (as happened in 1784; *ibid.*, XXXIV, 275, Rose to Cust. Comrs., 1784, Dec. 10), they seem never to have expressed themselves so forcibly to the Customs Board.

[1] See cases in above note.
[2] *Ibid.*, XXV, 228, Martin to Cust. Comrs., 1757, Feb. 10; cf. Cust. Ho. Lib., Extracts Board Minutes, II, "Treasury," 1757, Feb. 12. At this time the Commissioners were directed to be more explicit in their reports on petitions of smugglers and not only to state the case but also to give their opinion whether they thought the offenders proper subjects of favor.
[3] P.R.O., Patent Roll, 23 Chas. II, P. 2, No. 1, Mem. 33, dorse, [1671], Sept. 27.
[4] B.M., Add. MSS. 8133 C, ff. 1–4, "Commissioners of the Customs and Succession of the Commissioners," a printed item in Musgrave's papers, "Revenue of Customs."
[5] P.R.O., Patent Roll, 6 Anne, P. 6, No. 16, [1707], June 5.

EXECUTIVE CONTROL

of Customs Commissioners for Great Britain, and comprised seven Commissioners who resided in London to control the English and 4½ per cent duties, five in Edinburgh to supervise the Scottish and salt duties, and two at the outports under the direction of the Treasury.[1] This scheme of administration was continued until 1742, when separate boards were again established for England and Scotland [2] which remained distinct until 1823. Though the Scottish customs organization was patterned on the same lines as the English, and at times was under the same management, certain problems of administration peculiar to Scotland so affected the enforcement of the system in Scotland as to make a discussion of that department a separate story in itself. The same is true of the plantation customs. The colonial customs department was under the control of the English Board until 1767, before which date the Customs Commissioners at London had the appointment of colonial officers, regulated the plantation establishments, and influenced colonial policy in their recommendations to the Treasury and the Board of Trade upon various plantation matters. In 1767, however, a separate Board was constituted for the American Plantations.[3] Enforcement of colonial customs laws is an aspect of the customs organization which cannot be treated in a study confined to the machinery for the collection of revenue at a British port. Finally, the Irish customs during the period were under the administration of Commissioners of the Revenue in Ireland and did not come under the management of the English Customs Commissioners until the nineteenth century.

There was never a complete change in the personnel of the Board during the period.[4] As a place on the Board fell vacant, a Commis-

---

[1] P.R.O., Patent Roll, 9 Geo. I, P. 2, No. 12, [1723], June 27. See also B.M., Add. MSS. 8133 C, f. 3, "Commissioners of the Customs and Succession of the Commissioners."

[2] P.R.O., Patent Roll, 15 [incorrectly dated; should be 16] Geo. II, P. 5, Nos. 3–4, [1742], Sept. 9. See also B.M., Add. MSS. 8133 C, f. 3, "Commissioners of the Customs and Succession of the Commissioners."

[3] P.R.O., Patent Roll, 7 Geo. III, P. 5, No. 11, [1767], Sept. 8.

[4] B.M., Add. MSS. 8133 C, ff. 1–4, "Commissioners of the Customs and Succession of the Commissioners." The largest number of Commissioners who, because of death or for other reasons, were superseded in any one year was four, which occurred but three times during the entire period under consideration. Upon one other occasion three places were filled with new men. Except for these, no more than two changes on the commission were ever made at one time. Altogether, there were forty-five of the ninety years spanned by the period during which no letter patent was issued.

sioner was added and the commission was renewed with the insertion of his name in place of that of his predecessor.¹ Thus there was preserved a continuity which may partly account for the comparatively little change in policy. A similar continuity of the existence of the Board itself was ensured by statute. By 7–8 William III it was provided that no commission should become void upon the death of a sovereign, unless the sovereign should in the meantime be superseded by a successor; but that it should remain in force for six months after the decease of the monarch.²

Political considerations influenced the appointment of the Customs Commissioners as late as 1852.³ Such was undoubtedly the case to an even greater degree in the eighteenth century, though it has been impossible to explore the vast masses of correspondence which would yield evidence. Such political appointees necessarily had to become administrative officers at the Board, however; and the long tenure in office of many of the Commissioners shows a certain subordination of political influence to effective administration.⁴

Early in the period the Customs Commissioners in some cases acted individually, as is indicated in a letter from Blathwayt in 1701 signifying the King's approval of one of the Commissioners' taking care of shipping and trade and of another's inspecting weekly the account of customs receipts and vouchers ⁵; and in the appointment of Commissioner Godolphin at the same date to check the coast traffic generally in accordance with the Navigation Laws.⁶ Undoubtedly throughout the greater part of the century, however, the Customs

---

¹ E. g., *Cal. Treas. Books and Papers*, 1731–1734, p. 137, Royal warrant of 1731, Aug. 9, to Attorney or Solicitor-General.

² 7–8 Wm. III, c. 27.

³ *Report from the Select Committee on Customs; together with the Proceedings of the Committee, Minutes of Evidence, Appendix, and Index*, H.C. 498, p. 833 (1852), Part II, Minutes of Evidence, viii.

⁴ For example, Sir John Stanley, 1708–1744; Sir John Evelyn, 1721–1763; Edward Hooper, 1748–1793; Brian Fairfax, 1723–1750; Henry Pelham, 1758–1787; Sir William Musgrave, 1763–1785. Robert Beatson, *A Political Index to the Histories of Great Britain & Ireland: or, A Complete Register of the Hereditary Honours, Public Offices, and Persons in Office, from the Earliest Periods to the Present Time* (London, 1806), II, 357–362.

⁵ *Cal. Treas. Papers*, 1697–1701–2, p. 524, Blathwayt to Lowndes, 1701, Aug. 15.

⁶ P.R.O., Patent Roll, 13 Wm. III, P. 3, No. 1, [1701], Dec. 18; see B.M., Harl. MSS. 2263, f. 206, a docket of the customs commission of May, 1708, in which Godolphin's powers were continued. By appointment of 1701, Godolphin was exempted from the usual Board meetings.

Commissioners acted as a Board,[1] though naturally individual commissioners gave decisions upon less important matters of business. In 1780 the collective aspect of the Board's position seems to have been further defined when the Commissioners resolved that all general letters containing final orders, except those transmitting certain Treasury and Council orders, were in the future to be signed by the Board.[2]

Extensive privileges and powers were conferred on the Commissioners by the original patent of 1671.[3] They were not to be sued in court or molested by the Crown for anything they might do under the authority of their commission. Neither could they be charged with any money arising in receipt of customs nor were they obliged to render any account, a privilege which was upheld at a later date (1738) when the Court of Exchequer decided that the Customs Commissioners could not be charged in their private or public capacity, they not being accountable.[4] The Board were also exempted by patent from jury service and from bearing any civil or military office.[5] For their work in administration of the customs system the Commissioners were granted a salary of £2,000, a sum which, in 1696, had been reduced to £1,000, at which figure it remained throughout the period.[6]

The patent granted the Commissioners "full power & authority to manage & cause to be leavyed and Collected" the customs duties, to execute all parliamentary acts relating thereto, and "to doe or cause to be done all other matter & things whatsoever which by any Commissioners for the tyme being intrusted with the Receipt and management of our Customes can or may lawfully be done." It commanded

[1] As indicated in the correspondence of the Board with various outports, and from a study of the Board's business in the extracts from its minutes.
[2] Cust. Ho. Lib., Extracts Board Minutes, V, 189, 1780, July 28.
[3] P.R.O., Patent Roll, 23 Chas. II, P. 2, No. 1, Mem. 34, dorse, [1671], Sept. 27.
[4] Cust. Ho. Lib., Extracts Board Minutes, I, "Commissioners," 1738, June 6.
[5] This last provision was extended in the way of a disability when by 12–13 Wm. III, c. 10, s. 89, no member of the House of Commons could be a Customs Commissioner after the dissolution of the Parliament then in session.
[6] The first reduction took place in 1675 when the salary was cut to £1,200. In 1689–90 the remuneration was fixed at £1,000. (See B.M., Add. MSS. 8133 C, f. 2, "Commissioners of the Customs and Succession of the Commissioners.") The Commissioners considered the allowance of £1,000 far from adequate. (See *Cal. Treas. Papers,* 1697–1701–2, p. 529, Cust. Comrs. to Lords of Treas., 1701, Sept. 23; P.R.O., Chatham Papers, Bdl. 283, Cust. Comrs. to Lords of Treas., 1791, Jan.) By approximately the end of the period taxes had reduced the salary to a net income of £750. The Commissioners, however, received an additional £200, granted to them in 1722, for their services in superintending quarantine.

the Commissioners to see that the collectors remitted their receipts to the Receiver-General and returned their accounts regularly to the Board. It gave the Commissioners control over customs officers in matters of appointment pursuant to Treasury warrant and of dismissal and security. It granted them power to administer oaths and search ships, authorized them to make certain disbursements on the establishment and to compound seizures under forty shillings in value in duties, and permitted them the exercise of authority along lines which are too detailed to enumerate. As time went on, various aspects of these powers were further defined by practice and by opinion of the Attorney-General.[1]

The position of the Customs Commissioners in the machinery of state was that of a body of ministers through whom a higher controlling power operated to secure enforcement of trade laws, yet who were themselves responsible for the due execution of such laws. This character of the Board's status is indicated in a petition of a ship's captain to the Lords of the Treasury in 1725, wherein he stated the Commissioners' former opinion upon his case. They had insisted that the petitioner had some muslin on which the duty had not been paid, and that, since the Crown's evidence was positive, they could not depart from anything the evidence affirmed, "they being only Ministerial and not Invested with any dispensing Power for which Reasons they cannot agree to anything less than the Single Value of what

[1] See Cust. Ho. Lib., "Opinions of Counsel (England)," 4 vols., 1727–1781. In connection with the Commissioners' authority over their officers, more particularly over the patentees, Thurlow, Attorney-General, stated in 1774 (Aug. 20), "The powers contained in the patent Granted to the Commissioners are very General (in the Phrase of them) tho' very large; and may Depend in some degree upon practice for their Explanation, I cannot at present undertake to say Decisively that there can be no Office or breach of Employment in the Revenue of Customs, which may be so arranged & Constituted that the Commissioners have no Authority to change, or even Regulate it, if ever that should be in Question. It would be necessary to look very Minutely into the Establishment, and to consider every part of it with great Attention; But as the present Case involves no such Question, directly at least, I shall pass on to the other Questions, only observing that I take the General Scheme & plan of managing and ordering the levying and Collecting of the Customs to be put under their Authority, & Consequently all the inferior Officers employed in the Subordinate parts of it are equally bound to to [sic] conform to such Regulations as they think Necessary for Carrying on the General Plan of the Business, whether they Hold their Offices by patent under the great Seal, or by warrant of the Treasury or of the Commissioners themselves; or whether they hold During pleasure (as all officers of such a Revenue ought to hold their places) or for a more permanent Estate." Enclosure in Stiles to Rose, 1783, Jan. 29. P.R.O., Treasury Papers, Bdl. 584, Nos. 43–44.

EXECUTIVE CONTROL

Your Pet^r Stands Charged with by the said Evidence."[1] The lack of a dispensing power was again declared by the Commissioners in connection with a case in 1781, when they reported to the Treasury that the legislature having "in such express Terms" prohibited the use of certain East India articles and annexed heavy penalties thereto, "this Board has no power to dispense therewith."[2] If the power of the eighteenth-century Customs Board approximated that belonging to the Commissioners in 1851, as in some respects it did, though the Board had not the power to relax a statute, it could relax penalties to a certain degree, and it also had the power to remit a penalty imposed on a man convicted before a magistrate. The Lords of the Treasury, on the other hand, certainly had the authority to relax the law upon occasion, and acted through the Commissioners accordingly.[3]

The activities of the Board of Customs Commissioners were very widespread. Every aspect of practical administration, from the *minutiæ* of customs procedure to a broad program of governmental trade policy, came within their jurisdiction. The Commissioners gave much of their time to the details of pure routine work in the Port of London alone; they regulated the business of all the outports by general letters and dealt with the specific problems of individual ports; they directed the affairs of the Central Office and supervised the personnel of the entire department. These activities had to do with the superintendence of the actual customs machinery. There were others which related to the preservation of relationships with the mercantile community and state departments: the Commissioners conferred with merchants and gave decisions upon their petitions; through the Treasury they secured the assistance of other government offices for the more effective enforcement of customs laws. Still other activities involved the exercise of Board influence upon the commercial system of the day: the Commissioners frequently advised the Treasury on revenue and trade matters and recommended and prepared bills for Parliament.

[1] P.R.O., Treas. Out-letters, Cust., XVIII, 506–507, Petition of a Ship Commander to Lords of Treas., 1725.
[2] P.R.O., Treasury Papers, Bdl. 569, No. 157, Cust. Comrs. to Lords of Treas., 1781, Jan. 2. In 1766 the Attorney-General gave his opinion that the Board had no discretionary power to allow their officers a moiety in seizure cases when they did not comply with a certain act regulating seizure conduct. Cust. Ho. Lib., Extracts Board Minutes, III, 341, 1766, Mar. 15; see also Jan. 7.
[3] *First Rept. Sel. Com. on Cust.*, H.C. 209, pp. 109, 110 (1851), Minutes of Evidence, xi.

From this it may be seen that the duties of the Board of Customs were so varied in nature and so wide in scope that an attempt to consider all of them would only result in an incomplete summary and a welter of trivialities which would obscure any representative outline of the *agenda* of the Board. For the sake of clarity, those duties which are most characteristic of the many functions belonging to the Board may be grouped under five headings: regulation of customs procedure; prosecution of evasions of customs laws; supervision of personnel; consideration of merchants' petitions; and formulation of customs policy. It must be noted, however, that in actual practice no such hard-and-fast classification existed; frequently an activity was of equal importance to several of these divisions.

The first of these groups of functions, regulation of procedure in the customs, could be taken to include almost every duty belonging to the Board; but for the purpose of this outline it will be confined to supervision of the practical management of shipping and the due return of money and accounts arising therefrom. In London the Commissioners were closely occupied with petty affairs relating to individual shipments in that port: for instance, among other functions they selected officers for the discharge of every incoming vessel; they gave their permission for entries in certain cases and for the amending of entries and landing of goods; they directed the clearance of specific cargoes, signed debentures which authorized the repayment of any duties which had been paid at importation, and ordered the delivery of goods out of the warehouse. Besides giving attention to specific cases of importation and exportation, the Board was continually issuing minor regulations for the improvement of the London service: it laid down rules from time to time respecting the station of ships in the river; the landing, weighing, and warehousing of goods; allowances to merchants or masters for damage to goods and for draught, portage, and stores permitted on board; computation of duties, debentures, discounts, and bounties; payment of duties or security by bond; and returns of money and accounts into the Exchequer. By innumerable direct instructions and orders to officers the Customs Commissioners in their turn provided for enforcement of these regulations. Early in the period the Commissioners had been concerned with even more trifling details of the London business; a good part of their time had been taken up with signing and examining many shipping documents, certificates, and bills. One by one

EXECUTIVE CONTROL

these duties were discarded[1] and the Board came to be employed more and more with broader aspects of administration; but to the end of the period the Commissioners were occupied with an almost unbelievable number of routine matters in the Port of London.

It is obvious that the superintendence of the outport business had of necessity to take a more general form, though any questionable case, however insignificant, might be submitted to the Board by correspondence. The customs machinery operated in all the outports under the general letters and orders which the Board issued from time to time and through specific communications with individual ports. The Commissioners transmitted Council and Treasury orders, informed the chief officers of the outports of new regulations, advised the collectors on points of procedure of which they were ignorant, gave directions upon particular cases of importation and exportation, granted authority for certain action, directed the inspection of specific parts of the business, and ordered complete surveys of the ports. The Board also examined various daily and weekly accounts relating to imports and exports in the Port of London, scrutinized similar monthly, quarterly, and annual reports from the outports, and required records of the state of the revenue from time to time. Through the system of accounts the Board had the general supervision of the business of the staff in the Central Office.

Since the Customs Commissioners had the responsibility of enforcing the customs laws, they dealt as a matter of course with violation of such laws, though a separate department of the Central Office had charge of the legal side of the business. The Commissioners granted writs of assistance and gave permission to officers to search upon specific information of illegal practice; with their solicitors they decided upon prosecutions of seizures and bonds and small compositions of duties; when certain goods had been condemned, the Commissioners authorized their sale and delivery out of the warehouse, and in the case of certain commodities in the outports, their removal to Lon-

[1] The Board relinquished the following duties as indicated in Cust. Ho. Lib., Extracts Board Minutes: comparison of certificates of damage and over-entries and corn debentures (I, "Certificates," 1708, Oct. 25), examination of portage bills (II, "Portage," 1709, May 6), signing of certificates of return for the discharge of coast bonds (I, "Commissioners," 1715, Jan. 13), marking of the duplicates of ships' reports (I, "Commissioners," 1716, June 22), signing of cockets, warrants, etc. (I, "Bench Officers," 1718, Dec. 10; "Commissioners," 1729, Apr. 30; II, "Warrants," 1747, Mar. 17), and signing of certificates of outport plantation bonds (IV, 141, 1790, Oct. 1).

don for like disposal. The Board supervised the distribution of the shares of seizures as rewards and recommended officers and informers to the favor of the Lords of the Treasury on occasion. Upon reference of the Treasury Board the Commissioners reported as to whether law cases were deserving of *noli prosequi,* composition, or discharge, and whether persons imprisoned for fraudulent practices or debt should be released. To cope with illicit trade, the Board gave orders for the more effective guard of the coasts, establishing additional officers and providing new cruisers or changing their station. It secured Admiralty and military assistance in enforcement of customs regulations and influenced the passing of acts for the prevention of smuggling.

It was through the regulation of customs officers and the entire customs establishment, however, that uniformity in customs policy was attained and its enforcement secured. With the exception of certain powers which the Lords of the Treasury exercised directly, the Board of Customs was the administrative authority in control of personnel. The nature of such supervision will be discussed at greater length in Chapter VI; an indication of the functions of the Board in this connection will suffice at this point. By presentment of an officer to the Treasury and the issue of their deputation upon the Treasury warrant, the Commissioners appointed customs officers on the establishment. They named the extra men employed on incidents as well. From time to time the Commissioners recommended the creation of additional customs offices or the rearrangement of existing staff at various ports. They passed judgment upon the qualifications of officers, their security, training, place of residence, and the like. The Commissioners regulated the conduct of the staff on the one hand by means of approbation, promotion, and increase of salary and on the other by the fining and dismissal of officers. They gave orders for payments of salaries pursuant to Treasury warrant; administered relief to disabled customs officers and deserving widows and children of officers; and established the Superannuation Fund. They permitted men to apply to the Lords of the Treasury for leave of absence in certain cases and granted such leave themselves. Occasionally they altered the duties of individual officers; criticized instructions to new appointees; issued orders for improvement of the work in a particular department; considered collectors' reports on the conduct of officers; and directed inspections of personnel. The Board ordered disbursements on the customs establishment, such as the discharge of officers' salaries, incidents, and rewards, and the payment of portages, debentures, and bounties to merchants; directed the building, leasing, purchase, and repairing of custom-houses and the provision of adequate furnishings; and made arrangements for the maintenance of established sloops and their repair. Everything, in short, that affected the efficiency of the establishment, and consequently the welfare of the revenue, came under the jurisdiction of the Customs Commissioners.

A system of petitions and written communications provided the chief means of contact between the customs and the commercial interests and made the Board accessible to the customs officers. The consideration of such papers, together with those of similar nature referred to the Commissioners by the Lords of the Treasury, constituted a fourth major branch of the Board's activities. The most important of these applications received the attention and decision of the Board as a whole, while petitions of lesser note were dealt with by individual Commissioners. Merchants, officers, and private persons, as the case might be, applied to the Board upon such subjects as treatment of cargoes, behavior of customs officers, bonds, debts, points of customs law, informations of frauds and smuggling with elaborate schemes for prevention, and requests for places on the establishment, promotions, rewards, increases in salaries, and the like. The Board also heard merchants and officers in person upon their petitions. The accumulation of such business was clearly described in 1783 when it was stated that, apart from correspondence with the Treasury and other public offices, the Board received and answered annually, on an average, 10,000 petitions from the Port of London alone and 9,000 letters from the outports.[1]

[1] The Commissioners dealt with the London petitions themselves and personally attended the reading of and dictated the directions for the answers to the outport letters. Besides all of this business, Stiles informed Burke that the Commissioners further give "the strictest attention, not only to the Conduct of the Officers in general, but also to every part of the Public Accounts, as represented in my Letter of yesterday's date,—directions are constantly issuing for the building,—the equipment,—the repairs, and stations, of Forty two Cruisers, carrying upwards of five hundred Guns, and manned by near one thousand Mariners,—and also of a great number of Boats stationed along the Coast. Attention is likewise daily given to the crowd of Prosecutions, against Offenders, carrying on by the four Solicitors.—To all these, is added the Care of the Quarantine Service and the management of the Revenue, and the correspondence with the Officers in the Plantations. With such a heavy load of various business,—no part of which can be postponed on account of the daily arrival of Ships and other Occurrences, for which the Merchants are constantly soliciting dispatch,—it cannot surely be ex-

The more formal construction of customs policy necessitated work of still another order. The Commissioners informed the Treasury of conditions in various divisions of the service and requested authority to alter them from time to time. With due regard to precedents, they reported on petitions referred to them by the Treasury. They issued directions to the proper officers for the preparation of accounts and reports [1] to be laid before the Treasury and Parliament and proposed and drew up clauses to be incorporated with parliamentary bills for improvement of the revenue. The Commissioners interpreted customs laws in their practical directions to officers and recommendations to the Treasury and transmitted to the ports Treasury and Council commands which provided for uniformity in procedure. They obtained the coöperation of various departments and government officials and consulted with merchants, private individuals, and officers on fiscal measures. Though the Lords of the Treasury were the final authority in the determination of customs policy, the Customs Commissioners, by their practical control over the enforcement of customs laws, were largely responsible for the general character of the administration.

Board activities were not confined to customs matters alone. The result of serious investigation along this line will some day lay upon the Commissioners considerable responsibility for the general character of Britain's economic program during the period. They were constantly consulted upon proposed alterations of laws and impending

---

pected that the Commissioners should, in their own Persons, actually prepare any Accounts that may be called for by their Superiors,—or retain the minute particulars thereof in their memory, either collectively or individually, . . . neither is this conceived to be the practice at any other Board." (P.R.O., Treasury Papers, Bdl. 584, Nos. 55–56, Stiles to Burke, 1783, Oct. 17. Cf. *Repts. of Comrs.*, 1787, III, 367, App. No. 7, "Fourteenth Rept.," 1785.) In 1791, the Commissioners, in application to the Treasury for an increase in salary, stated that exclusive of the correspondence with the public offices and the plantations, they had, on an average of the preceding five years, annually dealt with upwards of 12,000 petitions from persons in the Port of London and above 10,400 letters from the officers in the outports, besides a considerable number of outport petitions. P.R.O., Chatham Papers, Bdl. 283, Cust. Comrs. to Lords of Treas., 1791, Jan.

[1] A conception of the work which might be involved in the preparation of such reports may be had from a unique instance in 1783, when, upon the Treasury's requesting information respecting smuggling during three years, the Commissioners "gave immediate directions for all the Letters received from the Out-Ports for that period, amounting to almost Thirty thousand to be revised, and the material passages to be extracted." They also ordered the officer who had charge of the riding officers' journals and the one who examined the journals of the masters and mates of customs cruisers to furnish any information which their books might contain. P.R.O., Treasury Papers, Bdl. 584, Nos. 56–57, Stiles to Burke. 1783, Oct. 17.

EXECUTIVE CONTROL

bills regulating British industry and colonial trade [1]; and they drafted clauses of such bills to be presented from time to time to Parliament.[2] While customs and commerce affairs are frequently not to be distinguished one from the other, there is no question but that the Commissioners' influence upon the economic order of the day transcended the demands of mere customs policy.

This survey of the work of the Board gives some insight into the position of the Commissioners in the organization of the customs system. Every part of the customs business came under their direct supervision, and the amount of attention given to minute detail is almost inconceivable when set against the vast range of activities to which the Commissioners bent their energies.

A survey of powers and functions would be of little value without an outline of the manner in which the Board transacted its enormous amount of business. The Secretary of the Customs, appointed by the patent of 1671, was the most important officer in the department after the Commissioners themselves, for it was through him that the

---

[1] For example, with reference to a petition of Liverpool merchants trading to the West Indies, praying an alteration in the act of 15 Charles II respecting the importation of lumber, the Commissioners reported to the Treasury, 1776, Dec. 6, "That the subsequent Relaxations from the before mentioned Acts [of 12 Chas. II, c. 18, and 15 Chas. II, c. 7] by other Statutes, allowing the Inhabitants of the Plantations to carry several Articles of their own Produce directly to other parts of Europe, seem greatly to have contributed to give them a Spirit of Independency and Enterprize in Trade and Navigation, that may with great probability be considered as one of the Sources of the present Rebellion in the British Colonies, and therefore any further deviations, should not as We conceive, be admitted without the greatest Caution and most Urgent Necessity." (P.R.O., Treasury Papers, Bdl. 523, Nos. 66–67.) In another case the Commissioners disapproved of an alteration (suggested by the East India Company) in the duties on muslins and calicoes, wherein their emphasis on certain aspects of trade policy is apparent: such alterations would be prejudicial to the customs revenue and of ill consequence to British linen and cotton manufactures. (*Ibid.*, Bdl. 481, Nos. 174, 179, Cust. Comrs. to Lords of Treas., 1771, Apr. 30.) See also the Commissioners' report to the Treasury on the memorial of the London merchants trading to the Carolinas and Georgia and of the agent of South Carolina praying a reduction of the present import duty on rice. (*Ibid.*, Bdl. 480, Nos. 354–355, 1770, Mar. 30.) See their opinion with respect to the colonial fishery trade. (*Ibid.*, Bdl. 470, Nos. 176, 183, 184, Cust. Comrs. to Lords of Treas., 1769, Feb. 18.) There are numerous other instances for the period to be found in the Treasury records.

[2] In 1770, for example, the Commissioners recommended to the Treasury that mahogany (which had been subject to duties if imported from a foreign plantation) might be admitted free from all parts of America in order to employ many persons in manufacture, to increase exportation, "and enable Us to vie with Our Neighbours at Foreign Marketts." In this memorial the Commissioners enclosed the draft of clauses to that effect. *Ibid.*, Bdl. 475, No. 404, Cust. Comrs. to Lords of Treas., 1770, Sept. 11.

Board's connection with all aspects of the customs business was maintained. The Secretary attended the Board constantly. He laid before it the reports on officers and the departmental books and accounts for the Commissioners' examination and presented all applications made to the Board and took orders upon them. He gave his opinion on questions of business when desired and attended "to all Matters of Information whereby the Commissioners may be the better enabled to guard against, and (as farr as may be within their reach) to redress, any neglects irregularitys or abuses which may happen, as well in the Long-room, as in any other part of that great and complicated System subject to their Management." He reported to the Board on his conferences with individuals calling at the Custom House, and his attendance upon the Treasury or Parliament; and assisted the Board "in giving orders provisionally upon such sudden and emergent occasions as sometimes happen when the Board is not sitting, & which require some immediate directions; and in a carefull attention to those Affairs which frequently occurr by extraordinary References and orders from the Council & Treasury Boards."[1] With respect to the general business of his department, the Secretary saw that petitions were referred to the proper officers, drafted many of the Board's reports and letters, and made sure that orders and minutes were drawn up at the Board's direction and communicated to the proper officers or parties. He superintended the clerks in their execution of the orders received from the Commissioners and in their proper treatment of officers' books and informations of various kinds turned into the office; he received and dealt with applications of persons appearing on business at the Custom House; and he represented the Commissioners at the Treasury, before the Houses of Parliament, and occasionally at the Board of Trade.[2] During the ninety years of the period, nine secretaries served the Commissioners; two of them remained in office for one year only, and one for two years; two secretaries, Charles Carkesse (1709–1741) and William Wood (1742–1765),

---

[1] See B.M., Add. MSS. 32864, ff. 389–390, enclosure relating to the business of the Long Room and the Secretary's office as described by Commissioner Hooper in his letter to Newcastle, 1756, Apr. 23.

[2] For the duties and business of the Secretary, see also *Repts. of Comrs.*, 1787, III, 367, App. No. 7, "Fourteenth Rept.," 1785; Cust. Ho. Lib., Extracts Board Minutes, II, III, V, "Secretary"; *Rules of the Water-side* (1715), pp. 76–77; and various types of his communications in the Treasury Out-letters, Customs, and Treasury Papers.

EXECUTIVE CONTROL 69

transacted the business of the department for fifty-five years.[1] This constancy of personnel may in part explain the comparatively little change in the general character of administration throughout the century.

The principal business of the Secretary's office came under the supervision of two chief clerks: the Clerk for the Western Ports and the Northern Clerk. It was the duty of the former of these officers to receive all communications concerning the western ports (of which there were forty-two in 1785), to sort such papers, refer certain of them to the proper officers for report, select those for the Board, and be present at their reading before the Board or read them to the Commissioners himself. He received the Board's instructions upon these papers and was authorized to execute the preparation of a letter, report, or other paper. He drew up rough copies of letters on special matters which were to be submitted with the transcripts for the Board's signature, and he read the first drafts to the Board. The function of the Northern Clerk was to superintend the business having to do with the northern ports of England (of which there were twenty-seven in 1785) in exactly the same way that the Western Clerk supervised the business of the ports of his district.[2]

The colonial business during part of the period required the attention of a Plantation Clerk [3] to whom all matters relating to plantation customs were committed. This officer received all plantation letters directed to the Commissioners and laid the books of their entry regularly before the Board; he examined and reported on colonial accounts of ships, bonds, and certificates and made out commissions for plantation officers. He received the orders of the Board upon all

---

[1] For these dates, see the appointment of secretaries which marked the beginning and end of each tenure of service. P.R.O., Treas. Out-letters, Cust., XV, 250–251; XXII, 168–169, 249; XXVIII, 214.

[2] The northern ports in 1756 included all of those "from Beaumaris on the west, round the North of England to Malden on the East, both inclusive," while the western ports embraced those "from Rochester round to Aberdovy, both inclusive." (B.M., Add. MSS. 32864, f. 389, enclosure in Hooper's letter to Newcastle, 1756, Apr. 23.) For a statement of the ports early in the period, see *Rules of the Water-side* (1715), p. 77. On the business of the chief clerks, see *ibid.*, p. 77; B.M., Add. MSS. 32864, ff. 389, 390–391; *Repts. of Comrs.*, 1787, III, 399–400, App. No. 21, 401, App. No. 22, "Fourteenth Rept.," 1785; Cust. Ho. Lib., Extracts Board Minutes, I, "Commissioners," 1735, Apr. 11; II, "Secretary," 1722, Apr. 4; IV, 187, 1778, Apr. 22; 190, 1779, Dec. 16; 1780, Mar. 18; 191, 1780, Apr. 19; V, 436–438, 1781, Nov. 23.

[3] The Western Clerk acted as Plantation Clerk for more than half the period.

plantation affairs and drafted them into form for despatch to the proper officers, and he recorded plantation certificates and the registers of ships bound to the colonies.[1]

The Chief Clerk of the Bond Office, which office was a separate branch of the Secretary's department, prepared all bonds for the due exportation of goods and those given in connection with the delivery of certain goods from the warehouse, and he certified the receipt of security on such bonds; he further recorded various shipping documents and kept accounts which were related directly to the bond business.[2] The Minute Clerk, who made out the drafts of each day's minutes and kept the minute book,[3] a Petition Clerk who (after 1765) received miscellaneous applications to the customs office and the reports of officers on such applications,[4] and the First Copying Clerk in the Secretary's Office were among the other most important clerks in the department. The actual transcribing, filing, and preparation of the departmental papers were done by the body of junior clerks who were superintended by the First Copying Clerk. With the growth of the customs business, the total number of clerks to the Secretary, besides the chief clerks, was fixed at fourteen by a Board minute of 1775.[5] Advancement in the higher offices of the department usually followed a fairly definite mode of succession: the Western Clerk became Secretary, the Northern Clerk as a rule filled the place of the Western Clerk,[6] and the junior clerks were moved up according to an order settled by minutes of 1778 and 1780.[7] In 1782, with refer-

---

[1] *Repts. of Comrs.*, 1787, III, 403, App. No. 24, "Fourteenth Rept.," 1785; Cust. Ho. Lib., Extracts Board Minutes, III, 389, 1758, Dec. 15; 392, 1763, Nov. 3; 393-394, 1764, July 26; 394-395, 1764, Aug. 30, and other references having to do with plantations in III, V.

[2] For instance, he kept accounts of certain goods that were prohibited from importation or subject to special regulation, listed certain debentures, and saw to the entry and issuance of particular cockets. *Repts. of Comrs.*, 1787, III, 403-404, App. No. 25, "Fourteenth Rept.," 1785.

[3] See Cust. Ho. Lib., Extracts Board Minutes, III, entries under "Minute Clerk."

[4] *Ibid.*, III, V, entries under "Petition Clerk."

[5] *Ibid.*, III, 499, 1775, Apr. 13; cf. *Repts. of Comrs.*, 1787, III, 82, "Fourteenth Rept.," 1785.

[6] For examples of the usual practice, with few exceptions, see Cust. Ho. Lib., Extracts Board Minutes, entries under "Secretary" in II, III, V, in particular for 1741, 1765, 1767, 1781, 1782. See also P.R.O., Treasury Papers, Bdl. 569, Nos. 162-163, Cust. Comrs. to Lords of Treas., 1781, Nov.

[7] Cust. Ho. Lib., Extracts Board Minutes, V, 427, 1778, Apr. 8; 432-433, 1780, Dec. 13; cf. V, 440-441, 1782, Nov. 21.

ence to the succession of the junior clerks to the office of the First Copying Clerk, it was stated that a clerk need not expect to be promoted to be Northern Clerk by right, but by qualification. Clerks aspiring to that position were required to have knowledge of the duties of all officers as contained in Crouch's *Complete Guide to Out Port Collectors,* to be well "versed" in the business of the Secretary's office in order to be able to "remind" the Commissioners and find quickly the printed instructions, minutes, and letters established for the government of customs officers in any particular case, and to command a knowledge of dates and the information of Treasury reports.[1]

The offices and Board Room of the Commissioners, together with the department of the Secretary and his clerks, were in the east end of the Custom House.[2] A door-keeper and messengers attended the Board for the despatch of the many references on petitions and memorials, summons of officers and other persons to attend the Board, orders for the entry, delivery, or prosecution of goods, and directions daily delivered in connection with the London business. The Commissioners appear to have met every weekday, though Board meetings seem to have been held but rarely on Saturdays and Mondays.[3] Occasionally the Board found it necessary to meet in extra sessions to consider matters demanding special attention or to make up arrears in business.[4] When such was the case, the Commissioners sometimes met in the early morning, but more usually they dined together and sat as a Board one or two afternoons a week. At times even holidays were sacrificed to the press of business. The Commissioners, however, were relieved from strict attendance on Board meetings by a system of absent days arranged according to a scheme of rotation.

[1] Cust. Ho. Lib., Extracts Board Minutes, V, 440-441, 1782, Nov. 21. In this minute the Commissioners declared that when the nomination of the Northern Clerk fell to them they would select the best qualified man from the Secretary's office or elsewhere, as was done formerly in the cases of Manley, Harnage, Stanley, Lowe, and many others.

[2] Except for certain times, as when the new Custom House was under construction or when repairs were being made.

[3] Several entries in Cust. Ho. Lib., Extracts Board Minutes, I, III, IV, under "Commissioners" indicate morning as the time of meeting. "Morning" at that time, however, included the early afternoon. For meetings on Saturdays and Mondays, see *ibid.,* I, "Commissioners," 1729, Apr. 24; IV, 197, 1782, Apr. 27; 205, 1787, Apr. 26, May 18; 207-208, 1788, Apr. 16.

[4] See *ibid.,* III, 88, 1764, July 26; IV, 197, 1782, Apr. 27; 202, 1785, May 4. The Board met every Thursday afternoon for such purposes in 1715, 1716, and 1717, as indicated by minute of 1782, Apr. 27.

Their indulgence in absent "weeks," in vacations of several months, and in summer "week-ends" (that sometimes extended from Friday until the following Tuesday, during which times towards the close of the period they might have the use of the Custom House yacht for a sail), indicates that they were not too burdened with the cares of office,[1] and confirms complaints against their frequent holidays.[2]

Except on the rare occasions when conscientious economy forbade it, breakfasting together at the Custom House usually cleared the ground for the business of the day.[3] There were minor changes during the period in the arrangement of the morning's program, but a definite procedure in the business, which appears to have been gen-

[1] Cust. Ho. Lib., Extracts Board Minutes, III, 708, 1781, Feb. 14; IV, 197, 1782, Apr. 27; 207–208, 1788, Apr. 16.

[2] A rough document in the Additional Manuscripts (undated and with no indication of authorship), entitled "The Com^{rs} Attend^{ce}," is a scathing attack on the frequent and long absences of the Commissioners. The writer implied that there was not a sufficient number of Commissioners present and indicated that they did not sit for a long enough time to attend to all the matters that came before them. He furthermore could not allow it as reasonable that "any Com^r should spend 2 or 3 months at a time in the Country on acc^{tt} of his private affairs, much less for his diversion; and I may venture to say that thô the looking after his private affairs is always made the pretence, yet that, for the most part, his Country diversions are the true cause of his absence." If the Commissioners did not give a complete attendance at the Board, one of two consequences would follow: business would either be done in a hurry or not despatched in due time, "And t'is hard to say by which of those ways the Revenue, or the Subject has suffer'd most." (B.M., Add. MSS. 18903, ff. 78, 79, 82.) Early in the period another writer, who offered excellent suggestions for reform in various branches of the customs, recommended diligent attendance on the part of the Commissioners themselves. The matters under the Board's management were "so many & so various as must frequently oblige the Com^{rs} to divide themselfs, that different matters may be under their respective considerations at the same time the better to prepare those matters for the determination and dispatch of the Board; which method . . . cannot be practised if less than six attend the service, four being the Quorum directed by their Comiss^n for the dispatch of all acts of the Board." The author advised reviving an old Treasury order of 1711 which directed the Commissioners to lay before the Lords a monthly account of their number and of the officers under them who were absent, which would oblige the Commissioners "to be diligent in their own attend^{ce}." (B.M., Add. MSS. 18903, f. 93.) The Commissioners were as quick to defend their "attendance," however, as they were loth to discontinue cherished holidays. In a report to the Treasury in 1783, wherein they contended that certain customs holidays did not affect the efficiency of the service, they ended, "And it is but common Justice to Ourselves to affirm to Your Lordships, that the early, and regular attendance and attention given by this Board, the better to conduct and accelerate the public Business has been at no time exceeded by the most assiduous of Our Predecessors." P.R.O., Treasury Papers, Bdl. 587, No. 355, 1783, June 5.

[3] Cust. Ho. Lib., Extracts Board Minutes, I, "Commissioners," 1719, Apr. 27; III, 88, 1766, Feb. 25; 90, 1770, July 27; IV, 200, 1783, Dec. 4; 203–204, 1786, June 30; 213, 1791, Apr. 27.

EXECUTIVE CONTROL

erålly followed, was defined by a minute of 1766.[1] In the morning the Commissioners gave directions on petitions and papers coming from the lobby of the London Custom House; at one o'clock they proceeded to read the minutes of the preceding day. The first instance of the Commissioner in the chair signing the minutes appears in May of 1705, and the practice of reading the minutes at the following session of the Board was provided for by minutes of 1711, 1742, and 1757.[2] The Board then considered such matters as were referred from the Treasury or Council, and reports to be made to those offices. Other papers, appointed by a previous Board order for the business of the day, followed, together with the papers of the Western and Northern Clerks which demanded immediate attention.

The chairmanship of the Board was determined in 1705 by the Commissioners agreeing to act in rotation, an arrangement that apparently was continued until 1788, when two warrant chairmen were appointed to preside at all meetings of the Board, to be relieved only on Mondays in the winter and Saturdays and Mondays in the summer by other Board members in rotation.[3] This would appear to have been the first step towards the establishment of the permanent chairman of modern times.

Specific days were designated by the Board for the consideration of certain matters: thus plantation letters were read on one morning

---

[1] Cust. Ho. Lib., Extracts Board Minutes, III, 89, 1766, Oct. 31. In describing the manner in which the business was carried on, the writer of the paper entitled "The Com^{rs} Attend^{ce}" states, "From 10 a clock (which is as soon as the Com^{rs} enter upon business) till between two & three, when the Board usually rises [?], they are imployed in giving answers to Merch^{ts}, and others upon their daily applications for the discharge of Goods seized, or stopt by the officers, in hearing & determining disputes between Merch^{ts} and officers ab^t the Entry of Goods, or between officer & officer touching the right of Seizure & in signing Debentures, Certif^{tes}, Portage Bils, Plate Cocq^{ts}, orders for paym^t of money, & the like. During the intermediate times of their being at leasure [?], and very often while those matters are before the Board, a clerk is reading Port letters, upon which directions are given, & minutes taken in order to his preparing answers. The usual time of their attend^{ce} at the Board being for the most part, thus imployed, what time have they to look into, and give a necess^{ry} dispatch to such other matters, I will venture to say of much more conseq^{ce}, as are under their managem^t. It will be said that they generally sitt one day in the week till 5 to dispatch those matters; I allow they do, but they seldom Enter upon the particular business appointed for that day till ab^t 2 a clock, so that there are not more than 3 hours in a week allowed for the dispatch of so many various matters as, if duly consider'd, woud require more than treble that time." B.M., Add. MSS. 18903, ff. 78–79.

[2] Cust. Ho. Lib., Extracts Board Minutes, II, "Secretary," 1705, May; I, "Commissioners," 1711, Feb. 19; 1742, July 9; II, "Secretary," 1757, Mar. 8.

[3] *Ibid.*, I, "Commissioners," 1705, Mar. 18; IV, 207–208, 1788, Apr. 16.

of the week,[1] and particular books of the Receiver-General, Controller-General, London collectors, and general officers were placed before the Board on certain other days for examination.[2] The London business and communications from the outports were dealt with daily, as were Treasury and Council papers whenever they arrived.[3] In 1784 it was provided that answers required to be made to the general outport letters should be laid before the Board when the returns from all but ten ports had been received or at the end of one month from the letter of order.[4]

Numerous minutes, particularly late in the period, regulated the receipt of Board letters and orders upon them. Thus it was provided that only the Secretary and the Western and Northern Clerks could open the letters of the Board [5]; and, later, sealed letters addressed to the Commissioners were to be taken unopened to the Chairman if the Board was sitting; if not, then to the Secretary or senior clerk in his absence.[6] Directions for the preparation of a letter or report had to receive the initials of one Commissioner,[7] though the Secretary and Western and Northern Clerks could give orders of reference.[8] Before letters, prepared by the Copying Clerks, could be submitted for the signature of the Board, they had to receive the approval and initials of the Secretary or one of the principal clerks,[9] and the draft had to be read by the clerks to the Board before it was signed.[10] In 1780 it was decided that no final order could pass without the initials of one Commissioner,[11] and all general letters containing final orders had to receive the Board's signature, except such as transmitted copies of quarantine and Treasury and Council orders.[12]

Documents were frequently referred for report to the solicitors,

[1] The day appointed for the reading of plantation letters was specified as Friday in 1705, Wednesday in 1748, and Thursday in 1779. Cust. Ho. Lib., Extracts Board Minutes, II, "Secretary," 1705, June 22; 1748, Sept. 20; IV, 188, 1779, Feb. 13.
[2] See for example *ibid.*, II, "Secretary," 1719, Nov. 10; "Commissioners," 1742, Oct. 13; III, 337–338, 1761, June 5.
[3] See reference, *ibid.*, II, "Secretary," 1722, Apr. 4; I, "Commissioners," 1709, May 22; III, 89, 1766, Oct. 31.
[4] *Ibid.*, V, 445, 1784, May 14.
[5] *Ibid.*, I, "Commissioners," 1735, Apr. 11.
[6] *Ibid.*, III, 88, 1766, Sept. 17.
[7] *Ibid.*, IV, 189, 1779, Apr. 8.
[8] *Ibid.*, IV, 190, 1780, Mar. 18; see also IV, 191, 1780, Apr. 19.
[9] *Ibid.*, IV, 187, 1778, Apr. 22.
[10] *Ibid.*, IV, 190, 1779, Dec. 16.
[11] *Ibid.*, IV, 190, 1780, Mar. 18.
[12] *Ibid.*, IV, 192, 1780, July 28.

EXECUTIVE CONTROL

general-surveyors (towards the close of the period), and Bench Officers in the Long Room. In virtue of their position as supervisors of officers' conduct, the general-surveyors acted as the official advisers to the Board.[1] The solicitors advised the Board upon any legal proceedings or points of customs law,[2] while "the duty of the bench officers [chief officers of the Port of London] has been always deemed to be that of advising the Board upon various questions that occur in practice." [3] By 1851 this business was considered to take up more time than any of the other duties of the Bench Officers.[4] When occasion demanded, business was referred to the principal outport officers as well. This system of referring numerous papers to officers after they had come to the Board was not too efficient, though it appears to have been regulated for the better in 1783. In that year a minute directed that collectors and controllers should give notice in their ports when they were ready to transmit all memorials and applications to the Board, and that upon receiving such documents they should themselves submit them to the correct officers and then forward the reports with their observations thereon, so that the whole matter might come up ready for the Board's consideration in the first instance without loss of time. This order was not meant to prevent merchants or others from sending their petitions directly to the Board.[5] The reference system, however, whereby the Chief Clerks gave orders on papers of reference, seems to have lent itself to some abuse at a later date, in the adoption of an indiscriminate use of reference with respect to all cases that came before the Commissioners for decision and from want of sufficient regulations relating to the time allowed to the officers to make their reports.[6]

The Board granted personal interviews to merchants, officers, and private individuals. Merchants usually came on matters of applications or memorials having to do with particular shipments or

---

[1] *Second Rept. Sel. Com. on Cust.*, H.C. 604, p. 92 (1851), Part I, Minutes of Evidence, xi. See *infra*, Ch. III, pp. 114–115.
[2] Such reports of the solicitors are to be found throughout the Treasury Out-letters, Customs. See *infra*, Ch. III, pp. 94, 95, 96–97.
[3] *Second Rept. Sel. Com. on Cust.*, H.C. 604, p. 198 (1851), Part I, Minutes of Evidence, xi. See *infra*, Ch. IV, p. 132.
[4] *Ibid.*, p. 197.
[5] Cust. Ho. Lib., Extracts Board Minutes, IV, 198–199, 1783, Feb. 11.
[6] *First, Second, Third, Fourth, Fifth, and Sixth Reports of the Commissioners appointed to inquire into the departments of the Customs and Excise; and Of the Proceedings of the Lords Commissioners of the Treasury thereupon* (Customs), H.C. 46, pp. 4–5 (1820), "First Report," 1818, vi.

customs practice, or to advise the Board upon matters of policy. London officers were summoned before the Board for various reasons: the Bench Officers usually reported on accounts and questions of customs procedure, while general-surveyors and solicitors, as has been noted, attended frequently because of the number of general orders of reference; other officers were called in from time to time on the business relating to their departments or to give a report or opinion; many were interviewed on being appointed or were heard before the Commissioners proceeded to their dismissal. Private individuals and public officials conferred with the Board upon special business.

Any outline of the position of the Board would be incomplete without more direct reference to its connection with the business and life in the London Custom House. The deputies to the chief patentees responsible for the London business were under the direct control of the Commissioners[1]; and in a case in 1720 deputies in the Long Room acquainted the Board that it had a right to make such a disposition in that Room as would be for the better carrying-on of the service.[2] The general governance of the Long Room business by the Bench Officers[3] came under the eye of the Board. One or more of the Commissioners themselves at certain times during the period sat on the Bench in direction of the business.[4] Thus in 1703 the Commissioners, taking notice that "due solemnity" was not used at the Bench in administering the oath, decided that they should officiate at the Bench in turn for one week each.[5] Whether the actual presence of the Commissioners in the Long Room was a usual thing matters relatively little, however, for few points of the London business were too insignificant to receive the direction of the Commissioners by written paper or oral order in reference.

Responsibility for the upkeep of the London Custom House was vested in a House-keeper who was considered an attendant upon

[1] With respect to the powers of the Board over the Bench Officers, see *supra*, Ch. I, pp. 19–20.
[2] Cust. Ho. Lib., Extracts Board Minutes, I, "Bench Officers," 1720, Sept. 15.
[3] On the business of the Bench Officers, see *infra*, Ch. IV, pp. 130–133.
[4] Henry Chamberlain, *A New and Compleat History and Survey of the Cities of London and Westminster . . . The Borough of Southwark, and Parts adjacent: from the Earliest Accounts to the Year 1770* (London, 1771), p. 552. Cf. *London*, edited by Charles Knight (London, 1842), II, 408, in Ch. L, "The Custom House," by J. J. Platt.
[5] Cust. Ho. Lib., Extracts Board Minutes, I, "Commissioners," 1703, June 22. It is doubtful if such an arrangement was continued for long.

EXECUTIVE CONTROL

the Board and was directly answerable to the Commissioners.[1] For some years this office was held by a woman,[2] presumably a lady of position and influence in one case at least, who was responsible for several servants who did the menial work about the establishment.[3] Though the House-keeper was connected in one way or another with everything that concerned the domestic administration of the Custom House, her main duties required that she be responsible for certain cleaning in the building, see that the watchmen were at their stations and that fires were secured and officers out of their offices by nine in the evening, deliver coal and candles to the Custom House staff, purchase supplies from tradesmen, and contract with jobbers for new work and repairs about the Custom House. She also provided the Commissioners' breakfast, superintended their stables, and purchased hay and straw for their horses.[4] For this work the House-keeper was granted a salary and an allowance for servants. Her accounts were checked by a controller [5]; but such control did not prevent abuses, for in 1783 drastic reforms were ordered upon the discovery that the House-keeper at that time was being far too thrifty in her own interests.[6] Mrs. Bridget Kelly had been selling partly used candles and taking the proceeds [7]; she had converted coal to her own use and evidently had taken advantage

[1] In the early part of the period the positions of House-keeper and Door-keeper had been filled by one person, but in 1709 they were held to be inconsistent and Godolphin made separate appointments. P.R.O., Treas. Out-letters, Cust., XV, 164–165, Cust. Comrs to Lord High Treasurer; Treasury warrant, 1709, May 10.
[2] See Cust. Ho. Lib., Extracts Board Minutes, I, "Housekeeper," 1740, Oct. 15, and other entries under "Housekeeper" in I, III, IV. See also P.R.O., Treas. Out-letters, Cust., XXIV, 389, Treasury warrant, 1754, July 17; XXVIII, 212, Treasury warrant, 1765, Aug. 2; XXIX, 332, Treasury warrant, 1770, May 16. In 1783 at a time when one of the women house-keepers was causing the Board considerable annoyance, Stiles informed Burke that for many years the office of House-keeper had been held by a man, and "indeed various branches of the Housekeeper's duty, seem to require that it should still be executed by Men in Person, who should be constantly resident in the House." P.R.O., Treasury Papers, Bdl. 589, No. 33, 1783, Oct. 22.
[3] By Treasury warrants of 1741, Aug. 5, and 1762, May 25, mentioned in Cust. Ho. Lib., Extracts Board Minutes, IV, 523, 1783, July 30.
[4] See *ibid.*, I, III, IV, entries under "House-keeper."
[5] At least from 1766 on, and perhaps earlier. (*Ibid.*, III, 216, 1766, Apr. 12.) The office of the controller was directed to be discontinued on the first vacancy by minute of 1783, Nov. 13. *Ibid.*, IV, 530.
[6] *Ibid.*, IV, 521–523, 1783, July 30; 524–527, 1783, Oct. 23; 528, 1783, Nov. 7.
[7] Representations were made to the Board that candles and coals were sold in such large quantities out of the Custom House as to affect the trade of the shop-keepers in the neighborhood. P.R.O., Treasury Papers, Bdl. 589, No. 34, Stiles to Burke, 1783, Oct. 22.

of her contract with the Customs Commissioners for furnishing wood for fires. She had hired fewer servants, appropriated part of her servant allowance, and demanded money for unnecessary work. The irate Board, evidently loth to dismiss her, took away many of her privileges and resolved unanimously that she should not have any emoluments other than her own and servants' wages from the Crown.

In review, a fair appraisal of the efficiency of the Boards is difficult, but certain features of their administration may be noted. Without exception, the Boards throughout the period were conscientious, occasionally almost to a fault in their concern with petty details of routine. For the most part administration was sound. Decisions on petitions show evidence of fair and sagacious judgment: the Commissioners did not strain at gnats on a point of customs law, but tempered their decision according to the circumstances of the case whenever they could and took care to avoid the establishment of dangerous precedents. The Board made continual attempts to improve the effectiveness of the service by extending the organization, encouraging officers, bettering the regulation of routine business, and having regard to the dangers of patent offices, fees, and the like. The Commissioners, however, cannot be entirely freed from responsibility for the poor condition of many of the ports, for the too frequent connivance of customs officials in fraud and smuggling, and for the indifferent personnel which meant a proportionate degree of inefficiency. Until the close of the period there was no concerted attempt at the badly needed reform of the system, partly perhaps because the Commissioners' hands were tied by the limitation of their powers, partly because of such immutable institutions as sinecures, fees, and customs duties, and partly also because eighteenth-century public opinion did not demand reform. Many of their efforts, while commendable enough, were often temporary expedients, provided mainly to answer the exigency of the moment and not with an eye to future development. That the revenue was as productive as it was,[1] despite the system which had to be enforced, is evidence of a certain degree of judicious administration by the Board of Customs Commissioners.

Nearly every main department of state and many local government officials were connected in some way with the execution of

[1] See *infra*, Ch. VII, p. 243.

customs laws. The Privy Council or a committee was immediately concerned with the direction of several departments of customs business. The Commissioners on rare occasions attended the Council, and after 1782 were frequently consulted by the special Committee of the Council on Trade, appointed in that year to take over the functions of the old Board of Trade.[1] Orders in Council which concerned the customs establishment alone or required the compliance of the Commissioners in execution of part of a general order relating to the customs were transmitted by the Lords of the Treasury to the Customs Board with the customary Treasury direction, "Let the Comm^{rs} of his Ma^{ty} Customs take care that this order of Councill be duly complyd with [2] Whitehall." [3] Orders of Council were executed at times without the Treasury order, though the Customs Board seems to have felt somewhat diffident about acting independently.[4] Customs reports upon Orders of Council or references of the Treasury Board and customs documents which required the attention of the Privy Council usually appear to have reached that body and the Secretaries of State through the Treasury, though there was direct communication as well.[5]

[1] For references to such attendance, see entries under "Commissioners" in Cust. Ho. Lib., Extracts Board Minutes, I, III, IV.

[2] This instruction was obviously meant to end with the word "with"; but in the original the period is missing.

[3] There are numerous instances in the Treasury Out-letters, Customs, for the period. See, for a typical example, XIII, 290, endorsement on Order in Council of 1696, Oct. 2.

[4] When the Lords of the Treasury were not in session, the Customs Commissioners on several occasions were empowered to execute the orders without the Treasury warrant. (E. g., ibid., XXVI, 137, West to Cust. Comrs., 1760, Aug. 3; XXVII, 200, Martin to Cust. Comrs., 1762, Aug. 3; Cust. Ho. Lib., Extracts Board Minutes, I, "Commissioners," 1721, Aug. 11.) In 1762 the Treasury directed the Commissioners to comply with Orders in Council for taking the embargo off provision ships before the Treasury warrant thereon was issued, even though the Treasury was in session; and acquainted the Commissioners that the proper forms of warrants would be signed thereafter for their justification upon such Orders of Council being returned to the Treasury for that purpose. (P.R.O., Treas. Out-letters, Cust., XXVII, 208, Martin to Cust. Comrs., 1762, Oct. 12.) The following year, the Customs Board desired that when the Lords of the Treasury were not adjourned the Orders of Council might be referred to them; but the directions which followed required that Orders of Council were to be immediately executed and afterwards returned to the Treasury to receive the sanction of the Lords. Cust. Ho. Lib., Extracts Board Minutes, III, 429, 1763, Feb. 1, 17.

[5] For instances of direct report, see P.R.O., Treasury Papers, Bdl. 483, No. 28, extract of a memorial of Cust. Comrs. to Privy Council, 1770, Nov. 12; and ibid.,

Of miscellaneous customs matters which came to the attention of the Council, there were some with which that body was especially concerned. The Lords of the Council had the immediate direction of quarantine enforcement by the Commissioners: they issued instructions to the customs concerning performance of quarantine by ships arriving from infected parts; they gave countless orders permitting specific ships to discharge and unload without further observation of quarantine; and they required customs reports and the attendance of the Commissioners from time to time on the subject of that service.[1] The Council directed the enforcement of embargo and gave permissions in the form of orders for individual ships to pro-

---

Bdl. 630, Nos. 352–373, copy of report of Cust. Comrs. to Lords of the Committee of Council for Trade and Plantations, 1786, Mar. 31. From a case in 1783 the Lords of the Treasury appear to have disapproved of the Commissioners' applying directly to the Council on matters which the Treasury felt belonged to their immediate jurisdiction. In a letter of Oct. 15, 1783, Stiles returned to Burke an account of customs applications which had been made to the Council on the subject of smuggling by large armed vessels, and stated, "But, as by some expressions in that Letter [Burke's letter of Aug. 30], and in your subsequent one dated the 9th Instant, it should seem as if their Lordships had entertained some unfavorable Sentiments, on account of an Application from this Board directly to the Council-Office ('passing by the Lords of the Treasury'). I am directed to transmit you the said Account, without further delay, by which their Lordships will see, that the Instances are no more than *three*,—and that this method of Application has only been adopted, when the Parties were not subject to any Punishment by the Laws of the Revenue,—but seemed to be arming in a piratical, or rebellious manner, in defiance of the general Laws and Peace of the Realm,— consequently in the judgment of this Board, the matter came most properly under the cognizance of the Council, and that it required *Haste*,—least the Vessels should depart out of Port, before any Embargo could be laid thereon, in case the Council Board should think it expedient to give such, or any other Orders relative thereto. Under these circumstances, the Commissioners thought it advisable, to transmit the representations of their Officers immediately to the Council-Office, for the sake of dispatch only, without the most distant intention of the smallest disrespect to the Board of Treasury,—for whom the Commissioners, both collectively and individually, always entertain the highest deference." *Ibid.*, Bdl. 583, Nos. 362–363. See enclosure, Nos. 358, 359. See also P.R.O., Treas. Outletters, Cust., XXXIII, 426–427, Burke to Cust. Comrs., 1783, Oct. 9.

[1] For directions and orders to the Customs Department on quarantine, see for example *ibid.*, XV, 351–353, Order in Council, 1711, Sept. 6; Oxford's direction, 1711, Sept. 7; and XXIV, 356–361, Order of Council, 1754, Mar. 1; Treasury direction, 1754, Mar. 4. For an example of an order for the discharge of particular ships, see *ibid.*, XV, 269, 1709, Feb. 26; Godolphin's direction, 1709, Mar. 2; XVII, 356, Treasury warrant, 1720, Feb. 14, on Order in Council of 1720, Feb. 10. For a reference to reports necessary to be made to the Council, see *ibid.*, XVIII, 156–157, Treasury warrant, 1722, Dec. 19. For instances of the attendance of the Commissioners on the Council upon the subject of quarantine, see Cust. Ho. Lib., Extracts Board Minutes, II, "Quarantin," 1720, Aug. 25; 1721, Apr. 26; 1729, Jan. 26; I, "Commissioners," 1743, Oct. 26.

EXECUTIVE CONTROL

ceed on their voyages notwithstanding the embargo [1] and for the removal of military stores in times of war.[2] The State Papers Domestic for the years 1744 and 1745 bear evidence that during military hostilities customs officers were called upon by Council orders to guard the coasts, inspect packet-boats, return intelligence of the appearance of an enemy fleet, and detain various persons entering England.

The Secretaries of State and the Under-Secretaries were individually concerned with various customs matters. They seem to have had no little influence over the personnel of the customs establishment. In the State Papers Domestic are to be found numerous applications to them from individuals and their friends for customs positions,[3] and memoranda of persons "to be laid before My Lord Duke [Newcastle]" for appointment to customs offices.[4] The Secretaries and their subordinates individually gave directions in connection with such matters as quarantine,[5] prevention of ships from sailing,[6] examination [7] or detention of passengers, and other miscellaneous items. Enforcement of customs laws against smuggling gave rise to much correspondence between the Secretaries and the Customs Department. Numerous informations of smuggling and seizure cases were laid before the Secretaries,[8] together with various plans for

---

[1] E. g., P.R.O., Treas. Out-letters, Cust., XIII, 255, Order of Council 1696, Mar. 26; Treasury direction, 1696, Apr. 1; XXVII, 82–83, Order of Council, 1762, Feb. 15; Treasury direction, 1762, Feb. 23; see *Cal. Treas. Books and Papers*, 1739–1741, p. 349.

[2] E. g., P.R.O., Treas. Out-letters, Cust., XXV, 274–277, June–December, 1757.

[3] For several examples, see: P.R.O., Descriptive List of State Papers Domestic, George I, references to Vols. VIII, No. 49, Hamilton to Stanhope, 1717, Feb. 23; XXXII, No. 65, St. Hill to Townshend, 1722, July; XII, No. 86, Gore to Craggs, 1718, July 17; P.R.O., State Papers Domestic, George II, Bdl. 44, John and William Scutt to Newcastle, 1737, Nov. 10; Bdl. 40, Boys to Newcastle, 1736-7, Mar. 7; cf. Bdl. 40, Newcastle to Brereton, 1737, Apr. 5. See also Hist. MSS. Com., *Fifteenth Rept., Report on the Manuscripts of His Grace The Duke of Portland, K.G., preserved at Welbeck Abbey*, VIII [Cd. 3475], p. 368 (1907).

[4] State Papers Domestic, Geo. II, Bdl. 39, Memoranda for Andrew Stone, 1736, Dec.; Memoranda for "my Lord Duke" (most of which are for customs positions, either for specific posts or to "some other Place in the Customs"), 1736, Aug.

[5] P.R.O., Desc. List State Papers Dom., Geo. I, ref. to Vol. XXIII, No. 19, Delafaye to Carkesse, 1720, Sept. 9.

[6] P.R.O., State Papers Domestic, Geo. II, Bdl. 116, Wood to Aldworth, 1751, Apr. 3, hoping "to receive his Grace the Duke of Bedfords Orders as soon as possible."

[7] P.R.O., Desc. List State Papers Dom., Geo. I, ref. to Vol. III, No. 85, Townshend to Customs, 1715, July 30.

[8] In connection with informations against smuggling, West, in a letter to Stone, refers to the act of last session of Parliament whereby "all Informations against

82 ORGANIZATION OF THE ENGLISH CUSTOMS

the suppression of the nefarious trade,[1] and on occasion the customs were advised of them.[2] The Board communicated with the Secretaries on matters pertaining to French ships engaged in smuggling.[3] (In one case at least, the Secretary of the Treasury, on behalf of the Customs Department, described the activity of the French ships in such illicit practices as serious enough to warrant a representation to the Court of France, and requested that such representation be made accordingly.[4]) When dragoons were needed to combat smuggling, the order of a Secretary or of the Privy Council to the Secretary at War was apparently necessary for their removal from one station to another.[5] The Customs Department occasionally acquainted the Secretaries' office with proceedings against illicit practices [6] and sought the assistance of the Secretaries in the prosecution of criminals. Such assistance would include the offering of rewards for the arrest of smugglers,[7] orders for the commitment to jail of arrested men,[8] and protection for individuals who went to distant parts to give evidence or secure witnesses against persons under

---

Smuglers which shall be transmitted to his Maj[ts] Principal Secretaries of State shall be immediately laid before his Majesty in his Privy Council and therefore Their Lordships [Lords of the Treasury] desire his Grace will be pleased to lay the said Papers before his Majesty in Council according to the directions of the said Act." P.R.O., State Papers Domestic, Geo. II, Bdl. 88, 1746, Oct. 2.

[1] E. g., P.R.O., Desc. List State Papers Dom., Geo. I, ref. to Vols. XX, No. 7, Gordin to Secretary of State, 1720, Jan. 18; XXIX, No. 5, J. S. to Townshend, 1721, Nov. 6.

[2] E. g., see Carkesse's acknowledgment of information to Tilson, *ibid.*, ref. to Vol. XLII, No. 54, Carkesse to Tilson, 1723, Mar. 16.

[3] E. g., P.R.O., Desc. List State Papers Dom., Geo. I, ref. to Vols. XLII, No. 120, Cust. Comrs. to Carteret, 1723, Apr. 3; No. 138, Cust. Comrs. to Carteret, 1723, Apr. 10; LII, No. 29, Cust. Comrs. to Newcastle, 1724, Sept. 12.

[4] P.R.O., Calendar (manuscript) State Papers Domestic, George II, 1727-1729, I, 191, Scrope to Delafaye, 1729, June 20.

[5] For an example of procedure with regard to the movement of troops, see an instance of 1748, P.R.O., State Papers Domestic, Geo. II, Bdl. 107, No. 67, Wood to Scrope, 1748, July 11, and West to Secretary at War (Henry Fox), 1748, July 14; cf. No. 59. In connection with a Secretary's order for the movement of troops to quell a riot, see Mark A. Thomson, *The Secretaries of State, 1681-1782* (Oxford, 1932), p. 107.

[6] E. g., P.R.O., Desc. List State Papers Dom., Geo. I, ref. to Vol. XXVII, No. 90, Manley to Delafaye, 1721, July 29; cf. ref. to Vol. XLII, No. 122a, Carkesse to Tilson, 1723, Apr. 3.

[7] E. g., *ibid.*, ref. to Vol. XXVIII, No. 14, Customs to Townshend, 1721, Aug. 15; see also ref. to Vol. XLVI, No. 7, Lowndes to Delafaye, 1723, Nov. 5.

[8] P.R.O., State Papers Domestic, Geo. II, Bdl. 83, Wood to Stone, 1746, Apr. 18, 22. See Thomson, *Secretaries of State*, p. 111.

EXECUTIVE CONTROL

prosecution.¹ Petitions for relief or pardon which came to the hands of the Secretaries from smugglers or others who were under sentence of imprisonment, transportation, or death were occasionally referred for report to the Customs Board ²; and that Board "likewise made the usual Application to One of His Majesty's principal Secretary's of State requesting the Kings most Gracious pardon" for the person making discovery of certain of his accomplices in the murder of a customs officer.³

The two departments were brought into close contact on minor subjects. The passage of the King's messengers through the ports of the south and east coasts on their way to and from the Continent was a cause of friction between the customs and state offices. Only too often the messengers were found guilty of maneuvering smuggled goods past the customs officers, as a letter from the Harwich collector suggests forcibly to the Board in 1746: "This we humbly hope is a sufficient proof what difficultys we labour under at this Port by such practices as these as we must either risque the disobliging the great officers of the Crown or suffer an illicit trade to be carried on. And after this detection no one can wonder how the millinery shops in London come to be fill'd with prohibited Dresden needle-work and other goods of Germany." ⁴ The customs officers in their turn seem to have been extremely conscientious and somewhat too curious in the examination of the messengers, for the Customs Commissioners received emphatic protests from the Secretaries' office against the unnecessary delays of messengers in the detention and search of their baggage. Delafaye's letter to Carkesse on one such occasion is as amusing as it is scathing. After reviewing a particularly inconvenient case (the first· instance of its kind during his thirty years' employment in the office), upon which he "cou'd not help being moved at this Insult both upon my Lord Duke of Newcastle & Mr Walpole . . . [but which he imputed rather] to the Officers at Dover being

¹ P.R.O., Desc. List State Papers Dom., Geo. I, ref. to Vols. XLII, No. 7, Cust. Comrs., to Carteret, 1723, Mar. 2; XLVIII, No. 6, Cust. Comrs. to Townshend, 1724, Jan. 7.
² For such an instance, see *ibid.*, ref. to Vol. XLVI, No. 15, Petitions of Lewis and Vaines to Lords Justices, 1723, Nov. 9, in connection with which is indicated a communication of Carkesse to Delafaye. See also ref. to Vol. XLVIII, No. 21, Cust. Comrs., to Carteret, 1724, Jan. 18.
³ P.R.O., Treasury Papers, Bdl. 607, No. 52, Stiles to Rose, 1784, July 24.
⁴ Cust. Ho. Lib., Sel. from Cust. Outport Recds., East Coast, 1923, p. 92, Harwich, Collector to Board, 1744-1748, 1746, July 15.

very strict in their Duty (which I hope they are in all other respects) than to a designed affront, . . . [he ended by] Supposing the Messengers themselves should bring over any small Matter of Goods, it can be but a trifle but as to that let them a' Gods Name be search'd to their Skin, but pray let it be done with Dispatch, & let the Kings Pacquets & Letters meet with as much regard at least from his own Officers as they do from those in France."[1] In studying the relations between the Secretaries of State and the Customs Department one is impressed on the one hand by the triviality of the customs business laid before the Secretaries, and on the other hand by their attention to detail.

The connection between the Customs Board and Parliament has been touched upon to some extent above.[2] The Customs Commissioners were responsible to Parliament through the Treasury.[3] In the beginning of the eighteenth century parliamentary disability had been imposed upon the Commissioners,[4] and from that time on the relationship of the customs with Parliament was confined to the channel of the Treasury. Nevertheless, parliamentary legislation affecting the customs service usually found its inception with the Customs Board. It was customary before parliamentary sessions for the Lords of the Treasury to desire the Customs Commissioners to consider the customs laws then in force and to make recommendations for any necessary alterations or additions. Upon the Treasury's request the Commissioners referred to the proper officers for any suggestions for improvement of the business of their respective departments or the

---

[1] P.R.O., State Papers Domestic, Geo. II, VI, ff. 15–16, Delafaye to Carkesse, 1728, Apr. 4. Other communications passed between these two; see P.R.O., MS. Cal. State Papers Dom., Geo. II, 1727–1729, I, 87, Carkesse to Delafaye, 1728, June 14; 113, Carkesse to Delafaye, 1728, Dec. 31. See also reference to Craggs' complaints to the customs in 1718 and 1719, P.R.O., Desc. List State Papers Dom., Geo. I, ref. to Vols. XIII, Nos. 49, 54; XVIII, No. 19; P.R.O., Treas. Out-letters, Cust., XXIII, 584, Lords of Treas. to Lord Chamberlain, 1750, Aug. 3.

[2] See *supra*, pp. 45–46, 49, 66–67, 68.

[3] Actually through the Chancellor of the Exchequer in 1852. *Rept. Sel. Com. on Cust.*, H.C. 498, p. 808 (1852), Part II, Minutes of Evidence, viii.

[4] 12–13 Wm. III, c. 10, s. 89, stipulated that no member of the House of Commons should act as a Customs Commissioner after the dissolution of the Parliament then sitting. At the time of this act, six of seven Commissioners were members of Parliament. At the following election in December of 1701, four Commissioners retained their positions as Customs Commissioners and lost their seat, while two relinquished their Board position and were reëlected. Henry Atton, "Commissioners of Customs, Excise, Hearth Money, and Inland Revenue," an unpublished study in the Custom House Library, p. 136.

EXECUTIVE CONTROL

customs as a whole and themselves considered and proposed clauses to the Lords of the Treasury. The Lords examined these drafts and, if they approved, directed the Commissioners to cause a bill to be prepared immediately and sent to them in order to be laid before Parliament for passing the clause into law.[1] The Commissioners as an entire Board, a Committee, or in odd numbers attended upon both Houses of Parliament from time to time on customs matters and with annual accounts and upon Committees of the House investigating revenue and trade questions. Occasionally individual customs officers were present, with or without the Commissioners, to explain any accounts or other business.[2] The Customs Board had no little influence upon the course of parliamentary legislation dealing with any matters which came within the jurisdiction of the Customs Department.

Fairly close coöperation between the Customs Commissioners and the Board of Trade was to be expected.[3] The two Boards corresponded through their secretaries[4]; on rare occasions they met together as well,[5] and the Secretary to the Customs Commissioners frequently attended the Board of Trade upon trade and plantation matters.[6] The criticism of the Customs Commissioners was frequently sought by the Board of Trade on colonial acts affecting commerce, instructions to certain plantation officials, and proposed regulation of colonial shipping. The Board of Trade was furnished with customs statistics on imports and exports and the state of certain branches of trade in general and of colonial trade in particular, while both Boards advised each other upon the enforcement of trade laws at home and in the plantations and supplied miscellaneous items of information on subjects having to do with commerce and the

---

[1] The Treasury Out-letters, Customs, contain numerous references in this connection. As examples, see XXV, 407, West to Cust. Comrs., 1758, Aug. 2; 444, Martin to Cust. Comrs., 1758, Dec. 1.
[2] For references to such attendance, see entries under "Commissioners" in Cust. Ho. Lib., Extracts Board Minutes, I, III, IV.
[3] See A. B. Keith, *Const. Hist. of First Brit. Empire*, pp. 278–279.
[4] The volumes of the *Journal of the Commissioners for Trade and Plantations* contain numerous references to such correspondence. E. g., see 1734-5–1741, p. 181, 1737, May 18.
[5] E. g., see *ibid.*, 1718–1722, pp. 45–46, for the attendance of two Customs Commissioners ("coming to the Board as desired") with Carkesse, regarding premiums on pitch and tar from the plantations, 1718-9, Mar. 12.
[6] E. g., see Carkesse's attendance on a draft of instructions relating to trade and navigation. *Ibid.*, 1734-5–1741, p. 205, 1737, July 13; see *ibid.*, 1718–1722, p. 179, 1720, July 6.

86 ORGANIZATION OF THE ENGLISH CUSTOMS

colonies. Nevertheless, the refusal of the Customs Commissioners upon several occasions to report to the Board of Trade, unless commanded by the Lords of the Treasury or the Privy Council, would seem to indicate the assertion of an independent position by the Customs Board as regards its relations with the Board of Trade, as well as to emphasize the limited powers of the Commissioners of Trade and Plantations.[1]

Coöperation between the Customs and Excise Boards was a necessity. During the period covered by this study the excise officers collected duties for the most part upon home products while customs officers received the duties upon imported goods. There were several foreign commodities, however, notably tea, coffee, brandy, and other liquors, that were subject to excise duties as well as customs duties, and the officers of both departments were employed in their collection.[2] Furthermore, though smuggled goods might be slipped past the

---

[1] A hesitation of the Customs Commissioners to give their opinion upon certain acts of Assembly may have been due to a departmental quarrel as Keith (*Const. Hist. of First Brit. Empire*, p. 279) supposes. (See *Journ. Comrs. for Trade and Plant.*, 1728-9-1734, pp. 164, 165, 168, 175.) Two more serious refusals of later date would seem to indicate that the Board of Customs was somewhat jealous of its own position. A minute of the Customs Board for 1758, Nov. 22, reports the attendance of two Commissioners upon the Duke of Newcastle on an order of reference received from the Board of Trade for preventing frauds in the execution of the revenue laws in the Plantations "by which it appears the Commissioners desired to be excused from entering into the Subject of the said Reference unless commanded thereto by the King and Council or the Lords of the Treasury agreeable to their practice and Constitution and the said Reference etc. ordered to be returned to the Board of Trade." (Cust. Ho. Lib., Extracts Board Minutes, III, 39.) In the following year another like refusal is recorded, but this time the Lords of the Treasury appear to have ordered the proper report made. William Wood in a letter to West of 1759, Mar. 6, regarding the receipt of a request of the Board of Trade for a report in connection with frauds and abuses in execution of plantation revenue laws, writes, "I am directed to send you the inclosed Copy of Mr. Pownal's Letter, in order that the Commissioners may receive their Lordships Directions, whether their Report should be made to the Lords of Trade; It being the Constitution and practice of this Board, in Matters of Revenue, only to receive Directions from, and to make Reports to the Lords Commissioners of the Treasury, or his Majesty in Council." (P.R.O., Treasury Papers, Bdl. 392, No. 34. See also, Nos. 35-36, 38-39. See *supra*, pp. 46-47 (esp. n. 1, p. 47). Cf. reference to a like refusal by the Admiralty to attend to a matter requested by the Board of Trade. Arthur Basye, *The Lords Commissioners of Trade and Plantations commonly known as the Board of Trade 1748-1782* (New Haven, 1925), p. 64.

[2] See reference to instances of such relations in connection with certain goods. Cust. Ho. Lib., Extracts Board Minutes, I, "Collectors in the Out Ports," 1724, Dec. 11. See entries having to do with excise, *ibid.*, I, IV. For the relationship of the customs and salt departments in the collection of the salt duties, see Hughes, *Stud. in Admin. and Finance*, p. 184.

customs officers, they still might be seized by excise officers who had been granted deputations by the Customs Commissioners, empowered by the Treasury from time to time [1]; and customs officers, in turn, could seize imported articles subject to excise as well as customs duties. In both cases the officer seizing the goods was obliged to report to the other department. It was upon the coöperation between the practical officers of both services that the relationship of the Excise and Customs Boards depended. The Commissioners of both departments corresponded and conferred together upon various subjects touching the improvement of their respective services: they gave information to each other,[2] consulted with and advised each other upon measures affecting both services,[3] and entered into joint agreements in regulation of their officers. As for the customs and excise officers themselves, they hated each other as only men can hate who see fortunes carried off before their very eyes. Rivalry in the rummage of a vessel or seizure of goods was intense, despite the careful regulations laid down to govern official procedure in search and seizure. Even an agreement between the two Boards in 1754 upon a regulation whereby the officers who were first on board a ship had the right of rummage without interference did not settle the difficulty [4]; and the wrangling continued without end. The Custom Board's direction to one collector "to enjoyn & recommend it to all the officers of your Port to behave decently & to live in unity & harmony with the Officers of Excise" is pitiful pleading.[5]

Time and again throughout the eighteenth century customs officers were in desperate need of naval and military assistance to cope with the smugglers who defied them at every turn. The usual procedure in securing Admiralty support was for the Customs Commissioners to apply to the Treasury that the Lords might express their desire

[1] P.R.O., Treas. Out-letters, Cust., XVII, 135, Treasury warrant, 1718, Dec. 23; XXVI, 336, Treasury warrant, 1761, May 19.
[2] E. g., Cust. Ho. Lib., Extracts Board Minutes, I, "Commissioners," 1734, Sept. 18.
[3] E. g., of personal "discourse," see *ibid.*, I, "Commissioners," 1705, Nov. 9; see also 1725, Mar. 9, 17, wherein the Customs Commissioners requested the perusal by the Excise Commissioners of the draft of a bill to prevent collusive seizures, and agreed to certain alterations proposed by the Excise Commissioners.
[4] *Ibid.*, I, "Inspectors of the River," 1754, Dec. 4 (enforcement of minute of 1725, Apr. 20); Cust. Ho. Lib., Sel. from Cust. Outport Recds., East Coast, 1931, p. 71, Boston, Collector to Board and Board to Collector, Stanley to Gentlemen, 1767, Oct. 10; *ibid.*, East Coast, 1923, pp. 9-10, Maldon, Board to Collector, 1743-1762, 1755, Aug. 12.
[5] *Ibid.*, p. 10.

for such support to the Lords of the Admiralty, upon whose order cruisers or men-of-war were stationed, or, if already stationed, were directed to assist the customs officers.[1] Commanders of Admiralty vessels were granted deputations to seize by the Customs Commissioners [2] and were given elaborate instructions for their procedure against illicit trade. These instructions provided for coöperation with the collector of the port and directed that a constant watch be kept for smuggling or illegal vessels within the district. Communications with customs cruisers and riding officers were to be maintained by a system of signals for giving and receiving notice of suspicious vessels on the coast or other important intelligence. Particular procedure was to be followed upon a seizure.[3] In consideration of their help the commanders received a suitable share of the proceeds of the seizure.[4] Records show a lively interest on the part of the Admiralty Department in smuggling and the evident effectiveness of Admiralty assistance.[5] On the whole, Admiralty boats seem to have become quite indispensable to the customs, for a minute of 1784 provided that an account of the arrival and sailing of the ships and cutters in the Navy employed in the suppression of smuggling was to be forwarded monthly to the Lords of the Admiralty [6]; and Admiralty expenditure in the suppression of smuggling was considerable.[7] If the Admiralty Department assisted the customs against smuggling, the customs aided the Admiralty in its turn in impressment of men for the fleet, in its concentration of customs vessels under Admiralty command in

---

[1] See for example of general procedure, Cust. Ho. Lib., Sel. from Cust. Outport Recds., South Coast, 1925, p. 99, Southampton, Board to Collector, 1719, Nov. 28; for request through the Lords of the Treasury, see P.R.O., Treasury Papers, Bdl. 429, No. 251, Cust. Comrs. to Lords of Treas., 1764, July 12. There are also instances of direct communication between the Customs and Admiralty Boards.

[2] That the Customs Department was apparently obliged to defend Admiralty officers in justifiable seizures is indicated in a case in 1784 wherein the Treasury, at the request of the Admiralty, directed that an Admiralty commander be defended by a customs solicitor in a prosecution resulting from his having seized a smuggling cutter. P.R.O., Treas. Out-letters, Cust., XXXIV, 273, Steele to Cust. Comrs., 1784, Dec. 1.

[3] P.R.O., Treasury Papers, Bdl. 402, Nos. 94–95, "Instructions to the Commanders of the Cruisers on the Coast of Great Britain." See also Cust. Ho. Lib., Extracts Board Minutes, III, 448, 1765, Feb. 27.

[4] See *infra*, Ch. VIII, p. 287.

[5] E. g., Cust. Ho. Lib., Sel. from Cust. Outport Recds., South Coast, 1922, Poole, Collector to Board, 1762–1767, 1764, Aug. 14.

[6] Cust. Ho. Lib., Extracts Board Minutes, IV, 25, 1784, Oct. 7.

[7] See *infra*, Ch. V, p. 178.

EXECUTIVE CONTROL

time of war, and in matters pertaining to prizes, privateers, and the like.[1]

As for the need for military assistance, a letter of the Board to the Exeter collector in 1740, wherein he is directed to acquaint all the officers at his port "that whenever they shall go out to make seizures they are to take care to have a sufficient military force with them"[2] is indicative of the helpless state to which the customs was reduced. When soldiers were needed to aid the customs officers in any one place, it appears to have been customary for a representation to that effect to be made by the Customs Commissioners to the Lords of the Treasury. If the Treasury Board approved, the application was sent to the Secretary at War, who, upon receiving it, procured the order of His Majesty in Council which enjoined the movement and station of the troops, and required their assistance to the customs officers upon proper application being made to the commanding officer.[3] There was direct communication as well between the Commissioners and the Secretary at War,—procedure which seems to have become more usual during the latter part of the period.[4] Finally in 1787 a Treasury letter directed that when customs officers were in need of military assistance, the Customs Commissioners should in the first instance apply to the Secretary at War, who, if the service admitted it, would afford the assistance required.[5] For their services

---

[1] See *supra*, Ch. I, pp. 41, 43–44.
[2] Cust. Ho. Lib., Sel. from Cust. Outport Recds., South Coast, 1922, p. 175, Exeter, Board to Collector, 1728–1744, 1740, Jan. 11.
[3] For example of such procedure, see *Cal. Treas. Books and Papers, 1731–1734*, p. 247, session of 1732, Aug. 8.
[4] In 1783, for example, Stiles informed Sheridan that the Customs Board "on representations being made to them, of the *force,* and *violence* of the Smugglers at Deale, repeatedly applied to the Secretary at War . . . for the assistance of the Military to protect the Officers of this Revenue at that Port in the execution of their Duty; all which applications were attended to by the Secretary at War, and early directions given accordingly for the Quartering of detachments of Troops at Deale, and in the neighbourhood thereof." P.R.O., Treasury Papers, Bdl. 585, Nos. 166–167, 1783, Nov. 5.
[5] "The Secretary of War having represented unto My Lords Comm[rs] of His Majesty's Treasury that it would save Trouble if when your Officers have Occasion for the Assistance of the Military in the Discharge of their Duty you were to make your Application for such Purpose immediately to his Office, I am commanded by their Lordships therefore to direct you upon such Occasions to apply in the 1st Instance to His Majestys Secretary at War who will (if the Service should admit of it) always afford the Assistance required." P.R.O., Treas. Outletters, Cust., XXXIV, 160, Steele to Cust. Comrs., 1787, Jan. 25.

the soldiers received a share of the seizures.[1] The Treasury Books and Papers for the period bear evidence of willing coöperation on the part of the several Secretaries at War in measures directed against illicit trade [2]; and the military seem to have been stationed not in vain when, in one case, the Treasury had to allow £200 "to supply a Regiment of Soldiers with Shoes & Stockings instead of those wore out in the Service to look after Owlers & Smugglers." [3]

Occasionally the Customs Commissioners and the Postmaster-General consulted together and corresponded on such subjects as fraudulent importations through the mails [4] and infringement of customs laws by smuggling by packet-boats [5]; and at times the Customs Commissioners requested that the Postmaster-General be directed to detain mails addressed to certain merchants who had failed on their bonds.[6]

Customs business, as might be expected, was closely bound up with law. One of the primary functions of the Attorney-General was to advise departments of the civil service upon legal matters. The Customs Board frequently found it necessary to secure the opinion of

[1] See *infra*, Ch. VIII, p. 287.
[2] During the latter part of the period especially, the War Office was much concerned with such measures. See enclosure in a letter of Lewis to Steele, 1784, Mar. 26, entitled "Considerations on the most probable means of suppressing Smuggling, by a new disposition of eight Dragoon Regiments along the Coast." P.R.O., Treasury Papers, Bdl. 602, Nos. 289–291. Cf. the Customs Commissioners' report to the Treasury on the "Considerations." *Ibid.*, Bdl. 602, Nos. 279–281, Stiles to Steele, 1784, May 6.
[3] Cust. Ho. Lib., Extracts Board Minutes, II, "Treasury," 1721, Mar. 2.
[4] E. g., *ibid.*, II, "Post Office," 1741, July 9, 17; P.R.O., Treasury Papers, Bdl. 490, No. 87, Treasury minute, 1772, Feb. 25; No. 165, Le Despencer and Thynne to Lords of Treas., 1772, Mar. 18.
[5] This was constantly a thorn in the side of the customs administration. Upon numerous occasions captains of packet-boats were prosecuted for frauds, despite representations in their behalf and requests for leniency by the Postmaster-General to the Treasury. A report of the Customs Commissioners to the Lords of the Treasury on a particular case in 1774 is illustrative of these conditions and indicates how serious such smuggling had become: "We Report that notwithstanding Our frequent Representations and Complaints to the Post Master General for some time past, Seizures have continued to be made from the Packet Boats almost every Voyage to a considerable Amount. . . . Finding that Our past forbearance had produced no good Effect and that the Quantities of Goods in the present Cases were very large," the Commissioners ordered the seizure and prosecution of these two vessels. The Commissioners did not recommend granting the request of the Postmaster-General for remission of His Majesty's part of the proceeds of the seizure. P.R.O., Treasury Papers, Bdl. 507, Nos. 253, 256, 1774, Sept. 30.
[6] E. g., P.R.O., State Papers Domestic, Geo. II, Bdl. 114, Cust. Comrs. to Duke of Bedford, 1750, July 27.

the Attorney-General or Solicitor-General on customs cases involving interpretation of the law, the definition of the power of the Commissioners, enforcement of the Navigation Acts, and cognate subjects.[1] If a particularly important or difficult legal action had to be taken by the Board of Customs, the law officers of the Crown were usually consulted. If they assumed the entire management of a case, the Customs Department relinquished its direction and the customs law officers were obliged to defer to the Attorney-General.[2] Cases often went to the Attorney-General through the solicitor of the customs or the Treasury, but the Customs Commissioners themselves consulted the Attorney-General direct in correspondence and conference.[3]

Besides assistance from these central departments and national services, the Customs Board enlisted the support of several local and municipal government officials. By the Commissioners' patent of 1671, justices of the peace, mayors, sheriffs, and other officials were obliged to help in the enforcement of customs law.[4] Consuls and persons abroad also communicated at times useful intelligence of smuggling and transmitted information regarding the landing of goods in accordance with the Navigation Act and similar matters.[5]

In conclusion, the details of executive control may be briefly summarized. The Lords of the Treasury constituted the ultimate authority over the customs system; the Board of Customs Commissioners was entrusted with its practical administration; various departments and officials of national and local government assisted in its enforcement, the Treasury, Commissioners, and other executive bodies working together to maintain an extensive and tremendously powerful organization.

[1] The Treasury Out-letters, Customs, contain instances of this.

[2] Based on *Second Rept. Sel. Com. on Cust.*, H.C. 604, pp. 923, 924 (1851), Part II, Minutes of Evidence, xi. Presumably the practice was the same in the eighteenth century.

[3] For an instance of personal attendance, see Cust. Ho. Lib., Extracts Board Minutes, I, "Commissioners," 1742, Nov. 6.

[4] See *infra*, Ch. V, p. 186. On the powers of the justices of the peace in connection with customs enforcement, see B.M., Add. MSS. 32523, f. 252, "A Digest of the Book of Rates, & some other laws Relating to the Customs."

[5] See, for example, an instance of the payment of the expenses of a Hamburg resident for his services in obtaining information on the illicit trade between Hamburg and England. (P.R.O., Treas. Out-letters, Cust., XXXI, 187, Treasury warrant, 1775, July 26.) See the information relative to smuggling, sent by the consul at Malaga to Lord Carmarthen, and in turn referred by Fraser to Rose, 1785, Mar. 25. (P.R.O., Treasury Papers, Bdl. 618, Nos. 102, 104.) See report of Cust. Comrs. to Lords of Treas., 1764, Oct. 16, on the extracts of several letters from ministers and consuls abroad relative to smuggling. *Ibid.*, Bdl. 429, Nos. 301–303.

CHAPTER III

THE CENTRAL OFFICE

In attendance upon the Board of Customs Commissioners in the London Custom House was a group of officers, not confined to any particular port, who discharged a certain share of the administrative business of the service and provided a central department for the receipt of revenue and the preparation of official accounts. This department included five different classes of officials: officers dealing with law business, cashiers and paymasters, controllers and examiners of the general accounts of the customs, inspectors of personnel, and officers keeping accounts respecting trade.[1] The legal experts supervised prosecutions for violation of customs laws and defended and advised the Board on questions of policy. The staff of the central customs treasury received the money arising from duties, fines and forfeitures, and petty receipts from all the ports; paid out charges of management, shares of seizures, debentures, bounties, and all other sums warranted by the Treasury and the Commissioners; and returned the net revenue into the Exchequer. Several controllers and examiners acted as checks upon the cashiers and prepared the departmental accounts of the customs. Inspectors of the officers' conduct represented the Board in a centralized control over the personnel of the establishment. Special officers, whose appointment was prompted by an awakened sense of the value to be derived from commercial statistics, prepared accounts of various aspects of trade which were submitted from time to time to the Treasury and Parliament. For the purposes of this study these officers will be described collectively as the Central Office of the Customs.

At the time of the creation of the Board of Customs Commissioners, the necessity for an especially trained officer to deal with the law

[1] The outline of offices used in this chapter is that given by an establishment book in the Custom House Library, "A list of the Commissioners and Officers of His Majesty's Customs in England, Wales, and in the Plantations with their Respective Salaries, to 1782," pp. 4–10. This book will henceforth be cited as "Estab., Eng., Wales, and Plant. to 1782." The "Fourteenth Report," 1785, of the Commissioners of Accounts in *Repts. of Comrs.*, 1787, III, 82–86, has also been followed in the list of officers. These records have been supplemented by various volumes of Customs Registers: Series I, Customs Quarterly Establishments, in the Public Record Office.

THE CENTRAL OFFICE 93

business of the customs was recognized by the establishment of the office of solicitor of the customs. One solicitor, with the help of an assistant and another person who acted as a solicitor, dealt with practically all customs matters of a legal nature until 1725, when, owing to a great increase in his business arising from the many frauds committed and the many laws passed relating to them, another solicitor was established. At this date the work of these officials became confined to separate districts: one solicitor transacted all the law business arising in London and in the northern ports of England and Wales, while the other performed the same duty as regards the ports of western England and Wales, of Kent, and of Sussex.[1] Over three years later, the business of the solicitors having increased "so much by the Frauds daily discovered & other Prosecutions," a third solicitor was appointed to carry on prosecutions of bonds and criminal cases in Crown Office or in Doctors' Commons and upon appeals or other business placed before the Council from the Plantations, Jersey, Guernsey, and Man.[2] To these three solicitors in the latter part of the period, a fourth was added by appointment of the Board of Customs to supervise prosecutions on coast bonds.[3] In 1718 the audit of the solicitor's accounts of money received for compositions and the prosecutor's share of seizures was delegated to a proper officer, that duty "being an Obstruction to the Commissioners in their Management."[4] Clerks and messengers attached to the first three solicitors completed the organization of this department. The remuneration of the solicitors consisted of their salaries on the establishment and professional fees, payable either by the defendants who were prosecuted or out of the produce of seizures.[5] They were granted allowances in addition for the provision of their clerks and messengers, for coals and candles, waterage, coach hire and chamber rent.[6]

[1] P.R.O., Treas. Out-letters, Cust., XVIII, 534-535, 536, Treasury constitution, 1725, Sept. 29; cf. 536-537, Treasury constitution, 1725, Sept. 28; cf. 541, Cust. Comrs. to Lords of Treas., 1725, Aug. 13. By the end of the period, however, the division of work appears to have been somewhat different, for these two officers were known respectively as the Solicitor for London and the Western Ports of England and Wales and the Solicitor for the Northern Ports.
[2] Ibid., XIX, 329-330, Treasury constitution, 1728-9, Feb. 28.
[3] As listed in P.R.O., Customs Registers: Series I, Cust. Quart. Estab., and mentioned in Cust. Ho. Lib., Extracts Board Minutes, II, "Sollicitors."
[4] Ibid., II, "Sollicitors," 1718, Dec. 31. See also minute for 1721, Aug. 29; and I, "Inspector of Prosecutions," 1725, Jan. 11.
[5] See *Repts. of Comrs.*, 1787, III, 83, "Fourteenth Rept.," 1785.
[6] See P.R.O., Treasury Papers, Bdl. 390, No. 178, Cust. Comrs. (Scotland) to Lords of Treas., 1759, July 19; Nos. 179-180, Swainston (Solicitor for Scotland)

The duties of the solicitors may roughly be grouped under four headings: they prosecuted goods illegally imported and seized, together with persons who offended against the Acts of Trade and the customs laws; they paid into the Exchequer the net proceeds arising from the prosecutor's share of seizures; they defended the Board and the customs officers in legal actions; and they advised the Commissioners upon every matter which involved a question of legality or court procedure and upon numerous other issues as well. The position of the solicitors in the scheme of customs administration may be indicated by a brief comment on each function.[1]

When the Customs Commissioners had been notified of a seizure they immediately referred the case to the proper solicitor for his opinion as to what directions should be given to the seizing officer.[2] Upon consideration of the case the solicitor reported his observations to the Board and offered his recommendation as to whether or not it was advisable to prosecute.[3] If the Board decided to bring an action, he prepared for the trial, securing the writ of appraisement if the prosecution was to be made in the Court of Exchequer[4] and corresponding with the officer in direction of the prosecution.[5] In general a similar procedure was followed in cases of personal prosecutions. When a particularly important case arose, the Solicitor of the Treasury and the law officers of the Crown were usually consulted.[6] The customs solicitor at such times prepared a statement of the case for

---

to Lords of Treas. [probably 1759]. In 1781 the allowances for clerks and messengers were placed on the establishment. (P.R.O., Treas. Out-letters, Cust., XXXII, 270–271, Cust. Comrs. to Lords of Treas., 1781, Mar. 1; Treasury warrant, 1781, Mar. 17.) In 1784 the Customs Commissioners canceled the additional sums granted for chamber rent, coach hire, and similar items. Cust. Ho. Lib., Extracts Board Minutes, V, 501, 1784, May 2.

[1] Though these duties in general were common to all the solicitors, the participation in them of each solicitor was determined by the nature of his office.

[2] See Cust. Ho. Lib., Extracts Board Minutes, III, 504–505, 1761, May 19. With reference to accounts of seizures sent to London, see for example Cust. Ho. Lib., London to Harwich, 1699–1788, p. 47, Carkesse to Harwich, 1737, Mar. 26.

[3] See Cust. Ho. Lib., Extracts Board Minutes, II, "Sollicitors," 1731, Mar. 9.

[4] Crouch, *Complete Guide to Officers* (1732), p. 288. The solicitor had the authority to require the attendance of Long Room officers at trials. (See Cust. Ho. Lib., Extracts Board Minutes, II, "Sollicitors," 1741, Nov. 26.) He might also order that outport witnesses be brought to London when necessary. *Ibid.,* II, "Witnesses," 1730, Dec. 16.

[5] Crouch, *Complete Guide to Officers* (1732), p. 287. On procedure in seizure cases, see *infra*, Ch. VIII, pp. 273–285.

[6] For example, see P.R.O., Treas. Out-letters, Cust., XXIX, 218, Bradshaw to Cust. Comrs., 1769, Dec. 11.

the Attorney-General and occasionally yielded the management of it to that officer. When necessary he appeared for the customs upon appeals to the Council or its proper committee.[1]

Compositions, wherein a sum mutually agreed upon by the customs and the defendant was paid by the latter to effect a discharge of his seizure or debt, naturally fell within the province of the solicitors. An application for such a composition was referred by the Board to the solicitor for his opinion as to whether or not the case was deserving,[2] and after directions had been given for the composition, the solicitor received the deposit or a part of it.[3] The position of the law officers in this connection seems to have become more firmly established as the Board sought to do away with irregularities when individual officers compounded independently,[4] and brought the matter of composition more closely under their control and that of the Treasury.[5]

When bonds which had been given by merchants in lieu of duties became due, they were delivered over to the solicitors by the Receiver-General, in whose custody as cashier of the customs they had been kept. Upon fair notice being given to the parties concerned, the solicitors brought action upon the bonds in default of payment.[6]

After goods had been condemned or compounded or bonds had been forfeited, the solicitors received the money arising by the prosecutor's share of seizures, the Crown's share of compositions, or the penalties on bonds.[7] From these sums the solicitors deducted law charges and the officers' shares and paid the remainder into the Exchequer.[8] Their accounts were passed by their Auditor.

When any suit was brought against a customs officer, and the

[1] According to the warrant by which the third solicitor was established.
[2] In connection with the solicitors' reports, see Cust. Ho. Lib., Extracts Board Minutes, I, "Compositions," 1719, Feb. 12; II, "Seizures," 1747, Dec. 23; III, 96, 1765, Dec. 13; 1767, Oct. 7.
[3] See *ibid.*, I, "Compositions," 1726, Feb. 9; *Repts. of Comrs.*, 1787, III, 37, "Thirteenth Rept.," 1785.
[4] Cust. Ho. Lib., Letters to Dartmouth, 1715–16 To 1731, p. 229, Carkesse to Dartmouth, 1726, Mar. 2; Cust. Ho. Lib., Extracts Board Minutes, I, "Informations and Informers," 1731, July 24; II, "Officers," 1743, Feb. 13. See also I, "Compositions," 1720, July 13.
[5] For references to the position of the Treasury in the matter of compositions, see entries in *ibid.*, I, III, IV, "Compositions."
[6] Of the many references in connection with bonds, see *ibid.*, II, "Sollicitors," 1713, July 15; 1733, Nov. 20; 1749, Feb. 6.
[7] For specific references to such receipts of solicitors, see *ibid.*, II, "Sollicitors," 1721, Jan. 10; 1726, Feb. 9; 1727, Aug. 16; III, 258, 1769, Feb. 15.
[8] See *Repts. of Comrs.*, 1787, III, 37, "Thirteenth Rept.," 1785.

96 ORGANIZATION OF THE ENGLISH CUSTOMS

Board upon investigation found that he had executed his duty in accordance with established rules or directions, he was defended by the solicitors at the Crown's charge.[1] If it was necessary for the Commissioners to be represented legally in any matter, the solicitors took such action.[2]

As advisers to the Board the solicitors held a position of great importance in the scheme of administration. So necessary was it that they should be available for consultation with the Commissioners at any time that the constant presence of one of them in the Custom House was required in the early years [3]; at approximately the close of the period, it appears that all the solicitors as far as possible were desired to be present every Board day in order to report when necessary upon all questions referred to them in various branches of their business.[4] Besides pronouncing upon all cases of seizure and personal informations and advising the Commissioners as to whether or not a practice was legal [5] and whether the Commissioners were empowered in a certain action, the solicitors considered methods for improvement of certain parts of the business [6] and prepared clauses and bills for Parliament.[7] They were also responsible for a system of regular reports to the Board in regard to prosecutions and their proceedings thereupon.[8] Together with the general-surveyors the solici-

---

[1] See *infra*, Ch. VIII, p. 286.

[2] E. g., Cust. Ho. Lib., Extracts Board Minutes, V, 499, 1780, Oct. 20.

[3] See *ibid.*, II, "Sollicitors," 1724, Nov. 24 [which ordered the attendance of the one solicitor or his assistant]; 1728, Dec. 11. By a minute of 1736 (Mar. 2), however, attendance on Saturdays and Mondays was dispensed with. *Ibid.*, II, "Sollicitors."

[4] *Ibid.*, V, 506–507, 1788, Oct. 30; cf. *Repts. of Comrs.*, 1787, III, 407, App. No. 28, 408, App. Nos. 29, 30, "Fourteenth Rept.," 1785.

[5] See, for example in this connection, Cust. Ho. Lib., Extracts Board Minutes, II, "Sollicitors," 1734, Dec. 6.

[6] E. g., *ibid.*, II, "Sollicitors," 1718, Dec. 11.

[7] In 1765 the Solicitor for the Northern Ports was granted £100 for preparing bills for Parliament. The following year he received £200 for the same service, an allowance which was continued to him annually for at least the next nine years. *Ibid.*, III, 537–538, 1765, June 5; 538, 1766, June 25.

[8] At the end of every term the solicitors were obliged to lay before the Board a list of prosecutions and what had been done upon them. (See *ibid.*, II, "Sollicitors," 1713, Feb. 23; 1714, Apr. 8; 1730, Dec. 16.) They also had to submit a list of persons subsisted as witnesses at the charge of the customs with their opinion as to whether it was necessary to continue them. (*Ibid.*, II, "Sollicitors," 1731, May 12.) The Solicitor for Bonds was required to send to the Board a monthly list of bonds delivered to him, and the proceedings thereon. (*Ibid.*, II, "Sollicitors," 1749, Feb. 6.) Early in the period the solicitors had to return to the Board after each

tors appear to have been the most useful officers to the Board in the practical administration of the system.

A survey of the department of the law business would be incomplete without mention of two other officers who, though their business had become quite useless, seem to have had a happy faculty of appropriating fat allowances during the period. The patent office of Inspector of Prosecutions, executed by deputy, was erected in 1686. In the early days of the Board's commission, any informer could prosecute seizure cases without the knowledge of the Commissioners; hence an Inspector of Prosecutions was established to see that informations of smuggled goods were prosecuted for the customs and the produce upon condemnation paid to the customs and the Exchequer. In the reign of George I, however, the power to prosecute such cases was no longer permitted freely to any one, but was confined to those prosecuting in the name of the Attorney-General and to the customs and excise officers.[1] Since the Customs Commissioners thus had direct knowledge of all legal proceedings on custom cases, the most important part of the original duty of the Inspector of Prosecutions appears to have lapsed.[2] Throughout the remainder of the period this officer was evidently more concerned with seeing that the money arising from seizures and fines and forfeitures was paid by the proper officers into the Exchequer.[3] He kept records of all seizures and prosecutions and reported upon them to the Board, and from time to time he received from the officers their accounts of payments due or discharged into the Exchequer.[4] Since the Board was informed

---

term an account of the money arising from the prosecutors' share of seizures; in 1769 an annual account of all of their receipts was required. *Ibid.*, II, "Sollicitors," 1721, Jan. 10; III, 258, 1769, Feb. 15. Various other reports were made from time to time.

[1] By 12 Geo. I, c. 28, s. 28.
[2] See *Repts. of Comrs.*, 1787, III, 100, "Fourteenth Rept.," 1785.
[3] *Ibid.*, III, 409, App. No. 31.
[4] The Inspector of Prosecutions was informed by the solicitors of what sums they had paid into the Exchequer as the Crown's money; from an officer known as the Accountant of Petty Receipts he secured certificates stating the amount of the Crown's share of seizures due that treasury from two other cashiers; and from the minutes of the Board he was acquainted with what payments of composition money had been ordered to be made into the Exchequer. These records the Inspector compared quarterly with an account, received from the Exchequer, of all sums paid into that office under seizures, fines, and forfeitures. *Ibid.*, III, 100, 409, App. No. 31. For other references to the Inspector of Prosecutions, see Cust. Ho. Lib., Extracts Board Minutes, I, III, IV, "Inspector of Prosecutions."

by these other officers of such remittances and had a direct check upon them, the intervention of the Inspector of Prosecutions was found by the Commissioners of Accounts to be unnecessary and his office useless.[1]

The remaining office in the Law Department, that of the Register of Seizures, dating back at least as far as the commission, was held by patent and executed by deputy. After a seizure had been made, the collector of the port sent a detailed account of it to the Register as well as to the Commissioners [2]; and upon the Board's order to prosecute, the outport officer corresponded with the Register of Seizures together with the solicitors in his proceedings.[3] In connection with the registration and examination in this office of two legal documents, the indenture of appraisement and the writ of delivery, the Commissioners of Accounts in 1785 observed that the function of the Register of Seizures was quite unnecessary and were of the opinion that the rest of his duty could have been transacted elsewhere in the department.[4]

The offices both of Inspector of Prosecutions and Register of Seizures were sinecures and served no useful purpose. The upkeep of these offices, furthermore, entailed heavy expense by reason of the poundage allowed to the Inspector and the salaries and fees which were paid to the Register.[5] Because of these considerations the Com-

[1] *Repts. of Comrs.*, 1787, III, 100, "Fourteenth Rept.," 1785.
[2] See Crouch, *Complete Guide to Officers* (1732), p. 285.
[3] *Ibid.*, p. 287.
[4] *Repts. of Comrs.*, 1787, III, 101, "Fourteenth Rept.," 1785. The indenture of appraisement, a document in which was listed the goods with their appraised value, was returned by the collector to this office for registration by the Register of Seizures before it could be proclaimed in prosecution in the Exchequer. After the goods had been condemned, the Register of Seizures received a writ of delivery, an instrument empowering their sale, which he compared with the indenture to see that the goods listed in both documents agreed. Upon his satisfaction, the writ of delivery, with his certificate, was transmitted to the warehouse-keeper (or collector) for execution. Because these two documents were both executed by the same officer—the collector or warehouse-keeper—jointly with other officers, the intervention of the Register of Seizures to see that the two instruments agreed was unnecessary. *Ibid.*, III, 101, 410–411, App. No. 32. For further information on this officer, see Cust. Ho. Lib., Extracts Board Minutes, II, III, "Register of Seizures."

[5] The Inspector of Prosecutions was allowed a poundage of 5 per cent upon the King's share of the produce of seizures paid into the Exchequer, a sum which amounted, on an average of ten years ending in 1781, to £3,676. 13s. 3½d. per annum. By an act of that year, however, the poundage was decreased, and this officer received a Treasury warrant to make up the difference to £2,000. (*Repts. of Comrs.*, 1787, III, 83, 100–101, "Fourteenth Rept.," 1785. See also P.R.O., Treasury Papers, Bdl. 596, Nos. 144–145, Poyntz to Lords of Treas.) The Register of Seiz-

THE CENTRAL OFFICE

missioners of Accounts recommended that these offices be abolished [1] and that the execution of all customs law business be confined to the solicitors. It was not until 1798, however, that such abolition was effected.[2]

The customs receipts were not all paid into one treasury. There were two divisions of the revenue department in the Central Office to which the proceeds of London and the outports were returned. In one section was received all money arising from duties and bonds, while in the other were lodged sums resulting from penalties for infringement of customs laws.

The principal officer in the first division, through which the bulk of the customs revenue reached the Exchequer, was the Receiver-General, who had formerly been Cashier to the Customs Farmers when the customs were in farm. The remuneration of this official during the period had come to take the form of several salaries, a poundage allowance, various fees, and several gratuities upon the payments made in his office. A part of the business of the office was executed by the Receiver-General himself, though a considerable share of it was dealt with by his assistants, tellers, clerks, and messenger, who were paid salaries and received similar fees and gratuities.[3]

The Receiver-General had charge of both receipts and disbursements.[4] Every day until two o'clock his office in the London Custom House was open to receive payments in cash and debentures for duties collected during the day by the Collectors-Inwards and Coastwise in the Port of London. At the end of every week, he received all the money taken in during the week (with the exception of a small proportion retained for current expenses) from these same receivers and

---

ures was paid two salaries and granted a 5s. fee on certificates where the King's share amounted to £10 or more. *Repts. of Comrs.*, 1787, III, 83, "Fourteenth Rept.," 1785.

[1] See *ibid.*, III, 99, 100, 101.
[2] 38 Geo. III, c. 86, s. 1.
[3] On the remuneration of these officers and the execution of the business, see *Repts. of Comrs.*, 1787, III, 84, 411, App. 33, "Fourteenth Rept.," 1785. Cf. B.M., Add. MSS. 32900, f. 452, "Mr Page's Paper [to Newcastle] concerning The Office of Receiver General of the Customs" [1759?]; and P.R.O., Chatham Papers, Bdl. 284, "The Statement of the Office of the Receiver General of the Customs."
[4] For a survey of the functions of the Receiver-General in the latter part of the period, see *Repts. of Comrs.*, 1787, III, 200–202, App. No. 3, 254–256, App. 37, "Thirteenth Rept.," 1785. For a brief abstract of the office in the beginning of the century, see B.M., Add. MSS. 18903, ff. 8, 9. "Abs^t of the Rep^t ab^t the Office of Rec^r Gen^{ll}." Miscellaneous references may be found in Cust. Ho. Lib., Extracts Board Minutes, II, III, V, entries under "Receiver General."

from the Collector-Outwards as well, whose receipts did not warrant daily payments. All duties were appropriated under their proper heads in the accounts returned by their respective officers.[1] The outport collectors sent the net produce of their ports in the form of bills and notes, accompanied by the proper accounts containing the correct appropriation of duties, to the Receiver-General from time to time as they received it.[2] Tobacco bonds were returned monthly by the London collector to the Receiver and were held in his department until they were discharged or prosecuted by the solicitors.[3]

Money from sources other than the London and outport collectors swelled the coffers of the Receiver-General. At times individual merchants in London paid duties and temporary deposits covering the duties on some goods directly to this cashier.[4] All amounts paid in connection with tobacco bonds, such as deposits, interest, and sums for their discharge, were lodged by the merchants with the Receiver-General.[5] The plantation collectors in their turn remitted the proceeds of the colonial customs to the Receiver-General,[6] and the Scottish Receiver-General did the same for the collection in North Britain.[7]

Out of all these receipts the Receiver-General made payments of various kinds. He discharged drawbacks of duties, certificates, portage bills, salaries, and other charges on the establishment, together with miscellaneous items of expenditure authorized by Treasury warrant and order of the Customs Board.[8] Since the outport collectors financed the management of their own ports as far as possible from their own receipts, a large part of such disbursements apparently went for the upkeep of the London establishment.[9]

---

[1] See *Repts. of Comrs.*, 1787, III, 26–27, 29, "Thirteenth Rept.," 1785.

[2] For a detailed account of such remittances see Crouch, *Complete Guide to Officers* (1732), pp. 255–261.

[3] *Repts. of Comrs.*, 1787, III, 28, "Thirteenth Rept.," 1785. In the early part of the period the Receiver-General received London wine and tobacco bonds weekly. B.M., Add. MSS. 18903, f. 8, "Abs^t of the Rep^t ab^t the Office of Rec^r Gen^{11}."

[4] *Repts. of Comrs.*, 1787, III, 17, 19, 20, 255–256, App. No. 37, "Thirteenth Rept.," 1785.

[5] *Ibid.*, III, 33.

[6] B.M., Add. MSS. 18903, f. 8, "Abs^t of the Rep^t Ab^t the Office of Rec^r Gen^{11}." See *Repts. of Comrs.*, 1787, III, 33, "Thirteenth Rept.," 1785.

[7] *Ibid.*, III, 140, "Fifteenth Rept.," 1786. See description of irregularities in connection with these returns. Atton and Holland, *The King's Customs*, I, 360–361.

[8] *Repts. of Comrs.*, 1787, III, 33, "Thirteenth Rept.," 1785; B.M., Add. MSS. 18903, f. 8, "Abs^t of the Rep^t Ab^t the Office of Rec^r Gen^{11}."

[9] Imprests, by which an outport collector was forced to borrow money from London or some other port with which to pay his necessary expenses, were not infrequent. See *infra*, Ch. VI, pp. 216–217.

On the last day of the week the Receiver-General made up his books of receipts and payments. Four accounts were prepared: one each for the Lords of the Treasury, the Customs Commissioners, the Exchequer, and the Supervisor of the Receiver-General's Receipts and Payments. Sometime during the following week the Receiver-General paid his balance into the Exchequer.[1] At the end of the financial year, which ran to January 5 inclusive,[2] the annual account of the customs was presented by the Receiver-General for audit to the Auditor of the Imprest, after which it was passed through the Treasury and Exchequer.[3] Such accounts, however, frequently did not reach the Auditor until they had been long overdue,—usually to the extent of two years.[4]

The Supervisor of the Receiver-General's Receipts and Payments acted as a control on the London receipts of the Receiver-General. He checked the weekly collections of the Receiver-General by comparing his weekly accounts with those of the London collectors and examined the record of bonds delivered into the office with the schedule of bonds returned by the London officer. Any merchants' deposits or payments on bonds to the Receiver-General were certified to the Supervisor, and interest on such bonds was calculated by that officer. Thus the Supervisor of the Receiver-General's Receipts and Payments had complete knowledge and check of the London receipts in the Central Office. The outport returns were examined by the Controller-General,[5] who is considered in the next class of officers.

The Supervisor also had the examination of all disbursements made by the Receiver-General. He secured daily entries of all expenditures, and at the end of the week his clerks compared such sums with the

[1] *Repts. of Comrs.*, 1787, III, 81, "Thirteenth Rept.," 1785. See also B.M., Add. MSS. 18903, f. 30, "Methods of passing Debentures in the Port of London" [1714].

[2] *Repts. of Comrs.*, 1787, III, 139, "Fifteenth Rept.," 1786. The date of the annual accounts of the customs was altered from Michaelmas to Christmas in 1697–8. P.R.O., Treas. Out-letters Cust., XIII, 419, Treasury warrant, 1697–8, Mar. 12 [erratum for Apr. 12?]. See also P.R.O., Treasury Papers, Vol. 49, No. 166, Cust. Comrs. to Lords of Treas., 1697, Nov. 30.

[3] *Repts. of Comrs.*, 1787, III, 7, "Thirteenth Rept.," 1785. For a description of the audit of the Receiver-General's account, see pp. 5–7.

[4] Atton and Holland, *The King's Customs*, I, 359.

[5] By his original constitution in 1703 the Supervisor was directed to act as a check on the Receiver-General as regarded the outport remittances by bills of exchange. This instruction, however, was omitted in succeeding constitutions, an omission which appears to have continued throughout the period, despite at least one recommendation for its insertion. See P.R.O., Treasury Papers, Bdl. 313, Nos. 40–41, "Report [to Cust. Comrs.] on the Instructions to the Comptroller of the Receipts and Payments of the Receiver General," 1743–4 [after Feb. 28].

instruments which authorized them, such as a debenture or the minute of the Customs Board or the Treasury warrant. Every quarter a further examination of this kind was made. Payments of money into the Exchequer by the Receiver-General were checked by the Supervisor's comparison of the tallies with the amounts listed as paid.[1]

The Supervisor of the Receiver-General's Receipts and Payments was the old Comptroller of the Issues and Payments of the Receiver-General, appointed in 1703.[2] The office, held by constitution and remunerated by salary, was executed by a deputy and clerks.[3] Because it existed as a sinecure, the Commissioners of Accounts in 1785 recommended the discontinuance of the useless part of the office.[4]

The second division of the revenue department had the receipt of practically all the money arising from fines and forfeitures, together with other sums that did not fall within the province of the Receiver-General.[5] There were two chief officers of receipt in this branch: the Receiver of Fines and Forfeitures for the Outports with his Controller and clerks, and a like Receiver for London with his deputy. This division also included four other officers: the Accountant of Petty Receipts, with several clerks, a Pay-master of Incidents, and the Receiver of the Superannuation Fund and his Controller.

When certain goods had been condemned or were forfeited in default of payment of duties or claim, they were sold at public auction upon the Board's order. It was the duty of the Receiver of Fines and Forfeitures to receive the proceeds of such sales from the collector, who was also the warehouse-keeper in a port, and, after defraying the necessary expenses, to remit the balance into the Exchequer. The London Receiver (who until approximately the end of the period was also warehouse-keeper of that port) himself paid from the produce of the sale all sale charges, together with the seizing officers' portion of the proceeds. After 1781, the remainder, known as the Crown's

---

[1] With respect to the duties of the Supervisor, see *Repts. of Comrs.*, 1787, III, 32–34, "Thirteenth Rept.," 1785. For an indication of such duties in the early part of the period, see B.M., Add. MSS. 18903, f. 8, "Abs^t of the Rep^t ab^t the Office of Rec^r Gen^{11};" and f. 30, "Methods of passing Debentures in the Port of London," [1714].

[2] P.R.O., Treas. Out-letters, Cust., XIV, 282–283, Treasury constitution, 1703, Aug. 26; see also 306–307, constitution, 1703, Jan. 12.

[3] *Repts. of Comrs.*, 1787, III, 84, "Fourteenth Rept.," 1785.

[4] *Ibid.*, III, 105–106.

[5] It must be remembered, however, that the solicitors remitted the proceeds of fines or compositions on seizures to the Exchequer. *Ibid.*, III, 143, "Fifteenth Rept.," 1786.

THE CENTRAL OFFICE

share, was further liable for payments of salaries, incidents, and imprests, pursuant to the Board's order. Whatever was left after all these disbursements had been made was paid by the London Receiver of Fines and Forfeitures into the Exchequer upon the direction of the Board, under the head of fines and forfeitures.[1] The Accountant of Petty Receipts audited his account after each sale, which meant about five times a year.

The outport collectors returned the Crown's share of the proceeds of such forfeitures directly to the Receiver of Fines and Forfeitures for the Outports after having retained enough of the proceeds of their sales to reward the officers and pay various expenses of management. Until 1774 the Outport Receiver paid his balance quarterly into the Exchequer after any payments had been deducted and his report had been made to the Board. By that date, however, increased receipts necessitated monthly payments, and in 1777 fortnightly remittances.[2] After 1783, when the Receiver took over the work of an officer known as the Pay-master of Incidents,[3] who had existed throughout the period for the purpose of paying out small sums under the head of incidents, these outport shares of the Crown became exhausted; hence, instead of there being remittances into the Exchequer, applications for imprests were necessary. Every two weeks, and again once every quarter—at least in the latter part of the period—the accounts

---

[1] See *Repts. of Comrs.*, 1787, III, 38–39, "Thirteenth Rept.," 1785.
[2] P.R.O., Treasury Papers, Bdl. 530, No. 282, Cust. Comrs. to Lords of Treas., 1777, Aug. 5. In a report to the Treasury earlier in 1777 upon a memorial of the Receiver of Fines and Forfeitures, praying that he might pay his money into the Exchequer quarterly instead of monthly, the Customs Commissioners were of opinion that monthly payments should be continued, not only on account of the increased receipts but also in order that this officer might be placed on the same footing with the London Receiver and the outport collectors, who made their remittances monthly, and with the Receiver-General, who made his payments weekly. In this report the Commissioners represented the following comparison of the medium of payments into the Exchequer by the Outport Receiver of Fines and Forfeitures:

  1745 and 1746............£2,129 per quarter
  1765 and 1766............£8,522 per quarter
  1775 and 1776............£6,491 per month

(*Ibid.*, Bdl. 530, Nos. 223–224, Cust. Comrs. to Lords of Treas., 1777, Jan. 17.) The Receiver, however, did not pay the money monthly into the Exchequer as directed by the Commissioners. In 1777 he was found to owe a balance to the Crown of £20,042. 4s. 7d., and his bonds were put in suit. (See *ibid.*, Bdl. 530, Nos. 283–284, Cust. Comrs. to Lords of Treas., 1777, Aug. 5.) Five years later his successor absconded, and his bond likewise was put in suit for the recovery of £7,456. 2s. 11¼d. Cust. Ho. Lib., Extracts Board Minutes, IV, 416, 1782, Apr. 24.
[3] *Ibid.*, V, 224, 1783, Feb. 19; 225, 1783, June 17.

of the Outport Receiver of Fines and Forfeitures were checked by the Accountant.[1]

The work of the office of Receiver of Fines and Forfeitures for London, instituted in 1728,[2] was transacted by the Warehouse-keeper for the Collector-Inwards, who until approximately 1782 or 1783 was the Deputy Receiver as well; after that date the offices were separated.[3] The London Receiver had a remuneration of several allowances and fees on sales.[4] The Receiver of Fines and Forfeitures for the Outports, who also came into service in 1728, held office at first by warrant and then by constitution.[5] Under this latter instrument he but rarely visited his office to superintend the business, most of which was transacted by his clerk.[6] The principal was paid by various poundages until 1765 when his recompense took the form of a salary.[7] The Controller of the Receiver of Fines and Forfeitures for the Outports, who was privy to all receipts of this Receiver and with him prepared and signed the accounts,[8] was instituted as well in 1728, and like the Receiver was paid by salary in lieu of poundage from 1777 on.[9]

The Accountant of Petty Receipts acted as a check on all collectors and on the two Receivers of Fines and Forfeitures touching their accounts of seizures and of the disposition of the proceeds of the sales.[10] He examined records of all seizures; made entries of all remittances to this treasury from London and the outports under the

[1] For a survey of these functions of the Receiver, see *Repts. of Comrs.*, 1787, III, 38–40, "Thirteenth Rept.," 1785.
[2] P.R.O., Treas. Out-letters, Cust., XIX, 322–326, Cust. Comrs. to Lords of Treas., 1728, Mar. 27; Treasury warrant, 1728-9, Feb. 11. Provision for the execution of the business of this officer had been made before this date.
[3] *Repts. of Comrs.*, 1787, III, 271, App. No. 51, "Thirteenth Rept.," 1785.
[4] See *ibid.*, III, 84, 415, App. No. 37, "Fourteenth Rept.," 1785.
[5] See *infra*, Ch. VI, p. 197, n. 3. As in the case of the other Receiver, arrangements had been made for the transaction of the business of this office before its establishment by Treasury appointment in 1728.
[6] *Repts. of Comrs.*, 1787, III, 416, App. No. 38, "Fourteenth Rept.," 1785.
[7] See P.R.O., Treasury Papers, Bdl. 542, Nos. 65–66, Cust. Comrs. to Lords of Treas., 1777, Jan. 2; cf. P.R.O., Treas. Out-letters, Cust., XXVIII, 214, 215, Treasury constitution, 1765, June 3. See also *Repts. of Comrs.*, 1787, III, 84, "Fourteenth Rept.," 1785.
[8] See *ibid.*, III, 417, App. No. 39, 418, App. No. 40.
[9] P.R.O., Treasury Papers, Bdl. 542, No. 136, Shafto to Lords of Treas., 1777, Oct. 20, and enclosures Nos. 137, 138; Nos. 139–140, Cust. Comrs. to Lords of Treas., 1778, June 30. See also *Repts. of Comrs.*, 1787, III, 84, "Fourteenth Rept.," 1785.
[10] See *ibid.*, III, 418, App. No. 41; cf. Cust. Ho. Lib., Extracts Board Minutes, IV, 10–11, 1783, Jan. 15.

THE CENTRAL OFFICE

head of fines and forfeitures; and checked these receipts and the payments therefrom. The Accountant passed the accounts of the Receiver of Fines and Forfeitures for London after every sale, and from time to time recommended to the Board what share of the balance in the hands of that Receiver might be paid into the Exchequer. He examined the accounts of the Receiver of Fines and Forfeitures for the Outports every fortnight (from 1777) and again every quarter.[1] In the case of both Receivers the tallies of their payments into the Exchequer were given to him as proof of their remittances.[2] The Accountant of Petty Receipts, apparently appointed in 1727,[3] held office by constitution and attended only occasionally to sign the necessary accounts. Most of the business of his department seems to have been done by clerks whom he appointed.[4] Remuneration consisted of poundage until 1783, when provision for a fixed salary was made.[5]

One other officer, unconnected with the receipts of fines and forfeitures, belonged to this second branch of the central revenue department. The Receiver of the Superannuation Fund, with his Controller, was appointed in 1713 to receive all sums to be applied to "the relief of Officers when worn out by age after long and faithful service, or otherwise disabled in the execution of their duty, & that are in want & not in a condition to support themselves & families."[6] At first the fund was confined to certain classes of officers; qualifications for admittance were high; and the reserve depended precariously upon small deductions from the salaries of a few officers, odd contributions in the form of mulcts, unclaimed rewards of soldiers who had assisted in seizures, and a part of the salaries of absent officers. During the period, however, the fund was extended in application to include more

---

[1] On the examination of these accounts, see *Repts. of Comrs.*, 1787, III, 39–40, "Thirteenth Rept.," 1785. See also Cust. Ho. Lib., Extracts Board Minutes, IV, 8, 1777, Aug. 5.

[2] At least during the latter part of the period. When in 1783 the work of the Paymaster of Incidents was taken over by the Receiver of Fines and Forfeitures for the Outports, the Accountant of Petty Receipts transacted the business respecting that office which had been done by the Controller-General. See *ibid.*, IV, 12, 1783, Mar. 8.

[3] *Ibid.*, I, "Accomptant of Petty Receipts," 1727, May 26, June 21.

[4] *Repts. of Comrs.* 1787, III, 418, App. No. 41, "Fourteenth Rept.," 1785.

[5] This took effect in 1788. Cust. Ho. Lib., Extracts Board Minutes, IV, 10, 1783, Jan. 15; 13, 1788, Feb. 26.

[6] *Ibid.*, V, 18, 1780, Sept. 13; II, "Superannuation," 1713, Aug. 19. For a survey of the establishment and history of the fund, see *ibid.*, II, III, V, entries under "Superannuation"; and *infra*, Ch. VI, pp. 236–237.

divisions of officers, and enlarged, though it fell short of being adequate in its relief of superannuates.[1] Every quarter the outport collectors transmitted to the Receiver the account of their money collected for the Superannuation Fund, while their controllers sent duplicates of such records to the department of the Controller-General in order for the receipts to be checked. The London officers paid their mulcts directly to the Receiver, while deductions from their salaries were made by the Receiver-General. From his receipts, the Receiver of the Superannuation Fund pensioned any qualified officer with an annual allowance during life, based on his salary. The remuneration of the Receiver and his Controller consisted of allowances out of the fund apparently until 1771, when it took the form of salaries by incidents.[2]

From the foregoing survey of the revenue branch of the Central Office it may be seen that several customs offices besides the office of the Receiver-General existed for the payment of customs receipts into the Exchequer. The Commissioners of Accounts in 1785 recommended that all these subsidiary treasuries should be abolished and the sums arising by fines and forfeitures and the produce of sales should be paid directly by the solicitors, the warehouse-keeper in London, and the outport collectors into the office of the Receiver-General. They proposed further that all payments from these sums, whether into the Exchequer or for expenses of management, be made by the Receiver-General. Thus the offices of Receivers of Fines and Forfeitures for London and the Outports would become unnecessary. The work of the Controller on the Outport Receiver and that of the Accountant of Petty Receipts would be taken over by the Controller-General, since the Receiver-General would pass his accounts of the fine and forfeiture branch in the same office in which he passed the rest of his accounts. Altogether, all departments of receipt in the central treasury, with the exception of that of the Receiver-General and possibly that of the Receiver of the Superannuation Fund, would be suppressed and their duty transferred to the department of the Receiver-General. Such an arrangement was designed to concentrate the great branches of receipt and payment in the one office of the Receiver-General, and thus to simplify the organization of the central treasury as well as to effect a large saving in the expense of the

[1] See *Commons Reports*, 1803, XII, 81, App. D. 4, "Fourth Rept. Sel. Com. on Finance," 1797.
[2] Cust. Ho. Lib., Extracts Board Minutes, III, 564, 1771, Mar. 15.

departments.¹ Although the Customs Commissioners concurred in such a plan of reform, they hesitated to undertake the necessary reorganization²; and the offices were allowed to continue unchanged until the act of 1798 which subjected them when vacant to abolition or to such regulation as the Customs Board should deem necessary.³

A group of officers known as the Controllers and Examiners of the General Accounts acted as a check on the main branch of the customs treasury and constituted the office for the preparation of the official accounts of the customs. It has been indicated above that the remittances of money to the Receiver-General arising from duties in the Port of London were controlled by the Supervisor of the Receiver-General's Receipts and Payments; while the payments of the proceeds of fines and forfeitures—both from the outports and from London—to the two Receivers of Fines and Forfeitures were checked by the Controller on the Outport Receiver and the Accountant of Petty Receipts respectively. It remains to account for the examination of one great department of the customs revenue sent into the office of the Receiver-General, the proceeds of duties in the outports. It was the business of the Controller-General and the several examiners of the outport accounts to serve as checks on that share of the receipts of the central customs treasury. As a matter of course these officers acted as controllers on the outport collectors as well. Since all the accounts of the Receiver-General and those of the outport collectors were transmitted finally to this office, the general accounts of the customs were compiled there. It must be noted, however, that no return was ever rendered to Parliament of the net proceeds of fines and forfeitures for London and the outports, since those proceeds were not under the cognizance of the Controller-General. Thus no perfect account of the customs was ever laid before Parliament during the period.⁴

This department of the Controllers and Examiners of the General Accounts included the Controller-General; four offices for the examination of the outport accounts—those of the Examiner of the Outport Books, the Surveyor of the Outport Accounts, the Inspector of the Outport Collectors' Accounts and Vouchers, and the Inspector of the Exchequer Books in the Outports; and two odd checks—an

---
¹ *Repts. of Comrs.*, 1787, III, 106-107, "Fourteenth Rept.," 1785.
² *Commons Reports*, 1803, XII, 57, "Fourth Rept. Sel. Com. Finance," 1797.
³ 38 Geo. III, c. 86, s. 6, 7, 8.
⁴ *Repts. of Comrs.*, 1787, III, 197, "Fifteenth Rept.," 1786.

108 ORGANIZATION OF THE ENGLISH CUSTOMS

Examiner of the Sufficiency of Officers' Securities and an Examiner of the Inferior Officers' Day Pay Bills. With the exception of the Inspector of the Outport Collectors' Accounts and Vouchers, appointed apparently in 1707,[1] the Inspector of the Exchequer Books in the Outports, established in 1712,[2] and possibly the Surveyor of the Outport Accounts,[3] provision for the transaction of the work of these offices had been made before the beginning of the eighteenth century. By the end of the century over half the offices, those of the Controller-General, the Surveyor, and the two Inspectors, had become sinecures.[4] The persons who filled these positions were paid by salaries with the exception of the Controller-General—who received in addition one third of the poundage on the coinage duty—and several clerks who had various gratuities or fees as well.[5]

In this department, the Controller-General, a patent officer established in 1671, occupied by far the most important position, for he examined and kept the accounts of the receipts and payments of all of the collectors in England. Until 1714 the entire responsibility of the office had devolved upon the Controller-General, but in that year the business was found too great for one person to carry alone with only irregular clerical assistance, and an Assistant or Chief Clerk, who had been employed in the office for many years, was established.[6] Fourteen years later, however, the office of Assistant was "sunk," and the salary attached to it was applied to the payment of two chief clerks in the Controller-General's office [7] who, together with their subordinates, transacted the work of the Controller-General throughout the period, and for whom he was responsible.

Every quarter the various collectors in the outports returned to the Board a complete account of the receipts and payments in their ports. These accounts were inspected and compared by several examiners with like accounts that were returned quarterly to the Board by the customers and controllers who acted as checks on the collectors.

---

[1] As indicated by P.R.O., Customs Registers: Series I, Cust. Quart. Estab., No. 80.
[2] See *supra*, Ch. I, pp. 8–9.
[3] This office may, however, have been a continuation of that of the old surveyor.
[4] *Repts. of Comrs.*, 1787, III, 101, 108, 422, App. No. 43, 424, App. No. 44, 425, App. No. 45, 426, App. No. 46, "Fourteenth Rept.," 1785.
[5] *Ibid.*, III, 85.
[6] P.R.O., Treas. Out-letters, Cust., XVI, 207–208, Treasury constitution, 1714–5, Feb. 22. Cf. *Rules of the Water-side* (1715), p. 80.
[7] P.R.O., Treas. Out-letters, Cust., XIX, 310, Treasury warrant, 1728, Dec. 11.

THE CENTRAL OFFICE

From these records the Controller-General was enabled to pass the collectors' accounts in his General Account.

The Receiver-General's account was passed by the Controller-General as that of a collector. From time to time, as the various collectors in the outports remitted their proceeds to the Receiver-General, their controllers sent accounts of such remittances to the Controller-General.[1] Weekly records of payments to the Receiver-General, prepared by the London collectors and signed by their controllers, were also transmitted to the Controller-General. Such sums, indicated by both the outport and London officers' accounts as having been paid to the Receiver-General, were compared by the Controller-General with the former's weekly certificates of receipts [2]; and from that examination the Controller-General formulated his account of receipts due to the Crown and payable into the Exchequer for which the Receiver-General could be held accountable.[3] From all the records of receipts and payments in London and the outports, together with the proper vouchers, the Controller-General made up his account and submitted it annually to the Auditor of the Imprest.[4] During the year the Controller-General stated the collectors' accounts regularly to the Board; he laid before the Commissioners, for transmission to the Treasury, the collectors' monthly balances as taken from their monthly abstracts, together with a general account at Christmas [5]; he informed the Commissioners at regular intervals of the accounts of collectors who were dead, dismissed, or removed [6]; and notified them

[1] As directed by Treasury warrant of 1697-8, Mar. 12 [erratum for Apr. 12?], P.R.O., Treas. Out-letters, Cust., XIII, 419.

[2] This record of receipts the Controller-General received from the Customs Commissioners to whom the Receiver-General had originally submitted it.

[3] The Receiver-General of course did not pay all of these receipts into the Exchequer, for from them he had to make disbursements. These payments were checked by the Supervisor of the Receiver-General's Receipts and Payments who returned an account of them to the Auditor of the Imprest, in whose office the Receiver-General passed his account.

[4] I have pieced together this sketch of the functions of the Controller-General from a description of the way in which the general accounts of the customs were passed, as included in *Repts. of Comrs.*, 1787, III, 5-13, 31-37, *passim*, "Thirteenth Rept.," 1785, and from miscellaneous minutes, of which the most useful are those in connection with the accounts of the London officers: Cust. Ho. Lib., Extracts Board Minutes, IV, 230, 1776, Jan. 23; 237, 1785, Jan. 26, 29; 238, 1785, July 6.

[5] *Ibid.*, I, "Comptroller General," 1735, July 3. See also *Repts. of Comrs.*, 1787, III, 35, "Thirteenth Rept.," 1785.

[6] For various references, see Cust. Ho. Lib., Extracts Board Minutes, I, "Comptroller General," 1713, July 15; 1726, Nov. 17; 1736, Mar. 10; 1742, Oct. 13; 1752, July 21.

as to what books were wanting when the collectors were remiss in sending up their accounts.[1] From time to time he attended Parliament with the accounts.[2]

The story of the way in which the business of this office was actually carried on would be amusing if it did not contain so serious an indictment against the system of duties and the machinery set up for their collection and account. The complicated appropriation of every duty on every article under many heads, and the deduction of payments from specific branches of duties must have turned more than one outport collector gray-headed. As duties increased during the period, so the collectors' accounts fell behind and the business of the office of the Controller-General became clogged. With the large increase of duties in the reign of Anne, the general account of the customs seems to have fallen into its first serious arrears in the century, for in 1717 the Customs Commissioners allowed the Controller-General £200 upon condition that the general accounts of the customs were not more than two years in arrears. Many a time after that the Controller-General was ordered to report why the accounts were so far behind, contrary to the Treasury warrant of that year.[3] By 1725 the accounts had become so greatly retarded [4] that £250 per annum for clerks had to be allowed the Controller-General appointed in that year.[5] This grant proved a good investment; the accounts were brought forward, and in 1736 the allowance was confirmed and an additional £100 given the Controller-General "on Condition that the said Accounts are kept up as they are at Present." [6] Subsequent arrears in succeeding years accompanied the imposition of new and high duties; thus another £190 was allowed in 1772 for five additional clerks on condition that two years' accounts be completed and passed within one year, such allowance to be discontinued when the arrears

---

[1] See Cust. Ho. Lib., Extracts Board Minutes, I, "Accounts," 1713, Apr. 10; I, "Comptroller General," 1741, Feb. 19; 1742, Dec. 8.

[2] E. g., *ibid.*, I, "Comptroller General," 1728, Feb. 21.

[3] *Ibid.*, I, "Comptroller General," 1720, Aug. 10; I, "Accounts," 1720, Dec. 29, Jan. 3; 1724, Jan. 15; 1726, Oct. 4, Nov. 16; 1728, Aug. 7, 14, 15, 22.

[4] According to a memorial of one of the Controllers-General, the accounts of the customs in 1725 had been delivered to the Auditors no further than Christmas, 1719, and the coal account no further than May 15, 1708. P.R.O., Treasury Papers, Bdl. 530, No. 274, Parsons to Lords of Treas. [read 1777, April].

[5] 1725 is the date of this grant according to Parsons' memorial, but a customs minute places it at 1728. See Cust. Ho. Lib., Extracts Board Minutes, I, "Comptroller General," 1736, Sept. 9.

[6] See *ibid.*, I, "Comptroller General," 1736, Sept. 9; and P.R.O., Treasury Papers, Bdl. 530, No. 274, Parsons to Lords of Treas. [read 1777, April].

THE CENTRAL OFFICE

were brought up.[1] Within a few years this grant was withdrawn,[2] though a further allowance of £80 was made in 1777 for two additional clerks to cease "whenever the Consolidation of the Customs shall take place."[3]

It has been stated above that the branch for the examination of outport accounts comprised four main offices: that of the Examiners of the Outport Books, the Surveyor of Outport Accounts, the Inspector of Outport Collectors' Accounts and Vouchers, and the Inspector of Exchequer Books in the Outports. A brief comment on each will serve to distinguish the duties of those officers. The four Examiners of the Outport Collectors' Accounts took the collectors' vouchers and quarterly accounts of receipts and payments sent to the Board and inspected them closely to see that duties and discounts, drawbacks and bounties were accurately computed and properly listed. These collectors' books then went to the Surveyor of the Outport Accounts in order for him to compare them with the controllers' and customers' records as a check upon the collector. From this office the collectors' books were delivered to the Controller-General. The Inspector of Outport Collectors' Accounts and Vouchers received from the Board or the collectors a separate quarterly account of payments by them of salaries, incidents, and all expenses attached to the port, which he compared with the collectors' vouchers of such payments to see that they were justified by the proper authority. From all the expenses defrayed by the collectors he made up a separate account for the Controller-General.[4] The Inspectorship of Exchequer Books had become a useless office since the return of such books had become generally disregarded.[5] By 1785 no duty or business remained to the office, yet the principal received a salary of £300 a year.[6]

The remaining two officers of this division may be dismissed quickly. One, the Examiner of the Sufficiency of Officers' Securities,

---

[1] Cust. Ho. Lib., Extracts Board Minutes, III, 99, 1772, Oct. 6.

[2] P.R.O., Treasury Papers, Bdl. 530, No. 274, Parsons to Lords of Treas. [read 1777, April].

[3] Cust. Ho. Lib., Extracts Board Minutes, IV, 230, 1777, July 1. In 1788 the allowance ceased as a result of the consolidation. *Ibid.,* IV, 238, 1788, Mar. 29.

[4] For this account of the functions of these officers, see *Repts. of Comrs.,* 1787, III, 35–36, "Thirteenth Rept.," 1785. The Extracts of Board Minutes contain short references to the business of these offices under their respective heads, which references supplement the account in the Commissioners' report. Cf. *Rules of the Water-side* (1715), p. 79.

[5] See *supra,* Ch. I, pp. 8–9.

[6] *Repts. of Comrs.,* 1787, III, 101, "Fourteenth Rept.," 1785.

received regular lists of persons offered by the customs officers as securities; made inquiry about such securities—whether they were dead, insufficient, or not to be found; certified the ability to pay of persons proposed as securities; and reported his observations to the Board annually.[1] The Examiner of the Inferior Officers' Day Pay Bills inspected the bills of the inferior London officers who were paid for their work by the day, and from them made out lists for the Receiver-General in accordance with which the men were paid.[2]

From this short survey it may be seen that the outport accounts were examined by seven officers who were entirely outside the department of the Controller-General where the accounts were eventually passed. The duty of one of these offices, that of the Inspector of Exchequer Books, was absolutely useless; two other offices, that of the Surveyor of Outport Accounts and Inspector of Outport Accounts and Vouchers, were sinecures, the principals of which for many years executed none of their duties [3]; all the officers were transacting business that properly belonged to the department of the Controller-General. In view of these considerations the Commissioners of Accounts in 1785 recommended the abolition of all these offices, and the incorporation of their work with that of the Controller-General [4]; but as in the case of officers previously mentioned, no alterations along these lines were made until 1798.[5]

Immediate responsibility for the conduct of the inferior officers of the customs rested with their superiors in London and with the collectors and controllers in the outports. It was important, however, that there should be an instrument of control unconnected with the officers of any one port, and directly representative of the Customs

[1] Cust. Ho. Lib., Extracts Board Minutes, I, III, V, entries under "Examiner of Officers' Securities." This officer also solicited the payment of debts outstanding in the plantations. For example of reference, see P.R.O., Treas. Out-letters, Cust., XXIV, 406, Treasury warrant, 1754, Nov. 6.

[2] See Cust. Ho. Lib., Extracts Board Minutes, III, 599, 1764, Dec. 15. The Examiner of the Inferior Officers' Day Pay Bills was Clerk to the Tide-surveyors until 1770. *Ibid.,* III, 152, 1770, Aug. 31.

[3] In 1785 it was reported that the Inspector of the Outport Collectors' Accounts had done no part of the business for over forty years. (*Repts. of Comrs.,* 1787, III, 426, App. 46, "Fourteenth Rept.," 1785.) Clerks transacted all of the business despite the Board's order to the Inspector in 1743 that he attend to his duty in person "in regard his Office is of too much Consequence to admit of Delay, and requires the Inspection of the Principal to see that the Clerks do their Duty." Cust. Ho. Lib., Extracts Board Minutes, I, "Inspector of Outport Collectors Accompts," 1743, Oct. 6.

[4] *Repts. of Comrs.,* 1787, III, 99, 101, 107–108, "Fourteenth Rept.," 1785.

[5] 38 Geo. III, c. 86, s. 1, 2, 3, 4, 6, 7 8.

THE CENTRAL OFFICE

Board. Strangely enough, it was not until 1771 that the offices which had been established to such an end were centralized in London.

In the early part of the eighteenth century, a kind of personnel officer, known as a surveyor-general, was reëstablished to supervise the conduct of the customs staff within a particular area. As the years went on, more of these officers were appointed as they became necessary,[1] until in the latter part of the period they numbered seven. These seven officers resided in certain districts into which the ports were divided, where they dealt with individual irregularities and made general surveys of the establishments. In 1771 the Customs Commissioners, dissatisfied with the form of control over the personnel of the outport system and probably mindful of the need for attendants to deal with the delinquencies of the London officers, proposed to the Lords of the Treasury that the local surveyors-general should be discontinued as vacancies might occur, and that there should be appointed in their stead four general-surveyors [2] to be resident in London, who should be ready to go on any mission into the outports and to superintend the conduct of the London officers under the directions of the Board.[3] The Lords of the Treasury issued their order accord-

[1] See P.R.O., Customs Registers: Series I, Cust. Quart. Estab.

[2] In the memorial the term "Surveyors General" is used; but because these officers were frequently known as "general-surveyors" and because that term distinguishes this department from the old surveyors-general, who were entirely distinct, it has been used throughout this study.

[3] In this memorial the Customs Commissioners represented that notwithstanding the fact that £2,120 were expended for the support of the seven surveyors-general, whenever it was necessary to examine the conduct of officers or the state of the ports or the nature of the illicit trade in several of the counties, they were obliged to send down skilful persons from London at an additional expense to the revenue. The Commissioners further stated that since most of the surveyors-general were resident in their respective districts, all of them at a considerable distance from London, the Board could not have their advice upon any emergency; and before the surveyors could get to London to receive the Board's instructions, there was danger that delinquent officers might discover the intentions of the Commissioners and so be prepared for any investigation. Finally, most of the surveyors-general had been appointed from among the country gentlemen without any previous instruction in the customs business, "and though We have no particular reason to be dissatisfied with the Conduct of these Gentlemen," reported the Commissioners, "yet, We can scarce persuade Ourselves, that they can sufficiently inform themselves of the Computation of the Duties, and other General Business of this Revenue, as well as the particular practical part of each Officer, from the Collector, down to the meanest Tidesmen without much application, and without a frequent attention to the practice of the Officers in this Port, where these Gentlemen very seldom repair, and would perhaps deem it an hardship so to do." P.R.O., Treasury Papers, Bdl. 483, No. 471, Cust. Comrs. to Lords of Treas., 1771, Oct. 4. See also No. 472.

ingly. In the following year, 1772, two general-surveyors were appointed by constitution at a fixed salary,[1] and the other two were established some time later. In 1785 all but three of the offices of the old surveyors-general had been abolished.[2]

The duties of the general-surveyors may be roughly summarized under three headings: they examined all complaints against officers and reported upon them to the Board; they made surveys of the outports; and they issued instructions for the conduct of officers. When a complaint arising in London was lodged against a customs officer, it was referred by the Board to the general-surveyors, who proceeded to investigate the case. They formed a charge against the officer, heard him in his defense, and reported their proceedings and stated their opinion to the Board. Upon the information of any outport irregularity, the general-surveyors sometimes went to the port in question, there to probe into the true state of affairs for themselves. The nature of the cases which came before these officers varied; they not only dealt with complaints against officers but also inquired into disputes between officers and into the frequent disagreements of the officers with the merchants.

From time to time the general-surveyors were desired by the Treasury or Customs Boards to make complete surveys of the ports. Upon such occasions the efficiency of every officer came under close scrutiny and all parts of the business were given careful examination. The reports upon such surveys were always of great importance, for they were often followed by orders for the alterations necessary to the improvement of the service.[3]

The general-surveyors were concerned with the positive side of personnel regulation as well. They prepared and issued instructions to officers governing their conduct and their procedure in the execution of the duty of their particular offices. They made recommendations to the Board, and they appear to have worked out plans for the better expedition of the business in various parts of the service. Two of them attended daily at all Board meetings to give any necessary advice.[4] So important did the general-surveyors become that in 1851

[1] Cust. Ho. Lib., Extracts Board Minutes, III, 575, 1772, Feb. 25; 576, 1772, Nov. 10, Dec. 8. In reality three were appointed, one of whom was superseded. See *ibid.*, III, 575, 1772, May 15; 576, 1773, Jan. 15.
[2] *Repts. of Comrs.* 1787, III, 368, App. No. 7, "Fourteenth Rept.," 1785.
[3] In Chapter V the nature of such surveys is considered at greater length.
[4] With respect to these duties of the general-surveyors, see *Repts. of Comrs.*, 1787, III, 428–429, App. No. 49, "Fourteenth Rept.," 1785; and Cust. Ho. Lib., Extracts Board Minutes, IV, entries under "General Surveyors."

THE CENTRAL OFFICE

the Deputy Chairman of the Board stated that "formerly they were said to be the right-hands, and even it went so far as to be said that they were the brains of the Commissioners."[1]

Two other offices, that of the Surveyor-General[2] and that of the Examiners of Riding Officers' Journals, must be included in the inspectorate of personnel. The office of Surveyor-General had been in existence long before the eighteenth century. At that date, however, that part of his duty which involved investigation of the conduct of officers apparently lapsed, and the Surveyor-General became essentially a check on the assessment and receipt of all the import and export duties in the Port of London. With other chief officers of the port, he had the superintendence of the accounting department of the business.[3] A sufficient check upon the collection of duties was, however, provided by other departments in London, and this office, which was a sinecure and had outworn its usefulness, should have been suppressed long before it was terminated in 1798.[4]

The riding officers were established at certain points along the coast to patrol their districts by day and night in order to detect any smuggling vessels and to seize run goods. They were obliged to keep journals of each day's activities, of which one copy had to be sent to London to be inspected. In 1717 two officers were appointed as Examiners of Riding Officers' Journals,[5] one of them to check over the books of riding officers in the northern ports, and the other those of officers in the western ports. These officers continued in their duties

---

[1] *Second Rept. Sel. Com. on Cust.*, H.C. 604, p. 92 (1851), Part I, Minutes of Evidence, xi. In 1786 the Commissioners reported to the Treasury, "The Advantage derived to the Revenue from this useful Institution during its Existence for more than 14 Years, has not only manifested the Importance of it, but has fully evinced that it is essentially and indispensably necessary for the good Management of the Revenue under our Care, and We should be wanting in Justice to the Memorialists if We did not represent to their Lordships that their Zeal and Ability in the Execution of the extensive and laborious Duties of their Office have been eminent and meritorious." In this report on a memorial of the general-surveyors praying relief because of the smallness of their incomes, the Customs Board recommended an addition of £200 per annum to the salary of each of the officers. It was warranted accordingly. P.R.O., Treas. Out-letters, Cust., XXXIV, 429–431, Cust. Comrs. to Lords of Treas., 1786, Jan. 20; Treasury warrant, 1786, July 22.
[2] Not to be confused with the surveyors-general and general-surveyors just mentioned, nor with the Surveyor of the Port of London mentioned in Chapter IV.
[3] See *infra*, Ch. IV, p. 137.
[4] 38 Geo. III, c. 86, s. 6, 7, 8.
[5] Cust. Ho. Lib., Extracts Board Minutes, I, "Instructions," 1717, Dec. 18. For a further reference to the position of these officers, see Crouch, *Complete Guide to Officers* (1732), p. 6.

until 1781, when the office for the western ports was brought to an end and that of the northern ports was ordered to fall in when it became vacant.[1]

It would seem that, by the latter part of the period, the group of officers known as Inspectors of Officers' Conduct had in general demonstrated their inutility, for every office had either been abolished entirely, had changed into another form, or was marked out for discontinuance by the Commissioners of Accounts in 1785.

Officers for keeping records respecting trade comprised the fifth and last division of the Central Office. In 1696 upon a presentment of the Customs Commissioners, the Lords of the Treasury instituted the office of Inspector-General of Imports and Exports to keep an account of goods shipped in and out of British ports and the places to and from which goods were sent; and, once a year or as often as should be required, to present a balance of trade between England and any other country.[2] The Inspector who succeeded to the office in 1703 and his successors were further required to keep an account of the shipping in which the imports and exports were made and to examine as well into the increase in the freight of foreign shipping and into any decay of British trade with foreign parts.[3] Such inspectors were directed to obey orders alike from the Lords of the Treasury, the Customs Commissioners, or the Commissioners for Trade and Plantations. Of the several offices established for the compilation of trade accounts, that of the Inspector-General of Imports and Exports was the most important.

Records of every entry of goods imported into London, accounts of over-entries and damages, and shipping bills of exports or their copies were sent regularly to the Inspector. The outports returned similar quarterly accounts.[4] From all of these documents a record of the quantity of every commodity was made, distinguishing the country of provenance and destination and stating the value in money cal-

[1] Cust. Ho. Lib., Extracts Board Minutes, IV, 380, 1781, Nov. 28.

[2] P.R.O., Treas. Out-letters, Cust., XIII, 294–295, Treasury constitution, 1696, Sept. 11.

[3] *Ibid.*, XIV, 272, Treasury constitution, 1703, June 3. Similar constitutions of later date are to be found in the Treasury Out-letters, Customs. For a description of the office, see P.R.O., Treasury Papers, Vol. 184, No. 157, Martyn to "My Lord," 1714, Nov. 18.

[4] These accounts were sometimes in arrears; thus, in 1715 the Inspector-General observed that "divers of the outports are fallen into many errours, derogating from the true scheme & method whereby the Coll^{rs} are requir'd to keep those acc^{ts} in a pticular manner." Cust. Ho. Lib., Letters to Dartmouth, 1675–6 to 1715, p. 318, Martyn to Dartmouth, 1715, July 14.

culated according to fixed rates.¹ From all the entries returned to this office from London and the outports, the account was prepared of the balance of trade between England and each foreign country and the British plantations. From time to time the Inspector was ordered by Parliament, the Council, the Treasury, the Board of Trade, or the Customs Board to prepare special accounts upon various aspects of the business.² The records compiled in this office unfortunately do not accurately represent the state of trade, but their indication of the tendencies of commercial policy make them of considerable interest.

The work of the Register-General of Trading Ships may be traced to a commission of 1701 which directed one of the Customs Commissioners, Godolphin, to keep a register of all trading ships and to check the particulars of vessels engaged in outport shipping.³ The actual office of the Register-General, however, was established in 1707 when, pursuant to the Act of Union which required the entry of all the ships of Scotland in the register of all trading vessels of England, Godolphin was authorized to keep such a register for all of Great Britain.⁴ It was in this office that a record was filed of the registration of all ships engaged in the plantation trade. Since such vessels had by the Navigation Act to be of British build, they had to be registered accordingly by oath of one or more of the owners before the collector of a port. The duplicate of this registration was sent to the Customs Commissioners at London and entered in a general register presumably kept in the office of the Register-General.⁵ To this office were also returned monthly accounts of all ships which entered as sailing coastwise and to or from a foreign port, with particulars as to cargo, tonnage, number of men, and whether British or foreign.⁶ Quarterly outport accounts of various commodities shipped coastwise and in and out were transmitted to this department as well.⁷ Once a year two general ac-

---

¹ These records are in the P.R.O. as Ledgers of Imports and Exports.
² For numerous miscellaneous references to the work of the Inspector, see Cust. Ho. Lib., Extracts Board Minutes, I, III, IV, entries under "Inspector of Imports and Exports."
³ P.R.O., Patent Roll, 13 Wm. III, P. 3, No. 1, [1701], Dec. 18; P.R.O., Treas. Out-letters, Cust., XIV, 182, Treasury warrant, 1702, May 13.
⁴ P.R.O., Treasury Papers, Vol. 103, No. 94, Cust. Comrs. to Lords of Treas., 1707, Oct. 21, and minute. I have no reference to the warrant itself, but by minute on this report, a warrant to this effect was directed to be prepared. See also P.R.O., Customs Registers: Series I, Cust. Quart. Estab., No. 80.
⁵ See Crouch, *Complete Guide to Officers* (1732), p. 90; cf. *Rules of the Waterside* (1715), p. 78.
⁶ See Crouch, *Complete Guide to Officers* (1732), pp. 36, 86–87, 239.
⁷ *Ibid.*, pp. 36, 84–85, 237.

counts were returned: one containing the number of ships belonging to the port, with their tonnage and number of men, the other giving the number of British and foreign ships which had traded to and from the port during the year, with an indication of their tonnage and voyages. From these records the Register-General of Trading Ships drew up an annual account of all ships trading to or from each foreign and British port during the year.[1] Thus a close check was kept upon Britain's position in the carrying trade.

Both these offices were sinecures. That of the Inspector-General of Imports and Exports was held by constitution and executed by an Assistant and clerks during the greater part of the period,[2] while that of the Register of Ships was held by patent and executed by a Chief and other clerks. In both departments the staff of clerks who transacted the business of their offices were appointed and paid by their principals,[3] and the clerks of the Register-General had some small fees as well.[4] Because of the uselessness and expense of the incumbents of these offices, the Commissioners of Accounts in 1785 advised their discontinuance and recommended that the duties and profits of the offices should be vested in those who actually did the work.[5] Within a short time the sinecure part of the Inspector-General's office was brought to an end [6]; but that part of the Register-General's position remained until it was marked out for discontinuance in 1798.[7]

In a review of these five departments, which included the law staff, cashiers, controllers, inspectors of officers' conduct, and officers of trade accounts, it is evident that the general outlines of the Central Office, as regards most of these departments, had been drawn before the eighteenth century. The three main law offices had been created; the offices of the Controller-General and of all but two of the other examiners [8] had been instituted at least as far back as the commission; one of the two offices for keeping accounts of trade was established

---

[1] *Repts. of Comrs.*, 1787, III, 431, App. No. 51, "Fourteenth Rept.," 1785.

[2] The Assistant was appointed August 16, 1722. P.R.O., Treas. Out-letters, Cust., XVIII, 125–127.

[3] *Repts. of Comrs.*, 1787, III, 431–432, App. No. 51, 432, App. No. 52, "Fourteenth Rept.," 1785.

[4] *Ibid.*, III, 86.

[5] *Ibid.*, III, 105–106.

[6] See P.R.O., Chatham Papers, Bdl. 285, "A List of Offices annexed to the Bill proposed in 1783 which are not included in the present Scheme [1792] with the reasons for their Omission."

[7] 38 Geo. III, c. 86, s. 2, 3, 4.

[8] Possibly three examiners, if the establishment of the office of Surveyor of the Outport Accounts was of later date.

THE CENTRAL OFFICE

in 1696, while the work of the other was begun in the opening years of the century. In the cashiers' division, while the Supervisor's office and the fines and forfeitures and superannuation fund departments date from the early part of the period, the department of the Receiver-General had been created before that time. In the inspectorate of personnel, also, two offices originated considerably before the eighteenth century. Thus, with the exception of only parts of these several branches, the general organization of the Central Office had been laid down before 1696.

The alterations which were made between 1696 and 1786 show for the most part expansion within the departments, either in the addition of extra officers like those already existing or in the establishment of several new ones to deal with various aspects of increasing business. There are instances of the discontinuance of offices, but they are rare. In general there was comparatively little change during the eighteenth century. This very fact was the chief explanation for the complexity in the organization of the Central Office.

Many offices had become redundant during the period but nevertheless had been allowed to continue. In their "Fourteenth Report" in 1785 the Commissioners of Accounts recommended that fourteen of these offices (or over half of the entire number existing in the department at that date) should be abolished.[1] Of these fourteen, there were three offices where the business was useful but the officer who held the place as a sinecure was useless, namely, those of the Supervisor of the Receiver-General's Receipts and Payments, the Inspector-General of Imports and Exports, and the Register-General of Trading Ships Belonging to Great Britain. There were four other sinecure offices where the duty attached was unnecessary and the whole office should have been abolished long before 1798, namely, those of the Inspector of Prosecutions, the Register of Seizures, the Surveyor-General, and the Inspector and Examiner of Exchequer Books in the Outports. Finally, there were seven offices, several of them sinecures, where the business was worth-while but the similarity of duty with that of other offices required either consolidation or the suppression of one of them and the transfer of duty to the other, namely, those of the Receivers of Fines and Forfeitures for London and for the Outports with the Controller, the Accountant of Petty Receipts, the Surveyor of Outport Accounts, the Inspector of Outport Accounts, and the four Examiners of Outport Accounts. Had the necessary reforms

[1] *Repts. of Comrs.*, 1787, III, 99–108, "Fourteenth Rept.," 1785.

been brought about in the various divisions, the law office would have included only the solicitors; the central treasury would have consisted only of the department of the Receiver-General and his Supervisor and possibly of the Receiver of the Money for the Superannuation Fund; the control section would have been confined to the offices of the Controller-General and the two odd examiners; the general-surveyors alone would have composed the division for the superintendence of personnel; the business of the accountants of trade and shipping would have been vested in the officers who actually did the work.

Upon evidence of such unnecessary duplication in the Central Office the question arises as to why such offices were allowed to continue for so long. Four reasons may be offered, all of which were responsible in some degree for the state of the department. In some instances the office was held by patent, and as such persisted unquestioned throughout the period [1]; sinecures were not confined to the customs service, but were common in many public departments and were centuries old in their origin. Undoubtedly the influence of patronage accounted for the continuation of some offices. In other cases the office was originally created to transact useful business, but with a change in that business it gradually became useless. Finally, some offices, such as those falling into the third class, had important duties, and any alteration would have necessitated other provisions for the performance of their functions. This last was doubtless an important consideration, for it was put by the Customs Commissioners before the Committee on Finance in 1797 as being a difficulty in the way of the reform of several offices.[2] It was not until 1798 that provision for the improvement of this administration was made.[3] The continuance of these

[1] The case of the Duke of Manchester is of interest in this connection. In the defense of his office as Collector-Outwards in the Port of London, the Duke stated [about 1783?], "On this undisputed & uninterrupted Possession I found my Right & if it can be set aside by such Antiquated & Dormant Statutes, will venture to Pronounce that few Properties in the Kingdom can be safe, however Guarded they may appear to the Possessor, by the Sanction of Time & the Protection of Deeds & Settlements." P.R.O., Chatham Papers, Bdl. 284, "D of Manchester Custom House Office."

[2] *Commons Reports,* 1803, XII, 57, "Fourth Rept. Sel. Com. on Finance," 1797.

[3] 38 Geo. III, c. 86, s. 1, 2, 3, 4, 6, 7, 8. Some of these offices were condemned by the Bill of 1783, which was defeated, and most of them listed as well in the draft of a bill in 1792. (For references, see *supra,* Ch. I, p. 24, n. 4, p. 25, n. 2. See also P.R.O., Chatham Papers, Bdl. 285, "Customs Fees etc. Notes respecting the proposal intended to be made in 1792," and enclosure No. 8.) By 1797 several altera-

many useless offices throughout the century imposed needless expense upon the government and complicated the business of the departments within the Central Office.

---

tions had been made (see *Commons Reports,* 1803, XII, 57–58, "Fourth Rept. Sel. Com. on Finance," 1797), though sweeping reform was not effected until 1798.

CHAPTER IV

THE ORGANIZATION OF THE PORT OF LONDON

During the eighteenth century London enjoyed a marked supremacy over the outports as one of the greatest centers of world trade. In her close contact with the hinterland and accessibility to the open seas, she occupied a strategic position which made her the port of internal distribution and Britain's largest market. Certain trades—the East India, Greenland, Italian silk, and African trades—were largely confined to London, and the head offices of the foreign trading companies were located there. The wealth and power of the London merchants were not approached by any similar group. Because there were more moneyed men in London and large sums were concentrated in the city through the commission and brokerage business for the merchants of the towns and the outports, bills of exchange and insurance were more cheaply negotiated, and credit was more readily obtainable, there than elsewhere. Further, capital was attracted to London as the seat of the national bank and the head of the financial operations of the government. All these considerations, and many others, gave London an early and unrivaled predominance in trade and shipping, in wealth and finance.[1]

Statisticians have estimated that between the middle of Henry VIII's reign and the second quarter of the eighteenth century, London paid annually 70 to 90 per cent of the customs duties of England.[2] After 1720 the rise of the outports is evident and the decentralization of English trade set in. Though the records of the Inspector-General do not represent accurate valuations, and for that reason conclusions based on their statistics alone cannot be taken as valid, they may be used to give some idea of tendencies in trade. According to those accounts, even after the outport competition was well under way (in 1750), over 66 per cent of Britain's exports found their way to foreign parts through the London cocket office, while

---

[1] Ray Bert Westerfield, "Middlemen in English Business Particularly between 1660 and 1760," *Transactions of the Connecticut Academy of Arts and Sciences* (May, 1915), XIX, 419–421, 423, for more detail on London's commercial ascendancy.

[2] *Ibid.*, XIX, 418, n. I have been unable to go beyond Westerfield for this statement.

ORGANIZATION OF THE PORT OF LONDON 123

over 71 per cent of the imports reached consumers by way of the Collector-Inwards in the Port of London.[1] Of the total tonnage entered at British ports at the middle of the century (1751) nearly 49 per cent was discharged in the Port of London, while nearly 25 per cent of the tonnage out was cleared there.[2]

The century saw a marked increase in vessels, tonnage, and value of imports and exports entering in and out of London. A comparison of shipping in 1702 and in 1794 reveals nearly three times as many vessels and approximately four times as much tonnage registered at the end of the period as at its beginning.[3] According to the Inspector-General's accounts, the value of imports increased more than 250 per cent, while exports nearly doubled during roughly the same time.[4] With respect both to ships and to the value of their cargoes, the second half of the century was the period of greatest increase.

London has a further significance for a survey of the eighteenth-century customs in that it consistently served as a model for the outports, and every attempt was made to bring them into conformity with the established practice in London.[5] For these reasons it is well to examine in some detail the organization of the Port of London as it existed during the period.

The jurisdiction of the port was defined by the Exchequer as extending from the North Foreland in the Isle of Thanet, north along an imaginary line to the opposite point, the Naze, on the Essex coast, and from there west to London Bridge, the whole area forming a great and very acute triangle. The rights of Sandwich and Ipswich as ports, however, were guaranteed.[6] Deal and Margate appear to have

---

[1] *Parliamentary Papers*, XLVII, Repts., XVII, H.C. No. 129, App. D, App. C c c (1796), "Report from the Committee appointed to enquire into the best Mode of providing sufficient Accomodation for the increased Trade and Shipping of the Port of London."

[2] *Parliamentary Papers*, XLVII, *Repts.*, XVII, H.C. No. 129, App. G, App. O o o (1796), "Rept. from Com. on Port of London."

	London	Outports
Tonnage Inwards, 1751	234,369 tons	245,485 tons
Tonnage Outwards, 1751	173,843 tons	522,802 tons

The calculations of Westerfield respecting this tonnage appear to be erroneous.

[3] *Parliamentary Papers*, XLVII, *Repts.*, XVII, H.C. No. 129, p. v (1796), "Rept. from Com. on Port of London." These figures do not include the coastwise trade.

[4] *Parliamentary Papers*, XLVII, *Repts.*, XVII, H.C. No. 129, App. D. (1796), "Rept. from Com. on Port of London."

[5] The methods employed toward that end are described in Chapter V.

[6] *A General Law-Treatise of Naval Trade and Commerce*, I, 152–153.

been the furthermost points to which customs guard of incoming ships extended, while most of the inward vessels were boarded at Gravesend. The center of customs administration was the Custom House which stood to the east of London Bridge and Billingsgate on the north bank of the Thames, flanked on both sides by the small official port quays, sufferance wharves, and warehouses.

The condition of the Thames at this period differed considerably from that of the present day. Its curve around the Isle of Dogs, narrowness, shallowness, and the rapidity of its tides below London Bridge caused serious delays in shipping and danger to vessels. At low tide it lost one third of its breadth and left high upon the mud bottom the coasting vessels and other ships that chanced to be anchored near shore. The negligence of masters and of individuals who had charge of moorings in the river enhanced the difficulties arising from its crowded state. Masters could drop anchor wherever they might choose, and small boats often took up the valuable berths of deep draught which should have been reserved for the greater vessels. At times these boats were so arranged that a ship actually could not pass. Neglect of the river with regard to dredging and upkeep added to its inadequacy. Malpractices at the time of the unlading of ships occasioned delay in clearance of cargoes and provided opportunities for plunder: thus, through the neglect of customs officers, ships were known to stand in the river for well over a month without final clearance; vessels began to unload when only a part of their shipment was entered; masters left their boats during the time of unlading, which gave opportunity to pilferers to help themselves; and the drawing of huge samples wasted the cargo.[1] Pilfering was notoriously rife throughout the century, and shipments were frequently despoiled at nearly every stage in the discharge [2] by organized bands of rob-

---

[1] On the condition of the Thames, see *Parliamentary Papers*, XLVII, *Repts.*, XVII, H.C. No. 129, pp. xi–xiv (1796), "Rept. from Com. on Port of London;" *Parliamentary Papers*, LIII, *Repts.*, XXIII, H.C. No. 154, pp. 68–70, App. D. 1 (1799), "Second Report from the Select Committee upon the Improvement of the Port of London." See also, for example, Cust. Ho. Lib., Extracts Board Minutes, I, "Inspectors of the River," 1716, July 4.

[2] E. g., P.R.O., Treasury Papers, Bdl. 338, Nos. 21–24, A statement of grocers, a sugar-refiner, William Clark and John Brookes to the Lords of the Treasury concerning depredations committed in sugar on ships in the Thames. At one time, according to these men, the losses in sugar by frauds on the river amounted to £70,000 a year. The organization for this plunderage was a clever one, probably typical of that by which many other cargoes were exploited: while the ship awaited the papers necessary for her delivery, the crew made away with what sugar they could; the persons who unloaded her (known as "lumpers") filled sacks and the

ORGANIZATION OF THE PORT OF LONDON 125

bers.[1] Merchants' complaints seem to have availed little. Even the united opposition of the merchants against such abuses [2] had but a temporary salutary effect, and the plundering continued unabated.

Lining the Thames from the Tower to London Bridge were the official port quays, all small and crowded. By actual measurement they extended but 488 yards along the river, while one of the quays was confined to the incredibly small space of twenty-three feet. The extent of the legal quays in 1796 was no greater than it had been when they were established by act of 1 Elizabeth, regardless of the fact that a great increase in business must have rendered extension necessary.[3] Serious evils arose in consequence of the quays being too limited: loaded lighters were frequently detained at the legal quays for want of room, and merchants were often obliged to resort to sufferance wharves which were sometimes inconvenient.[4] Delays in discharge were costly; frequently cargoes suffered not only plunder [5] but sea-damage.[6] There were also evils consequent upon poor regulation of the quays: the export and import trades were frequently mixed together at one place and time; goods over and above the amount orig-

---

pockets of their large canvas trousers with the sugar and carried away enormous quantities of it when they went ashore for their breakfasts, dinners, and suppers; the lighterman who managed the boats which brought the sugar to the Custom House would contrive not to reach the quay on a particular tide, and moor out in order to smuggle to his fellows some of the sugar from the lighter; the cooper, who was placed on board to repair broken casks, stole as much sugar as he could, often by sending his bag to shore, pretending to need nails. Though customs officers were on board the ship, they seldom or never interfered in these activities, for they too had a share in the proceeds, and at night they themselves frequently assisted in the nefarious practices. The ship, in short, was described as one general scene of robbery and plunder from the time she began to work until her cargo was delivered. And the same was said to be true of other vessels carrying rum, indigo, and other West India products. Frauds in East India cargoes were even worse. For further reference to Thames pilferage, see *Parliamentary Papers*, XLVII, *Repts.*, XVII, H.C. No. 129, pp. xiv, xxvi, xxvii (1796), "Rept. from Com. on Port of London."

[1] Sir J. G. Broodbank, *History of the Port of London* (London, 1921), I, 83.

[2] See P.R.O., Treasury Papers, Bdl. 446, Nos. 184–185, Robinson, Staples, and Thomson, London merchants, to Lords of Treas. [endorsement of 1766, June 18]. See P.R.O., State Papers Domestic, Geo. II, Bdl. 115, No. 5, London merchants to Lords Justices. In 2 Geo. III, apparently at the instigation of the merchants, an act was passed to prevent frauds by persons navigating certain river craft.

[3] *Parliamentary Papers*, XLVII, *Repts.*, XVII, H.C. No. 129, p. xiv (1796), "Rept. from Com. on Port of London."

[4] *Parliamentary Papers*, XLVII, *Repts.*, XVII, H.C. No. 129, p. xvi (1796), "Rept. from Com. on Port of London."

[5] *Parliamentary Papers*, LIII, *Repts.*, XXIII, H.C. No. 154, p. 70, App. D. 1 (1799), "Second Rept. from Sel. Com. on Port of London."

[6] See *infra*, note, for example of such damage.

inally entered by the merchant crowded the quays, awaiting payment of duties; liquors were sometimes gauged at one wharf and landed at another; there were often not enough customs officers and only too many customs holidays. These and many other abuses constituted a real discouragement to trade.[1] Spirited remonstrances were made by the merchants throughout the period against the conditions of the London quays,[2] but no improvement was effected and inconveniences were permitted to continue.

By Exchequer Roll of 19 Charles II, pursuant to an act of 13 and 14 Charles II, the principal officers or farmers of the customs were authorized to permit shipping and landing of goods at places other than the lawful quays.[3] Thus, as business increased and legal quays

[1] *Parliamentary Papers*, XLVII, *Repts.*, XVII, H.C. No. 129, p. xvi (1796), "Rept. from Com. on Port of London."

[2] In 1762 and 1764 the London merchants begged the extension of the lawful quays of the Port of London by the addition of new wharves set out by a commission. (For such a method, see *infra*, Ch. V, p. 168.) Upon both occasions the commissions were created, and the commissioners therein named made a return specifying certain pieces of ground; but in both instances the returns were ended by the Court of King's Bench. With respect to the merchants' representations of 1762 and the commission which issued thereupon, see B.M., Add. MSS. 35906, ff. 205–206, 207, 209, 211, 213, 219–221, 227; and P.R.O., Treasury Papers, Bdl. 435, Nos. 35, 36. For various papers on the efforts of 1764 and 1765, see *ibid.*, Bdl. 435, Nos. 27, 37, 38; Bdl. 445, Nos. 317, 318; and P.R.O., Treas. Out-letters, Cust., XXVIII, 187–190. See also Charles Capper, *The Port and Trade of London* (London, 1862), pp. 144–145.

[3] P.R.O., Treasury Papers, Bdl. 408, No. 88, Cust. Comrs. to Lords of Treas., 1761, Aug. 12. This report is of interest in connection with the Commissioners' exercise of this authority. In 1761 ten or twelve ships from South Carolina loaded with rice, which had been entered and upon which duty had been paid, lay in the Thames undischarged because there was no room for them at the legal quays, and the Customs Commissioners refused to grant permission for their cargo to be unshipped at a sufferance wharf. Some of the rice had been unloaded into lighters and suffered damage. In desperation the merchants petitioned the Lords of the Treasury to grant them relief. Upon the petition being referred to them, the Customs Board reported that they had always been very tender in the use of their authority to permit unloading at a sufferance quay, except in cases of single ships and of absolute necessity, and that on this occasion they had not been able to grant so general a request for so many ships without the approbation of the Treasury and without proof of immediate necessity. Having been attended by the merchants concerned and the proper officers, however, and it having been alleged that part of the cargoes were damaged and that it would be a considerable time before they could be regularly landed at lawful quays, the Board stated that it had no objection in this case to granting the petitioners' request if the Lords approved, hoping that such a favor might not subsequently be drawn into precedent without the special authority of the Lords of the Treasury. By 1783 the Commissioners may have been a little more lenient in matters of this kind, for in that year they informed the Treasury Board that they never refused permission for landing goods at a sufferance wharf upon application being made for that purpose, and that when sufficient

ORGANIZATION OF THE PORT OF LONDON 127

became insufficient, sufferance wharves were appointed for the discharge of goods. By 1795 these had a frontage on the river of more than 1,200 yards [1] and afforded considerable relief from the overcrowded condition of the legal quays. Although the sufferance wharves were regulated by the Customs Commissioners, many of them were owned privately by wharfingers and often they were inconvenient for the use of the merchants. Some of them were situated at a great distance from the legal quays; to several there was no access by land save through the dwelling-houses of the proprietors; others excluded all goods but those belonging to the proprietor; extra fees had to be paid to customs officers for goods landed at those places. In 1789 the Customs Commissioners remedied many of those abuses by means of much-needed reforms.[2]

Along the river and for a short distance inland were scattered many warehouses where goods were stored until they were delivered out or condemned; but it was not until the Warehousing Act of 1803 that the modern system of warehouses came into being. Some distance down the river at Deptford was the Tobacco Burning Ground or "the King's Tobacco Pipe," as it was popularly known, where damaged and bad tobacco was destroyed, and seized ships that were of no use to the service were burned.[3]

Most of the streets leading to the Custom House were very narrow, crooked, and steep, which caused continual crowding and made them dangerous to traffic. Because of their narrowness, carts had to go on the quays and goods had to remain on the quays for some length of time, which added to their crowded condition. Confusion in the streets not only delayed shipping but encouraged all kinds of petty pilfering.[4]

---

proof was laid before them that a cargo was damaged and required despatch, or in cases of absolute want or scarcity of lighters, or when ships had on board stores for His Majesty's dockyards, or on any other real exigency, they almost constantly consented to the removal of the ship from the stream to such sufferance quays or the King's Yards as the case might be. *Ibid.,* Bdl. 587, No. 360, Cust. Comrs. to Lords of Treas., 1783, June 6.

[1] Actually 3,676 feet. *Parliamentary Papers,* XLVII, *Repts.,* XVII, H.C. No. 129, p. xxv (1796), "Rept. from Com. on Port of London."

[2] *Parliamentary Papers,* LIII, *Repts.,* XXIII, H.C. No. 154, pp. 163-164, App. G. 26 (1799), "Second Rept. from Sel. Com. on Port of London."

[3] See Cust. Ho. Lib., Extracts Board Minutes, II, "Tobacco Ground," III, V, "Tobacco Burning Ground." It is a curious fact that at one time a woman was given the responsibility of bringing the damaged tobacco from the quays to the burning ground. *Ibid.,* III, 636, 1762, Sept. 7.

[4] On the condition of the streets, see *Parliamentary Papers,* LIII, *Repts.,* XXIII, H.C. No. 154, pp. 154-156, App. G. 17 (1799), "Second Rept. from Sel. Com. on

128 ORGANIZATION OF THE ENGLISH CUSTOMS

The Custom House was the center of a scene of hubbub; here lighters, carts, and scales operated in a medley of bustle. Skippers and officers, glutmen,[1] and passengers hurried about their respective duties in such a way that Gwynn writes in 1766, "it is astonishing how so much business can possibly be carried on in a place which is so extremely crowded, and consequently perpetually confused. Those only can form an idea of it whose business or curiosity prompt them to become spectators of this scene of hurry and confusion."[2]

There were two Custom Houses during the century, neither of them at any date large enough to accommodate the business of the Port of London; indeed, various additions had to be made to the main buildings time and again. The first Custom House, planned by Christopher Wren, was burned in 1714-5. Its successor may be considered the seat of customs administration during the century. Built of brick and stone, it "was designed to stand for ages."[3] The center, set back from the river and parallel with it, was long and narrow, while the wings extended toward the river. Below each wing ran a colonnade passage of the Tuscan order, while the upper story was adorned with Ionic columns. Underneath on each side were large warehouses for the reception of goods, and entrances which led through into the streets on the north side. The Custom House was on two floors, the middle part of the upper one being occupied by a magnificent room known as the Long Room, where the accounting offices of the Port of London were located. At the east end of the Custom House appear to have been the offices of the Commissioners and presumably those of the central department.[4]

The most striking feature of the building was the Long Room, extending nearly the whole length of the House. Unfortunately information about the interior and business of the room is meager owing to the destruction of practically all the official Board and London records in the Custom House fire of 1814. From an old print of the

---

Port of London"; *Parliamentary Papers*, XLVII, *Repts.*, XVII, H.C. No. 129, App. E e (1796), "Rept. from Com. on Port of London."

[1] Glutmen were extra laborers who assisted in the waterside business.

[2] John Gwynn, *London and Westminster Improved* (London, 1766), p. 106.

[3] For a brief description of the London Custom House see John Entick, *New and Accurate History and Survey of London* (1766), IV, 325-326; Knight, *London* (1842), II, 408. William Maitland, *History and Survey of London* (London, 1756), II, opp. p. 1033, includes a picture of the Custom House.

[4] P.R.O., Treas. Out-letters, Cust., XVIII, 93, Cust. Comrs. to Lords of Treas., 1721, Mar. 14; see XVIII, 94, Treasury warrant, 1722, Mar. 30.

ORGANIZATION OF THE PORT OF LONDON 129

Long Room,[1] several casual references in contemporary descriptions of London, and a few of the extracts from the Board Minutes, something of the life in the room may still be reconstructed. The public entrance was on the north side near the west end. The attention of any one entering the room would immediately be drawn to the raised platform at the far east end, on which at one time sat one or more of the Customs Commissioners and the Bench Officers or chief officials of London Port, in superintendence of the business of the room. Behind the Bench was a door through which the officials might retire into an adjoining room when their presence was not required on the Bench. Along the river side of the room were rows of counters, separated into offices for the different branches of business by low wooden divisions. Above each office was posted the table of fees which belonged to it,[2] and late in the period officers were directed to have the names of their offices painted over their seats.[3] On the opposite side of the room were tables and a number of similar counters. These compact sections with several officers in each must have been sadly crowded, for a return of the Bench Officers to a Board minute in 1721 indicates that three feet were allowed to each officer and clerk in the Long Room.[4] Indeed upon a minute of the Board in 1720 which forbade clerks and other persons to sit outside the counters in the Long Room, the patent officers at the Bench presented a memorial to the Commissioners desiring them to reconsider the order.[5] Insufficient space would surely be the only reason for such a request, and crowded numbers must account for the odd minute which directed that air trunks were to be attached to the ceiling "to convey the foul vapor," on a proposal "of Rev. Dr. Hales."[6] Toward the close of the period, conditions had become so intolerable that an additional Long Room had to be provided, and in 1774 several offices, among them that of the coast and coal business, were removed into it.[7]

On rush days at the Custom House the line of merchants, brokers,[8]

[1] The print, dated 1808, is in the library of the Custom House.
[2] As indicated by Cust. Ho. Lib., Extracts Board Minutes, I, "Long Room," 1725, Mar. 3.
[3] *Ibid.*, III, 345, 1767, Apr. 30.
[4] *Ibid.*, I, "Long Room," 1721, June 12.
[5] *Ibid.*, I, "Long Room," 1720, Sept. 15.
[6] *Ibid.*, III, 312, 1760, Sept. 30.
[7] *Ibid.*, III, 312, 1774, July 27; 313, 1774, Aug. 23.
[8] At the beginning of the period the Custom House was full of stock-jobbers, brokers, wharfingers, and watermen who daily crowded at the seats of the officers to the disturbance of the merchants or their known brokers, whereby, "diverse times

and masters appears to have formed at the public door on the north side of the room and extended down the middle to the east end where entries were made before the Bench Officers. From there the merchant went to the particular division in which he needed to transact his business. What a gay cosmopolitan scene a busy day must have afforded! Orientals in their turbans and flowing gowns, Chinamen with sleek queues, hale and crude colonials, professional brokers from the City, weather-beaten skippers, and occasional dignified London merchants or smartly dressed dandies—all equipped with their papers and any necessary money-bags—stood in line together and supped their tea and ate their buns, bought from a buxom lass or an attentive fellow who served them while they waited. Of the Long Room Defoe could say that "the Croud of People who appear there, and the Business they do, is not to be explained by Words, nothing of that Kind in *Europe* is like it." [1] The tremendous sums that daily were paid for duties may well have excited his even keener enthusiasm: "In the long room it's a pretty pleasure to see the multitude of payments that are made there in a morning. I heard Count Tallard say, that nothing gave him so true and great an idea of the richness and grandeur of this nation as this, when he saw it after the Peace of Ryswick." [2]

At times one or more of the Commissioners themselves superintended the business of the Long Room.[3] As they surrendered some of their lesser duties, however, and became fewer in numbers when the English and Scottish establishments were separated, it is doubtful if they very often attended there in person. The practical direction of the business was given to the Bench Officers, the chief officials of the Port of London, who sat in august ceremony on the raised platform at the east end of the Long Room. They were the deputies of the

---

Errors have happened to the Inconvenience and prejudice of his Ma[ty] Customes and Ignorant persons who have trusted Such pretended Clerks to pass Entrys for them, have been deceived of their Money mistaken Entrys have passed and some times no Entrys at all. and also diverse other private and Sinisters designes are there negotiated & transacted by them." In 1697 upon a memorial of the Commissioners, the Lords of the Treasury directed that the Usher should turn such persons out and that the customs officers should not permit them to sit in the Custom House. At various other times throughout the period, the Usher was obliged to expel such undesirables, particularly fraudulent brokers. P.R.O., Treas. Out-letters, Cust., XIII, 349, Treasury warrant, 1697, June 3.

[1] Daniel Defoe, *A Tour Thro' the whole Island of Great Britain*, edited by G. D. H. Cole (London, 1927), I, 344.

[2] Daniel Defoe, *A Journey through England*, I, 237, as quoted by Peter Cunningham, *A Handbook for London Port Past and Present* (London, 1849), I, 254.

[3] See *supra*, Ch. II, p. 76.

ORGANIZATION OF THE PORT OF LONDON 131

Collector-Inwards, of the Collector-Outwards, of the Controller, of the Surveyor of the Port of London, and of the Surveyor-General; and no other officer, unless he held a deputation from the royal patentees, had a right to sit upon the Bench.[1] The patent parts of these offices were the political plums of the customs, and a list of their principals would constitute an imposing array of some of the proudest names of the eighteenth-century British peerage. Thus, at the end of the period in 1792, the First Earl of Liverpool was Collector-Inwards, the Duke of Manchester Collector-Outwards, the Duke of Newcastle, and afterwards the Earl of Guilford, Controller In and Out, and Lord Stowel Surveyor of Subsidies and Petty Customs. These men never attended at the Custom House except upon their admittance to office, on which occasion they appear to have been accompanied to the Bench with much pomp by the Commissioners themselves. They did none of the work of their offices but merely appointed their deputies and clerks and drew the lucrative emoluments accruing to the office by patent.[2] There was friction at times between the Board and these patentees with regard to the execution of the duty by the deputies,

---

[1] Cust. Ho. Lib., Extracts Board Minutes, I, "Bench Officers," 1698, Dec. 13. The Usher of the Long Room was a Bench Officer, but he did not rank in importance with these men.

[2] *First Rept. Comrs. of Cust. on Cust.* [Cd. 2186], p. 5, H.C. (1857), iii. A number of these patents were of long standing: for example, the Earl of Manchester was appointed Collector-Outwards by patent of 27 Chas. II, Mar. 18, as indicated in Cust. Ho. Lib., Extracts Board Minutes, I, "Bench Officers," 1714, Aug. 4. A more serious feature of some of the patents was their grant for a duration of several lives, "when so many accidents might any day throw it [the responsibility for the execution of the office of Collector-Outwards] upon persons neither wise enough to take so proper a part, nor capable (as in the case of executors and trustees) to make such concessions as might be eventually necessary to the public interest." (Hist. MSS. Com., *Fourteenth Rept.*, App. Part IV, *The Manuscripts of Lord Kenyon* [Cd. 7571], p. 513 (1894), Thurlow to ——, 1783, Jan. 4.) For the Duke of Manchester's defense of his patent, see P.R.O., Chatham Papers, Bdl. 284, "D of Manchester Custom House Office."

The income from these offices was considerable. Their annual average value for the years 1772-1774, after all payments to deputies and for taxes had been made, was as follows:

Collector-Inwards (Sir Horatio Mann), £2,153. 13s. 8½d.
Collector-Outwards (George, Duke of Manchester), £1,944. 0s. 5d.
Controller Inwards and Outwards (Henry, Duke of Newcastle), £1,433. 2s. 6d.
Surveyor-General (Right Honorable Lord Pelham), £1,519. 1s. 5½d.
Surveyor of London Port (Henry, Lord Stanwell), £1,302. 15s. 4d.

B.M., Add. MSS. 8133, ff. 8–9, "An Account of the Officers employed in the Revenue of the Customs in England with the Value of their Places, arising from Salaries Fees and other Perquisites," Part II. See also P.R.O., Chatham Papers, Bdl. 285, "An Extract from the Lists of Useless & Sinecure Offices, mark'd A. & B.," enclosure in Musgrave to Shelburne, 1782, Dec. 10.

but in such cases the authority of the Board and the responsibility of the principal were clearly defined.[1]

The Bench Officers, as the controlling officers of the Port of London, saw that all laws and regulations relating to customs and trade were carried into effect in that port. They communicated with the solicitors and general-surveyors and the head officers of the landing and shipping departments respecting various parts of the business, and dealt with merchants and their agents upon questions arising in connection with their cargoes. Early in the period at least, they were desired to inspect the work at the waterside personally from time to time, by going over the quays and noting any negligence and absence of officers; but their immediate province was the superintendence of the business of the Long Room. Each of these officers was responsible for the work of his own department: he assigned the duties to his clerks, checked their attendance, saw that all orders relating to their business were duly observed, inspected their books, and settled his balances daily. All entries of ships were made before two of the Bench officers, at which time the necessary oaths were administered by them. The most important function of these officers, however, was that of advising the Board upon various questions that arose in practice; and they seem to have had no little part in determining the policy of the institution. Thus they gave notice of revenue laws that were expiring, indicated any weak points in them, made suggestions as to what new legislation should be proposed to Parliament, gave their observations on depending bills, and prepared necessary accounts called for by Parliament and the Treasury.[2]

An officer known as the Usher of the Long Room [3] arouses some curiosity, since early in the period he combined the duty of a Housekeeper of the Custom House with that of a Bench Officer in the Long

---

[1] See *supra*, Ch. I, pp. 19-20.

[2] The duties of the Bench Officers in the eighteenth century were undoubtedly the same as those performed in 1851, as indicated by the Collector of the Customs in London in that year. (*Second Rept. Sel. Com. on Cust.*, H.C. 604, pp. 196-198 (1851), Part I, Minutes of Evidence, xi; see also *Repts. of Comrs.*, 1787, III, 433, App. No. 54, "Fourteenth Rept.," 1785.) For the relationship of the Bench Officers to parliamentary legislation and accounts, see for examples Cust. Ho. Lib., Extracts Board Minutes, I, "Commissioners," 1723, May 7; 1709, Nov. 25; IV, 18, 1781, Jan. 9. Regarding their survey of the quays, see for instance *ibid.*, II, "Quays," 1718, July 8. In connection with the preparation of accounts, see *ibid.*, IV, 80, 1776, Jan. 23; 81, 1777, Sept. 3.

[3] See *Rules of the Water-side* (1715), p. 84; *Repts. of Comrs.*, 1787, III, 464-465, App. No. 81, "Fourteenth Rept.," 1785; Cust. Ho. Lib., Extracts Board Minutes, II, entries under "Usher Long Room."

ORGANIZATION OF THE PORT OF LONDON 133

Room. Upon the appointment of a separate person as House-keeper, the duties of the Usher appear to have been confined to the Long Room. There he acted as a kind of general supervisor who not only kept order in the Room but also transmitted the Board's orders to the patent officers and saw to the enforcement of Long Room regulations laid down by the Commissioners. As a Bench Officer he was closely connected with the administration of oaths in the export business.

The accounting of the customs business in the Port of London was done by four distinct classes of officials who had their desks in the Long Room: those who dealt with imports only, those who were concerned primarily with exports, those who served as officers for imports and exports alike, and those who acted as additional checks on the foreign business in and out.[1]

The department of the Collector-Inwards had the supervision of the import business, for it was in this division that entries of goods inwards were made and the duties on them computed and paid.[2] The Chief Deputy of the Collector-Inwards, as the executive officer of this class, was responsible for the transaction of the entire business of the department by the several deputies and clerks and for the collection of all import duties and their remittance to the Receiver-General. Entries of all ships arriving in London from abroad were made by masters before the Deputy Collector-Inwards and another Bench Officer.[3] These reports were deposited with the Clerk of the Ships' Entries, whose Assistant laid before a Commissioner a daily account of all vessels entering inwards in order that he might appoint the proper officers to discharge them.[4] Import duties were assessed by the Clerk

---

[1] Cust. Ho. Lib., Estab., Eng., Wales, Plant. to 1782, pp. 10–15; *Repts. of Comrs.*, 1787, III, 86–89, "Fourteenth Rept.," 1785. For the organization of offices in this chapter the establishment book known as Estab., Eng., Wales, Plant. to 1782 has been followed (in conjunction with the "Fourteenth Report" of the Commissioners of Accounts) since it is the most comprehensive of the establishment books, including, as it does, dates of the creation and abolition of many offices and of various regulations governing them. Because these two sources are used, the numbers of officers under certain divisions in this chapter are not necessarily those of the year 1786, as indicated by the establishment book of that year; for this reason slight deviations will be noted in some cases. Such numbers do, however, mark the extent of the London establishment at approximately the close of the period.

[2] See *Rules of the Water-side* (1715), p. 81.

[3] *Repts. of Comrs.*, 1787, III, 16, "Thirteenth Rept.," 1785.

[4] *Ibid.*, III, 437, App. No. 58, 444, App. No. 63, "Fourteenth Rept.," 1785; see Cust. Ho. Lib., Extracts Board Minutes, I, entries under "Clerk of the Ships Entries."

of the Rates when business was not too heavy,[1] and there were three separate Computers of special duties as well.[2] The actual collection of duties and receipt of bonds was in the hands of three Receivers—those of the Grand Receipt and of the Plantation and Wine Duties respectively. Separate collectors of these two latter branches were necessary because of the importance of the commodities and the difficulty in the computation of their duties; one receiver was sufficient to attend to the receipt on all other goods at importation.[3]

The system of controls on the collection of all duties in the Long Room will be examined in connection with the division of officers for both the import and export business. In the department of the Collector-Inwards, however, were two Examiners and a Clerk of the Warrants (or Copying Clerk of the Entries Inwards) who checked the computation and receipt of the duties.[4] When goods were reexported, debentures were granted to the merchant after a comparison of the goods listed on them as shipped had been made with the entries of all shipments kept by the Clerk of the Certificates under the Collector-Inwards.[5] The Receivers paid out the sums for debentures and imprests.

Several other officers are recorded as belonging to this department, but their business became quite useless during the period. The patent office of Collector of Petty Customs Inwards still existed; but what few duties remained under the heading of Petty Customs were received by the Collector-Inwards, and the other work belonging to this officer, the registration of alien entries, could have been done

---

[1] *Repts. of Comrs.*, 1787, III, 16, "Thirteenth Rept.," 1785. This officer also reckoned the duties repaid on debentures and the allowances for damage and overentry. P.R.O., Treas. Out-letters, Cust., XXXII, 47, deputation to Clerk of Rates, 1778, Mar. 30.

[2] There was a Computer of the Imposts on Tobacco, a Computer of the Fifteen Per cent on Muslins and White Calicoes, and a Computer of Unrated East India Goods. Cust. Ho. Lib., Estab., Eng., Wales, Plant. to 1782, pp. 11–12. For the duties of the Computer of the Fifteen Per cent on Muslins, see *Repts. of Comrs.*, 1787, III, 450–451, App. No. 71, "Fourteenth Rept.," 1785.

[3] *Ibid.*, III, 446–447, App. No. 65, 447, App. No. 66, 448, App. No. 67. On the receipt of bonds, see B.M., Add. MSS. 18903, f. 29, "The Method of taking Bonds for the Duties of goods imported," 1714, Oct. 26.

[4] There was an Examiner of all Duties Inwards except Wines and Currants and an Examiner of the Duties on Wines and Currants. (Cust. Ho. Lib., Estab., Eng., Wales, Plant. to 1782, p. 12.) These officers are mentioned also in Cust. Ho. Lib., Extracts Board Minutes. For reference to the Clerk of the Warrants, see *Repts. of Comrs.*, 1787, III, 17, 227, App. No. 18, "Thirteenth Rept.," 1785.

[5] *Ibid.*, III, 463–464, App. No. 80, "Fourteenth Rept.," 1785.

ORGANIZATION OF THE PORT OF LONDON 135

elsewhere.[1] Similarly, the only business of the Register of Warrants, transacted by deputy, was to keep copies of the entries of all vessels which reported inwards at the Port of London and return them at specified times to the Exchequer. Such a relic of a practice of the farming days should long before have been abolished.[2]

The officers in the Long Room engaged in the export business constituted that branch of the office of the Collector-Outwards known as the Cocket Office.[3] It was in this department that entries of ships clearing from the Port of London were made, the proper bonds taken, and export duties paid. The patent officer of this division, the Collector-Outwards, executed the entire duty of the office by a Chief Deputy, another deputy, an assistant, a Receiver, and several cocket-writers. When a ship sailed on an outward voyage, it was entered by the master or owner with the deputy of the Collector-Outwards who computed the duties, took an account of them, and paid them weekly into the Central Office. This officer also calculated bounties, made out any bonds that might be required on a particular exportation, and granted certificates which testified to the landing of goods at importation.[4] Since outward duties were few, no special officer was necessary for their calculation; the deputy assessed them and they were collected by the Receiver, who as Chief Cocket-writer made out the cocket for the merchant which authorized the export officers at the waterside to permit the shipping of the goods.[5]

As in the import division, the computation and receipt of duties was controlled by a group of officers who acted as checks on both imports and exports. Within the department of the Collector-Outwards, however, was the Copying Clerk Outwards, who compared the documents containing descriptions of the goods and sent an entry of each bill to the Inspector-General of Imports and Exports.[6] The Usher of the Long Room, whose deputy participated in the administration of oaths taken on goods exported and on debentures, together

---

[1] *Repts. of Comrs.*, 1787, III, 109, 449, App. No. 69.
[2] *Ibid.*, III, 102–103, 425, App. No. 45, "Fourteenth Rept.," 1785.
[3] The other branch was the Coast Office, described in a later division.
[4] For information on the Collector-Outwards, see *ibid.*, III, 238–239, App. No. 25, "Thirteenth Rept.," 1785; P.R.O., Treas. Out-letters, Cust., XVIII, 380–381, Treasury warrant, 1723, Nov. 25; *Rules of the Water-side* (1715), p. 81. See also *Repts. of Comrs.*, 1787, III, 457–458, App. No. 74, "Fourteenth Rept.," 1785.
[5] See *ibid.*, III, 460, App. No. 77.
[6] *Ibid.*, III, 24, "Thirteenth Rept.," 1785.

with two watchmen who came under his supervision, must be included in the division of officers in the Long Room for the export business.[1]

A useless fragment of the early days of this export organization under the Commission existed in the office of the Collector of the Great Customs on Wool and Leather Exported. Since the export of wool had been discouraged, this Collector had come to have only the receipt of duties on exported leather and the supervision of coastwise shipping of wool.[2] A Controller checked the Collector in these few duties.[3] The work of this office, which had become much diminished, properly fell in the department of the Collector-Outwards, and these two offices which were held by patent should have been discontinued.[4]

The group of officers in the Long Room employed in the division which dealt with both imports and exports operated for the most part as checks upon the Collectors Inwards and Outwards. The most important officer in this department was the Controller of the Customs in the Port of London, the official check on the collection of all the duties. With the Collector he had the joint safe-keeping of deposits and bonds given in payment of duties, and he returned regular accounts thereof to the proper officers in the Central Office. From 1712 on he also approved merchants' securities for the duties on goods imported.[5] The office, held by patent, was executed by a Chief Deputy, who as a Bench Officer was responsible for the work of the department, and by separate deputies, with their clerks, for the import, export, and coastwise business. The Deputy Controller-Inwards was a check on the receipt of all duties paid at importation. He made a separate computation of such duties, compared his calculation with that of other checks, and every week examined the receipts and payments of the Receivers with his own account. He had a like control over the computation and payment of drawbacks.[6] The Deputy Controller-Outwards had the same kind of a check on duties paid to the Collector-Outwards at exportation as did the Deputy Controller-Inwards on the import account, and he also examined the computation and payment of bounties.[7] The work of the Deputy Controller-

---

[1] See *Repts. of Comrs.*, 1787, III, 464–465, App. No. 81, "Fourteenth Rept.," 1785.
[2] See *Rules of the Water-side* (1715), p. 83; and *Repts. of Comrs.*, 1787, III, 461, App. No. 78, "Fourteenth Rept.," 1785.
[3] *Ibid.*, III, 462–463, App. No. 79.
[4] *Ibid.*, III, 110.
[5] P.R.O., Treas. Out-letters, Cust., XIV, 10, Treasury warrant, 1712, Feb. 20.
[6] See *Repts. of Comrs.*, 1787, III, 228, App. No. 19, "Thirteenth Rept.," 1785.
[7] *Ibid.*, III, 242, App. No. 28.

ORGANIZATION OF THE PORT OF LONDON 137

Coastwise will be described in connection with the organization of the Coast Department.

It would seem as though this office furnished an adequate control over the calculation and receipt of duties. In the eighteenth century, however, two other offices existed for the same general purpose, those of the Surveyor of the Port of London and the Surveyor-General, mentioned in Chapter III. The first of these offices, held by patent, was executed by a Chief Deputy who acted as a check on the computation and receipt of duties paid inwards, and by a Deputy Outwards who held the same position with respect to duties paid at exportation, together with several clerks.[1] Because the business transacted in this office was duplicated in other departments, the entire office and its deputies and clerks should have been discontinued. The Surveyor-General likewise constituted a check on imports and exports. As a patent officer, he discharged his duty by clerks and deputies, of whom one acted as Chief Deputy, another as a control on the Grand and Plantation Receipts, and still a third as a check on the Wine Branch and duties outwards.[2] This office also was useless, since its function was adequately performed elsewhere.[3]

One other officer, the Customer of Cloth and Petty Customs (Outwards), with his Controller, is included in this section on the establishment list. His sole business was to receive duties on white woollen cloth shipped out and to collect fees from alien exporters to be divided between himself, the Controller, the Surveyor, and the Survey-General. The Collector-Outwards should properly have taken over the collection of the duties, and this office, with that of its Controller, also should have been abolished.[4]

Additional checks on the import and export business were provided by five jerquers with their clerks and by the Register of Certificate Cockets or Debentures with his assistants. The office of the jerquers

---

[1] For the duties of this office, see *Repts. of Comrs.*, 1787, III, 23–24, 229–230, App. No. 20, 243, App. No. 29; *ibid.*, III, 437–438, App. No. 59, 556–557, App. No. 143, "Fourteenth Rept.," 1785. Cf. *Rules of the Water-side* (1715), p. 82.

[2] For reference to the work of the Surveyor-General, see *ibid.*, p. 82; *Repts. of Comrs.*, 1787, III, 123–124, 230–231, App. No. 21, 244, App. No. 30, "Thirteenth Rept.," 1785; *ibid.*, III, 427–428, App. No. 48, 556–557, App. No. 144, "Fourteenth Rept.," 1785.

[3] See recommendation of the abolition of this office as well as that of the Surveyor of the Port of London by the Commissioners of Accounts in 1785. *Ibid.*, III, 99, 102.

[4] *Ibid.*, III, 109–110. With respect to the Customer of Cloth and Petty Customs (Outwards), see *ibid.*, III, 435–436, App. No. 57. On the controller, see *ibid.*, III, 436–437, App. No. 58. Cf. *Rules of the Water-side* (1715), p. 83.

had been in existence before the eighteenth century, but two of them were added during this period.¹ These five officials divided their work in general according to the port from which ships arrived. The Northern and Southern European Jerquers dealt with cargoes from the ports of North and South Europe respectively. The Wine Officer attended to all ships having ten tun of wine or more on board. The Southern Plantation Jerquer looked after vessels coming from the plantations, while the one of the Northern Plantation, who was appointed in 1776,² seems to have taken over the ships that the other officers did not want.³

It was the duty of the jerquer⁴ to compare the description of the cargo on the master's report with the books of the land-waiters who had supervised the landing and weighing of the goods in order to see that they agreed. All allowances made by the land-waiters for damage, tare, and the like were examined to see that they were fair and their computations accurate. The jerquers acted as a close check on the land-waiters, reporting to the Board from time to time those officers who were negligent in turning in their books or careless in the preparation of them.⁵ Finally, these officers compared the land-waiters' books with the accounts of the tide-waiters who supervised the delivery of the ship, and kept a record of the goods unloaded. Upon finding that the master had made a correct report, the jerquer calculated the allowance of portage money due him.

The Register of Certificate Cockets and his clerks had the granting of debentures. After a debenture had been examined by the proper checks and the drawback computed, it was brought to this officer,

---

¹ The fourth jerquer was added in 1727-8 (see P.R.O., Treas. Out-letters, Cust., XIX, 193, Treasury warrant?, 1727, Feb. 23) and the other in 1776 (see note below).

² *Ibid.*, XXXI, 115, Cust. Comrs. to Lords of Treas., 1776, Feb. 11; Treasury warrant, 1776, Dec. 23.

³ See Cust. Ho. Lib., Extracts Board Minutes, III, 224, 1773, July 2. The duties of this jerquer were prescribed in 1773. See *ibid.*, III, 225, 1773, Dec. 1; 228, 1777 Jan. 28, Feb. 8.

⁴ For miscellaneous references to the duties of the jerquers, see *ibid.*, I, III, IV, entries under "Jerquers;" *Repts. of Comrs.*, 1787, III, 471-472, App. No. 83, 473, App. No. 84, "Fourteenth Rept.," 1785.

⁵ Land-waiters were subject to penalties for not delivering their books to the jerquers within a specified time; upon various occasions they suffered loss of salary and suspension and were obliged to secure a jerquer's certificate for absence unless their accounts were up to date. The jerquers reported delinquents to the Board and annually at Christmas laid their observations on the conduct of the land-waiters before the Commissioners. See numerous references in this connection in Cust. Ho. Lib., Extracts Board Minutes, I, III, IV, entries under "Jerquers."

ORGANIZATION OF THE PORT OF LONDON

who in turn gave it his examination, wrote an order for payment, signed it, and delivered it to the Commissioners for their signature. Upon its being authorized, he gave it to the merchant.[1]

A comparison of the offices of the Long Room in the late eighteenth century with those of the first establishment under the commission in 1671 [2] reveals the age of organization. With the exception, in the import department, of the Computers and two special clerks,[3] and, in the control division, of the Register of Certificate Cockets and one jerquer, it appears that all the offices that have been discussed were in existence in 1671. The entire Long Room department, then, dates in its final form at least as far back as the first organization under the Commission. The only alteration during the period was the addition of extra clerks and deputies to deal with the increase in business. Such little change, however, is deplorable in view of the continuation of many sinecures and useless offices. The offices of Collector-Inwards, Collector-Outwards, Controller Inwards and Outwards, and Usher of the Long Room had been converted into sinecures of which the patent part should have been abolished.[4] The duty attached to the sinecure offices of the Surveyor-General, the Surveyor of the Port of London, and the Register of Warrants was entirely worthless.[5] The

---

[1] See *Repts. of Comrs.*, 1787, III, 475, App. No. 87, "Fourteenth Rept.," 1785. Cf. P.R.O., Treasury Papers, Bdl. 507, Nos. 266–267, Cust. Comrs. to Lords of Treas., 1774, Nov. 22. This memorial sheds light upon conditions prevailing in the service, as well as upon the reasons for the establishment of this office. The Commissioners state, "That from the hurry or negligence with which the Clerks to the Patent Officers usually transact their business various Errors and informalities have been frequently discovered in the Computation of the Drawbacks and in other parts of the said Debentures to the prejudice of the Revenue which was also further subject to very great loss by persons not duly Authorized getting possession of Debentures and receiving the same which were afterwards obliged to be paid again to the proper Merchants entitled thereto. To prevent these Evils it was found necessary upwards of Sixty Years ago to Establish an Officer by the Name of the Register of Debentures and Certificate Cockets. . . . The Lords of the Treasury having always been very attentive to provide able and diligent Men for this important Employment, we have the pleasure to observe that it has fully answered the purposes of its Original Institution. But the Patent Officers having lately fallen into some of their former Inaccuracies we have been obliged to issue some further orders for their Government which the better to keep them to their duty will be attended with every considerable Additional trouble to the Register." In view of the additional business delegated to this office, the Commissioners recommended an increase in salary.

[2] Cust. Ho. Lib., An Establishment of the Officers of the Customs belonging to the Outports, 1671.

[3] Clerk of the Rates, Clerk of the Certificates.

[4] *Repts. of Comrs.*, 1787, III, 105–106, "Fourteenth Rept.," 1785.

[5] *Ibid.*, III, 99, 102–103.

three extra collectors, the Customer of Cloth and Petty Customs Outwards, the Collector of Petty Customs Inwards, and the Collector of the Great Customs on Wool and Leather Exported, were redundant, since their duties properly belonged to the Collectors for the import and export duties. The principals, together with their two Controllers, all of whom held office by patent, and four of whom were sinecurists, should have been dispensed with.[1] No alterations in these offices, however, were made until 1798.[2]

The officers of all these departments were paid by salaries and fees, and many of them by gratuities as well. The proportion of fees and gratuities to salaries in the various divisions as reported in 1785 is of some interest. In the import department, the ratio was nearly three and two thirds to one[3]; in the export section it was more than seventeen to one[4]; in the control division it was well over four and two thirds to one[5]; and in the class of additional checks, it was not quite half and half, salaries amounting to more than one sixth as much again as fees.[6]

Out on the wharves along the river-front and on board ships quayed or moored in the channel was the vast body of officers for the import, export, and coastwise business at the waterside. By approximately the end of the period, about 400 officers—not including the extra men—were engaged in the unlading, landing, examining, weighing, and warehousing of goods, concentrated from all parts of the world within the narrow limits of the Pool of London.[7] When it is considered that this number represents the import staff alone and includes neither the officers who saw to the clearing of goods outwards and coastwise nor the personnel of the warehouses and special departments nor the land- and water-guards, some estimate may be reached of the magnitude of the waterside organization for the practical business inwards.

The nucleus of the import system was the land-waiter, appointed by deputation of the Customs Commissioners upon a Treasury warrant. He had the supervision of the landing of all goods imported and the responsibility of seeing that they agreed with the warrant

---

[1] *Repts. of Comrs.*, 1787, III, 109–110.
[2] 38 Geo. III, c. 86, s. 1, 2, 3, 4, 5, 6, 7.
[3] *Repts. of Comrs.*, 1787, III, 87–88, "Fourteenth Rept.," 1785.
[4] *Ibid.*, III, 88.
[5] *Ibid.*, III, 87.
[6] *Ibid.*, III, 89.
[7] *Ibid.*, III, 90. Cf. Cust. Ho. Lib., Estab., Eng., Wales, Plant. to 1782, pp. 14–21.

ORGANIZATION OF THE PORT OF LONDON

for landing them, made out upon the merchant's entry and payment of duty.[1] There were thirty-seven land-waiters during the greater part of the period,[2] and nineteen more patent king's-waiters who transacted the same duty by their nineteen deputies. Land-waiters were assigned to the discharge of specific ships by the Customs Commissioners in rotation every week. A register of all vessels reporting inwards at the Port of London was laid before the appointing Commissioner daily, together with lists of land-waiters who were already stationed and the names of those who had no ships or were unavailable because of illness or absence. Above the name of the vessel the Commissioner wrote the names of the two land-waiters whom he chose to clear it. Despite occasional efforts to ensure a respectable equality in the appointment of such officers, the arrangement was unfair, since some land-waiters were continually employed with many ships which yielded good fees, while others had only spasmodic work and earned about one third as much.[3]

Upon the delivery of a ship, the land-waiter attended the unlading; supervised the weighing of the goods, making the proper allowances for damage, draught, and tare; and entered the marks, numbers, and weight of the articles in his Blue Book. Upon comparing the quantity of goods actually landed with the quantity on the warrant, and finding a surplus for which the merchant had not paid duties, he informed the importer, who made a post-entry and paid the necessary sums. Undoubtedly the bait of a fat fee induced the land-waiters to give merchants credit in such cases far too frequently, to the detriment of the revenue. After the ship had been entirely discharged and all duties paid, the officers referred their books to the land-surveyor for approval and then deposited them with the jerquers. The land-waiter, as "an officer of great trust," was subject to strict regulations which were enforced by the land-surveyors: he could not work singly

---

[1] For references to the general duties of the land-waiter, see *Repts. of Comrs.*, 1787, III, 482–483, App. No. 91, 472, App. No. 83, "Fourteenth Rept.," 1785; *Rules of the Water-side* (1715), p. 86; and, with particular reference to the outport land-waiter, Crouch, *Complete Guide to Officers* (1732), p. 5.

[2] Six of these men were added by Treasury warrant, dated 1718, Jan. 15. P.R.O., Treas. Out-letters, Cust., XVII, 144.

[3] With respect to the appointment of land-waiters to ships, see *Repts. of Comrs.*, 1787, III, 90, 485–486, App. No. 94, "Fourteenth Rept.," 1785. A minute of 1708 ordered that those land-waiters out of work should be preferably employed to those who had one or more ships undischarged. (Cust. Ho. Lib., Extracts Board Minutes, I, "Land Waiters," 1708, June 24.) By numerous other minutes as well, land-waiters were ordered not to apply to the Board for ships. See *ibid.*, I, "Land Waiters," 1712, Oct. 20; 1733, June 20; 1755, Aug. 13.

without his partner as a check, nor could he work at noon while the land-surveyor was gone to dinner; he was obliged to notify his superior officer of any irregularity and to secure his approval of allowances made; his books had to be carefully prepared with no erasures and returned to the jerquers within a specified time. These and many other minutes had for their end the protection of the revenue against fraudulent officers, and failure to comply therewith meant severe penalties.[1]

Throughout most of the period, nine land-surveyors, stationed for the most part at the Upper, Middle, and Lower Stations on the quays between the Tower and London Bridge, supervised the conduct of the land-waiters.[2] It was in the land-surveyors' office that the daily attendance of the land-waiters was checked and permission granted for temporary absence. From time to time the land-surveyors went over the quays to see that the land-waiters did their duty and observed the regulations governing them. They were present when goods of particular value were examined by these officers, and they settled or approved allowances for tare and damage, of which last they gave notice to the Bench Officers. Complaints against land-waiters were referred to the land-surveyor for investigation, and he reported regularly to the Board on the behavior of those men, particularly as regarded the return of their books to the jerquers. So important was this duty as a check on the land-waiters that the Board in 1781 stated that should any land-surveyor fail to report on the irregularity of a land-waiter, if the negligent land-surveyor could not be identified, a mulct would be inflicted on the whole staff.[3]

Since the land-surveyors were the superintending officers of the waterside import department, they had the management of others than land-waiters as well. They appointed constables [4] and gaugers [5] to the

[1] There are numerous minutes against delay in the delivery of books to jerquers and improper credit on post-entries. The minute for 1771, March 2, summarizes the main regulations made during the century. (Cust. Ho. Lib., Extracts Board Minutes, III, 294–296.) Various minutes under the heading "Land Waiters" in *ibid.*, I, and "Landingwaiters" in III, V, have to do with minor regulations.

[2] For a general account of numbers, location, and duties of the land-surveyors, see *Repts. of Comrs.*, 1787, III, 480–481, App. No. 89, "Fourteenth Rept.," 1785; *Rules of the Water-side* (1715), pp. 86, 92; and entries in Cust. Ho. Lib., Extracts Board Minutes, I, "Land Surveyors," III, V, "Landing Surveyors."

[3] *Ibid.*, V, 19–20, 1781, Sept. 28. Laxity in this office warranted an exceedingly harsh communication from the Commissioners in 1778. *Ibid.*, V, 13, 1778, Dec. 8.

[4] *Ibid.*, I, "Land Surveyors," 1740, Oct. 17.

[5] See *ibid.*, I, "Guagers," 1728, June 27.

ORGANIZATION OF THE PORT OF LONDON 143

proper stations on the quays; they supervised the Appointers of the Weighers [1]—upon whose selection of weighers they passed their approval—and searchers for a few years in the latter part of the period [2]; every Christmas they laid before the Board an account of the ages, abilities, and capacities of all officers under their survey—the land-waiters, weighers, and noon-tenders (men who relieved the watchmen at mid-day).[3] Two special surveyors, appointed to this staff in the early part of the period, assisted the land-surveyors in the examination of paper and baggage respectively.[4] An officer known as the Surveyor of the Quays had a check upon the attendance of all land-surveyors and other waterside officers.[5] By the seventeen-eighties, however, the inutility of these three offices had been demonstrated, and the Board resolved upon their discontinuance.[6]

Assisting in the unloading, carrying, weighing, and storing of goods were many petty officers on the quays whose places provided "pretty Livelihoods for the inferior Rank of People." The weighing department included a large number of these men. By approximately the end of the period about 225 weighers were stationed in the King's Warehouse, in the warehouses of East India goods, tobacco, cambrics, sugars, and bugles, and at the three stations on the quays in the import and export business, while about 212 extra weighers were employed from time to time when the work was particularly heavy.[7] Twenty-five of the weighers, known as the Weighers in Fee, were established by Treasury warrant, and as senior officers were always appointed

---

[1] Cust. Ho. Lib., Extracts Board Minutes, V, 11–12, 1778, July 31.

[2] *Ibid.*, III, 288, 1775, Aug. 9, Nov. 29; V, 6, 1776, Mar. 15, 19; 8, 1777, Oct. 2; 19, 1780, Oct. 13.

[3] *Ibid.*, I, "Land Surveyors," 1732, Oct. 6; III, 287, 1768, Dec. 29.

[4] See Cust. Ho. Lib., Estab., Eng., Wales, Plant. to 1782, p. 14. See also Cust. Ho. Lib., Extracts Board Minutes, II, "Surveyor of Baggage," "Surveyor of Paper."

[5] See *ibid.*, II, V, entries under "Surveyor of the Quays."

[6] Though this decision as it affected the Surveyor of Paper and the Surveyor of Baggage was made in 1783, a new Surveyor of Baggage was established in 1784 by Treasury warrant, the Treasury not having been apprised of the Board's minute for laying aside the office. See Cust. Ho. Lib., Estab., Eng., Wales, Plant. to 1782, p. 14; and Cust. Ho. Lib., Extracts Board Minutes, IV, 74, 1784, Jan. 13. With respect to the Surveyor of the Quays, see *ibid.*, V, 583, 1780, Nov. 29, Dec. 16; 1788, Apr. 11.

[7] With respect to these numbers, see *Repts. of Comrs.*, 1787, III, 90, "Fourteenth Rept.," 1785; Cust. Ho. Lib., Estab., Eng., Wales, Plant. to 1782, pp. 18–19. For numbers of weighers and instances of their increase during the period, see Cust. Ho. Lib., Extracts Board Minutes, entries under "Weighers" in II, III, V.

first to a ship. The Preferable Men, who numbered approximately 200, came next in the employment. It was the duty of the weighers to weigh the goods which had been landed and to call the result to the land-waiters or other officers with whom they worked for entry in the accounts. They also opened and repacked goods for examination at importation or before exportation.[1] Three gaugers gauged all commodities capable of liquid measure and, like the weighers, gave their figures to the land-waiter after the measurement had been made.[2] During the greater part of the period apparently, the weighers were under the immediate direction of three of their own Weighers in Fee. As Appointers of the Weighers, these officers selected the men for each ship entered inwards and delivered the lists of them to the land-waiters. The land-surveyors acted as a final check on the weighers.

Watchmen stationed about the Custom House, on the quays, and on board lighters guarded goods against pilferage after the other officers had finished their day's work. Forty-two of these men constituted the established department,[3] though near the close of the period the number of established and preferable men together totaled eighty-four and many extra men had been provided.[4] In 1725 one of the watchmen was designated an Appointer of the Watchmen,[5] and he was established as such five years later.[6] In the evenings he took the watchmen over the quays and left certain of them where the land-waiters had been working. Later in the evening he visited them to see that they were at work, and during the night the tide-surveyors and River Inspectors made the rounds to see that they were on duty. Watchmen were employed in turns, young men generally being placed on lighters and older officers on the shore and in warehouses.[7] Eighteen noon-tenders relieved the watchmen for two hours every noon, to receive bills from lighters bringing in goods from the ships to the land-

---

[1] On the weighing department in general, see Cust. Ho. Lib., Extracts Board Minutes, entries under "Weighers" in II, III, V; *Repts. of Comrs.*, 1787, III, 90, 487–488, App. No. 95, "Fourteenth Rept.," 1785.

[2] *Ibid.*, III, 484, App. No. 92; Cust. Ho. Lib., Extracts Board Minutes, I, entries under "Guagers," IV, "Gaugers."

[3] See *Rules of the Water-side* (1715), p. 92; Cust. Ho. Lib., Estab., Eng., Wales, Plant. to 1782, p. 21.

[4] *Repts. of Comrs.*, 1787, III, 90, "Fourteenth Rept.," 1785. See also Cust. Ho. Lib., Extracts Board Minutes, II, III, V, entries under "Watchmen."

[5] *Ibid.*, II, "Watchmen," 1725, July 14. Before this date and even after, the appointment of the watchmen was under the general supervision of the tide-surveyors.

[6] *Ibid.*, II, "Watchmen," 1730, Feb. 26.

[7] See *ibid.*, II, "Watchmen," 1727, Apr. 12. This appears to have been a practice throughout the period.

ORGANIZATION OF THE PORT OF LONDON 145

waiters and to take care of the goods on shore while the weighers were at dinner.[1]

The main offices for the import business at the waterside, those of the land- and king's-waiter, land-surveyor, weigher, and watchmen, were very old, all of them having been created long before 1696. The eighteenth century saw a tremendous increase in the number of officers who filled these positions and, unfortunately, the persistence of the nineteen patent king's-waiters who were not discontinued until 1798.[2] With the possible exception of the watchmen, all the men took fees or gratuities, some of them authorized, many of them not. And all but the deputy king's-waiters had salaries.[3] The land-surveyors received a salary and fees and, after 1764,[4] £35—equally divided among them—for every sale which they superintended in the Long Room. For some years the first six of the land-surveyors were given in addition a present of spices from the East India Company valued at £5. 4s. The land-waiters had small salaries and fees from the merchant, according to the number and value of the ships to which they were appointed; the deputy king's-waiters received only fees and gratuities, though their principals drew a good salary and fees besides.[5] Weighers in Fee had a salary and fees and gratuities, while the Preferable Men were paid by incidents and day pay. Watchmen earned a salary and so did the gaugers. If the latter were employed on the lawful quays, they got gratuities also; and if on the sufferance wharves, fees. Altogether, as reported in 1785, salaries exceeded the other emoluments of these officers by more than one eighth. The use of fees for the remuneration of these waterside officers constituted one of the greatest needs of reform during the period.

The searcher, who was the central officer of the export department, superintended the outward business on the quay. His position was one demanding the utmost skill and integrity, for, with no supervision but that of another searcher, he certified the shipping of all goods entitled to a drawback or bounty in accordance with which the debentures

---

[1] See Cust. Ho. Lib., Extracts Board Minutes, II, entries under "Noon-Tenders," V, "Noontenders"; *Repts. of Comrs.*, 1787, III, 487, App. No. 95, "Fourteenth Rept.," 1785.
[2] 38 Geo. III, c. 86, s. 2, 3, 4.
[3] With respect to the payment of officers at the waterside for the import business, see *Repts. of Comrs.*, 1787, III, 90–91, "Fourteenth Rept.," 1785.
[4] See Cust. Ho. Lib., Extracts Board Minutes, III, 286, 1763, July 20, Oct. 12; 1764, Feb. 28.
[5] For reference to abuses of patent king's-waiters in pecuniary exactions upon the appointment of their deputies, see P.R.O., Treas. Out-letters, Cust., XVIII, 377, Cust. Comrs. to Lords of Treas., 1723, May 16.

were made out for the merchant. So responsible a position did the searchers hold that the Commissioners in 1785 informed them that they would not admit private affairs or trifling accidents as an excuse for neglect of duty "in Officers who have such an important trust as the drawing upon the Revenue by their Certificates for upwards of Two Millions annually." [1] Upon receiving from the exporter the cocket which contained the entry of all articles to be cleared on a particular vessel, the searcher attended the shipping of the cargo. He checked all packages, as they were placed on board ship, by comparing the weight, number, or measure with those marks specified on the cocket. Frequently he required goods to be opened and weighed that he might the better examine them to prevent any fraudulent exportation. After they had been loaded, he deposited the cocket, with the endorsements upon it, in the searchers' office, whence upon proper examination it was sent to Gravesend to be compared by the searchers there with the lading of the ship when it passed that point on its outward voyage. The debenture was made out in the searchers' office according to the quantity certified as shipped.

There were two branches in the London searchers' department which had grown out of the old office of patent searcher.[2] One division consisted of the chief patent searcher and his deputy and five undersearchers and their deputies, while the other division was staffed by five controlling searchers and their principal officer, the Surveyor of the Searchers.[3] Although as early as 1700 the Customs Commissioners

---

[1] Cust. Ho. Lib., Extracts Board Minutes, V, 412, 1785, Feb. 22.

[2] Originally the chief patent searcher had executed the office by five deputies. Upon the increase of trade, it was decided that the trust and profits accruing to this office should be divided, and five additional patent searchers were created in place of the five deputies, their duty in turn being transacted by their five deputies. This organization continued until the customs were farmed under Charles II, at which time the farmers appointed two surveyors and five controlling searchers to act as a check for them upon the Chief and five sub-searchers. When the customs were put into commission in 1671, this organization was retained, the controlling searchers continuing to check the deputed searchers in all parts of their business. P.R.O., Treasury Papers, Vol. 79, No. 34, Perhaps 1701 or 1702. "An Abstract of the Constitucōn and Practice of the Searchers Office in the Port of London as Established by Law."

[3] For references to the chief offices of the searchers' department and their duties, see *Repts. of Comrs.*, 1787, III, 91–92, 496–497, App. No. 99, 498–499, App. No. 100, 499, App. No. 101, 500, App. No. 102, 502–503, App. No. 104, 503, App. No. 105, "Fourteenth Rept.," 1785. See also Cust. Ho. Lib., Estab., Eng., Wales, Plant. to 1782, pp. 21–22, and Cust. Ho. Lib., Extracts Board Minutes, II, III, V, entries under "Searchers." For an indication of a state of the office early in the period, see *Rules of the Water-side* (1715), pp. 84–85.

ORGANIZATION OF THE PORT OF LONDON 147

had represented the inadequacy of these numbers to deal with the export business,[1] it was not until 1775 and 1776, upon the great increase in the export trade, that another five controlling [2] and five deputy searchers [3] were added to the respective departments. Each of the branches had separate offices with their own clerks. The controlling searchers acted as checks on the deputy searchers, attending them in their examination of goods and with them comparing the marks and numbers of the packages with the entries on the cockets. Both the deputy and controlling searchers delivered to their respective offices their particular papers as evidence of the goods shipped, which accounts were afterwards compared. The deputy who executed the duty of the Chief Patent Searcher and the head clerk in his office, together with several other clerks, had the final examination of the records for each ship. The Debenture Clerk delivered the debenture to a merchant after he had verified the actual shipping of the goods. Assisting the searchers at the lading of the ship were a number of petty officers [4]: coopers, weighers, and several men for specialized duties connected with goods to be exported.

The Surveyor of the Controlling Searchers had supervision over the controlling searchers, and in 1788 his authority was completely extended over the deputies to the under-patent searchers as well.[5] It was his business to see that the goods which had been entered out-

---

[1] P.R.O., Treasury Papers, Vol. 70, No. 169, Cust. Comrs. to Lords of Treas., 1700, Sept. 28.

[2] The addition of these men is indicated by minute of 1775, Aug. 9, Cust. Ho. Lib., Extracts Board Minutes, III, 488; and P.R.O., Customs Registers: Series I, Cust. Quart. Estab., No. 357.

[3] See P.R.O., Treas. Out-letters, Cust., XXXI, 136, Treasury warrant, 1776, Mar. 5. The Customs Commissioners, in their memorial to the Treasury on the necessity of extension in the searchers' department, represented the amount of drawbacks on foreign goods exported at London to be £1,450,132 per annum on a medium of five years ending 1774; the annual total of bounties on the same medium was stated to be £126,422. These drawbacks and bounties had been certified by only five patent (deputy) and five controlling searchers. P.R.O., Treasury Papers, Bdl. 507, No. 232, Cust. Comrs. to Lords of Treas., 1774, Aug. 19.

[4] See *Repts. of Comrs.*, 1787, III, 505, App. No. 107, "Fourteenth Rept.," 1785. A Chief Packer to the Searchers served between 1777 and 1787. (Cust. Ho. Lib., Extracts Board Minutes, V, 396, 1777, Feb. 1; 214, 1787, Sept. 12.) Officers with specialized duties, not mentioned individually above but listed in the Establishment Book of 1782, p. 22, are: Commissioners' Clerk in the Searchers' Office, Officer to assist the Searchers in taking an Account of Gun powder Shipt for Exportation, Officers for Cutting off the Stamps on Calicoes (and certain other goods) Exported, Assistant to the Searchers in Opening and Repacking Muslins and other Fine Goods.

[5] Cust. Ho. Lib., Extracts Board Minutes, V, 419, 1788, Dec. 4.

wards in the cocket were fairly shipped. For this purpose he stationed on the vessel the tide-waiters, who entered in their books an account of the goods shipped, and visited them daily to see that the goods were on board and guarded against relanding and pilferage. He certified the bills of these water-guard officers on the basis of which they received their day's pay.[1]

At Gravesend were stationed the deputies to two patent searchers and also a controlling searcher, who checked the ship's lading at that station with her cocket, victualing bill, and other papers sent from London after she had hoisted sail from the port. Upon being satisfied that the goods were on board, the Gravesend searcher delivered the cocket and other proper bills to the master, and the ship proceeded on her voyage.[2]

The principal office in this division of the waterside export business, that of the searchers, was one of the oldest in the customs. The plan of the two branches of the searchers' department had its origin when the customs were farmed under Charles II, while marked expansion within the department itself took place in the latter part of the eighteenth century. As in the import division, certain sinecures were allowed to continue in the form of six patent searchers' offices in London and two at Gravesend, which were not abolished until 1798.[3] The staff of this class had salaries paid by the Crown, with the exception of the deputies to the patent officers, the Debenture Clerk, and a few clerks who were paid chiefly by their principals. All but the Surveyor of the Searchers and a few assisting officers received fees or gratuities in addition.[4] Numerous minutes indicate too great a readiness on the part of these men to exact fees, which, as represented in 1785, amounted to more than three and a half times the salaries.[5]

The personnel of the coast and coal offices may be considered together as a separate department.[6] The Collector-Outwards and the

---

[1] *Repts. of Comrs.,* 1787, III, 501–502, App. No. 103, "Fourteenth Rept.," 1785.
[2] *Ibid.,* III, 505–506, App. No. 108. Cf. *Rules of the Water-side* (1715), p. 85.
[3] 38 Geo. III, c. 86, s. 2, 3, 4.
[4] The controlling searchers were not legally entitled to fees, but they might receive gratuities for extra services. (See Cust. Ho. Lib., Extracts Board Minutes, III, 359–360, 488, 1775, May 11; V, 406–407, 1783, Oct. 1.) It appears that such gratuities as they did receive and those taken by the patent and deputy searchers were divided among the patent, deputy, and controlling searchers. *Repts. of Comrs.,* 1787, III, 92, "Fourteenth Rept.," 1785.
[5] *Ibid.,* III, 92.
[6] For a list of the officers of the coast department, see *ibid.,* III, 94; Cust. Ho. Lib., Estab., Eng., Wales, Plant. to 1782, pp. 25–26. For information on the office

ORGANIZATION OF THE PORT OF LONDON 149

Controller of the Port of London were by patent Collector and Controller of the Coast Duties, though they actually took none of them, since duties coastwise on coal, cinders, and culm and on fish, salt, and malt from Scotland were received by collectors appointed specifically for that purpose, and those on wines shipped to London were paid at the outports. The deputy of the Collector-Outwards, however, with several clerks, received sufferances which were written permits authorizing shipments coastwise, produced by the master bringing his goods to London. These sufferances he endorsed and gave to the coast-waiters to execute, and he canceled them when the shipment had been landed. When goods were sent to an outport from London, he in turn granted like sufferances.[1] The Controller's deputy with his clerk acted as a check upon the Deputy Collector in this business and sent canceled coast bonds to the Exchequer and a list of uncertified bonds to the solicitor of the customs.[2] A Clerk of the Coast Business assisted in these transactions, executing the work of the Deputy Collector when he was absent.[3] Eighteen coast-waiters, distributed at the several stations along the quays, attended the landing and shipping of goods coastwise; examined and took an account thereof; and saw that they agreed with the sufferances. A Surveyor of the Coast-waiters superintended them.[4] This organization of the coast department was old; exactly the same establishment existed in 1786 as in 1696; there was not any noticeable increase even in the numbers of the principal officers.

The coal department, which was distinct from the coast division, accounts in some measure for the static state of the coastwise organization.[5] Coal was the one article subject to coast duty over which the customs had jurisdiction in London; and instead of the receipt of those duties falling to the coast department, a separate class of officers was established for their collection. A Collector of Coal Duties with his clerks computed and received the duties on coal brought coast-

---

in general, see Cust. Ho. Lib., Extracts Board Minutes, entries in I, "Coast Surveyor & Officers," III, IV, "Coastwaiters."

[1] *Repts. of Comrs.,* 1787, III, 525, App. No. 119, "Fourteenth Rept.," 1785.

[2] *Ibid.,* III, 527, App. No. 121. In the case of many commodities, bonds had to be given by the master to land his goods at the port which he gave as his destination upon shipment coastwise. See *infra,* Ch. VII, pp. 265–266.

[3] *Repts. of Comrs.,* 1787, III, 526, App. No. 120, "Fourteenth Rept.," 1785.

[4] *Ibid.,* III, 528, App. No. 122. The coast-waiters numbered seventeen in 1715. See *Rules of the Water-side* (1715), p. 88.

[5] For an outline of the coal offices, see Cust. Ho. Lib., Estab., Eng., Wales, Plant. to 1782, p. 25; and *Repts. of Comrs.,* 1787, III, 93, "Fourteenth Rept.," 1785.

wise, while the Controller and his clerk acted as a check upon him. The receipt from coal was paid into the office of the Receiver-General in the same way as were the proceeds of import duties, and the accounts of the Coal Collector and Controller were made up as were those of the Collector-Inwards and his Controller.[1] An Examiner, by a comparison of the quarter book kept by the Collector, the quarterly list of coal ships recorded by the Collector-Coastwise, and the coal-meters' account of coals delivered, checked the computation and receipt of the Collector for the preceding quarter.[2] Fifteen coal-meters, nominated by the Corporation of London,[3] attended the delivery of ships coming coastwise with coal, cinder, and culm; measured and weighed the goods; and took an exact account of the quantities delivered.[4]

The main officers of these departments had salaries paid by the Crown or by their principals as the case happened to be. With the exception of the Examiner in the Coast Business, all had customary fees as well, and the coast officers received gratuities for extra services. The proportion of fees to salaries in the coast department near the close of the period (1784) was more than two and a half to one,[5] while in the coal business the salaries exceeded the fees by about one fifth.[6]

Scattered along the quays from Billingsgate to the Tower were the numerous warehouses in which goods were stored as security for duties or to await condemnation after seizure. The King's Warehouses accommodated practically all commodities except East India goods, which were secured in separate warehouses under the control of the East India Company. The principal offices in the King's Warehouse had been established before the eighteenth century, and in general they did not alter except for additions to meet the increase in business. The East India system grew up in the eighteenth century.[7] With few exceptions, the staff of both divisions were paid by salaries, fees, and gratuities, while the men of the King's Warehouse had in addition a poundage on the produce of enumerated goods. In

[1] On the work of these officers, see *Repts. of Comrs.*, 1787, III, 19–20, 24–32 *passim*, "Thirteenth Rept.," 1785. With respect to the Controller, see also *ibid.*, III, 250–252, App. No. 35.
[2] *Ibid.*, III, 25.
[3] Cust. Ho. Lib., Estab., Eng., Wales, Plant. to 1782, p. 25.
[4] Crouch, *Complete Guide to Officers* (1732), p. 6. This account of outport coal-meters is equally applicable to those of London.
[5] *Repts. of Comrs.*, 1787, III, 94, "Fourteenth Rept.," 1785.
[6] *Ibid.*, III, 93.
[7] Cust. Ho. Lib., Estab., Eng., Wales, Plant. to 1782, pp. 23–24, 26–28.

ORGANIZATION OF THE PORT OF LONDON 151

the remuneration of the officers of the King's Warehouse in 1784, the amount of salaries and poundage was more than two and two thirds times as much as that of fees and gratuities,[1] while in the payment of the East India staff, salaries exceeded fees and gratuities by more than one fourth.[2]

Since the collector of a port was in law also the warehouse-keeper,[3] the deputy of the Collector-Inwards served as Warehouse-keeper of the King's Warehouse in the Port of London.[4] He had the responsibility for all goods stored, necessitating close check upon merchandise delivered in and out; and, as deputy to the Receiver of Fines and Forfeitures for London until near the close of the period, he received and paid to the Exchequer the proceeds from the sales of condemned goods.[5] The Warehouse-keeper of the Crown by deputy acted as a check upon the Warehouse-keeper of the Collector-Inwards, keeping an account of all receipts and disbursements of the latter officer.[6] The Surveyor of the Warehouse had the superintendence of the officers employed in the warehouse. He saw that articles brought for storage were examined and appraised according to the nature of the commodity and recorded the results of such examination. He also superintended the Long Room sales of condemned goods, directing the preparations and keeping an account of the proceeds.[7] Besides these officers and their assistants or clerks there were several other warehouse-keepers for particular commodities, two appraisers (who set a value upon merchandise seized, preparatory to its being prosecuted in the Court of Exchequer) with their deputies and a controller, lockers who assisted in the inspection and lotting of goods previous to their sale, weighers, a cooper, and several odd officers who examined goods or accounts.[8]

---

[1] *Repts. of Comrs.*, 1787, III, 93, "Fourteenth Rept.," 1785.
[2] *Ibid.*, III, 94-95.
[3] P.R.O., Treas. Out-letters, Cust., XVIII, 440, Cust. Comrs. to Lords of Treas., 1724, Apr. 22.
[4] See *Repts. of Comrs.*, 1787, III, 415, App. No. 37, "Fourteenth Rept.," 1785.
[5] See Cust. Ho. Lib., Extracts Board Minutes, II, "Warehouse Officers," III, V, "Warehouse (King's)."
[6] See e. g., *ibid.*, II, "Warehouse Officers," 1726, Oct. 14; *Repts. of Comrs.*, 1787, III, 514, App. No. 112, "Fourteenth Rept.," 1785.
[7] *Ibid.*, III, 513, App. No. 111; Cust. Ho. Lib., Extracts Board Minutes, II, "Warehouse Officers," III, V, "Warehouse (King's)." See also P.R.O., Chatham Papers, Bdl. 284, "Kings Ware House Custom House," 1783, Mar. 12.
[8] Cust. Ho. Lib., Estab., Eng., Wales, Plant. to 1782, p. 24. Cf. *Repts. of Comrs.*, 1787, III, 93, "Fourteenth Rept.," 1785. For more detailed information on the warehouse staff in general, see Cust. Ho. Lib., Extracts Board Minutes, II, "Ware-

The organization of the East India warehouses was similar to that of the King's Warehouse, except for the provision of a customs check upon the Company. In 1785 there were ten or more warehouses reserved for different kinds of East India commodities such as pepper, coffee, cocoanuts, which had been placed under a warehousing scheme, prohibited East India articles, and miscellaneous goods.[1] In each of these East India warehouses, one or more separate warehouse-keepers served as a control for the customs upon the warehouse-keeper of the Company. A central officer, the Surveyor, compared all the Company's warehouse-keepers' accounts of goods secured with those of the land-waiters who had landed and stored the merchandise and, after a further check, sent a warrant of the cargo to the office of the Collector-Inwards.[2] The Inspector of the Delivery of Unrated East Indian Goods supervised all officers on the part of the customs in the India warehouses and reported to the Board upon all matters relating to the East India business. He attended the examination of all articles secured and, with officers both of the customs and of the Company, took an account of them. On sales of tea, china, and unrated goods he checked the number of chests or quantity of the commodity brought by the Company to the sales, on the proceeds of which the duties were computed.[3] In 1784 fourteen warehouse-keepers, six controllers, three examiners, a jerquer, and a large number of lockers completed this class.[4]

The general organization of offices which existed during the eighteenth century for the import, export, and coastwise business has been described. There were two separate departments, however, for special branches of the customs business, namely, officers of the tobacco division and those of the 4½ per cent duty.

By the middle of the eighteenth century, the tobacco trade had practically broken down under the enormous quantities of smuggled stuff that were thrown upon the market. In an effort to shake the

---

house Officers," III, V, "Warehouse (King's)." On appraisers, see *ibid.*, I, entries under "Appraisers and Appraisement;" and *Repts. of Comrs.*, 1787, III, 515, App. No. 113, "Fourteenth Rept.," 1785. For lockers, see *ibid.*, III, 515, App. No. 113; and Cust. Ho. Lib., Extracts Board Minutes, III, V, "Lockers."

[1] Cust. Ho. Lib., Estab., Eng., Wales, Plant. to 1782, pp. 26–27; *Repts. of Comrs.*, 1787, III, 531, App. No. 125, "Fourteenth Rept.," 1785.

[2] *Ibid.*, 1787, III, 531–532, App. No. 125.

[3] *Ibid.*, III, 532–533, App. No. 126; see also Cust. Ho. Lib., Extracts Board Minutes, I, "East India Goods & Ships," 1758, Jan. 4, 20, Mar. 23.

[4] *Repts. of Comrs.*, 1787, III, 94, "Fourteenth Rept.," 1785; cf. Cust. Ho. Lib., Estab., Eng., Wales, Plant. to 1782, pp. 26–28.

ORGANIZATION OF THE PORT OF LONDON   153

hold of the illicit traders, the tobacco bill of 1751 was passed [1] after elaborate investigations into records of seizures and prosecutions had disclosed inefficiency and corruption in the customs.[2]

By that act the department of the Register-General of Tobacco was established in London to keep accounts of all tobacco imported and cleared and carried coastwise in all the ports of Great Britain. The office as finally settled consisted of the Register-General and his clerks, four other clerks for the inland tobacco business (two each under the Collector and Controller-Inwards), and several other officers. All these men had salaries, while the four special clerks and the lockers with their superintendent had fees and gratuities also. In 1784 the proportion of salaries to other emoluments was approximately nine to one.[3]

The Register-General kept a record of all tobacco imported into Britain. The London land-waiters gave him their accounts of hogsheads landed and the outport collectors and controllers did the same; if the shipment was warehoused, he was informed of it by the lockers. When the tobacco was exported, the Register-General received the searchers' bills of the number of hogsheads cleared, and thus he was able to cancel the original importation. When the commodity was sold, he was given a record of the number of hogsheads and discharged the account. If tobacco was removed from one place to another, the certificate authorizing such removal was registered in his office. Thus, theoretically at least, he had knowledge of the importation and disposal of every hogshead that came into Britain.[4] An assistant to the Register-General in Scotland kept a like account for all North Britain and returned an annual report to the London officer.[5]

---

[1] 24 Geo. II, c. 41.

[2] The Treasury Papers for the years immediately preceding 1750 contain numerous customs reports and representations and merchants' schemes to improve the collection of this duty. The bill of 1751 was drawn up by the merchants, the Customs Commissioners, and the Lords of the Treasury. Two of the papers which came before the Treasury in this connection are of particular interest, since in them may be found marked similarities to the scheme adopted. See Bdl. 332, No. 57, "Additions to be made to the present Heads"; No. 68, a paper of Mr. Bland headed "Tobacco, Cl. for preventing Frauds."

[3] *Repts. of Comrs.*, 1787, III, 95, "Fourteenth Rept.," 1785. On the organization of the tobacco office, cf. Cust. Ho. Lib., Estab., Eng., Wales, Plant. to 1782, p. 29.

[4] On the establishment of the Register-General, see P.R.O., Treas. Out-letters, Cust., XXIV, 87–88, Treasury constitution, 1751, Sept. 18. For further information on this officer, see *Repts. of Comrs.*, 1787, III, 541–542, App. No. 130, "Fourteenth Rept.," 1785; and Cust. Ho. Lib., Extracts Board Minutes, II, entries under "Register General of Tobacco," III, V, "Tobacco."

[5] There is a very interesting petition among the Treasury Papers (Bdl. 352,

Clerks under the Collector and Controller in the Custom House were appointed in 1753 as a greater convenience to the dealers who had had but the one tobacco office to which they could go for their certificates and business.[1] The Clerk checked accounts of tobacco imported and exported and delivered out for home consumption; he granted the necessary certificates for the removal of the shipment upon the application of the manufacturer; examined orders for delivery of the hogsheads from the warehouse; and provided a warrant for the computation of bonded duties when the merchant was ready to pay them.[2] Every month the vouchers of the Collector and Controller-Inwards were delivered to the Register-General, and every quarter the Clerks and the Register-General met together and examined their accounts. Annual statements of hogsheads that had been imported and remained undischarged for eighteen months were returned to the Register-General.[3]

The Register-General also had the superintendence of an assistant to the searchers who acted as Inspector of Manufactured Tobacco for Exportation.[4] This position was first arranged in 1770 for one Stone, an ordinary weigher who seems to have fairly bewitched the Board by his knowledge of the intricacies of the tobacco trade and his ability to detect frauds. Stone's responsibility imposed upon him more varied functions than that of a mere check on the export of manufactured tobacco; he inspected all seized tobacco before it was sent to the Tobacco Burning Ground, and acted as a kind of general supervisor of the tobacco business on the quays.[5] The Register-General also had supervision over the lockers in the tobacco warehouses, as a check upon their accounts and attendance.[6]

There were several other officers for the tobacco business, most of whom had been established in the early eighteenth century before the creation of the tobacco department.[7] Some of the landing and

---

No. 89) of date 1752, regarding the duties of one Gideon Schaw, Assistant Register General of Tobacco in Scotland.

[1] P.R.O., Treas. Out-letters, Cust., XXIV, 321–322, Treasury warrant, 1753, Oct. 31.

[2] *Repts. of Comrs.*, 1787, III, 542–543, App. No. 131, "Fourteenth Rept.," 1785.

[3] According to a minute of 1769, Aug. 25. Cust. Ho. Lib., Extracts Board Minutes, III, 35.

[4] *Ibid.*, III, 632, 1771, May 28.

[5] On Stone, see *ibid.*, II, "Searchers," 1770, Mar. 29, July 26, Dec. 22; III, 630–631, 1770, Mar. 29; 632, 1771, July 4.

[6] *Ibid.*, III, 626, 1767, Apr. 8; 627, 1767, June 19.

[7] See Cust. Ho. Lib., Estab., Eng., Wales, Plant. to 1782, pp. 29–30; and Cust. Ho. Lib., Extracts Board Minutes, II, III, V, entries under "Tobacco."

ORGANIZATION OF THE PORT OF LONDON 155

shipping of the commodity seems to have come under the superintendence of a special Surveyor. The Viewer and Examiner joined with the land-waiters in the examination of imported tobacco, with them determined allowances for damage, and saw that the damaged part was cut off and despatched to the Tobacco Ground to be burnt. There was so much pilfering of the damaged tobacco before it reached the kiln, however, that in 1767 the practice was begun of soaking it in tar water in order to make it entirely worthless.[1] An Inspector of the Tobacco Ground superintended the destruction of the stuff. The burning of tobacco seems to have occasioned the customs officers no little difficulty: in the outports it was not easy to find places where it could be burnt, for the smoke was unpleasant and it damaged the ground; in London it had to be burned at night. The use made of the tobacco ash, which was carefully preserved by strict orders from the Board and to the great annoyance of the customs officers, has been a subject of some curiosity. It would seem from a chance reference that it was used in the making of soap, since one outport collector referred to "an ignorant soap-boiler" as being the only possible person who might give him any small pittance for the ash,[2] and it is known that water poured over ashes produces a lye that is used in soap-making.

Altogether there were three stages in the customs history of the tobacco business of the eighteenth century. Until the fifties, though tobacco was one of the most productive and troublesome articles of commerce, it went through the same general customs machinery as did other commodities. From 1751 to 1789 a special organization struggled in vain against the abuses of high customs duties. Finally

[1] Cust. Ho. Lib., Extracts Board Minutes, III, 626, 1767, Mar. 28, July 29. See also Surveyor's Reports (London) Board's Orders Thereon 1768–1770. Not only damaged leaf was stolen: pilfering of good tobacco on the quays was so serious by 1786 that the King's Victualling Wharf had to be taken over for its warehousing. Of the many papers on the subject, see P.R.O., Treasury Papers, Bdl. 627, No. 316, Stephens to Rose, 1786, Feb. 22. See Stiles' letter to Rose, 1785, Feb. 11, concerning the Commissioners' interest in the Victualling Warehouses, wherein Stiles states that "Repeated representations have been made to this Board of the enormous thefts and outrages committed on the Quays, whereby the Merchants and the Revenue are constantly suffering very considerable losses on several species of Goods imported and exported, particularly in the article of Tobacco, which the Merchants are now afraid to strip in order to be weighed notwithstanding the protection afforded by the Constables who are paid by this Revenue, as the Thieves assemble in such large bodies, and are grown so audacious, that they are neither to be intimidated nor restrained." *Ibid.,* Bdl. 624, No. 112.

[2] Cust. Ho. Lib., Sel. from Cust. Outport Recds., South Coast, 1922, pp. 108–109, Weymouth, Collector to Board, 1735–1738, 1737, June 13.

in 1789 failure was recognized; tobacco was subjected to excise as well as customs duties and placed under a warehousing scheme.[1]

The 4½ per cent duty, levied on dead commodities exported from Barbadoes and the Leeward Islands, had been placed by patent under the control of the Customs Commissioners in 1686,[2] and continued to be received in the customs office throughout the eighteenth century. In the islands the duty was collected in the form of produce—generally sugar—which was sent by the collectors to an officer known as the Husband of the Four-and-a-Half Per Cent in London.[3] When the sugars reached London the Husband attended their weighing at landing, saw that they were carefully warehoused,[4] and several times a year put them up to auction (sales of sugar being increased in 1772 from two to four or more a year or whenever there were 500 casks of sugar in the warehouse [5]). From the proceeds of the sales the Husband paid certain salaries and pensions by patent, by privy seal, and by King's warrant,[6] and the remainder he remitted to the Receiver-General.[7] An Assistant served the Husband during part of the period.[8] In 1734 a Controller and an Examiner of the accounts of the Husband and Controller were appointed as checks,[9] and toward the close of the period a Warehouse-keeper was established. A cooper and two lockers completed the organization.[10] Since the 4½ per cent duty

---

[1] 29 Geo. III, c. 68.

[2] P.R.O., Patent Roll, 2 Jas. II, P. 9, dorse, No. 6, [1686], June 25.

[3] P.R.O., Chatham Papers, Bdl. 231, section headed "Four and an half per Cent" in manuscript booklet entitled "The Business done in the Treasury by the Officers —distinguishing each Particular Branch."

[4] See Cust. Ho. Lib., Extracts Board Minutes, I, "£4½ Pr Cent," 1734, Aug. 15.

[5] *Ibid.*, III, 173, 1772, Feb. 27.

[6] In the Custom House Library is the 4½ P C Minute Book, 1776–1829, which illustrates such payments. See also P.R.O., Chatham Papers, Bdl. 231, paper headed "Charge on the 4½ Per Cent Duty 1785."

[7] P.R.O., Treas. Out-letters, Cust., XXIII, 273–274, Cust. Comrs. to Lords of Treas., 1746–7, Mar. 24. According to a later account [1782 or 1783?] of the 4½ per cent in P.R.O., Chatham Papers, Bdl. 231, manuscript booklet entitled, "The Business done in the Treasury by the Officers—distinguishing each Particular Branch," the Husband paid the surplus into the Exchequer.

[8] As appears from Cust. Ho. Lib., Estab., Eng., Wales, Plant. to 1782, p. 28.

[9] *Ibid.*, pp. 28–29; Cust. Ho. Lib., Extracts Board Minutes, I, "£4½ Pr Cent," 1734, Aug. 15; *ibid.*, I, "Husband of the 4½ P Cent," 1734, Aug. 15. In 1781 the office of Examiner was directed to be discontinued. P.R.O., Treas. Out-letters, Cust., XXXII, 79, Robinson to Cust. Comrs., 1781, Nov. 21. See also P.R.O., Treasury Papers, Bdl. 564, No. 274, Cust. Comrs. to Lords of Treas., 1781, Nov.

[10] Cust. Ho. Lib., Estab., Eng., Wales, Plant. to 1782, p. 29; *Repts. of Comrs.*, 1787, III, 554, App. No. 141, "Fourteenth Rept.," 1785.

ORGANIZATION OF THE PORT OF LONDON

did not belong to the public, the charges of collecting it were not paid out of the customs revenue except in the case of the Warehousekeeper and the lockers, who received salaries.[1]

The officers at the Custom House, in the warehouses, and along the quays were far from constituting the entire body of customs officials. The authority of the service was asserted in some instances before a ship drew into the River. In the early part of the period it had been a practice to send tide-waiters from London to Gravesend, and from there by horseback to Deal and Margate to board the big merchantmen from Turkey and the East Indies and watch them to London. These tide-waiters, however, who were usually landsmen, were often sick in the passage, and advantage was taken of their illness to run goods. About 1723, in an effort to remedy this state of affairs, the Customs Commissioners appointed mariners to ride on the boats from Deal and Margate to Gravesend. These men also soon proved inefficient, many frauds being committed and few seizures made. In 1728 this arrangement of boarding officers was discarded, and instead four sloops were established by Treasury warrant at Deal and Sandwich to accompany the vessels to Gravesend.[2] Ships with less valuable cargoes were not brought under the surveillance of the customs until they reached that point.

At Gravesend and at the Boarding Station every ship from foreign parts was boarded by a tide-surveyor who took an account of the vessel, inspected her carefully to see that no goods were concealed to be run, and stationed the proper tide-waiters to guard her until she was cleared at London. The tide-surveyors, who were increased in number from eight to seventeen during the period,[3] had their positions at six stations along the Thames and took their turns in the direction of the business at each point. Higher up the river from Gravesend were the Homeward and Outward Bound Stations, where lay ships which were waiting their turns to enter inwards or clear outwards. The tide-surveyor at each of these places visited the ship and saw that the tide-waiters were on guard. When a vessel drew into the Clearing

---

[1] *Repts. of Comrs.*, 1787, III, 96.

[2] P.R.O., Treas. Out-letters, Cust., XIX, 231–233, Cust. Comrs. to Lords of Treas., 1727, Feb. 22; Treasury warrant, 1728, June 25.

[3] Nine of these officers were tide-waiters who acted as tide-surveyors. (*Repts. of Comrs.*, 1787, III, 550, App. No. 138, "Fourteenth Rept.," 1785.) For instances of additions to these officers, see Cust. Ho. Lib., Extracts Board Minutes, II, "Tide Surveyors," III, V, "Tidesurveyors."

Station it was unloaded, and the tide-surveyor there had the responsibility for a fair discharge. He visited the ship to be cleared, sent all small packages to the warehouses to be secured for the duties, called upon the tide-waiters at odd times to see that they worked efficiently, and discharged them when the ship was unloaded. The tide-surveyor at the Quay and Office Stations visited the tide-waiters by day and night to see that they were on duty, despatched the men on the Gravesend call, and cleared the ship. He also patrolled the quays to see that the watchmen were at their posts.[1] The tide-surveyors were the immediate supervisory officers over the tide-waiters, watchmen, and watermen. They appointed the tide-waiters to the ships, checked their attendance, discharged them, and signed their bills; they gave them directions in execution of their duty, reprimanded them when necessary, and reported delinquents to the River Inspector and the Board. They stationed watchmen, saw that they attended their duty, and did the same with respect to the watermen.[2] The journals of the tide-surveyors were placed before the Board weekly.[3] In their office, a Register of the Tide-waiters kept the necessary records of the employment, attendance, and conduct of these officers, and represented the same to the Board.[4] A separate Register was established for the watermen in 1777.[5]

The duty of the tide-waiters, stationed on all ships coming into the Port of London and upon those bound outwards with debenture goods on board, was to guard the cargo against fraudulent landing. When the land-waiters gave their orders for the delivery of the goods, the tide-waiters kept a careful record of all articles unloaded from the ship into the lighters and sent a note of them to the land-waiter on shore.

---

[1] *Repts. of Comrs.*, 1787, III, 549–550, App. No. 137, "Fourteenth Rept.," 1785; Cust. Ho. Lib., Estab., Eng., Wales, Plant. to 1782, p. 32. For a general survey of the tide-surveyors in the early part of the period, see *Rules of the Water-side* (1715), p. 87; Crouch, *Complete Guide to Officers* (1732), p. 5. For a reference to the rotation of the tide-surveyors, see Cust. Ho. Lib., Extracts Board Minutes, III, 599, 1766, Oct. 16.

[2] In connection with the duties of the tide-surveyors as supervisors over the inferior officers, see numerous entries under "Tide Surveyors" in *ibid.*, II, and "Tide-surveyors" in III, V.

[3] As is indicated by *ibid.*, II, "Tide Surveyors," 1744, Sept. 8.

[4] This officer was established in 1686. (P.R.O., Treas. Out-letters, Cust., X, 150, Treasury warrant, 1686, July 28.) For an indication of his duties, see entries in Cust. Ho. Lib., Extracts Board Minutes, II, "Register in Tide Surveyors' Office," III, "Register of the Tidewaiters."

[5] *Ibid.*, V, 354, 1776, June 7, Sept. 20; 1777, Jan. 8.

ORGANIZATION OF THE PORT OF LONDON 159

After the vessel had been discharged, their books were signed by the land-waiters and tide-surveyors, after which they were deposited with the jerquers.[1]

The tide-waiters were placed under strict regulations in an effort to protect cargoes against petty pilfering: for instance, if they were stationed on a ship they had to remain on it constantly—they could go on shore for provisions only under certain conditions; they were never allowed to sleep on shore, and they could not take their wives on board ship.[2] In 1787 seventy-six tide-waiters were suspended at one time for frauds and absence from their ships,[3] showing that these and other such regulations were far from effective. Life aboard ship was not the most idyllic in the world. The masters were inclined to be none too civil to these fellows who interfered with their private peccadilloes. Many a tide-waiter was discomfited by ill treatment and poor food and lodging. He was generally subsisted by the masters of the vessels while on duty, but allowances of such provisions were frequently denied him.[4] At such times, at least in the early years of the period, the Customs Commissioners retaliated by withholding a part of the master's portage.[5]

By approximately the end of the period there were 192 established tide-waiters (belonging to the Superior and Inferior Lists which were distinguished only by a difference of £5 in salary) and 356 preferable

---

[1] *Repts. of Comrs.*, 1787, III, 551, App. No. 139, "Fourteenth Rept.," 1785. For references to the general business of the tide-waiter, see *Rules of the Water-side* (1715), p. 87; Crouch, *Complete Guide to Officers* (1732), p. 5.

[2] For examples of such rules, see Cust. Ho. Lib., Extracts Board Minutes, III, 616, 1774, Nov. 16; 346, 1768, Jan. 2; 607, 1765, Sept. 5.

[3] *Ibid.*, V, 628, 1787, June 21.

[4] See *Repts. of Comrs.*, 1787, III, 551, App. No. 139, "Fourteenth Rept.," 1785.

[5] Cust. Ho. Lib., Extracts Board Minutes, II, "Tidesmen," 1707, Dec. 8; 1709, Mar. 31. "Portage," it will be recalled, was the allowance made to the master for the correct entry of his cargo. The practice of refusing a part of this allowance appears to have been authorized in 1671. A Treasury warrant of that year declared that portage had usually been permitted to masters in order to encourage trade and to defray such charges as the customs officers put upon them. The masters, however, had been maltreating the officers with regard to their provisions and lodgings, and yet they demanded the portage money. In the future, upon complaint of this nature being made, the Commissioners were directed to hear the case and were empowered to detain all or a part of the portage money and pay it to the abused customs officer. (*Cal. Treas. Books, 1669–1672*, Part II, p. 1146.) It would seem that at a later date some alteration in this connection was made, for in 1731 (Sept. 28) Yorke was of opinion that the master should permit the officers to take shelter in the vessel but that he was not obliged to allow them any part of the ship's provisions. P.R.O., Treasury Papers, Bdl. 466, No. 276.

tide-waiters who were paid a small weekly sum or day pay.[1] The established were always appointed first to ships, the preferable next, and any glutmen of course last.[2] An elaborate organization of officers guarded the East Indiamen[3]; on wine ships there appear to have been usually three tide-waiters stationed; on tobacco vessels, five; on Short-Traders, Hambro' boats, and Turkey and Leghorn vessels, four.[4] The oldest and most infirm of the tide-waiters were employed as Piazza Men on the Homeward and Outward Bound Stations.[5] The Gravesend service seems to have been the least desirable. The trip down was not an easy one; tide-waiters were punished if through negligence they did not arrive from London in time to board[6]; and once at Gravesend they were strictly supervised by being required to lodge in two and later three taverns designated by the Board.[7] Of these taverns, the "New" and the "Fountain" were the most famous in connection with the customs. The Commissioners allowed their proprietors money or coal and candles for the officers,[8] and the master of the "New Tavern" received £30 to provide horses to send up calls to London for tide-waiters.[9] One may well imagine how irksome a burden the tide-waiters found the Board's requirement of particular cleanliness on the Gravesend station. In 1778 the Commissioners ordered that when any tide-waiter should report to the tide-surveyor in the Gravesend office, and his clothing should appear very "ragged, dirty, or offensive," he should be required to "produce such necessaries as he may have brought with him, & if upon examination the whole of his apparel shall be found insufficient to keep him cleanly & decent when on duty," the Inspector was to command him to return to London, where he was to be put on the general list for the call;

---

[1] *Repts. of Comrs.*, 1787, III, 95, 551–552, App. No. 139, "Fourteenth Rept.," 1785; cf. Cust. Ho. Lib., Estab., Eng., Wales, Plant. to 1782, pp. 34, 39. In regard to alterations in the numbers of tide-waiters during the period, see various volumes of P.R.O., Customs Registers: Series I, Cust. Quart. Estab., and Cust. Ho. Lib., Extracts Board Minutes, II, "Tidesmen," III, V, "Tidewaiters."

[2] E. g., *ibid.*, II, "Tidesmen," 1713, Dec. 7.

[3] *Repts. of Comrs.*, 1787, III, 548, App. No. 136, "Fourteenth Rept.," 1785.

[4] According to Cust. Ho. Lib., Extracts Board Minutes, V, 633, 1790, Jan. 19.

[5] To be on this list a person had to be fifty years old, and at least ten years in the service, or have met with an accident in his employment. See for example *ibid.*, III, 386, 1766, May 13. For an indication of the position of the Piazza Men, see *ibid.*, II, III, "Piazza Men," V, "Piazza men."

[6] *Ibid.*, I, "Gravesend," 1725, June 23.

[7] *Ibid.*, I, "Gravesend," 1733, June 27; 200, 1763, Feb. 5.

[8] *Ibid.*, III, 199, 1759, July 18; 202, 1775, Dec. 30.

[9] *Ibid.*, III, 200, 1765, Nov. 8.

ORGANIZATION OF THE PORT OF LONDON

if, however, when he was sent down to Gravesend again he should once more be "found deficient in Necessaries," he was to be marked a defaulter and reported to the Board![1]

The remaining members of the water guard consisted of the watermen and the crews of customs boats. The watermen or boatmen were appointed to row the tide-surveyors' boats, though in some of the outports they served in the capacity of tide-waiters as well by watching on board ships.[2] Toward the close of the period there were fifty-six established and ninety-seven preferable men in this branch of the London service.[3] Several customs boats were employed under the jurisdiction of the Port of London to cruise against smugglers. The journals of their commanders were examined regularly by an officer especially appointed for the purpose.[4]

Superintending this vast water guard of tide-surveyors, tide-waiters, watermen, and watchmen, who together approximated between 800 and 850 near the close of the period,[5] were the four Inspectors of the River, all of whom were added during the period.[6] One of these officers attended at Gravesend, two on the River and on the East India service, and one at the office and upon the quays, the duty at all of these stations being equally shared by the men.[7] In their supervision of the water guard they patrolled the quays and visited the ships by day and night to see that their subordinate officers were doing their duty: they supervised the employment of these men, checked the attendance of tide-surveyors, and examined and certified bills for the payment of the tide-waiters and watermen, and the incidental pay of the tide-surveyors. They laid before the Board weekly

---

[1] Cust. Ho. Lib., Extracts Board Minutes, IV, 499, 1778, June 2.

[2] For a general indication of the duty of the watermen, see Crouch, *Complete Guide to Officers* (1732), p. 6; Cust. Ho. Lib., Extracts Board Minutes, II, III, V, entries under "Watermen."

[3] See *Repts. of Comrs.*, 1787, III, 95, "Fourteenth Rept.," 1785; Cust. Ho. Lib., Estab., Eng., Wales, Plant. to 1782, pp. 39, 41.

[4] On boats in the London service, see *ibid.*, p. 42; and various volumes of P.R.O., Customs Registers: Series I, Cust. Quart. Estab.

[5] Although these numbers include the watchmen (whom I have counted as well in the staff for the import business on page 140), several of them were not, however, employed on the quays. (Cf. Cust. Ho. Lib., Estab., Eng., Wales, Plant. to 1782, pp. 20, 21, 31–41; and *Repts. of Comrs.*, 1787, III, 90, 95, "Fourteenth Rept.," 1785.) There were in addition the crews of customs boats in the London service and an indefinite number of extra men.

[6] As appears by P.R.O., Customs Registers: Series I, Cust. Quart. Estab. Three of the Inspectors were added in the early years of the eighteenth century.

[7] See Cust. Ho. Lib., Extracts Board Minutes, IV, 583, 1776, June 7; 586, 1776, Oct. 29. Cf. III, 264, 1774, Nov. 11. An extra Inspector served from 1773 to 1776.

returns of the attendance and conduct of the officers, their monthly journals, and the usual Christmas accounts of the ages, capacities, and abilities of all the officers under their jurisdiction. They reported to the Board when necessary on their subordinates and upon any particular references of the Commissioners. As the superior officers of the river service, the Inspectors were responsible for the observance of proper regulations by ships in the river; thus they reported vessels that lay for thirty days in the river without entry of cargo and enforced rules forbidding boats to lie against a quay.[1]

The Surveyor for the Building and Repairing of Sloops and Boats, who appears to have taken over the duties of an Inspector appointed in 1728,[2] kept a register of all boats in the service of the water guard at London and the outports. He inspected the London boats and those brought to London for repair, and it appears that he surveyed all sloops which by minute of 1742 were sent to London annually for that purpose, except those of Bristol and Wales, which were dealt with in Bristol.[3] He examined estimates for the building or repairing of boats and laid them before the Board, reported to the Commissioners on accounts and bills for repairs of the outport craft which were referred to him, and contracted for new boats. Apparently these Surveyors were not always the most practical men, as is illustrated in a letter of the Weymouth collector to the Board in 1770 wherein he writes, "I acknowledge the receipt of a new boat . . . and find her very unfit in every respect, out of proper dimensions nor plan'd for going through the water in so swift a manner as the nature of the service do require."[4] In 1790 the Board directed that such boats in the future were to be built at the port required or at a neighboring port, where the officer for whom the boat was intended might supervise the construction.[5] As Inspector or Surveyor during the period, this officer also took care of the preservation of confiscated boats at the Tobacco Burning Ground and informed the Board of their condition from time to time. Whenever a new boat was needed for the

---

[1] For an outline of the duties of the Inspectors, see *Repts. of Comrs*, 1787, III, 548, App. No. 136, "Fourteenth Rept.," 1785; and Cust. Ho. Lib., Extracts Board Minutes, I, III, IV, entries under "Inspectors of the River." See esp. III, 262–263, 1774, Apr. 8.
[2] *Ibid.*, I, "Inspector of Boats & Sloops," 1728, July 30.
[3] *Ibid.*, I, "Inspector of Boats & Sloops," 1742, Mar. 15.
[4] Cust. Ho. Lib., Sel. from Cust. Outport Recds., South Coast, 1922, p. 119, Weymouth, Collector to Board, 1770–1772, 1770, July 4.
[5] Cust. Ho. Lib., Extracts Board Minutes, IV, 106–107, 1790, Oct. 13.

ORGANIZATION OF THE PORT OF LONDON 163

service, he reported as to whether one was available at the Ground.[1] In 1741, as Inspector, he was ordered to examine quarterly the journals of the commanders, mates, and other chief officers of the boats in the service of the customs, to see that these men were rendering efficient service.[2] With the Surveyor of the Act of Navigation, the Surveyor for the Building of Sloops inspected ships (or, in the case of the outports, the reports of ships) engaged in the Greenland Fishery Trade and the Labrador Whale Fisheries to see that they complied with the acts which gave premiums to such vessels.[3] Thus the Surveyor of Sloops acted in three capacities altogether: as Surveyor of Sloops, Examiner of the Water Guard Officers' Journals, and Inspector of Ships in the Whale and Herring Fisheries.[4]

The Surveyor for the Act of Navigation had the examination of ships to see that they met the requirements of the Navigation Act. All vessels entering London were registered in his office and a record kept of the names of the ship and master, tonnage, number of men, from whence the vessel came, her cargo, and other details. This officer, with the Surveyor of Sloops, inspected the ships fitted out for the fisheries, and he certified the building and tonnage of the vessel when necessary.[5]

All the principal offices of the water guard, except those of the Surveyor of Sloops, Register of the Watermen, and Inspectors of the River, were in existence before 1696,[6] though the numbers of men who performed their functions was increased greatly during the period. With the exception of a few petty clerks who received salaries from their principals, all of the officers received salaries from the Crown, and many of them got fees and gratuities. The proportion of

[1] In connection with the Surveyor's examination of boats at the Tobacco Burning Ground, see Cust. Ho. Lib., Extracts Board Minutes, I, "Inspector of Boats & Sloops," 1734, Oct. 22; 1735, Dec. 1; III, 584, 1769, June 23.
[2] See *ibid.*, I, "Examiner of Journals of the Commanders of Sloops," 1742, Aug. 19; I, "Inspector of Boats & Sloops," 1741, Feb. 22; II, "Masters of the Custom-House Sloops," 1742, Aug. 19.
[3] On the inspection of fishery boats, see *ibid.*, I, "Inspector of Boats & Sloops," 1754, Apr. 19; V, 567, 1776, Aug. 23; and *Repts. of Comrs.*, 1787, III, 546, App. No. 134, 547, App. No. 135, "Fourteenth Rept.," 1785. When ships of the herring fisheries were entitled to bounties, the documents were sent to this officer by the Board for his examination and report.
[4] For an account of these duties, see *ibid.*, III, 546, App. No. 134; and Cust. Ho. Lib., Extracts Board Minutes, I, entries under "Inspector of Boats & Sloops," III, V, "Surveyor for Sloops."
[5] See *ibid.*, II, III, V, entries under "Surveyor for the Act of Navigation," and *Repts. of Comrs.*, 1787, III, 547, App. No. 135, "Fourteenth Rept.," 1785
[6] Cust. Ho. Lib., Estab., Eng., Wales, Plant. to 1782, pp. 31-42, *passim.*

salaries to the other emoluments in 1784 was more than twenty-seven to one.[1]

In anticipation of the smugglers' evasion of officers at port and of the cruisers, the customs system had its "third line" in the land guard. Though this department of the service was far more elaborately developed in the outports,[2] there was a modest organization in London[3] which was continued until 1782.[4] Seventeen land-carriage men, added from time to time during the period, visited inns in London, Westminster, and Southwark and examined carriages of every kind to see that they carried no uncustomed or uncertified goods. They also inspected the warehouses at the inns upon occasion and were empowered to search for goods anywhere upon information. These men were under the superintendence of a Surveyor who performed the same duty as they did. Several riding officers completed the organization. The post of land-carriage officer existed in the seventeenth century, while that of the London riding officer appears to have been of early eighteenth-century origin.[5] Salaries were the only form of remuneration to these officers.[6]

Assisting in the lading, unlading, carrying, weighing, and storing of goods were many men on the quays who were not officially in the employ of the customs.[7] The wharfingers had the management of the lighters which brought the merchant's cargo from the ship to the quay; and they also had the "letting" of the several hundred private warehouses at the waterside, which were used by the merchant as places wherein to store his goods against the weather.[8] The lightermen attended the mooring of the craft under the direction of respon-

---

[1] *Repts. of Comrs.*, 1787, III, 96, "Fourteenth Rept.," 1785.

[2] See *infra*, Ch. V, pp. 182–185.

[3] On the London organization, see *Repts. of Comrs.*, 1787, III, 95, 545, App. No. 133; Cust. Ho. Lib., Estab., Eng., Wales, Plant. to 1782, pp. 30–31; *Rules of the Water-side* (1715), pp. 87–88; Cust. Ho. Lib., Extracts Board Minutes, I, various entries under "Land Carriage Officers."

[4] In 1782 the Board resolved to discontinue the land-carriage officers in London, and in 1783 and 1784 the same was done with the officers in Bristol and Newcastle respectively. *Ibid.*, V, 4, 1782, Dec. 18; 1783, Jan. 8; 1784, Apr. 10.

[5] Cust. Ho. Lib., Estab., Eng., Wales, Plant. to 1782, pp. 30–31.

[6] *Repts. of Comrs.*, 1787, III, 95, 545, App. No. 133, "Fourteenth Rept.," 1785.

[7] This survey is descriptive of the organization as it stood at approximately the end of the third decade of the century. It may be taken as fairly representative of the entire period.

[8] Edward Hatton, *Comes Commercii or The Trader's Companion* (London, 1723), p. 272. For further information on the wharfingers, see pp. 269, 270.

ORGANIZATION OF THE PORT OF LONDON 165

sible officers and manned the lighters. The porters, who were divided into four groups,[1] carried the goods from the ship to the place of weighing and from there to the storehouses or wagons.[2] Carmen hauled the goods to any place designated by the merchant.[3] Besides these workers, casual laborers known as the glutmen were taken on to deal with sudden rushes of work,[4] an irregularity that was responsible for much of the confusion in the system.

In conclusion, it may be said that the outlines of the London organization had been laid down before the dates covered by this study. While there were not many increases in offices as such, except in the more specialized departments, there was a large growth in numbers of officers as commerce expanded during the eighteenth century. Many useless offices that were an expense to the government and interfered with efficient execution of business were unnecessarily allowed to continue.[5] There were three sinecures which were of no service at all, namely, the Surveyor of Subsidies and Petty Customs in the Port of London, the Surveyor-General, and the Register of Warrants. In addition to these there were eight sinecure offices (held by thirty-two principals) whereof the duty was useful but the officer useless. These were the Controller Inwards and Outwards, Collector-Inwards, Collector-Outwards, Usher in the Long

---

[1] The Companies Porters were concerned in the landing and shipping of goods for Holland, France, Spain, Italy, Germany, Turkey, and Cape of Good Hope and beyond, and to certain ports on the Baltic; the Ticket Porters looked after the American goods and those of northern Baltic ports; the Tackle Men, societies of the ticket officers, were usually equipped with scales, weights, and the like to assist in the weighing of goods at the waterside between the buyer and seller; and the Fellowship Porters landed or shipped such goods as were measurable by dry measure, such as corn, salt, and similar commodities. Hatton, *Comes Commercii* (1723), pp. 274–275; Giles Jacob, *Lex Mercatoria: or, the Merchant's Companion* (London, 1729), p. 134.

[2] The Corporation of London controlled and regulated the lightermen and porters and certain watermen. See David Hughson, *London; Being an accurate History and Description of the British Metropolis and its Neighbourhood* (London, 1805), II, 67.

[3] All the carmen had to be licensed with a number and mark and were subject to numerous detailed regulations. The governors of Christ's Hospital had the power vested in them by the City of London to give to these men orders and rules of conduct which were fairly strict. Hatton, *Comes Commercii* (1723), pp. 277–284; Jacob, *Lex Mercatoria* (1729), pp. 134–135.

[4] See M. Dorothy George, *London Life in the Eighteenth Century* (London, 1925), p. 269.

[5] *Repts. of Comrs.*, 1787, III, 98–99, 102–103, 105, 109–110, "Fourteenth Rept.," 1785.

Room, nineteen King's-Waiters, Chief Patent Searcher, five Under-Patent Searchers, and two Patent Searchers at Gravesend.[1] Finally there were five offices (four of which were sinecures) whereof the business was or might have been transacted in another department. These were the Customer of Cloth and Petty Customs Outwards, Controller of the Customer of Cloth and Petty Customs Inwards and Outwards, Collector of Petty Customs Inwards, Customer of the Great Customs Outwards and his Controller. These numbers take no account of posts which had existed during a part of the period and were abolished or marked out for discontinuance before 1786. A reduction of these offices was necessary, but it would have been difficult to accomplish without revision of the whole method of carrying on the business. It remained for later reforms, begun in 1798,[2] to cut out the dead wood of the London organization.

[1] One of these offices was granted to two persons.
[2] 38 Geo. III, c. 86, s. 1, 2, 3, 4, 5, 6, 7, 8. As in the case of outport sinecures and offices of the Central Office, these useless and sinecure offices in the London organization were recommended for abolition in the unsuccessful Bill of 1783, and in the scheme of 1792. See references in Ch. I, p. 24, n. 4, p. 25, n. 2.

CHAPTER V

The Outports

An outport may be defined as any port other than London where foreign shipping was carried on, and where the duties payable thereon were received by a collector to be remitted to the Receiver-General and accounted for with the Controller-General in London.[1] Though all the outports answered to this description, there was a certain distinction: they were either head-ports or members, so designated at the time that they were set out by commission. Under the control of these two divisions was a third class known as creeks.

A head-port was distinguished by an appointment of three patent officers, the customer, controller, and searcher, who were possessed of authority over all the members and creeks which came within the jurisdiction of the head-port. A member was differentiated by its subjection to the head-port as regards the control of these patent officers; as a rule it was a smaller port as well. Except for the first distinction, however, the member was entirely independent of the head-port and like it in every respect. A creek was a point within the limits of the head- or member-port, at which the coast business only could be transacted by officers stationed by order of the Customs Commissioners, and very often it was merely a nook where officers were or had been placed "by way of Prevention of Frauds in the Customs."[2] Since a creek was not a legal place of commerce, no foreign shipping could be carried on unless a particular license was secured from the head- or member-port, subject to strict regulations, of which the most important was the requirement that duties be paid in advance at the head-port. Since the patent officers could not be resident upon all of their offices, they were obliged to appoint deputies at all members, while at the creeks deputies of the customer and controller were stationed for the coast business, and occasionally a collector of the coal duties; there was seldom a deputy of the searcher there, since that officer was confined to the foreign

[1] *Repts. of Comrs.*, 1787, III, 124, "Fifteenth Rept.," 1786.
[2] See *Law-Treatise of Naval Trade*, I, 143.

business. Any coal duties received at a creek were remitted to the collector of the head- or member-port and by him returned to the customs office.[1] The chief officers of the head- and member-ports separately accounted for their receipts and disbursements with the central officers in London.[2] Not all the head-ports had members, and those which did possessed varying numbers. For example, in 1786 neither Boston nor Bristol had subordinate members; Plymouth, on the other hand, had ten, while most of the ports seem to have had two, three, or four.[3]

The limits of a port or of an additional quay within a port were set out by commission founded on the authority of acts of Parliament based on 1 Elizabeth and 14 Charles II.[4] In such cases it was the practice for the Customs Commissioners, upon their being satisfied as to the advisability of creating the port, to instruct their solicitor to prepare the draught of such a commission. This form was then submitted to the Lords of the Treasury who, upon approving, directed their warrant to the King's Remembrancer for a commission to issue from the Court of Exchequer empowering the commissioners to assign the ports or quays.[5] The commission usually included several chief officers, merchants, and the principal magistrates of the town, who repaired to the port and marked out its limits and certified their proceedings to the Barons of the Exchequer.[6] In 1696 there were fifty head- and member-ports; in 1786 these numbered seventy-one.[7]

[1] Except in the case of Leigh, which, though a creek, accounted directly with the London office.

[2] This survey of the outports is contained in *Repts. of Comrs.*, 1787, III, 121–124, "Fifteenth Rept.," 1786.

[3] See *ibid.*, 594, App. No. 6.

[4] *Ibid.*, III, 121–122.

[5] A copy of a significant statement of this method (with particular reference to quays) made by Wyatt, a solicitor of the customs, was sent by William Wood, Customs Secretary, to Nelthorpe, First Clerk to the Secretary of the Scottish Commssioners, 1751, Aug. 13. (P.R.O., Treasury Papers, Bdl. 346, No. 111.) Ryder, Attorney-General, was of opinion at this time (1751, Nov. 28) that the method of proceeding in Scotland should be similar to that in England as stated in Wyatt's report. *Ibid.*, Bdl. 346, Nos. 114–115.

[6] E. g., see warrant for the commission for redefining the limits of Newcastle, pursuant to 14 Chas. II. P.R.O., Treas. Out-letters, Cust., XXIV, 235–238, 1753, Mar. 7; cf. for Bristol, *ibid.*, XVIII, 415-419, 1723, Feb. 15.

[7] For the list of ports in these years, see P.R.O., Customs Registers: Series I, Cust. Quart. Estab., Nos. 36, 430. The following ports existed in both 1696 and 1786:

| Barnstaple | Dartmouth | Looe | Portsmouth |
| Beaumaris | Deal | Lyme | Poulton |

THE OUTPORTS

The jurisdiction of the head-ports varied, though it frequently covered hundreds of miles. The extent along the coast appears at one time to have coincided roughly with the boundaries of counties, but as ports came to be added, deviations took place. Inland jurisdiction theoretically reached to the first bridge of any river or creek which emptied within the coast limits of the port,[1] while the circuit of the riding officers, at one period at least, extended ten miles in from the sea. The size of such an area alone offered a serious problem with respect to a sufficient patrol against illicit trade; but when the coast-line was cut by jagged inlets and winding creeks which were ideal hiding-places for smugglers and gave easy access into the interior, effective guard became almost an impossibility. The proximity of certain continental and island ports used as bases by the runners forced the administration almost to despair of ever preventing the pernicious trade and to concentrate instead upon seizure and condemnation in punishment of illicit importation.[2] French and Flemish ports, notably Dunkirk and Ostend, were convenient harbors for the loading of wines, repacking of tobacco, or preparation of Continental goods for landing on the coasts of Kent and Sussex.[3] The Channel Islands, particularly Jersey and Guernsey, both as

Berwick	Dover	Lynn	Rochester
Bideford	Exeter	Milford	Rye
Boston	Falmouth	Minehead	Sandwich
Bridgwater	Faversham	Newcastle	Southampton
Bristol	Fowy	Newhaven	Stockton
Carlisle	Harwich	Padstow	Sunderland
Chester	Hull	Penryn	Swansea
Chichester	Ipswich	Penzance	Truro
Colchester	Lancaster	Plymouth	Weymouth
Cowes	Liverpool	Poole	Whitby
	Whitehaven	Yarmouth	

Additional ports listed on the establishment for 1786 which were not in existence in 1696 are: Aberystwith, Aldeburgh, Arundel, Blackney and Clay, Bridlington, Cardiffe, Cardigan, Chepstow, Gloucester, Gweek, Ilfracombe, Llanelly, Maldon, Preston, Scarbrough, Scilly, Shoreham, Southwold, St. Ives, Wells, Wisbech, Woodbridge. Poulton is the only port to be found on the 1696 establishment which is not included on the 1786 list. In 1784 the head-ports numbered twenty (of which four had no dependent members), the member-ports fifty-one, and the creeks thirty-two. *Repts. of Comrs.*, 1787, III, 124, "Fifteenth Rept.," 1786.

[1] Statement of B. R. Leftwich, Esq., Librarian of the Custom House.
[2] The Treasury Papers contain dozens of communications relating to the position of those ports in the smuggling trade.
[3] E. g., *The Report, with the Appendix, from the Committee of the House of Commons appointed to enquire into the Frauds and Abuses in the Customs, to the Prejudice of Trade, and Diminution of the Revenue* (London, 1733), p. 13.

strongholds of tobacco smugglers [1] and as connecting links between France and England for the running of French wines and brandies, were a continual menace to the peace of Plymouth, Dartmouth, Penzance, and Falmouth. The Isle of Man [2] with its sheltering inlets furnished an ideal place of rendezvous for the tobacco runners who played fast and loose with the plantation shipments destined for the western ports of Bristol, Liverpool, Lancaster, and Whitehaven, or for export thence to the Continent. For prohibited and other foreign goods and for goods intended to be relanded in Britain after exportation thence by drawback, this island was a veritable "Common Warehouse." Indeed, customs enforcement in the very face of that obstruction was finally despaired of and openly avowed an impossibility by the purchase of the island in 1765 from the Duke of Athol at £70,000.[3] In short, many of the difficulties of outport administration were due to such considerations as sheer location and jurisdiction of ports and nature of the adjoining coasts.

The outport custom-houses for the most part were operated on the rental system during the eighteenth century. By this arrangement it was customary to lease a suitable building in the port from a private owner or from the town corporation for a specified term of years upon the basis of a rent mutually agreed upon. The more usual lease ran for twenty-one years, though there were many variations. Rents increased steadily throughout the period, an addition very often taking place upon the expiration of a lease.[4] The Customs Commissioners appear not always to have kept up with the advance in rents, a fact which frequently forced transaction of customs business in buildings ill fitted to such a use and which more than once proved of considerable embarrassment to the officers of the port.

This informal rental system had many disadvantages. Sometimes the customs officers were forced to evacuate the custom-house with

---

[1] E. g., *Rept. of Com.*, 1733, pp. 61, 63–64, App. No. 17.

[2] E. g., *ibid.*, p. 65, App. No. 17.

[3] There is a vast body of material in the Treasury Papers relating to this subject for several years preceding the purchase. In connection with the transaction, see especially Bdl. 392, No. 16; Bdl. 434, Nos. 302–303, 304–305, 306; Bdl. 441, No. 348. British ownership of the island did not end the illicit trade for which exorbitant duties provided a constant impetus. Thus in 1778 the Excise Commissioners informed the Lords of the Treasury that more teas and brandies were then being smuggled on certain western coasts of Britain than when the government of Man was in private hands. *Ibid.*, Bdl. 542, No. 228, Excise Comrs. to Lords of Treas., 1778, Mar. 24.

[4] This information is compiled from many minute references in outport correspondence contained in Cust. Ho. Lib., Selections from Customs Outport Records.

THE OUTPORTS

only a few weeks' notice in which to find another.[1] At other times, the officers would be reduced to taking an unsatisfactory or high-priced room or building simply because there was but one place in the town suitable for a custom-house, and, upon hesitating, would be told to "quit it or take & that soon."[2] There were furthermore the questions of increase in rent, and of insecurity of tenure which might result in certain cases from the death of the lessee[3] or of those responsible for the lease[4] or from irregularity with respect to a lease.[5] Apparently as time went on, the Board began to realize the weaknesses in this system of leasing, for its policy changed somewhat—at least as far as regards the more rapidly growing ports—into the outright purchase or building of custom-houses. The Hull collector in a letter to the Board in 1757, in which he represents the advance of rent by the corporation from £32 to £60, suggests, "Should the town continue to flourish in trade as at present I humbly submit it to your Honrs consideration whether it may not be adviseable to purchase or build as your Honours have thought proper to do at Liverpool and some other Ports."[6]

There were other evidences of carelessness with regard to the state of the outport establishment. The unsuitable location of many of the custom-houses caused inconvenience to the merchants and gave opportunities for corrupt practices. Thus there are instances of the custom-house having been located in a collector's house[7] or in a deputy controller's home[8] and of customs business being transacted in a public-house.[9] Some of the buildings or their furnishings were permitted to lapse into so ruinous a condition that they actually

---

[1] E. g., Cust. Ho. Lib., Sel. from Cust. Outport Recds., South Coast, 1922, p. 119, Weymouth, Collector to Board, 1770–1772, 1770, Oct. 5.
[2] E. g., *ibid.*, West Coast, 1926, pp. 87–88, Swansea, Collector to Board, Leysen Richard, Custom-house, Neath, to Collector and Controller at Swansea.
[3] E. g., *ibid.*, Northern England, 1924, p. 25, Whitehaven, Collector to Board, 1743, Feb. 8; *ibid.*, South Coast, 1922, p. 118, Weymouth, Collector to Board, 1763–1766, 1763, Apr. 30.
[4] E. g., *ibid.*, p. 151, Exeter, Collector to Board, 1756–1761, 1758, Sept. 9 (regarding the watch-house at Exmouth).
[5] E. g., *ibid.*, East Coast, 1923, p. 217, Hull, Collector to Board, 1756–1759, 1757, Jan. 7.
[6] *Ibid.*, p. 217, Hull, Collector to Board, 1756–1759, 1757, Jan. 7.
[7] P.R.O., Treas. Out-letters, Cust., XVII, 89, Cust. Comrs. to Lords of Treas., 1717, Nov. 7.
[8] Cust. Ho. Lib., Sel. from Cust. Outport Recds., West Coast, 1926, p. 123, Beaumaris, Board to Collector, 1724, Aug. 29.
[9] *Ibid.*, East Coast, 1923, p. 132, Yarmouth, Collector to Board, 1702–1708, To Officers at Lowestoft and Pakefield, 1708, Oct. 29.

hindered business. How disagreeable must have been the state of the poor Sunderland officers whose collector wrote: "the flat desks are become so very old, rotten and decayed the covering torn & the mouldering of the rotten wood raises so much dust and harbours vermin so that all our seats in the Custom Ho. are very offensive & almost become an hindrance to the dispatch of business"[1]; and how precarious that of the Cardiff men whose collector represented that: "The writing desk in our Custom House which has stood there time out of mind is now become so very infirm and so entirely worm eaten that for some months past it has not been used, the officers being in fear least it should fall on their legs."[2] Mistaken economy on the part of the Board seems to have been responsible for such conditions. Buildings, furthermore, were often insecure, and the custom-house chest more than once fell a prey to robbers.[3] Occasionally custom-houses were crowded and not large enough to accommodate commerce,[4] though lack of room on the quays was a more frequent complaint.[5] There is, perhaps, a temptation to exaggerate

---

[1] Cust. Ho. Lib., Sel. from Cust. Outport Recds., Northern England, 1924, p. 118, Sunderland, Collector to Board, 1739, Sept. 18.

[2] *Ibid.*, West Coast, 1926, p. 42, Cardiff, Collector to Board, 1767, Jan. 6.

[3] There are several instances. See, for example, *ibid.*, South Coast, 1925, p. 125, Southampton, Board to Collector, 1766, Aug. 7; South Coast, 1922, p. 132, Weymouth, Board to Collector, 1742–1748, 1747, Oct. 17. The collector of the port suffered most from such robberies. Upon a memorial of the collector of Bridlington, praying that the sum of £74. 9s. 2d. which was stolen from his custom-house (and which he himself had been obliged to make good) might be repaid him or other relief granted him, the Customs Commissioners reported to the Treasury, 1773, May 8: "And altho' there have been two Instances of this kind, in which favour has been shewn, yet as every Collector of the Customs is answerable in Law, and by the Bond given by him with Sureties at the time of his Appointment for the Crown's Money, until payment thereof into the hands of the Receiver General, and this without exception as to Fire, or any other unavoidable Accidents, as represented to Your Lordships by a Report of this Board of the 19th of July 1769—on a Petition of the late Collector of Dartmouth on a similar Case with the present;—And as the shewing of Favour where the Robbery is not fully and clearly proved by a Conviction of one or more of the Offenders, or otherwise, (which, is the present Case), would tend to weaken the responsibility of the Collectors of the Out Ports, and expose the Revenue to Frauds; We cannot therefore advise the granting the prayer of the Petitioner." P.R.O., Treasury Papers, Bdl. 499, Nos. 280–281.

[4] There are several instances of such conditions. See, for example, Cust. Ho. Lib., Sel. from Cust. Outport Recds., East Coast., 1923, p. 146, Yarmouth, Collector to Board, 1730–1735, To the Mayor, 1731, Feb. 16.

[5] This was especially true of such centers as Liverpool and Bristol and others of the rapidly growing outports. See for example P.R.O., Treasury Papers, Bdl. 486, No. 332, Master, Wardens and Commonalty of the Society of Merchants-

THE OUTPORTS

the poor condition of many of the outport custom-houses. It must be remembered in this connection that numerous ports transacted too little business to warrant the need of an elaborate establishment. On the other hand, there was often negligence and false economy which was costly to the best interests of the revenue.

Conspicuous features of outport organization may be brought into sharper relief by a comparison of the outports with the Port of London. The two structures were very much alike with respect to personnel and procedure in shipping. The officers engaged in the actual collection of the revenue at an outport—the collector, controller, searcher, surveyor, land-waiter, tide-waiter, and boatman—were the same as the key officers in each of the important departments of the London organization; and the men of both establishments were subject to the same general regulations with regard to absences, remuneration, and rules defining conduct and execution of duty within the particular office. The chief differences between the two staffs were in the number of officers employed and the arrangement of duty. The average outport establishment was much smaller than that of the London organization, and for this reason outport officers had more varied duties to perform than the more specialized officers in London. The outport collector, for instance, not only received the customs receipts but was directly responsible for the conduct of all the men in his port and acted as warehouse-keeper as well. An outport surveyor did the work of both a land-surveyor and tide-surveyor, or, in a very small port, the deputy searcher filled his own position and that of surveyor. The outport establishment was further distinguished by the three patent officers whose peculiar position has been examined at length in Chapter I.

Procedure in import, export, and coastwise trade was similar in London and the outports. The same rules governed entry of cargo, payment of duties, allowances, unloading, weighing, and storing of goods. Regard must be had to peculiarities arising only from differences in the business carried on with respect to certain trades, since several of them were centered in London. On the whole, owing to constant efforts to secure and maintain uniformity, the general outlines of the organizations at London and at the outports corresponded closely.

There were significant differences, however, that arose in actual ad-

---

Venturers of Bristol to Lords of Treas. [1770]; and Nos. 333, 334, Cust. Comrs. to Lords of Treas., 1771, Feb. 26.

ministration. Several problems which confronted the outport organization deserve special attention. First of all, there were those difficulties which sprang from the distance of outports from the center of control in London. Though a voluminous correspondence was carried on by the Board in letters to the individual ports and through general letters to all the ports, undoubtedly outport administration suffered from lack of closer contact. The Board's letters could not reach many of the ports for days, during which time an officer might puzzle in vain over the best procedure in a given case, or a smuggling vessel—of which the outport had no knowledge—might accomplish its mission because of lack of official information from London which might have stopped the illicit importation. It is impossible to estimate the importance of this factor of distance from London, but it may well have had most unfortunate effects on business. A letter, included in the Yarmouth records under the heading of "Collector to Board," and addressed to one William Smith, is probably not the only one of its kind: "Good Sir,—I am sensible of your kindness to me in the dispatch of the Board's Letters of late, the want of them sometimes being very inconvenient to the business of the Port and the kind expression in one of them was so great a variety that I had almost forgot where there was such a thing in nature,—besides their kind order for a writt of assistance for the Port."[1] At times the Board failed to appreciate conditions in some of the ports as was indicated, for instance, by their under-estimation of the staff needed in many places.[2] On the whole, however, Board directions appear remarkably intelligent considering the nature of communications in the eighteenth century.

In the matter of remittances the outports faced another difficulty with respect to their distance from the central offices. Since the entire outport revenue was involved, it is well to consider the subject of remittances at some length. Receipts from the outports were usually sent to London in the form of bills of exchange, though they might be in merchants' or bank notes,[3] and sometimes they were consigned in cash under guard.[4] Because the collector of the port was respon-

---

[1] Cust. Ho. Lib., Sel. from Cust. Outport Recds., East Coast, 1923, p. 133, Yarmouth, Collector to Board, 1714–1719, To Wm. Smith, 1717, Sept. 23.
[2] E. g., see *infra*, Ch. VI, pp. 228–229.
[3] See Crouch, *Complete Guide to Officers* (1732), pp. 255–256, 259–261.
[4] E. g., *Cal. Treas. Papers,* 1556–7–1696, p. 489, Cust. Comrs. to Lords of Treas., 1695–6, Feb. 14, and minute; cf. p. 495; Cust. Ho. Lib., Sel. from Cust. Outport Recds., South Coast, 1925, p. 102, Southampton, Board to Collector,

THE OUTPORTS

sible for the safety of such remittances and was charged with any expense attached to them, the Commissioners maintained a fine disregard of the particular manner in which such remittances were made, as is indicated in their report to the Treasury on the petition of the merchants of Lynn:

> Upon the whole, We beg leave to observe to Your Lordships, that, as Collectors are by the Condition of their Bonds to remit the King's Money, from time to time, at their own Risque, and are answerable for the same—until it is paid to the Receiver General, it would be very improper in this Board to interfere, with respect to the manner, in which, the Remittances are made, —the Collectors being alone responsible for the same.[1]

Bills of exchange were generally used as being the safest and most convenient form of remittance. When a collector wished to remit to London, he would pay his cash to some merchant or "substantial person" in the port in return for the merchant's bill upon his correspondent in London ordering him to pay the Receiver-General the sum indicated. The collector then sent the bill to London and the Receiver-General proceeded to cash it. The Receiver-General could cause bills of £20 or over to be prosecuted if they were refused, and if such bills were accepted but not paid within three days, they could be protested by a notary public. Such protests and the bill were returned to the collector, who repaid the bill by sending another to the Receiver-General. The collector in the meantime became charged with

---

1733, May 10. The Scottish Customs Commissioners forbade remittances in merchants' bills and permitted them only in bankers' notes or in specie. P.R.O., Treasury Minute Book, XXXVIII, p. 36, Treasury session, 1766, June 13.

[1] On this occasion the merchants protested against the collector's refusal to accept bank notes in payment of duties because of liability to robbery in remittance. (P.R.O., Treasury Papers, Bdl. 426, No. 318, Cust. Comrs. to Lords of Treas., 1763, Dec. 9. See also No. 319.) In another report to the Treasury in 1784, upon a petition of the merchants of Liverpool (praying that their bills on London for payment of duties might be taken by the Liverpool collector at sixty instead of thirty days), the Customs Commissioners informed the Lords that they had always avoided giving any directions to their collectors concerning the acceptance of a merchant's bill for duties, each collector being responsible as to the manner of transmitting the money, "which is always to be done at his risque and expence." The Commissioners, however, had restrained their collectors from receiving bills drawn at a date exceeding thirty days, several collectors having failed to transmit their money in due time, whereby public accounts had been retarded. The Liverpool merchants and collector had made several applications to be released from the instruction; but the Board at those times, as upon this occasion, did not favor granting the petition. *Ibid.*, Bdl. 597, Nos. 266–267.

the cost of the protest and interest until he was reimbursed by the merchant.[1]

Sometimes the collector found no opportunity of any kind for remitting his receipts, it being impossible to arrange bills of exchange or to secure a sufficient guard, and large sums of cash would accumulate for want of the opportunity of remittance.[2] Furthermore, though the expense attached to such remittances appears to have been small enough, it may have been something of a consideration at times, since the collector remitted at his own charge.[3] Huge balances remained in collectors' hands for weeks at a time. The Customs and Treasury regulations, minutes, and orders for accounts of money on hand and for more frequent remittances [4] give evidence of the difficult problem that remittances presented. The returns of outport accounts of receipts and disbursements to the Central Office were further retarded by lack of sufficient funds in the outports with which to pay expenses, thus causing delays while money was sent from London or from a neighboring outport.[5] The notorious arrears in the books of the Central Office strongly confirm the sad effects of delays in outport remittances and accounts.

Open running on the coast, which necessitated concentration on the land guard and water guard, constituted the second big problem of administration peculiar to the outports. The chief means of checking smuggling lay in the custom-house sloops and cruisers which guarded

---

[1] Crouch, *Complete Guide to Officers* (1732), pp. 255–256, 259–260. There is an interesting case of a bill being returned to the Swansea collector because it was payable in Chelsea and not in London, the draft having been drawn by the collector on his sister at Chelsea who had money of his in her hands. Cust. Ho. Lib., Sel. from Cust. Outport Recds., West Coast, 1926, p. 90, Swansea, Collector to Board, 1751, Aug. 12.

[2] E. g., *Cal. Treas. Papers*, 1556-7–1696, p. 495, Cust. Comrs. to Lords of Treas., 1695–6, Mar. 14; *Cal. Treas. Books and Papers, 1739–1741*, p. 491, 1741, Aug. 12.

[3] For instance, the Board in 1735–6 disallowed £1. 18s., which represented the cost of sending £500 from Weymouth to London, on the grounds that the collector was obliged to pay such expenses. Cust. Ho. Lib., Sel. from Cust. Outport Recds., South Coast, 1922, p. 127, Weymouth, Board to Collector, 1733–1738, 1735–6, Jan. 13.

[4] E. g., in the early part of the period, see P.R.O., Treas. Out-letters, Cust., XIV, 441–442, Godolphin to Cust. Comrs., 1706, Aug. 30; and Cust. Ho. Lib., Letters to Dartmouth, 1675–6 to 1715, pp. 213–214, [Board] to Dartmouth, 1706, Sept. 3. For example toward the close of the period, see Robinson's communications to the Customs Commissioners in 1775, 1776, and 1777. P.R.O., Treas. Out-letters, Cust., XXXI, 426, 437, 441, 464, 481; and P.R.O., Treasury Papers, Bdl. 523, No. 230, Stanley to Robinson, 1776, Mar. 20.

[5] See *infra*, Ch. VI, pp. 216–217.

THE OUTPORTS

the shores and in the riding officers and their supervisors who patrolled the coast.

The history of the water guard of the eighteenth century is that of a merry game between the customs and the smugglers, who vied in the numbers and efficiency of boats laid down, with the smugglers always one move ahead of the Commissioners. In the early part of the period the customs guard appears to have consisted almost entirely of modest smacks and sloops. It was not long, however, before the Customs Commissioners embarked upon a more elaborate scheme of boats. They strengthened the water guard by stationing more sloops, adding to the service cutters and cruisers which were made larger and larger, and, at one period, a system of six-oared boats which were bigger than those previously used for guard to the western coasts.[1] Still the smugglers always went one better. When the Commissioners established large boats in some places, the smugglers would resort to light, open craft which could lie in the shallows where the customs boats could not go or outrow the heavier cruisers, built mainly for sailing.[2] At one time on the western coast, the runners used a lug-sail vessel which permitted them to land their goods and sail immediately out to sea while the customs boat with its ordinary sail could but stand helplessly by and watch the escape. Indeed, such was the superiority of the lug-sail over the customs cutters that the Exeter collector and controller in 1770 offered to build a lugger at their own expense, by which they hoped to give a severe check to the runners on their coast.[3] Highly organized groups of smugglers used great armed cruisers which they continually enlarged so that their tonnage frequently reached 100 and 200 tons and occasionally touched 300, with many carriage guns and a crew of scores of men.[4]

[1] The increase in the water guard is indicated for the most part by miscellaneous references in Cust. Ho. Lib., Extracts Board Minutes, III, IV, "Cruizers," and in the Treasury material and outport correspondence. On the system of six-oared boats, see P.R.O., Treas. Out-letters, Cust., XXVIII, 130, Cooper to Cust. Comrs., 1766, Dec. 17; and XXVIII, 136, Cooper to Cust. Comrs., 1767, Mar. 4; P.R.O., Treasury Papers, Bdl. 459, Nos. 67–72, Cust. Comrs. to Lords of Treas., 1767, Feb. 21; Nos. 77–78, Cust. Comrs. to Lords of Treas., 1767, Apr. 29.

[2] E. g., Cust. Ho. Lib., Sel. from Cust. Outport Recds., Northern England, 1924, pp. 15–16, Whitehaven, Collector to Board, 1731, May 26; P.R.O., Treasury Papers, Bdl. 434, No. 347.

[3] Cust. Ho. Lib., Sel. from Cust. Outport Recds., South Coast, 1922, p. 160, Exeter, Collector to Board, 1766–1771, 1770, Aug. 4.

[4] E. g., in connection with the port of Portsmouth, see comment of B. R. Leftwich in *ibid.*, South Coast, 1925, p. 148.

The second half of the century saw the Board resolutely ordering the construction of boat after boat. During the years from 1763 to 1783 alone, the number of armed cutters of the service almost doubled (rising from twenty-two to forty-two), while tonnage, men, and guns were each increased by over 300 per cent, and the sum expended on the cruisers was raised from £14,046. 10s. 3d. to £42,845. 5s. 8d.[1] Such boats even then would have made a pitiful showing without the coöperation of Admiralty cruisers and men-of-war. The Admiralty expense account for assistance to the customs increased from £139,724 in 1767 to £220,220 in 1783, and the number of men employed by the Admiralty in this service increased from 2,687 to 4,235.[2] As the methods of the smugglers became more daring, efforts to cope with them became more determined. Only during several periods of war with France does the Board appear to have slackened the effectiveness of the water guard. At such times many of the sloops were laid aside, and the land guard was strengthened instead.[3]

Cruisers in the latter part of the period were maintained in two different ways—on the establishment and by contract, on "Principles of Service so different," observed a Parliamentary Committee in their report of 1784, "that it is impossible to suppose that both can be right, or equally eligible."[4] When the vessel was kept on the establishment, it belonged to the Crown and its expenses were paid quarterly out of the customs revenue. There were two kinds of contract: in one, the Crown furnished the vessel to a contractor free of charge, but the outfitting, repairs, victualing,[5] and wages of mariners were paid out of the produce of her seizures, and the remainder or the loss shared between the Crown and the contractor. In the other type of

---

[1] *Parliamentary Papers*, XXXVI, *Repts.*, VI, H. C. No. 58, p. 27, App. No. 1 (1783), "First Report from the Committee appointed to Enquire into the Illicit Practices used in Defrauding the Revenue." See also Cross, *Eighteenth Century Documents* [*Univ. of Mich. Publ.: Hist. and Pol. Science*, VII], p. 255.

[2] *Parliamentary Papers*, XXXVI, *Repts.*, VI, H.C. No. 58, p. 7 (1783), "First Rept. on Illicit Practices."

[3] *Cal. Treas. Papers*, 1697–1701–2, p. 250, Cust. Comrs. to Lords of Treas., 1698, Dec. 8; *Cal. Treas. Books and Papers*, 1742–1745, p. 489, Cust. Comrs. to Lords of Treas., 1744, June 21.

[4] *Parliamentary Papers*, XXXVI, *Repts.*, VI, H.C. No. 60, p. 6 (1784), "Third Report from the Committee appointed to Enquire into the Illicit Practices used in Defrauding the Revenue." For examples of such vessels, see B.M., Add. MSS. 8133 B, ff. 110–113.

[5] The usual allowance for victualing was 9d. per day for each man, and 1s. per lunar month for fires and candles. There were miscellaneous items as well.

contract the contractor provided the vessel at an allowance from the Crown of 4s. 6d. per ton per lunar month. For this allowance he was obliged to supply the outfit and provide for all improvements. As in the first arrangement, all expenses of salaries, victualing, and miscellaneous allowances were borne out of the produce of seizures, and the surplus divided or the failure made good equally between the Crown and contracting party.[1] The commanders, the mates, and sometimes a deputed mariner were appointed by the Board's commission.[2]

Only too often cruiser contracts were made with the collector and controller of an outport. Of twenty-four customs cruisers on contract in 1784, sixteen were under such management. Since the collector of a port was required to certify of what use the cruiser had been to the revenue, together with the items of expenditure, there was too great an opportunity for him to sacrifice the interests of the Crown to his own advantage, particularly as regarded his savings on victualing bills or repairs. The Commissioners of Accounts in 1786 observed that such an arrangement violated the principle that no interest in the performance of a service should rest in the person whose duty it was to execute the service, and recommended that customs officers should not be permitted to contract for such vessels.[3] In the following year, because contract cruisers had perpetrated frauds and the established

---

[1] *Repts. of Comrs.*, 1787, III, 145–148, "Fifteenth Rept.," 1786, describes the plan of maintenance of vessels. For the usual terms of contract, see P.R.O., Treasury Papers, Bdl. 516, Nos. 252–253, Stanley to Cooper, 1775, Apr. 7. It appears, however, that at one time there were some contracts used for vessels on the establishment wherein the Crown paid 4s. 6d. per ton per month for hire of the vessel and defrayed expenses of officers' wages, victualing, and other costs. (*Ibid.*, Bdl. 551, Nos. 177–178, Harvey to Lords of Treas., [read 1779, May]. The arrangement whereby the crews were paid salaries whether they made seizures or not was found to be open to abuse. According to Musgrave, "it was discovered that these like the other places in the Customs were beginning to be considered as pensions for old decayed Borough Voters." The Customs Commissioners therefore resolved that they would employ no new cruisers unless the commander would contract that all expenses should first be paid out of the produce of seizures and the net remainder be divided equally between the Crown and the crew; any loss was to be borne equally by the Crown and the commander. (Cross, *Eighteenth Century Documents* [*Uni. of Mich. Publ.: Hist. and Pol. Science*, VII], pp. 255–256.) This proved so strong an incentive to activity in the crew that apparently at one time all established cruisers were ordered to be laid aside unless the commanders would accept the terms of contract. See Cust. Ho. Lib., Extracts Board Minutes, IV, 271, 1783, Feb. 21, Sept. 4; 273, 1784, Dec. 16.

[2] Those of the established cruisers, pursuant to Treasury warrant.

[3] *Repts. of Comrs.*, 1787, III, 195–196, "Fifteenth Rept.," 1786.

cruisers had proved by far the most profitable, the cruisers by contract were discontinued.[1]

The greater number of the more important Board minutes and general letters for the regulation of cruisers had been issued by the middle of the century, and the duties of the officers and their crews had been fairly well fixed.[2] A review of the most important points of these instructions as they stood in 1781 will indicate the measures taken to provide for prevention of smuggling. Every commander was to keep a full complement of mariners on duty at all times, who were to be approved by him and by the collector, controller, and chief mate as able seamen. He was required to keep a journal which contained his observations as to winds, weather, and the station of the boat, and to submit a duplicate of the journal monthly to the collector of the outport to be sent to the Customs Commissioners. His cruiser was to be kept in constant motion; it was never to go into port except for provisions and then only for the shortest time possible. Communication regarding smugglers was to be held with the riding officers on the coast in the form of color signals by day and fires by night. Whenever the cruiser brought up in a bay, the commander was to send a boat ashore in search of any smugglers who might be lying low awaiting an opportunity for running. The commander was required to speak with all ships that were in the path of the cruiser, ascertaining where they were from and whither they were bound; and if a vessel acted suspiciously, attending it until it was clear of the coast. Any boat found hovering or at anchor within two leagues of the coast might be seized; and if any ship was found to have broken bulk and landed part of its cargo, such goods were subject to forfeiture. Numerous other instructions defined more closely the nature of goods and ships liable to seizure and the procedure of officers in making seizures.[3]

The commander of the boat was directly answerable to the collector of the port for enforcement of these regulations, and his correspond-

---

[1] *Commons Reports*, 1803, XII, 58, "Fourth Rept. Sel. Com. on Finance," 1797.

[2] In B.M., *Instructions to Officers in the Out Ports* are indicated the dates of such directions on the margin of the "Instructions for the Commanders and Mates of His Majesty's Cruisers, in the Service of the Customs," 1781.

[3] *Ibid.* This book of outport instructions, which contains sets of instructions directed to all of the principal officers in the outports, includes a body of "Instructions to Commanders of Sloops and Cutters." They are of the same general character as the instructions just summarized, with more emphasis on seizures.

THE OUTPORTS

ence with the custom-house was required at all times. The collector gave orders for specific movements of cruisers and directed better execution of duty when necessary. He advised the commander of any smuggling vessel of which he had intelligence, and the commander in turn gave the collector any useful information which he might have. The collector examined the journals of the commanders, representing any item of importance to the Board, and saw that the boats were well cared for and the mariners well provided for. It must be feared, however, that there was not always the desired contact between the ships' officers and the officers of the various ports.[1]

The greatest difficulty in the management of the cruisers was to keep them at sea. Many were the commanders lying in port on the excuse that they had run out of provisions or that the boat needed repairs. The requirement that sufficient provisions for two weeks or a month should be taken on board at a time, and that the collector should be notified whenever the boat was in port and should report to the Board accordingly, was designed at one period to prevent such laxity.[2] There were also complaints (some of them from the Admiralty) that in cases of seizures the customs cruisers were too often content with seizing only the goods and permitting the smuggling vessels to escape; and many were the orders, backed with the threat of penalties, against the practice.[3] Furthermore, there was often sad lack of good discipline on the boats. Mariners were not infrequently disobedient and mutinous (and the Board dealt hardly enough with such fellows by urging to have them impressed for the navy upon their

[1] E. g., Cust. Ho. Lib., Sel. from Cust. Outport Recds., South Coast, 1925, p. 56, Dartmouth, Board to Collector, 1765, Jan. 22.

[2] E. g., Cust. Ho. Lib., Letters to Dartmouth, 1675-6 to 1715, pp. 308-309, Carkesse to Dartmouth, 1714, Feb. 5; Board's Letters to the Port of Boston, Lincolnshire, February $\frac{1732}{3}$ to March $\frac{1745}{6}$, Carkesse to Boston, 1740, July 24. In 1776 the irregularity was so serious that Robinson, Treasury secretary, informed the Customs Commissioners that "It having been represented to My Lords Comm^{rs} of his Maj^{ts} Treasury that the Commanders of the Custom House Sloops do often stay at home and thereby trust the Care of their Vessels to their Mates or some other of their officers, And that it would be of Great benefit to the Revenue, if strict Orders were Given to them, to go to Sea and bring in all the Smuggling Vessels, Boats, and Men they meet with, by which many fine fellows might be procured for his Maj^{ts} Service, I am Command by their Lordships to acquaint you therewith & direct you to give Orders accordingly." P.R.O., Treas. Out-letters, Cust., XXXI, 468.

[3] E. g., Cust. Ho. Lib., Sel. from Cust. Outport Recds., South Coast, 1922, p. 222, Penzance, Board to Collector, 1761-1769, 1765, Jan. 8.

182   ORGANIZATION OF THE ENGLISH CUSTOMS

dismissal) [1]; commanders at times provided their men with unsatisfactory food [2]; and there were disagreements over shares of seizures between commanders and men.[3]

The Board made continued efforts to improve this aspect of the service, and with such success that Musgrave could state in 1782: "The good Effects of the Boards attention to this Service is proved by the produce of the King's share of Seizures which is encreased from £40,000 ℔ ann. to £80,000 ℔ ann. in the last 20 years of which last Sum—£50,000 has been taken by the Cruizers." [4] With what conviction must this commissioner have declared that "The principal dependance for the Guard of the Coast must be upon the Cruisers." [5]

The land guard reinforced the water guard as the second branch of preventive organization. Stationed a few miles distant from each other, riding surveyors or supervisors, with their several underofficers, constantly patrolled the coast to detect and prevent as much smuggling as possible, keeping in touch with one another so that concerted efforts could be made against the smugglers. The value of the riding officers was early appreciated by the administration, and that staff seems to have been of especial assistance during the first years of the period before the efficiency of the water guard was felt, and while the prevention of the export of wool constituted such a vexatious problem. Particularly useful were the riding officers of northern England who guarded the passes into Scotland against the inroads of the Scottish smugglers, whose cheap goods glutted the English markets. Until the Board made use of more powerful boats, the major part of preventive service in times of war with France was thrust upon the land guard, as has been indicated above.

From several sets of instructions issued to riding officers and riding surveyors at various times in the period, some outline of their duties may be constructed. The officers were required to provide themselves with a horse to patrol their particular districts by day and by night—

[1] E. g., Cust. Ho. Lib., Board's Letters to Boston, Feb., 1732-3 to Mar., 1745-6, Carkesse to Boston, 1734, Dec. 12.

[2] E. g., Cust. Ho. Lib., Sel. from Cust. Outport Recds., East Coast, 1923, pp. 200-201, King's Lynn, Board to Collector, 1731-1735, 1734, Oct. 5.

[3] A minute of 1745, Feb. 21 (enforcing former minutes of 1732), directed that commanders and mates of sloops should not have a share in seizures unless they were on board when such seizures were made. Cust. Ho. Lib., Extracts Board Minutes, II, "Sloops."

[4] Cross, *Eighteenth Century Documents* [*Uni. of Mich. Publ.: Hist. and Pol. Science*, VII], p. 256.

[5] *Ibid.*, p. 255.

if the night was favorable to illicit trade—and to go properly armed. They were ordered to visit all villages and towns within their particular district on the watch for any runners or for smuggled goods which had been hidden for later land-carriage to market. The officers at all times were to keep in close communication with their brother officers, advising them of any informations of smuggling on the coast and goods illicitly landed, and joining with them when necessary in searches or seizures. Communications also were to be maintained with the cruisers at sea. Of all these activities a record had to be kept in the form of a ledger and a journal. The officer was required to enter in detail the places and extent of his ride, time of departure, places visited, and any particulars connected therewith, such as meetings with brother officers, seizures, and the like. These journals were inspected by his riding supervisor and by an Examiner in London.

The riding surveyor or supervisor was directly responsible for the observance of the above regulations governing the riding officers. As often as possible he was to visit his men at their stations and examine their journals. If an officer had been guilty of some irregularity, the supervisor made note of it in his journals and delivered a charge against the man in writing. He regularly returned the officers' journals to the surveyor-general or in some cases to the collector, and reported quarterly on the conduct of his men. The supervisor offered his staff active assistance: whenever he had news of any run goods, he informed the officers through whose district they were likely to pass; and in order to detect such illicit practices more easily, he attempted to discover the smugglers' use of signals and agreed upon a proper system of signals with the sloop-masters.[1]

The surveyor-general of a district (during that part of the period when surveyors-general were stationed in the outports to superintend the ports of their districts) gave orders to the supervisors and their subordinates as occasion demanded and frequently inspected journals as well. The collector of a port, however, was responsible for the execution of duty by the land guard. He informed supervisors and officers of any run goods and gave them directions with respect to their work. Every time the supervisor was in the port he was expected to call upon the collector and controller to receive any orders

[1] This survey of the general duties of riding supervisors and riding officers is based on Cust. Ho. Lib., *Instructions to be Observed by Supervisors* (1734); *Instructions to be Observ'd by Riding Officers* (1734); B.M., *Instructions to Officers in the Out Ports*, "Instructions to a Supervisor or Surveyor of the Riding and other Preventive Officers," and outport correspondence.

that they might have and to inform them if anything "remarkable" had happened in his district. The collector, as has been noted, had a final check over the conduct of all the officers by his examination of their journals and accounts and observations upon them.

The life of the preventive officer was hard. By day and often by night he was expected to make his rounds in all kinds of weather, and often in circumstances of grave danger. Well might such officers be built of "sterner stuff"; well might they have answered to the qualifications recommended by the Weymouth collector in 1717: "wee are humbly of opinion that the persons imployed in this service be men that are hardy, unmarryed and are well acquainted with the country soe that they maynt have the clogg of a family and may be capable from their acquaintance to cultivate a friendship with the country people to have their assistance on occasion without which the service will not be soe well performed." [1] The temptation of the fireside was responsible for one form of delinquency on the part of the officers. There were various reports and charges made against their staying at home too many days or for too long in the day. The requirement that an officer record the exact times of his departure for duty of a morning and of his return at night was designed in some measure to prevent this. False entries in journals were always possible, but penalties on detection were severe. Strangely enough, in connection with an officer's patrol there were complaints that he had no horse. If, however, horses were always as difficult to secure as they were in the case of a poor fellow at Penzance who was suspected for not having one, and of other irregularities, pity rather than reprimand might well go out to an officer:

> To the first article, I beg leave to acquaint your Honble Board that on my admission as waiter and searcher at Marazion, I immediately bought a horse which in a few months I was so unfortunate to loose by death, I bought a second which turned out so vicious that I was obliged to part with him at a considerable disadvantage, I bought a third which was recommended to me as a good sound horse but turned out blind, I bought a fourth which after a year's service died by which severall horses I have not lost less than eighteen guineas since the death of the fourth. I have had a horse constantly at my call day and night and am determined as soon as opportunity offers to purchase one.[2]

[1] Cust. Ho. Lib., Sel. from Cust. Outport Recds., South Coast, 1922, p. 95, Weymouth, Collector to Board, 1716–1719, 1717, Sept. 28.
[2] *Ibid.*, pp. 201–202, Penzance, Collector to Board, 1748–1750, Benjamin Elliott to [Board ?].

Negligence of sufficient meeting and correspondence with brother officers was also a frequent charge.¹ The examination of journals and inspection by the supervisor were calculated in some degree to secure such consultation.

On the whole, though the land guard was undoubtedly useful in exacting penalties for infringement of customs laws, at no time in the period does it appear to have constituted a really effective force against the smugglers. In 1783 the Commissioners of the Revenue were reported to have observed "that their Inland Establishment is utterly unfit to suppress these Proceedings [running on the coast by force]; being calculated rather to detect Frauds than to resist Violence, and having hardly any Powers of Exertion upon the Coast, beyond the Detection of small illicit Importations and Exportations, attempted by Merchant Vessels, or by the Coasting Trade." ² According to Musgrave, the riding men were "of very little Service tho' a great Burthen to the Revenue and of late Years [before 1782] parliamentary Interest has recommended Apothecaries, Brewers & other Tradesmen to these employments who never ride but when their own occupations require it and fabricate Journals for the rest of the time. And it is generally reported that many of them are the relation of— & even that some of them are the Agents & Collectors for the Smuglers." These officers, declared the Commissioner, were not "sufficiently numerous" nor "resolute" enough to prove any serious obstacle to the large bodies of armed smugglers that infested the coasts. "Nor co^d they be encreased so as to render effectual Service unless one half of the Inhabitants co^d be hired to watch the other." ³

This last statement points to yet a third feature peculiar to outport organization—the relationship of the customs to several officials of local government and to the people of the country. In Chapter VI the problem that this factor raised in effective customs enforcement is indicated more fully. It will suffice at this point to call attention to the fact that the outport establishment was obliged to concern itself with the attitude of the officials and inhabitants of the port and countryside, for whether or not the customs could count for support upon those elements frequently influenced efficiency in preventing running,

¹ E. g., Cust. Ho. Lib., Letters From Whitby, 1721–1724, Richard Wilson to Gentlemen, 1722, Feb. 1.
² *Parliamentary Papers*, XXXVI, *Repts.*, VI, H.C. No. 58, p. 5 (1783), "First Rept. on Illicit Practices."
³ Cross, *Eighteenth Century Documents* [*Uni. of Mich. Publ.: Hist. and Pol. Science*, VII], p. 255.

186 ORGANIZATION OF THE ENGLISH CUSTOMS

in effecting seizures, and in securing their condemnation upon prosecution.

By the patent creating the Customs Board in 1671 the coöperation of officials of local government was ordered. The patent required that "all & singular our Officers & ministers Whoe now have or hereafter shall have any Office power or authority derived from or under our Lord high Admirall of England & alsoe all & every our Viceadmiralls Justices of Peace mayors Sherriffes Constables Bayliffes headborroughs & all other our Officers & Ministers Whatsoever That they & every of them be unto you and every of you & to all & every your Deputy Collectors ministers Servants & other Officers aydeing & assisting in Execuĉon of the p̄misses and obedient in all things as becometh under payne of our high displeasure and the utmost pill [peril] that may fall thereon."[1] Officially, then, customs enforcement received the support of these magistrates, but it must be feared that too often such encouragement remained merely theoretical. Some of the justices of the peace, who were the most prominent of these local officers and before whom certain seizure cases might be prosecuted,[2] were known at times to use their authority to the prejudice of the revenue.[3] As for the attitude of the populace, the phenomenal successes of the smuggling organizations against the combined efforts of the Customs, Excise, Admiralty, and War Departments bear witness to that ready support so frequently to be found in the villages and along the coasts.

With respect, then, to these three problems of distance from London, adequate land and water guard, and relationship to local officials and inhabitants, the outport customs organization dealt with difficulties peculiar to itself.

Having examined the general character of the outport system, it now remains to consider how these ports were brought into the general scheme of customs administration. There were two principles operating in the control of the outports by the Board and officers of the Central Office: first, to provide for the greatest possible efficiency in the collection and remittance of revenue; second, to bring the outports into conformity with the established practice in London. It would be idle to offer any further illustration of the first of these. As to the second, numerous Board communications indicate such a pur-

---

[1] P.R.O., Patent Roll, 23 Chas. II, P. 2, No. 1, Mem. 35, dorse, [1671], Sept. 27.
[2] See *infra*, Ch. VIII, pp. 277, 280.
[3] E. g., see *infra*, Ch. VI, p. 233.

pose, but perhaps the best single statement is to be found in instructions to officers sent on special surveys of the outports: "We recommend the bringing the practice in such Ports, to as near a Conformity with That of the Port of London as the Nature of the thing may well admit." [1] All instructions and orders sent out to the ports from London were directed toward these two ends.

The agents of the Board's centralized supervision were the collectors and controllers of the outports and the surveyors-general. In 1697-8 the importance of the controller was emphasized by a Treasury warrant which directed that he keep account of money and bills remitted to the Receiver-General by the outport collector and send duplicates thereof to the Controller-General in London.[2] The position of the controller in the outport management was further strengthened in 1706 by the Board's resolving to direct all its orders and letters to the collectors and controllers together and ordering them to join in their letters to the Board. The position which was held by the collector at that time is well described by the general letter which bore the Board's orders upon this occasion:

It being of late observed that several Letters and Orders directed from this Board to some of the Coll^{rs} in the Outports have been concealed by y^u from the Comptrollers or their Deputys, & other Officers concern'd therein, wth out being communicated to them, as they ought to have been; & more especially in all such matters as relate to the managem^t wth respect to the Rec^{ts} of money, remitting of Cash, & paym^t of Incidents & Debentures—and We Observing also that some Coll^{rs} to cover their ill designs have many times misrepresented matters to the Board wch hath in Several Instances obstructed the course of our managem^t— We have resolved that all our Letters Orders & Instructions (unless in some special & extraordinary cases) shall here after be directed to the Coll^{rs} & Comptrollers Joyntly, & in like manner we direct that the Comptroller do jointly with the Coll^{rs} in their Letters & Answers to us; that so there may be no pretence of Ignorance in either, or mistakes in the managem^t of the business of the Port.[3]

---

[1] P.R.O., Treasury Papers, Bdl. 433, Nos. 242–243, headed "Instructions for the Officers of the Customs appointed to Survey & Report the State of the several ports in England & Wales 1764." Though this set of instructions, addressed to the surveyor-general for Hants and Dorset and to another person, appears to be a rough draft, and indeed is headed as a "plan" on the back, this statement is borne out by instructions to certain surveyors of Scottish ports in that year. Cf. ibid., Bdl. 435 No. 237.

[2] P.R.O., Treas. Out-letters, Cust., XIII, 419, Treasury warrant, 1697-8, Mar. 12.

[3] Cust. Ho. Lib., Letters to Dartmouth, 1675–6 to 1715, p. 212 [Board] to Dartmouth, 1706, Aug. 29; cf. Cust. Ho. Lib., Extracts Board Minutes, I, "Collectors in the Outports," 1706, Aug. 21.

Additional responsibility was placed upon the controller two years later by a Treasury warrant which made it incumbent upon him to keep a joint custody of the cash.[1] The controller's position in connection with the management of the port seems to have been still more firmly established in 1725 and 1739. In a general order of the latter year, the collectors were further cautioned to take notice:

> that the Surveyor as well as the Comptroller is to be consulted & advised with in the conduct & management of the business in the port in general and that the Collector does upon all occasions, advise with the Comptroller, and not take upon him to give orders or directions relating to the management of the Port without first consulting him and having his consent; and he is not only to join in writing all Letters to the Board and all matters of business which has relation to the waterside, or to such part of the proceedings of the Port wherein the Surveyor has any care or Inspection, you are also to consult and advise with him, and have his approbation. But if at any time it shall happen that you differ in opinion, you are to make separate reports to the Board.[2]

With the last of these orders the co-responsibility of the controller appears to have been well defined.

The manner in which the Board directed the regulation of a port through the collectors and controllers may be summarized briefly. Through orders and instructions in correspondence with these officers, general procedure was prescribed and regulations for government were laid down. When new laws were passed, affecting the customs, the Board gave the collector directions for their enforcement or the observance of the new practice therein described. The discovery of an irregularity at one or two ports would frequently evoke a general Board letter to all the ports, warning them to be on the watch for similar practices.[3] Time and again the Board would notify the outports of smuggling vessels expected on their particular coasts and inform the officers in remarkable detail of the runners' plans.[4]

---

[1] Cust. Ho. Lib., Letters to Dartmouth, 1675–6 to 1715, p. 218, Board to Dartmouth, 1708, June 17; cf. Cust. Ho. Lib., Sel. from Cust. Outport Recds., Northern England, 1924, p. 228, Whitby, Collector to Board and General, 1728, Aug. 24.

[2] Cust. Ho. Lib., Board's Letters to Boston, Feb., 1732–3, to Mar., 1745–6, Carkesse to [Boston], 1739, Dec. 22.

[3] For example, upon an instance of French wine being entered as Spanish in one port, a general letter to other outport officers cautioned them to see that wines were not entered under wrong denominations. Cust. Ho. Lib., Letters to Dartmouth, 1715–16 to 1731, p. 43, Carkesse to Collector and Controller, 1717, Aug. [10 or 20].

[4] E. g., Cust. Ho. Lib., Board's Letters to Boston, Feb., 1732–3 to Mar., 1745–6, Carkesse to Boston, 1735, Apr. 30.

THE OUTPORTS   189

Since the collectors were responsible for the officers in the port, they gave the Board information of any delinquency or corruption, and the Board dealt with it accordingly. In order to inform themselves of the conduct of officers and to secure their execution of duty, the collectors examined journals, visited the men at the waterside and on board vessels,[1] and in some cases called at their members and neighboring ports at definite times, the better to examine into any irregular conditions.[2] Thus the conduct of the outport staff also came under the close surveillance of the Board.

The number of customs accounts, the care with which they had to be kept, the regularity and frequency of remittances of money and accounts to the Central Office, and the close examination they there received were all designed to bring the outport revenue administration, through the agency of the collectors and controllers, under the close superintendence of the Board and its attendants. Collectors were further obliged to correspond with law officers on informations and seizures, and thus close control was kept upon any cases liable to involve the customs in legal embarrassment, but more particularly with an eye to the revenue arising from successful prosecution of seized goods.

Finally, the Board used opportunities to meet officers personally. In the beginning of the period, whenever any collector happened to be in London on business, it was usual for the Commissioners to call for the survey of the port, and if there had been any charge against the officer, he was called in and "enjoined" or reprimanded as the case necessitated.[3] In 1716 the Board required that when a collector or any other officer above a land-waiter had leave to be in London, he was to appear before the Board at his first coming.[4]

The Commissioners did not depend entirely upon the chief officers of the outports in their supervision. They had direct representatives as well in the form of the surveyors-general who were stationed in various districts of the outports and, after 1771, their successors the general-surveyors, who had their offices in London. The position of

[1] E. g., Cust. Ho. Lib., London to Harwich, 1699–1788, p. 41, Board to Harwich, 1735, Nov. 15; cf. Cust. Ho. Lib., Extracts Board Minutes, I, "Collectors in the Out Ports," 1735, Nov. 12.
[2] E. g., Treas. Out-letters, Cust., XXIII, 492, Cust. Comrs. to Lords of Treas., 1749, July 27; e. g., Cust. Ho. Lib., Letter Book, Wells, 1712 to 1730, p. 28, Board to Wells Collector, 1712, Mar. 21.
[3] Cust. Ho. Lib., Extracts Board Minutes, I, "Collectors in the Out Ports," 1697, June 25.
[4] *Ibid.*, I, "Collectors in the Out Ports," 1716, Nov. 10.

190 ORGANIZATION OF THE ENGLISH CUSTOMS

the general-surveyors has been indicated at some length in the discussion of the Central Office in Chapter III.[1] A further comment on the surveyors-general as outport administrative officers is pertinent at this point. These men were general supervisors or inspectors over a district that included several ports, and as such were concerned with the broader aspects of administration within their particular area. Thus they visited the ports within their survey, inspected the work of the officers, informed the Board of irregularities, gave orders for improvement of the business, and reported upon difficulties peculiar to their ports, such as a particularly troublesome smuggling trade.[2]

The conduct by the surveyors-general and general-surveyors of the elaborate formal surveys of the ports that were made from time to time was one of their most important functions. These surveys were of considerable significance, for the reports on them were given the most careful attention, and the recommendations which they embodied for the improvement of the service were acted upon accordingly. The instructions issued upon the occasion of a survey in 1764 indicate the thoroughness of such investigations. Briefly, the most important of these directed that the surveyors examine into the way in which the chief and inferior officers did their duties, the state of the foreign and coast trade at the port, the number of ships and their tonnage trading to the port and the proportion of foreign tonnage to British, the chief smuggling vessels that frequented the port, and the reasons why the receipt of the port was not large enough to cover its expenses, if such chanced to be the case. The surveyors were desired to inspect all journals, account books, and office records, to see that the boats were kept in proper repair, and to report on the number and efficiency of sloops and the stations of riding supervisors and officers. They were required, as has been stated above, to bring the ports into conformity with procedure in the Port of London and to offer their observations as to how frauds in the port could be better suppressed.[3] In their re-

---

[1] See *supra*, Ch. III, pp. 113–115.

[2] E. g., P.R.O., Treasury Papers, Bdl. 433, No. 138, Cust. Comrs. to Lords of Treas., 1764, July 4.

[3] *Ibid.*, Bdl. 433, Nos. 238–243, [Plan of] "Instructions for the Officers of the Customs appointed to Survey & Report the State of the several ports in England & Wales, 1764." Cf. *ibid.*, Bdl. 435, Nos. 229–240, for like instructions taken from the report of Douglas and Holyburton on the survey of Inverness, 1764, Oct. 19. See various reports of Scottish surveys in this bundle. The instructions here referred to differ somewhat from a draft prepared by the Customs Commissioners from Danby's instructions of 1676. P.R.O., Treas. Out-letters, Cust., XVIII, 210–216, addressed to A.B.

THE OUTPORTS

turns, the surveyors were desired to answer each article separately, and such reports when completed usually formed a modest volume.

Occasionally the head officers of another port were appointed on such surveys or directed to make a particular investigation. Sometimes special officers sent out from London were ordered to investigate flagrant instances of inefficiency, corruption, or illicit trade along a specific coast.[1] At one time Commissioners themselves appear to have made visits to the ports, but by the latter part of the period they had certainly discontinued that duty and depended upon the reports of the general-surveyors.

Any comment on the nature of the Board's control over the outports must consider the relationship as it concerned both the Board and the port. The Board gave careful attention to petty outport matters and rendered judicious decisions for the most part. Occasionally there was failure to appreciate true conditions; too great a conservatism and an unwise economy sometimes prevailed in policy; and in rare instances there was delay or ineffective procedure in the business of the port for want of direction. In the port the inevitable lack of close supervision told in the way in which business was carried on; thus Crouch, in his preface to *A Complete Guide to Officers*, states: "I was encouraged in this Undertaking, by a Complaint, That some general prescribed Forms for the Transacting and Executing of the several Parts of the Business of the Customs, were very much wanted, and would be of great service towards promoting a general Method of Practice, throughout Great Britain; for that at present, the Methods were almost as various, as the Ports were numerous."[2] There was, furthermore, laxity in the collection of duties that gave the outports an advantage over London which in some measure was responsible for the decentralization of trade to the outports. Sometimes there were variations in duties according to the port of import; charges of collection were not infrequently lower at the outports than in London, and duties were unequally collected. There was less strict examination of goods at landing and shipping, and connivance in smuggling by outport officials.[3] The merchants did not hesitate to

---

[1] E. g., P.R.O., Treasury Papers, Bdl. 332, Nos. 128, 132–135, Cust. Comrs. to Lords of Treas., 1748, Dec. 16; cf. P.R.O., Treas. Out-letters, Cust., XVI, 109, Cust. Comrs. to Lord High Treasurer, 1713, Jan. 7.

[2] Crouch, *Complete Guide to Officers* (1732), p. iv.

[3] The material in the Treasury records bears evidence of such conditions. See also Westerfield, "Middlemen in English Business," *Trans. Conn. Acad. Arts and Sciences* (May, 1915), XIX, 424.

complain of these discriminations.[1] Far more serious than this condition was the allegation that enforcement of customs laws in some of the outports was more strict than in others because of advantages to be gained in parliamentary influence.[2] As for fraud, a study of the many papers which came to the attention of the Treasury during the period reveals that only too frequently the outports were the "Back Doors" for the illicit traders. The corruption in the outports, for example, was so serious that a proposal was considered, in connection with the prevention of tobacco frauds, to confine the importation of tobacco to certain ports.[3]

Altogether there existed in outport administration an informality that in large measure was responsible for the severe losses to the revenue throughout the period. Whatever the weak spots in that administration, however, the contribution of the outports to England's revenue and trade in the eighteenth century was considerable. Thus, to take the five outports in the class of ports that had an annual net produce of £50,000 or more during the years 1771–1780, the average gross receipt of Bristol was £252,630. 16s., of Liverpool £239,879, of Hull £88,706. 12s., of Whitehaven £85,746. 18s., and of Lynn £54,203. 14s.,[4] while the revenue from the lesser outports was correspondingly high. During the last fifty years of the century after the decentralization of the London commerce had set in, the outport trade grew by leaps and bounds. Though the actual figures of the Inspector-General of Imports and Exports cannot be relied upon as

---

[1] There are numerous cases of this kind. For example, the lower outport wine duties, though legal, constituted a genuine grievance of the London merchants. (See *Cal. Treas. Papers*, 1702–1707, p. 410, Cust. Comrs. to Lord High Treas., 1705–6, Feb. 1; P.R.O., Treasury Papers, Vol. 258, No. 2, Fisher to Walpole [1727?].) In 1728 the London iron merchants complained against irregularities in the weighing of iron at several of the outports. (Cust. Ho. Lib., Letters to Dartmouth, 1715–16 to 1731, p. 265, Carkesse to Dartmouth, 1728, July 9.) And there were several complaints on the part of both the London and the outport merchants against advantages given to the Hull merchants in the lax examination of their goods and connivance of officers. (*Cal. Treas. Books and Papers*, 1742–1745, p. 27, Cust. Comrs. to Lords of Treas., 1742, Apr. 15; P.R.O., Treasury Papers, Bdl. 332, No. 130, John and William Rosbe and Company to Lords of Treas., 1748, June 30; and No. 152, Everett Everard, in behalf of himself and other Lynn Regis merchants, to Lords of Treas., 1747, Mar. 21. Cf. Nos. 132–135, 156–158.)

[2] Westerfield, "Middlemen in English Business," *Trans. Conn. Acad. Arts and Sciences* (May, 1915), XIX, 424, indicates that this was alleged in *Increase and Decline*, p. 21.

[3] P.R.O., Treasury Papers, Bdl. 332, No. 74, an item headed "Tobacco," undated, with no indication of authorship.

[4] B.M., Add. MSS. 8133 C, f. 116.

THE OUTPORTS

correct valuations, they may be used to indicate roughly the increase in outport trade. Thus, the value of exports in the outports altered from £4,283,862. 8s. 11d. in 1750 to £13,920,316. 12s. 4d. in 1798 or by approximately 325 per cent, while the value of imports over the same period grew from £2,231,475. 7s. 9d. to £7,739,135. 5s. 11d. or nearly three and one half times.[1]

Bristol was the largest outport, her population and trade in 1760 amounting to about one seventh that of London. The fortunate situation of Bristol was responsible in large measure for her predominance. Her port was convenient for the American, West Indian, and Irish trade, while the Wye and the Severn gave access well into the interior, thus making her a central distributing point for the whole of the west of England. This factor was of considerable importance to the trade of Bristol, inasmuch as there was no other outport, with the exception of Liverpool, where a merchant could dispose of his entire cargo in bulk; instead he was obliged to sell part of it in London and take on part of his outgoing shipment there also.[2]

Although Bristol's trade increased, she was outstripped in time by Liverpool, who supplanted her in the nineteenth century as the second English port after London. The rise of Liverpool was phenomenal. Westerfield states that in six decades it increased seven times in population, and that its shipping grew from one thirtieth that of all England in 1702 to more than one sixth by 1792. The opening-up of the Lancashire and Yorkshire manufactures and the expansion of the American trade were primarily responsible for the tremendous growth of the port, though other factors played their part as well.[3] Small wonder, when this is considered, that lack of customs officers, boats, and quay room constituted recurrent complaints throughout the period; and little can the Customs Commissioners be blamed for failing sometimes to appreciate the state of affairs.

On the east coast the ports of Hull and Newcastle in particular took on a marked importance in the eighteenth century. It is of interest that several of the eastern ports should specialize almost entirely in one or two articles of trade: Hull was the center of corn, coal, and cloth exportation; Newcastle exported coal, grindstone, and salt; Yarmouth ran the herring fishery, and was interested in malt and coal

[1] *Parliamentary Papers*, LIII, *Repts.*, XXIII, H.C. No. 154, p. 90, App. D. 14 (1799), "Second Rept. from Sel. Com. on Port of London."
[2] Westerfield, "Middlemen in English Business," *Trans. Conn. Acad. Arts and Sciences* (May, 1915), XIX, 426–427.
[3] *Ibid.*, XIX, 427.

as well.[1] As the western ports were concerned primarily with the plantation and Irish trade, and the southern ports with the plantation and French trade, the importance of the eastern outports depended on the Scandinavian, eastern Continental, and coast commerce generally.

The significance of the outports goes further than their increase in size and trade, for they typify the great change in industry, commerce, and social life that was taking place in England during the eighteenth century. The commercial population gained a predominance that they had never before enjoyed, and the merchants of the eighteenth century were the forerunners of those who were to open up the great markets of the nineteenth-century empire.

[1] Westerfield, "Middlemen in English Business," *Trans. Conn. Acad. Arts and Sciences* (May, 1915), XIX, 416, 427-428.

CHAPTER VI

PERSONNEL

Much of the inefficiency and corruption in the eighteenth-century customs system can be explained by abuses in the appointment of officers, evils in the fee system and other forms of remuneration, and laxity in certain regulations defining the daily conduct of officers. At the same time, continuous efforts toward reform and the general improvement of the service were made during the period. The effects alike of such corruption and of the attempts of those in authority to cope with it can best be appreciated by a brief survey of the conditions.

With one exception, London and the outports were alike in the authorities and instruments by which customs officers held their positions.[1] Patronage took two main forms[2]: patent and warrant offices, "no person being to be esteemed an Officer of the Customes by the Act of Frauds 14. C. 2^d but Such as are appointed by his Ma^{ty} or Deputed by Us upon a warrant from the Treasury."[3] The former were held either by royal letters patent (in Latin until 1733) set in motion by a Treasury *fiat,* or by letters patent (always in English) of the Lords of the Treasury or the Lord High Treasurer.[4] In the outports these offices, which consisted of customer, controller, and searcher, were held during pleasure only; but in London some of the patent offices, and more particularly those of the Bench, were granted for life or in reversion.[5] As has been indicated above, the deputies to these patentees

---

[1] *Repts. of Comrs.,* 1787, III, 127, "Fifteenth Rept.," 1786.
[2] For a brief survey of the way in which all customs offices were held, see *ibid.,* III, 127; *Rules of the Water-side* (1715), pp. 89–94; and P.R.O., Chatham Papers, Bdl. 231, manuscript booklet entitled "The Business done in the Treasury by the Officers—distinguishing each Particular Branch," in section headed "English Customs."
[3] P.R.O., Treas. Out-letters, Cust., XVII, 217, Cust. Comrs. to Lords of Treas.; Treasury warrant, 1719, Nov. 6.
[4] From a note kindly supplied by William A. Shaw, editor of the *Calendar of Treasury Books and Papers.* There are numerous examples in the Treasury Out-letters, Customs.
[5] *Repts. of Comrs.,* 1787, III, 128, "Fifteenth Rept.," 1786.

were nominally appointed by their principals, who frequently acted in accordance with the wishes of the Customs or Treasury Boards.[1]

Offices of the second important class were held by the more regular form of Treasury warrant. Upon the Commissioners' presentment of a person for a specific position, the Lords of the Treasury sent their warrant to the Customs Board nominating the officer and empowering the Commissioners to issue their deputation. Though the Lords frequently signified whom they wished presented, in normal procedure the Commissioners recommended persons of their own choice.[2] The manner in which the Commissioners exercised their patronage in this connection is of some importance. Before 1703 the ports had been divided into districts under the care of particular Commissioners, each one of whom made the appointment to his respective district as a vacancy occurred. In that year, the Commissioners, being of opinion "that the present method is inconvenient and gives occasion for Reflection upon their management," altered the practice and decided instead that the Commissioner who should be in the chair at the time of the death or dismissal of any officer should nominate a successor to the Board for their approbation.[3] Subsequent minutes of 1708 and 1710 changed this procedure somewhat and provided that in the case of dismissal, patronage should go by ballot.[4] By the latter minute, however, the ballot was not to be used until after the presentation of persons who were subsisted at the Queen's charge, and of those who were under favorable consideration of the Board for services rendered. Upon receipt of a Treasury warrant for the appointment of a particular officer, the Commissioners always made inquiry as to whether he had been dismissed from the service and, in the case of land-surveyors, land-waiters, or coast-waiters, whether he was duly qualified by a knowledge of the business of the office. If the nominee was unsatisfactory, the warrant was returned to the

---

[1] See *supra*, Ch. I, pp. 14–17, 20–22. See also *infra*, pp. 200–201.

[2] With respect to the influence of the Lords of the Treasury upon the presentments, see *infra*, pp. 199–200.

[3] Cust. Ho. Lib., Extracts Board Minutes, I, "Commissioners," 1703, Aug. 5.

[4] *Ibid.*, I, "Commissioners," 1708, June 30; 1710, Aug. 15. It appears that vacancies by superannuation or resignation were in the same class as those by dismissal. (*Ibid.*, IV, 209, 1789, Mar. 20.) Minor alterations were made in the arrangement during the period. Further regulations in connection with the employment of the patronage may be found in *ibid.*, III, 90, 1770, July 27; 91, 1771, Nov. 27; 93, 1774, Dec. 8; IV, 207, 1788, Apr. 9. Redington, in the introduction to *Cal. Treas. Papers*, 1556-7–1696, pp. xlv–xlvi, gives a very good account of the way in which the patronage was exercised in 1689.

PERSONNEL 197

Treasury; if the person was willing to undergo the necessary course of instruction in his particular business, the deputation was detained until the certificate of his qualification had been received.[1]

Offices held by Treasury warrant were the most usual form of grant by authority of the Lords. There were several posts, however, which were held by constitution of the Treasury, whereby the appointment was taken entirely out of the hands of the Commissioners. In such cases the Lords of the Treasury issued no warrant which nominated the person and authorized the Customs Board to make the appointment, but themselves both nominated and appointed the officer.[2] The person so established thus derived his power immediately from the Lords of the Treasury, and the Commissioners had as a matter of course less control over officers who acted by constitution.[3] Cu-

---

[1] *Repts. of Comrs.*, 1787, III, 74-75, "Fourteenth Rept.," 1785.
[2] *Ibid.*, III, 74.
[3] This is well illustrated in connection with the office of the Receiver of Fines and Forfeitures. When that office was created in 1728 the Commissioners requested that it be done by Treasury warrant, "Which we the rather desire than by Constitution—forasmuch as the Persons appointed will be thereby more under Our Directions than they are if they Act by Constitution." (P.R.O., Treas. Out-letters, Cust., XIX, 325, Cust. Comrs. to Lords of Treas., 1728, Mar. 27.) The Treasury approved the request and the office continued as a warrant office until 1765, when it was changed to a constitution. That form of establishment proved to be detrimental to the revenue, and, in representing the matter to the Treasury in 1777 (Aug. 5), the Customs Commissioners set forth the limitations of their power over officers appointed by constitution and the danger therein. "The abovementioned Reasoning of Our Predecessors [in their request of 1728 wherein they desired establishment of the office by warrant instead of by constitution] is equally applicable to all other Officers whom the Boards of Treasury have thought fit to appoint by Constitution instead of directing Us by their Warrants to issue Our Deputations. . . . We have thought it Our Duty to make this Representation because it appears that tho' the 4th Clause of Our Patent gives Us full Powers over the Officers acting under Our Deputation— And the 14th Clause enjoins the Patent Officers to be obedient to this Board without which We could not execute Your Lordships Commands as We are thereby required— Yet no mention is made in Our said Patent of Officers appointed by Your Lordships Constitution from whence doubts have arisen

"1st—That where such Constitutions do not contain a Clause of Obedience to the Orders of this Board, the Officers acting thereby do not come under Our Management but are solely under Your Lordships direction from whom they derive their Authority.

"2d—That where the usual Clause of Obedience to Our Orders is inserted it is questioned whether We can enforce the same by Suspension, or the other usual methods of punishing disobedient and refractory Officers—much less that We can Cancel Your Lordships Commission and proceed to the dismission of the Offenders let their Conduct be ever so contumacious to Us, or dangerous to the Revenue.

"[The Customs Commissioners indicated that for these points to remain in doubt

198 ORGANIZATION OF THE ENGLISH CUSTOMS

riously enough, there were two officers in the customs—appraisers in the London King's Warehouse—who were appointed by special warrant of the Chancellor of the Exchequer.[1]

Besides the two chief classes, there were many other persons employed in subordinate positions in the customs, known as Incidental Officers, who owed their appointment directly to a commission or minute of the Customs Board without the intervention of the Treasury.[2] As a rule these were certain of the tide-waiters and other inferior officials whose remuneration was by incident payment.[3] The Commissioners' exercise of patronage in the incidental vacancies followed the same general rules which governed presentments to the Treasury.[4] There were other persons in the service of the customs who were not usually considered officers: clerks were appointed by their principals or by the Treasury or by or with the approbation of the Customs Board [5]; while London coal-meters, lightermen, porters, and glutmen were under the control of the Corporation of the City of London.[6]

The general character of eighteenth-century customs personnel must have been greatly influenced by the gradual usurpation of the

---

would be] prejudicial to the Service and a great Impediment to Our Management [for in any exigency they were unable to take immediate vigorous measures but could only state the matter to the Treasury Lords and await their orders. Therefore the Commissioners submitted] whether You will think fit to cause the 4th Clause in Our Patent to be amended so as to give Us the same Powers over the Officers acting under Your Lordships Constitution, as We thereby have over the Officers deputed by Us by virtue of Your Warrant, or else will be pleased to cancel Your Constitutions especially those of a more modern Creation and revert to the Antient and more general Practise of directing Us to appoint by Your Warrant because Your Lordships will equally have the disposal of the Place whether the Officer derives His Power immediately from Yourselves or from Us under Your Lordships Warrant." (P.R.O., Treasury Papers, Bdl. 530, Nos. 284–285.) Although the Treasury in 1777 apparently approved the appointment of the future Receiver by warrant (Cust. Ho. Lib., Extracts Board Minutes, IV, 410, 1777, Aug. 15), the office in 1778 was granted by a constitution which contained a clause of obedience to the Customs Commissioners. (P.R.O., Treas. Out-letters, Cust., XXXI, 128–129, Treasury constitution, 1778, Jan. 31.) This form of appointment appears to have continued in this office and many others during the remainder of the period.

[1] *Repts. of Comrs.*, 1787, III, 127, "Fifteenth Rept.," 1786.

[2] *Ibid.*, III, 74, "Fourteenth Rept.," 1785.

[3] See *infra*, p. 218.

[4] These and other regulations are embodied in a minute of 1766, May 13, which summarizes many rules previously made. Cust. Ho. Lib., Extracts Board Minutes, III, 342–344. See also III, 93, 1774, Dec. 8; IV, 209, 1789, Mar. 20.

[5] *Repts. of Comrs.*, 1787, III, 74, "Fourteenth Rept.," 1785.

[6] See Hughson, *London* (1805), II, 67. The direction of these men in the eighteenth century was undoubtedly as indicated by Hughson.

PERSONNEL

patronage on the part of the Treasury.[1] From this it should not be inferred that there was a systematic encroachment year by year throughout the period, for the interest of the Treasury Lords in civil patronage varied with the several administrations. Taken as a whole, however, there was a steady growth in Treasury control over customs appointments during the eighteenth century. Specific instances of such control make it possible to summarize the position of the Board in this connection. In the first part of the period the Treasury seem to have done little more than to alter some of the Commissioners' presentments to established offices,[2] and occasionally to recommend persons to the Customs Board to be presented to them for such vacancies.[3] In time recommendations for appointments[4] became more frequent, and the Lords urged the Commissioners to hasten their presentments to the vacancies.[5] Even when there were no vacancies, the Lords might direct that an object of their favor be admitted to the service and employed in some temporary position until an opening came and he could be appointed in the regular way. Promotions might be made in the same fashion.[6] Such eagerness became almost unfeeling impatience upon occasion, as when the Lords informed the Commissioners that they were aware that a particular officer was "dangerously Ill" and "(in case he sho^d dye)" desired that his place not be filled

---

[1] Hughes, in *Studies in Administration and Finance, 1558–1825*, presents material bearing on the subject of Treasury encroachment upon the patronage of revenue departments, more particularly that of the Salt Office.

[2] In 1711 the Lord High Treasurer "recommended to the Commissioners the Care of the Revenue, particularly the Tobacco Trade and said he had Reason to believe, the inferior Officers were faulty in their Duty and was pleased to let the Commissioners know he should be sometimes obliged to alter their Presentments, tho' it should be but rarely; and in Case he should establish any persons that were not fit or proper for the Respective Employments the Commissioners are at Liberty to represent their Opinion to him very freely." (Cust. Ho. Lib., Extracts Board Minutes, I, "Commissioners," 1711, Mar. 20.) In 1754, West, at the desire of Newcastle, directed the Commissioners to make a special inquiry into the merits of certain persons whom they had recommended, "as the Duke of Newcastle will always have the greatest Regard to your Recommendation." P.R.O., Treas. Out-letters, Cust., XXIV, 389, 1754, Sept. 11.

[3] The author of *Rules of the Water-side*, p. 90, states in 1715, "and also the Lord Treasurer has sometimes thought fit to direct the Commissioners of the Customs, to present unto him such Gentlemen as he has a Mind to prefer to such Employments as they shall find them qualify'd for."

[4] E. g., P.R.O., Treas. Out-letters, Cust., XXIII, 116, West to Sir, 1746, Dec. 11.

[5] E. g., *ibid.*, XXIII, 59, Scrope to Wood, 1745, Jan. 27.

[6] E. g., *ibid.*, XXIII, 58, Scrope to Cust. Comrs., 1745, Jan. 21, desiring that a certain London tide-waiter who had been recommended to the Treasury to be preferred to the office of coast-waiter be permitted to act as coast-waiter until a vacancy occurred for which he could be presented.

without their knowledge.[1] To ensure earlier notification of vacancies, it was provided in 1757 that notice was to be sent immediately to the Treasury as soon as any established officer was dismissed[2]; and finally in 1765 the Lords directed that presentments to vacancies were to be submitted weekly to them by the Commissioners.[3]

But the patronage of established offices did not satisfy the Treasury, and encroachment upon the appointments to other offices of the service began. Cleverly the Lords resorted to the device of creating more and more offices by constitution, which form of establishment, it may be recalled, took from the Commissioners their power of appointment and vested both that power and the power of nomination in the Treasury. The representation of the Customs Board to the Treasury on this matter in 1777 points to the principle of patronage control by the Treasury which was inherent in these as in other appointments.[4]

The Lords early singled out the places of the deputies to patentees for their own interests. At first only in isolated instances did they desire the Customs Commissioners to "procure" a particular person to be appointed deputy upon a vacancy[5]; but by the end of the period the Lords were sending numerous such directions to the Commissioners.[6] When a vacancy occurred or was expected in these as in other offices, the Lords might order that it remain unfilled until the Customs Board should hear from them[7]; and, apparently in order

[1] P.R.O., Treas. Out-letters, Cust., XXVI, 69, West to [Cust. Comrs.], 1759, Oct. 1.

[2] Cust. Ho. Lib., Extracts Board Minutes, I, "Commissioners," 1757, Mar. 8.

[3] ". . . as persons have been frequently recomended to them [the Lords of the Treasury], for Employments in the Customs upon Vacancies which have happened long before any signification thereof has come to this office from you; Their Lordps are desirous that for the future Presentments may be made to them on every Monday Morning, of such Vacancies of Officers under your Department, as shall have come to your Knowledge, and have not before been directed by any Warrants of their Lordships to be filled up." P.R.O., Treas. Out-letters, Cust., XXVIII, 94, Lowndes to Cust. Comrs., 1765, Nov. 15.

[4] See note 3, p. 197.

[5] E. g., P.R.O., Treas. Out-letters, Cust., XXV, 334, West to Cust. Comrs., 1758, Feb. 2, desiring them to "procure" one Williams to be appointed deputy customer at Newcastle upon the next vacancy which was daily expected.

[6] See *ibid.*, XXXIII, 4, for such letters for the years, 1782, 1783, and 1784. See *supra*, Ch. I, p. 20.

[7] E. g., *ibid.*, XXX, 470, Rowe to Cust. Comrs., 1775, Jan. 7, desiring that a deputy to the patent controller at Hull be not appointed until the Commissioners hear further from the Lords. See also *ibid.*, XXXII, 426, Robinson to Cust. Comrs., 1779, Dec. 20, stating that the Lords of the Treasury, having been informed that the office of deputy controller at Chepstow is likely to fall vacant, desire that the same be not disposed of until further notice.

that such vacancies should not be disposed of without at least their knowledge, the Lords directed in 1782 that in all future vacancies of deputies, the Commissioners should not admit them to their offices unless approved by the Treasury.[1]

Besides the established and deputy offices, there remained the incidental places on the customs staff to which the Customs Board nominally had the entire appointment.[2] Treasury interference in this patronage took place during the period, and by 1783, as far as the outport incidental offices were concerned, it appears to have been completely established. In that year the Commissioners resolved that the Treasury should be notified of all outport incidental vacancies in the same list with the established ones, though the London incidental vacancies should be entered in a separate book as Board Vacancies.[3] With few exceptions the influence of the Lords of the Treasury did not extend to the patronage of certain of the London incidental tide-waiters' offices which were within the control of the Customs Commissioners. The immunity of such offices to outside disposal was clearly indicated by Hooper, writing to Lowndes in 1765, when he begged leave "to assure his Ldp [Rockingham], thro' your means, that no Board of Treasury, or first Lord Commissioner of that Board, has ever (to the best of my knowledge and belief) broke in upon that Right to the disposal of the preferable List in the port of London which the Board of Customs has ever had and exercised." [4]

[1] See *supra*, Ch. I, p. 22.
[2] See *supra*, p. 198.
[3] Cust. Ho. Lib., Extracts Board Minutes, IV, 201, 1783, Dec. 4. I cannot say, however, that Treasury control of patronage was the sole source of this ruling, for it may have been connected with the efforts of the Customs Commissioners to discontinue offices on incidents.
[4] Hooper, a Customs Commissioner in 1765, observed that he had received a letter from Lowndes, Secretary to the Treasury Board, signifying "Lord Rockingham's desire that Richard Higgins should be placed on the preferable List of Tidesmen in the port of London, and that his Ldp having been informed that there are some vacancies in the said List, & that others may soon happen his Ldp would be glad they may be reserved for his disposal, and you desire me to communicate This in what Manner I shall judge most proper to the other Gentlemen in the Commission of the Customs. . . . Lord Rockingham, I dare say, has been induced to believe that what his Ldp is now pleased to desire, is agreeable to the practice of his predecessors. But I beg Leave to assure his Ldp, thro' your means, that no Board of Treasury, or first Lord Commissioner of that Board, has ever (to the best of my knowledge and belief) broke in upon that Right to the disposal of the preferable List in the port of London which the Board of Customs has ever had and exercised. [Hooper ends his reply by believing that Lord Rockingham will not be displeased with him] for not transmitting to the Board of Customs, your said letter; nor with the honest freedom I have now Taken, upon an affair wherein

By the end of the period the Lords had an extensive control over the customs offices, and the Commissioners were brought into conformity therewith. If there was any delay, for instance, in issuing their deputation pursuant to a Treasury warrant, the Board might receive a letter from the Lords repeating the directions that the appointment be made.[1] Even the Commissioners' hesitation to appoint officers because of unfitness for the service sometimes did not deter the Treasury from commanding that the man be instructed and the appointment take place as ordered.[2] At one time the Lords played so fast and loose with the patronage that they actually became confused with regard to their own proceedings. In 1782 a good land-waiter at Lyme Regis was superseded by the Commissioners in obedience to the commands of the Treasury. The Lords, upon receiving a petition from the land-waiter in question, asked the Commissioners why they had dismissed him. It was undoubtedly much to the Lords' surprise that the Commissioners informed them that they themselves had ordered it. The Treasury directed the reinstatement of the officer.[3] In short, the position of the Lords of the Treasury was like that of the Lord High Treasurer, whom a certain John Key described as being "in such a station that his countenance might be like rain upon the mown grass to him [Key] and his family."[4]

Considering the ramifications of patronage, it would appear that the customs offices of the eighteenth century sometimes existed less for the collection of revenue than for the collection of favors. In 1782 one Lisle, who had been a customs officer for many years, would "not mention the Abilities, or how well qualified every Officer is for his station, as their Appointments are Favors from their Members, and much more Attention being paid to their Interest as Votes, than to their Abilities and Education for the Duty of their Offices; owing to the Ignorance of some and Inattention of others, the Revenue suf-

---

the Commissioners of the Customs, and the Revenue under their management, are so materially concern'd." P.R.O., Treasury Papers, Bdl. 441, Nos. 423-424, 1765, Dec. 14.

[1] E. g., P.R.O., Treas. Out-letters, Cust., XXX, 403, Robinson to Cust. Comrs., 1772, Jan. 10, repeating the Lords' desire that William Flight be appointed as preferable tide-waiter at Liverpool, as requested in Robinson's letter of Jan. 2.

[2] E. g., see *supra*, Ch. II, p. 55, n. 7.

[3] *Ibid.*, XXXIII, 229, Lowe to [Secretary of Treasury?], 1782, Apr. 30; Treasury warrant, 1782, May 6.

[4] *Cal. Treas. Papers*, 1702-1707, p. 16, John Key to Lord High Treasurer, 1702, May 22.

fers to a vast amount, and Bribery and Corruption is much practis'd from the Collectors down to the Tidesmen and Extra men." [1] With regard to the patent offices, a statement of the Commissioners in 1694 is representative of their attitude throughout most of the period: "the Comm^{rs} have always look't upon them as bountyes, in the hands of the Crowne or yor Lord^{pps}, being generally bestowed upon persons, with power to execute by deputy; and therefore the Comm^{rs} have always been passive and easy in the transactions of those grants, when their Lord^{pps} have been pleased to referr them to this Board; not thinking it became them to enter into the consideration of the meritts or services for which they were bestowed, nor to concerne themselves soe much about the qualification of the person as to make provision for good deputies, who are to execute those offices." [2] As for the established offices, instances of interference in customs patronage by prominent state officials or other persons of influence points to the fact that the Customs Commissioners were frequently obliged to use their power of appointment to such vacancies in accordance with the desires of such individuals.[3] A statement in 1715, with reference to such influence, undoubtedly held true for the whole of the eighteenth century. Of presentments of the Commissioners, a writer observes that they "are for the most part agreed to by the Lord Treasurer, they never presenting any but who are well recommended for their Capacity and Fidelity to the Government (even after the Qualification as before mention'd) by Gentlemen of Note and Distinction, very often Members of Parliament, or the Peers of the Realm." [4] Commissioner Musgrave, in reporting to a Treasury Lord [?] on the value of several collectorships, observed in 1782 that "Tho' it has been usual for the Treasury to take the Recommendations from the Members of Parliament for the several *towns* Yet there is no necessity for it nor reason why your Lordship sh^d not oblige the Mem-

---

[1] Cross, *Eighteenth Century Documents* [*Univ. of Mich. Publ.: Hist. and Pol. Science,* VII], p. 246.
[2] *Cal. Treas. Papers,* 1556-7-1696, p. xlvii, statement of the Customs Commissioners, 1694, July 23.
[3] See a list of customs appointments for 1784 and 1785 with a record of the persons by whom the men were recommended. (P.R.O., Chatham Papers, Bdl. 283, booklet entitled "Account of Returns from the Custom House.") There are numerous instances of such influence. See for example Hist. MSS. Com., *Fourteenth Rept.,* App. Part I, *The Manuscripts of His Grace The Duke of Rutland, K.G. preserved at Belvoir Castle,* III [Cd. 7476], pp. 238-239, 41 (1894).
[4] *Rules of the Water-side* (1715), p. 90.

bers for the *Counties* or any other friend of Government with these Lucrative Appointments." [1]

Since, for the most part, the London incidental tide-waiters' offices were beyond the pale of Treasury influence, it is impossible to say how far political considerations decided appointments to those offices. It is equally difficult to ascertain just how far the interests of the revenue in those appointments were subordinated to the personal interests of the Commissioners. According to *The Rules of the Water-side*, however, the "Gift of an extraordinary Tidesman's Place is entirely in the Commissioners, and dispos'd of by them to Persons recommended by People of Credit and Substance, and such who have either an Acquaintance with the Commissioners, or Reason to expect a Favour from the Board, as in the Case of other Places; and that when a Person can write and read well, it is a happy Circumstance of Recommendation." [2] In cases of appointment either by the Treasury or by the Customs Board, special consideration was given to a person to whom those Boards were under obligation. Thus, in 1703, one John Carter, upon his petition for part of a debt owed to him and for employment in the customs, was given perusal of the establishment by the Commissioners. Upon his seeming to decline and insisting upon a patent office, the Commissioners thought that a patent office executed by a deputy might best suit him. [3]

Qualifications for admittance into the service varied. The expediencies of patronage may have caused the standard in choice of the more important outport officers to be lower than that for the inferior ones. A rule of 1705 which required that collectors should be appointed "out of Such psons as had been bred to Clerkship & other business in the Customes, And that the Collectors of the Lesser Ports should be preferred according to their Merritts to the Greater Ports," [4] became generally diregarded, for in 1785 the Commissioners of Ac-

---

[1] Cross, *Eighteenth Century Documents* [*Univ. of Mich. Publ.: Hist. and Pol. Science*, VII], p. 267.

[2] *Rules of the Water-side* (1715), p. 94.

[3] *Cal. Treas. Papers*, 1702–1707, pp. 192–193, Cust. Comrs. to Lord High Treasurer, 1703, Sept. 13. This is minuted, "There is no patent office vacant, but my Lord will consider this when there is a proper occasion."

[4] P.R.O., Treas. Out-letters, Cust., XIV, 406, Godolphin to Cust. Comrs., 1705, Jan. 31. For a case of subsequent observance of this rule, see *Cal. Treas. Papers*, 1702–1707, p. 438, Newcastle collector to John Bell, 1706 [about May 29]. For a case of willingness to override the regulation, see Treas. Out-letters, Cust., XV, 107, Cust. Comrs. to Lords of Treas., 1708, May 11; Treasury warrant, 1708, May 18.

PERSONNEL

counts reported that the only question raised in connection with the fitness of a collector was whether or not he had ever been dismissed from the service and could give the necessary security by bond.[1] The same was also true of the controller. Thus it happened that men utterly ignorant of the complicated accounts that had to be kept, and indifferent to the responsibilities attached to the office, were frequently appointed to the most important places in the customs. In 1782 Commissioner Musgrave deplored the fact that of late years collectors in general had been appointed "from Country Fox-hunters, Bankrupt Merchants, & Officers of the Army & Navy—without the least previous knowledge of the Business of the Revenue and too late in Life to acquire it—so that they are totally unfit to keep good order in the port or to be the representatives of the Board which they are required to be in many respects." [2] Not until 1787, when the Customs Commissioners decided that collectors and controllers should be instructed for six months in the business of their departments, was any formal training required for the admittance of either of these officers into the service.[3]

Such was not the case with the subordinate men, however. A regulation, proposed by the Commissioners in 1696 and apparently approved by the Treasury, provided that no one could be employed above the degree of tidesman, boatman, and preventive officer who had not been instructed for six months and whose qualification at the end of that time had not been properly certified.[4] Subsequent minutes reaffirmed

---

[1] *Repts. of Comrs.*, 1787, III, 181, "Fifteenth Rept.," 1786.

[2] Cross, *Eighteenth Century Documents* [*Univ. of Mich. Publ.: Hist. and Pol. Science*, VII], p. 250. A writer in the early part of the period stated that "It has for some time past been a practise to admit Persons, on the recomendacon of such who are altogether unexperienced in the business of the Customs, into offices, (even of the highest rank) in the out Ports; who at the time of their admiss^n are Inhabitants there, and have Relations concerned in the Trade of those Ports; And this is done for some special reasons, (which I shall forbear to mention) without regarding the abilities, or other qualifications of the Persons for the Imploym^{ts} to which they are recommended." B.M., Add. MSS. 18903, f. 88.

[3] *Commons Reports*, 1803, XII, 65, App. B. 1, "Fourth Rept. Sel. Com. on Finance," 1797.

[4] The Commissioners further resolved to present no man for collector, surveyor, or land-waiter without examining him as to his qualifications with regard to the port in which he was to serve, since some ports required more knowledge than others. (*Cal. Treas. Papers*, 1697-1701-2, pp. 560-561, Cust. Comrs. to Lords of Treas., 1701-2, Feb. 3.) The author of *Rules of the Water-side* (1715), pp. 88-89, states that attendance had to be by order of the Customs Commissioners. "Such Orders are obtain'd by a Petition, or by the Favour of Gentlemen who have Interest at the Board of Customs, and a Title to ask Favours from the Government; therefore it is a Favour to be instructed, in order to a Qualification." There are

the requirement of certain training for land-waiters, deputed searchers, and coast-waiters, and at the end of the period extended it to controllers, collectors, surveyors (when they had the care of the water guard), and jerquers.[1] All these men were obliged to undergo training at specific ports designated as instructing ports. Such places first appear to have been appointed in 1717, and later additions were made in 1733.[2] Though at one time irregularities caused London to be the only instructing port permitted for land-waiters, in 1759–1760 such ports were again established elsewhere,[3] and these remained, with the exception of a few alterations in 1785.[4]

Not until the close of the period does any definite age limit appear to have restricted the admission of officers, a fact which was responsible for the numbers of older men in the employment. In 1782 the Board took the first step toward restriction by setting fifty as the age over which tide-waiters, watermen, boatmen, coal-meters, and weighers could not be admitted to the service, while riding officers could not be over forty-five.[5] In 1786 and 1787 the age for practically all officers

---

numerous references to such instruction in outport correspondence and in Cust. Ho. Lib., Extracts Board Minutes, I, III, IV, under "Instructions."

[1] Cust. Ho. Lib., Extracts Board Minutes: for land-waiters, I, "Instructions," 1722, Sept. 13; for deputed searchers, II, "Searchers," 1733, Nov. 23; for coast-waiters, I, "Coast Surveyor & Officers," 1733, Nov. 28; for collectors and controllers, IV, 609, 1787, Aug. 15; for surveyors, IV, 596, 1787, Nov. 24; for jerquers, IV, 611, 1790, Aug. 27. In 1706 the Commissioners determined upon additional qualifications for land-surveyors, land-waiters, tide-waiters, and boatmen. (*Ibid.*, II, "Officers," 1706, Oct. 11.) Later minutes reaffirmed or extended several of these requirements. The lack of a necessary qualification could prove costly. In 1771 (Feb. 27) Stanley wrote Robinson that a tide-surveyor and all the boatmen at Lancaster having been drowned in 1753 through the unskilfulness and inexperience of the tide-surveyor in the management of a boat, the Commissioners "from a tender regard to the Lives of their Officers, as well as to prevent the Service from Suffering, have ever since required, previous to the admission of a TideSurveyor that he shall be Certified to be duly Qualified by the proper Officers." P.R.O., Treasury Papers, Bdl. 484, No. 361. Cf. Extracts Board Minutes, II, "Tide Surveyors," 1755, Apr. 11.

[2] *Ibid.*, I, "Instructing Ports," 1717, July 12; 1733, Jan. 29; II, "Whitehaven," 1733, Mar. 8.

[3] *Ibid.*, III, 336, 1760, May 12. The ports that appear to have been established at this time were London, Bristol, Plymouth, Exeter, Bideford, Barnstaple, Southampton, Lynn, Hull, Yarmouth, Liverpool, Chester, Newcastle, Whitehaven. P.R.O., Treasury Papers, Bdl. 392, Nos. 47–48, Cust. Comrs. to Lords of Treas., 1759, May 22.

[4] In 1785 Portsmouth was substituted for Southampton, and Bideford and Barnstaple were struck off the list. Cust. Ho. Lib., Extracts Board Minutes, IV, 607, 1785, Mar. 10.

[5] *Ibid.*, V, 148, 1782, Mar. 15; 151, 1782, Oct. 16.

PERSONNEL

including and below the land-surveyor was lowered to forty-five,[1] and in 1788 it was provided that no person under twenty-one could become an officer where security and oath were required.[2] With few exceptions it was observed that an officer could not be reëmployed once he had been dismissed,[3] though the Board in some instances relaxed the severity of its policy about the middle of the period.[4]

Miscellaneous regulations respecting the appointment of officers were designed to ensure integrity and efficiency of personnel. An Order in Council in 1714 directed that officers could not be admitted to serve in ports where they had been inhabitants.[5] "Can any one believe that a Coll^r, or other officer, unless he has more integrity than w^t is usual in this Age, will detect his Brother, Uncle, or other Relation of any fraud committed to the prejudice of the Revenue, (at least I've never heard one instance of it,) On the contrary is it not rather to be apprehended that the officer and his trading Relation will agree to share the profitt of such fraudulent Trade?"[6] Though the order of 1714 was neglected at times,[7] the Treasury and Customs Boards were fully aware of its advantages.[8]

---

[1] Cust. Ho. Lib., Extracts Board Minutes, IV, 167, 1786, Feb. 15; 109, 157, 1787, June 28; V, 28, 1786, Feb. 15; 725, 733, 1787, June 28.

[2] *Ibid.*, V, 171, 1788, Sept. 9.

[3] In a case in 1766 Fremantle informed Lowndes that it had "been the General Rule of this Board not to suffer any person who has been dismissed the Service to be again employed therein." (P.R.O., Treasury Papers, Bdl. 445, No. 9, Fremantle to Lowndes, 1766, July 17.) A dismissed customs officer in 1735 informed "My Lord" [Duke of Newcastle?] that "Their Honours [Customs Commissioners] I understand restore no Officer but what is particularly recōmended by a friend." (P.R.O., State Papers Domestic, Geo. II, Bdl. 36, Jno. Darby to My Lord, 1735, Sept. 10.) Such a recommendation by no means automatically restored a man. In a case in 1739, Carkesse informed Courand that since a particular officer had been dismissed for acting contrary to instructions, the Commissioners could not reinstate him, but they would be glad to oblige Courand in any other matter. *Ibid.*, Bdl. 50, No. 45, Carkesse to Courand, 1739, Mar. 5.

[4] Cust. Ho. Lib., Extracts Board Minutes, I, "Commissioners," 1746, Feb. 11.

[5] *Ibid.*, I, "Commissioners," 1714, June 28, July 8; P.R.O., Treas. Out-letters, Cust., XVI, 157, Order in Council, 1714, June 21. As far back as 1697 [possibly 1696] the Commissioners, in a report to the Treasury, stated "it to have been the constant Opinion of this Board to avoid as much as possible the Imploying Officers in such of the Out Ports where they have been related or Habituated." Cross, *Eighteenth Century Documents* [*Univ. of Mich. Publ.: Hist. and Pol. Science,* VII], pp. 262–263.

[6] B.M., Add. MSS. 18903, f. 88.

[7] B.M., Add. MSS. 18903, ff. 88–89.

[8] In a communication of 1766, Dec. 17, Cooper informed the Customs Commissioners that the Lords of the Treasury "acknowledge the Wisdom of the order in

The Commissioners also scrupulously enforced the rule forbidding customs officers to engage in trade or hold any other employment upon their admittance into the service. Many were the men who were obliged to explain in the most apologetic tone whether there was any truth in the rumor that they were bakers or apothecaries or ran grocery or linen shops or—gravest sin of all—kept a public-house.[1] In some instances officers apparently tried to evade the regulation by placing the business in the hands of a relative. An anonymous letter from King's Lynn to the Board in 1725 complained that several officers at that port kept public-houses "to the disgust of those who have no other methods of living and enter them under a colour in their daughters or some relations of their families name when they themselves are the real proprietors and a hindrance both to the Excise and Customs not only by engrossing sailors to their houses wch lays an obligation upon them to be kind, but prevents several of us brewers paying our honest duties." [2] In the case of an Exeter bridegroom who had married a "maiden woman" that kept "a little shop," one wonders how many years he might have taken to dispose of the stock, which he was "loth to sell away at once for half value," had not he been obliged to give an explanation to the Board.[3] If the flagrant coal frauds at Sunderland and Newcastle in 1782 were partly effected by the officers' neglect of duty—there being "no less than from 26 to 30 Officers of the Customs [the Treasury was informed] who carry on various Trades & Occupations incompatible & inconsistent with the Duties of their respective Appointments & contrary to Law & your Instructions,

---

Council of the 21st of June 1714, & being fully sensible how much the Appointment of Persons in the Customs out of the Natives of the Place & too long residence even of Foreigners in the same Place exposes the Officers of the Customs to Connections & influence that may hurt the Revenue Their Lps are resolved to guard against these inconveniencies according to the Spirit of the Order as far as circumstances Shall permit both in the original Nomination of the Officers & by an Occasional Rotation." P.R.O., Treas. Out-letters, Cust., XXVIII, 130.

[1] There are numerous references in connection with such occupations in Cust. Ho. Lib., Sel. from Cust. Outport Recds. With regard to shops, see *ibid.,* South Coast, 1925, p. 111, Southampton, Board to Collector, Joseph Rogers to Board, 1741, Apr. 9; on serving as an apothecary, see *ibid.,* East Coast, 1923, p. 161, Yarmouth, Collector to Board, 1756–1759, 1757, Nov. 9; as a baker, *ibid.,* South Coast, 1922, p. 65, Poole, Collector to Board, 1762–1767, 1767, Feb. 23.

[2] *Ibid.,* East Coast, 1923, pp. 192–193, King's Lynn, Board to Collector, 1724–1731, 1725, Nov. 9; see also *ibid.,* South Coast, 1922, p. 106, Weymouth, Collector to Board, 1735–1738, To Mr. Brown, 1736, Nov. 20.

[3] *Ibid.,* p. 140, Exeter, Collector to Board, 1743–1748, Patient Pope to Board, 1743, June 8.

by the Connivance of the coll^r of the said Port"—,there is small wonder that the Customs Board strongly insisted on a regulation forbidding such practices.[1]

Every officer, upon his admittance to the service, was required to give security for the due execution of his duty and to take an oath not to accept other than the legal fees and emoluments.[2] The Customs and Treasury Boards, supported after 1711 by an Order in Council which forbade the purchase or sale of any employment in the revenue,[3] discouraged transfer of offices whereby a consideration in money or a part of the salary was paid to an outgoing occupant by his successor, even to the extent of requiring an oath in some instances that no money was involved.[4] Such practices, it was contended, were "highly detrimental to the public service": able officers might resign from their employment and become pensioners, while the purchasers might be placed at a disadvantage compared with other officers of the same rank [5] and tempted to make up their salaries by defrauding the Crown or exacting from the merchants.[6] Though such surrender of offices was not countenanced in theory, it appears to have been managed only too often in actual practice. Thus, in 1782, Thomas Preston wrote Pitt that possibly he did not know "that some of the Landwaiters have paid large sums for their appointments, others are quartered upon, and supply daily bread to the Widows and Orphans of their Predeces-

---

[1] P.R.O., Treas. Out-letters, Cust., XXXII, 60, Robinson to Cust. Comrs., 1782, Feb. 20.
[2] Crouch, *Complete Guide to Officers* (1732), pp. 7–8. Cf. Cust. Ho. Lib., Extracts Board Minutes, I, "Commissioners," 1700, Aug. 31. Securities in some cases were increased as time went on; see reference for 1773, in connection with several outport collectors, *ibid.*, III, 83, 1773, Apr. 28. A minute of 1708 provided that for the securities of outport collectors, no persons resident or merchants be accepted. (*Ibid.*, I, "Collectors in the Out Ports," 1708, Apr. 8.) For an official account of the amount of securities given by the collectors in the outports, see P.R.O., Treasury Papers, Bdl. 339, No. 89.
[3] Cross, *Eighteenth Century Documents* [*Univ. of Mich. Publ.: Hist. and Pol. Science*, VII], pp. 261–262.
[4] Instances of an unfavorable attitude to such surrenders are numerous. See for example *Cal. Treas. Papers*, 1702–1707, p. 25, Cust. Comrs. to [Lord High Treasurer], 1702, June 15. Cf. *ibid.*, 1697–1701-2, p. 523, Cust. Comrs. to Lords of Treas., 1701, Aug. 9; Cust. Ho. Lib., Extracts Board Minutes, I, "Incidents," 1744, May 31. For the requirement of an oath, see *ibid.*, II, "Officers," 1718, Mar. 18; Cust. Ho. Lib., Sel. from Cust. Outport Recds., East Coast, 1923, p. 8, Maldon, Board to Collector, 1745–1762, 1748, Jan. 17. See also Hist. MSS. Com., *Eighteenth Rept., Report on the Manuscripts of the Marquess of Downshire, Preserved at Easthampstead Park, Berks*, I, Part II, p. 898 (1924).
[5] See Hughes, *Stud. in Admin. and Finance*, p. 272, n.
[6] See *Cal. Treas. Papers*, 1702–1707, p. xxviii; *ibid.*, 1714–1719, p. xix.

sors."[1] In a case of unusual interest in 1757, negotiations for a landwaiter's place were handled by a Charing Cross broker.[2]

Apart from its powers in the recruiting of new personnel, the Board of Customs was given by patent the power of dismissal of officers.[3] A minute of 1782, directing a communication to the Treasury, indicates the procedure of the Commissioners in such cases: "No Officer of the Revenue is ever punished by this Board till a formal Charge in writing has been delivered to him & He has been allowed 3 Days at least to put in his answer, and that He & his Witnesses are then heard publicly face to face against his Accusers & his Witnesses with liberty of mutual Cross Examination, and where there are any contradictory circumstances, the Board, like Juries, can only consider how the Weight & Credibility of the Evidence preponderates, & never pronounce sentence but upon such proof as would convict the Culprit in any Court of Justice."[4] It is doubtful if such an elaborate practice was followed with the inferior officers of the outports, though every man was always charged with his irregularity and given an opportunity to defend himself before the Board proceeded to his dismissal.[5] Well might the Commissioners be jealous of their power of dismissal, since that was their most effective instrument against neglect or inefficiency. The Commissioners' defense of their action in dismissing an officer in 1782 illustrates both this attitude and their policy in imposing such a penalty:

And the Secretary is also to observe [to Mr. Burke for the Lords of the Treasury] that the Commissioners being entrusted by His Majesty in a considerable Station under an Oath 'to execute that trust to the best of their Knowledge & Power.' They (equally with the Judges of the Law) have their consciences & reputations at Stake; and therefore have never proceeded but with the greatest care & deliberation to pronounce a Sentence that deprives any Man of his Character & Subsistence.—And that the Treasury have at all times been so convinced of the truth of this Observation, that the Commissioners cannot recollect an Instance of that Board having influenced the decision of the Commissioners in these Cases, And it is sincerely to be wished that the Treasury may invariably adhere to so salutary a rule because this Board having no means of rewarding, if they are also deprived of the power of punishing, they will lose every kind of controul over their Officers, & the

---

[1] P.R.O., Chatham Papers, Bdl. 284, Preston to Pitt, 1782, Feb. 18.
[2] P.R.O., Treasury Papers, Bdl. 380, Nos. 27–28, For Mr. West, 1758, Jan. 19.
[3] P.R.O., Patent Roll, 23 Chas. II, P. 2, No. 1, Mem. 34, dorse, [1671], Sept. 27.
[4] Cust. Ho. Lib., Extracts Board Minutes, IV, 196, 1782, Apr. 26.
[5] For examples, see P.R.O., Treasury Papers, Bdl. 530, Nos. 198–215, enclosures in No. 197, Howe to Robinson, 1777, Nov. 27.

PERSONNEL

effects of such a relaxation will be immediately felt at the Exchequer.—And that the power of punishing their Officers even by Dismission is founded on the 4th Clause of the Commissioners Patent (a Copy whereof is to be enclosed) for their Lordships' Satisfaction.[1]

This extract also demonstrates the handicap which the Board felt with respect to the power of rewarding officers, though in actual practice the Commissioners often influenced the grant of rewards by recommendations to the Treasury. In the same way they frequently determined promotions which were confirmed by the Lords. As far as can be ascertained, a standing rule of 1689 "to advance those who have well deserved in an inferior station"[2] seems to have been generally observed in the following century,[3] though it must be feared that only too often merit was sacrificed to favor through the influence of outside agencies.[4]

Any survey of the system of appointment leads to only one conclusion: it was open to abuse at every turn, and efficiency suffered accordingly. The unnecessary continuance of useless patent officers cumbered the organization. There was too much interference with the Commissioners' appointments, and the standard of personnel suffered in proportion. Though the Customs Board took various measures to prevent the buying and selling of offices, it appears that money only too often played its part in the disposal of employments. Untrained men were put into the higher positions, and, despite the instruction insisted upon for the lower ranks of officers, there was no system of examination, classification, or promotion. Not until well into the nineteenth century was there any marked improvement.

In addition to the foregoing abuses in appointment, there were certain elements in the system of remuneration of officers which were opposed to the best interests of the revenue. Though some attempt was made to bring such elements under control and to remedy their weaknesses, they nevertheless lingered on. The fee system, which consisted

---

[1] Cust. Ho. Lib., Extracts Board Minutes, IV, 197, 1782, Apr. 26. For a similar statement of the Customs Board to the Treasury in 1689, see *Cal. Treas. Papers,* 1556–7–1696, pp. xliv–xlv.

[2] *Ibid.,* 1556–7–1696, p. xlvi.

[3] In connection with the suppression of illicit trade in 1766, Cooper gave the Customs Board "the fullest assurance" that the Lords of the Treasury "shall be ready & pleased at all times to reward by promotion & succession in their respective Stations all such officers of whose Abilities & fidelity their Lps shall be convinced." P.R.O., Treas. Out-letters, Cust., XXVIII, 132, Cooper to Cust. Comrs., 1766, Dec. 17.

[4] See B.M., Add. MSS. 18903, f. 88.

of small payments to customs officers by merchants for various services, was the oldest form of remuneration in the customs. Even in its early days it had been subject to abuse. A law of 4 Henry IV, c. 21, forbade searchers to take other than the fees prescribed by the King, and between 1557 and 1626 many bills directed against exactions by the holders of the three original patent offices were introduced or revived in Parliament only to be lost. Apparently not until the Restoration were fees officially established by Parliament.[1] In 1662 the Commons settled tables of those fees which could legally be required by certain officers at several ports.[2] Additional fees were subsequently authorized, and, upon an address from the Commons to the King in 1715–6, it was ordered that Tables of Fees be put up in all public offices where they obtained. In accordance with this provision the Customs Commissioners in 1716 directed that such tables should be erected in the several custom-houses,[3] an order which was confirmed by the Treasury in 1724 and further enforced in 1776.[4] At the time of the investigation by the Commissioners of Accounts in 1784, sixty-nine of the seventy-two head- and member-ports and eleven of the thirty-two creeks had such tables of fees.[5]

These tables of fees were confined almost entirely to patent officers, and were by no means representative of the fees at a port. As time went on, many new fees had been allowed by Parliament to certain officers and ports and for special services; others had become established by agreement between officers and merchants or by usage; and still others were demanded upon no authority at all by deputed and established officers. At none of the ports, however, were there tables which included all the fees, which differed widely at the various places, and differed between heads and members of the same port.[6]

[1] *Repts. of Comrs.*, 1787, III, 182, "Fifteenth Rept.," 1786.
[2] *Ibid.*, III, 78–79, "Fourteenth Rept.," 1785; see also 12 Chas. II, c. 4, s. 24; 13–14 Chas. II, c. 11, s. 34.
[3] Cust. Ho. Lib., Letter Book. Blackney. 1711–23, pp. 60–61, Board to Blackney, 1716, Aug. 10; cf. *Repts. of Comrs.*, 1787, III, 162–163, "Fifteenth Rept.," 1786.
[4] *Ibid.*, III, 163; Cust. Ho. Lib., Extracts Board Minutes, IV, 395, 1776, Apr. 12.
[5] *Repts. of Comrs.*, 1787, III, 163, "Fifteenth Rept.," 1786. For a short survey of customs fees, see P.R.O., Chatham Papers, Bdl. 284, "Extracts from the Parliamentary Journals respecting the Fees taken by the Officers of the Customs" [1786?].
[6] See *ibid.*, Bdl. 285, "Custom House Fees Authorities under which they are Received at the several Ports in England"; *Repts. of Comrs.*, 1787, III, 164–165, 183–184, "Fifteenth Rept.," 1786; *ibid.*, III, 78, "Fourteenth Rept.," 1785. For a detailed schedule of fees due in London, see *ibid.*, III, 386–392, App. No. 15; *Rules of the Water-side* (1715), pp. 95–101.

Serious evils arose in connection with the fee system which affected merchants, officers, and the revenue alike. Since many officers received but a very small allowance on the customs establishment, they had to depend almost entirely upon fees for their support, and their demands were frequently exorbitant. As one writer put it in 1715, "And the Gentlemen of the Custom-house must excuse me, if I say many of them are either so desirous of getting Money, or stand so much in Need of it, that they will be apt to impose upon the Merchants, if they have not a better Justification for themselves, in Relation to what is due from them for Fees, than the Officers Words, or the Merchants Memories will be, except such as have had a long Experience."[1] The stranger, ignorant as to what fees could legally be demanded, was exploited again and again. Despatch in the delivery of a cargo was not infrequently effected by a merchant's willingness to hand out the additional sum.[2] Altogether the merchant was subjected to much embarrassment and imposition by the arrangement.[3]

The situation of the customs officer was hardly less pleasant. Some of the inferior men had no salaries, or the salary received was "so small as not to afford common Support." In such cases, unless a man accepted unauthorized fees he could scarcely keep body and soul together. On the other hand, if he did demand such fees and was caught, he suffered the penalty of dismissal and could not be reëmployed. An income derived from such a system was precarious, since it was affected by any fluctuations of business. The profit among officers of the same class was unequal, and subordinates were known to receive greater emoluments than their superiors.[4] Morale suffered accordingly.

It was the revenue, however, that suffered most from the fee system. Small orders went unexecuted because of prohibitive fees. Merchant-strangers in some cases were deterred from shipping because of their ignorance and uncertainty concerning these payments. Most dangerous of all, fees offered too great an encouragement for corrupt agreements with merchants to facilitate fraud and smuggling. The proper solution lay in the payment of the officers exclusively by those to whom they were responsible.[5]

---

[1] *Rules of the Water-side* (1715), p. viii.
[2] *Repts. of Comrs.*, 1787, III, 166, "Fifteenth Rept.," 1786.
[3] *Ibid.*, III, 184.
[4] *Ibid.*, III, 185.
[5] For the effect on the revenue of this mode of payment, see *ibid.*, III, 186–188; *Commons Reports*, 1803, XII, 81, App. D. 4, "Fourth Rept. Sel. Com. on Finance,"

214 ORGANIZATION OF THE ENGLISH CUSTOMS

Complaints against excessive or unwarranted fees were made by the merchants time and again.¹ The administration was well aware of the dangers involved and did all that it could to control fees, short of abolishing them: tables regulating patent fees were ordered to be put up in offices ²; men were enjoined not to receive any but the legal fees ³ and were punished by dismissal if they acted differently; and the Commissioners encouraged any prosecutions taken against officers for unlawful demands.⁴ Toward the close of the period, investigation into fees and like emoluments was begun,⁵ but it was not until after the report of the Commissioners of Accounts wherein strong recommendations were made for the abolition of fees that active measures toward reform were taken.⁶

1797. In 1783 it was stated that "the established Practice of Fees, which seems to be inseparable from a complicated and difficult System of Duties, added to the Pressure of Low Salaries and great Temptations, have combined to produce an Intimacy and Connection between the inferior Officers and the Merchants which is very prejudicial to the Public." *Parliamentary Papers*, XXXVI, *Repts.*, VI, H.C. No. 58, pp. 10–11 (1783), "First Rept. on Illicit Practices."

¹ See *Repts. of Comrs.*, 1787, III, 184, 865, App. No. 59, "Fifteenth Rept.," 1786; Cust. Ho. Lib., Extracts Board Minutes, IV, 399, 1784, Dec. 8. E. g., in specific cases, see *ibid.*, I, "Fees," 1724, July 15, and instance of 1708–9 when members of Parliament for the county of Stockton on Tees protested on behalf of merchants there against unreasonable fees, Cust. Ho. Lib., Sel. from Cust. Outport Recds., Northern England, 1924, pp. 172–173, Stockton on Tees, Board to Collector, 1708–9, Jan. 13.

² Cust. Ho. Lib., Extracts Board Minutes, I, "Fees," 1725, Mar. 3; III, 159, 1761, Apr. 29; 1764, Mar. 2; IV, 395, 1777, Oct. 24. See *supra*, p. 212.

³ Entries under "Fees" in *ibid.* contain numerous instances. E. g., III, 159, 1772, Jan. 31.

⁴ E. g., *ibid.*, IV, 395, 1776, Feb. 6. In this case, upon a merchant's complaint he was informed "that the Board are extremely desirous that all their Officers should receive exemplary punishment whenever they act contrary to Law, that he is fully at liberty to proceed before the proper Court of Justice, that being the course which the Legislature seems to have pointed out by giving double Costs & damages, besides which penalties the Board on conviction will peremptorily proceed to the dismission of the Offenders pursuant to the 24th Rule of the Book of Rates & 13th & 14th Chaˢ 2ⁿᵈ C. 11th Sec. 34th."

⁵ See *ibid.*, IV, 398, 1783, Sept. 3. In 1783 a bill which provided among other things for the abolition of fees and useless offices was introduced into Parliament, only to be dropped in Committee. P.R.O., Chatham Papers, Bdl. 285, "Proceedings respecting Custom Fees since the Introduction of the Bill in 1783."

⁶ In 1787 and 1788, outport and London merchants were consulted on the fees. In 1789, the Treasury, empowered by act of Parliament, appointed two Customs Commissioners in England and one in Scotland to inquire into the emoluments of customs officers. These Commissioners made three successive reports, wherein they favored an entire abolition of fees, or at least the abolition of fees taken by the waterside department. They suggested that salaries be readjusted, since many of the officers' incomes were inadequate to their trust, and proposed the establishment of a stable superannuation fund. In pursuance of many of the recommendations, a

PERSONNEL

Payment of officers by gratuity was liable to the same abuses as by fees. When business was transacted either out of its proper department, or outside the legal hours of work, or upon the sufferance quays, or with some additional trouble to officers, this form of recompense was due.[1] Therein lies the distinction between a fee and a gratuity, for a fee was paid for the execution of duty at legal times and places. The gratuity was sanctioned by 6 and 7 William III, which permitted the acceptance of a reward, though not its demand, for the performance of such extra duty.[2] There were two types of gratuities: those given by merchants to customs officers for work despatched under the circumstances described above and those granted by the Commissioners to particularly deserving officers for commendable services. Because the former class of gratuities was open to the same evils as fees, and because of complaints against the demands of officers for such sums, like recommendations were made to put an end to them.[3]

Salaries may be considered the official form of remuneration to officers. By *salaries* is meant such sums as were paid on the establishment or by dormant warrant, and as "incidents" by the standing orders of the Customs Commissioners to additional officers or to those who were given an extra allowance when their salaries on the establishment were insufficient.[4] At the end of every quarter, the Lords of the Treasury issued their warrant to the Customs Commissioners empowering them to give orders for the payment of salaries. Upon receipt of the warrant the Board sent a copy of the establishment to each port with an order specifying the amount of salaries and directing payment by the collector and the controller. When the establishment reached the port the collector published a notice to that effect and the officers called for their money. Before they were paid, however, the collector had

---

bill was prepared in 1792, but the expense of providing an adequate compensation for the officers in lieu of fees, and the difficulty of the arrangement, prevented any further proceedings at that time. (*Ibid.*, Bdl. 285, "Proceedings respecting Custom Fees since the Introduction of the Bill in 1783.") The three reports of the Commissioners and other papers relating to the subject are in this bundle. See also *Commons Reports*, 1803, XII, 58, 60, 65, App. B. 1, "Fourth Rept. Sel. Com. on Finance," 1797; *Repts. of Comrs.*, 1787, III, 188; "Fifteenth Rept.," 1786, entries under "Fees" in Cust. Ho. Lib., Extracts Board Minutes, I, III, IV.

[1] *Repts. of Comrs.*, 1787, III, 80, "Fourteenth Rept.," 1785.
[2] 6 and 7 Wm. III, c. 7, s. 14; *Repts. of Comrs.*, 1787, III, 79, "Fourteenth Rept.," 1785; *ibid.*, III, 159–160, "Fifteenth Rept.," 1786.
[3] *Ibid.*, III, 188, 849, App. No. 51, 865, App. No. 59; *ibid.*, III, 369, App. No. 7, "Fourteenth Rept.," 1785.
[4] *Ibid.*, III, 137, "Fifteenth Rept.," 1786; Crouch, *Complete Guide to Officers* (1732), p. 245.

to make small deductions on every pound for the Superannuation Fund and for taxes unless the salary did not exceed £60 [1]; he was obliged to see that the securities were still valid, and that regulations in connection with particular officers had been observed. A receipt of payment was taken from each officer and returned with the account of salaries and order for their payment to the Inspector of the Outport Collectors' Accounts.[2] In London the Receiver-General defrayed salaries, and the Pay-master of Incidents discharged the bills of the London incidental officers.[3]

The inadequacy of the funds which provided the salaries was often a nuisance. In the very early part of the period, collectors paid salaries out of the receipts from the branch of duties known as the Old Customs. By 1710 this was found insufficient, and in that year the receipts of this branch and of additional duties known as the United Branches were opened to payments.[4] Finally in 1761 all heads of duties (coinage branch excepted) were made liable for charges of management.[5] Even then it frequently happened that there was not enough money in an outport for payment of salaries or other expenses. In one quarter in 1714 an unfortunate collector at Yarmouth had only 4s. 2d. with which to pay incidents and salaries amounting to £300.[6] In such cases the Commissioners usually granted an imprest for money on the collector of a neighboring port, by which arrangement the needy collector was tided over until his receipts were sufficient to meet his payments.[7]

---

[1] In connection with the exemption from the land-tax, see P.R.O., Chatham Papers, Bdl. 231, manuscript booklet entitled "The Business done in the Treasury by the Officers—distinguishing each Particular Branch;" Crouch, *Complete Guide to Officers* (1732), p. 250, n.

[2] For an account of general procedure, see *ibid.*, pp. 241, 244–245.

[3] See for example Cust. Ho. Lib., Extracts Board Minutes, II, "Officers," 1716, May 25; III, 346, 1767, June 17.

[4] P.R.O., Treas. Out-letters, Cust., XV, 281–282, Cust. Comrs. to Lord High Treasurer; Treasury warrant, 1710, Apr. 25. For an example of the order which went to the outports, see Cust. Ho. Lib., Letters to Dartmouth, 1675-6 to 1715, p. 250, Board to Dartmouth, 1710, May 20. The United Branches consisted of the Customs, the Impost on Wine and Vinegar, the Impost on Tobacco, the Impost of 1690 and the Additional Impost of 1692, and the New Duty on Whalefins.

[5] P.R.O., Treasury Papers, Bdl. 408, No. 83, Cust. Comrs. to Lords of Treas., 1761, July 18; see also enclosure No. 86. See *Repts. of Comrs.*, 1787, III, 78, "Fourteenth Rept.," 1785.

[6] Cust. Ho. Lib., Sel. from Cust. Outport Recds., East Coast, 1923, pp. 132–133, Yarmouth, Collector to Board, 1714-1719, 1714, Jan. 28.

[7] For procedure with regard to an imprest, see Crouch, *Complete Guide to Officers* (1732), p. 253.

PERSONNEL 217

The inconvenience of such a system is put forcibly by the Weymouth collector in a letter to [the Board?] of March, 1745. "I am really surprised have not yet heard from you on account of the imprest sent in my letter of 15 January 1745 for £273" 15" 1 on Bristoll, the poor under officers I very much pitty being so long out of their salaries. I beg you would favour the forwarding thereof as I hope no mischance has happened therein & you will add to the many favours I have already received etc."[1] Such imprests were responsible for arrears in the collectors' official accounts as well.[2]

There were yet other unsatisfactory aspects of the salary system. Salaries in general were low,[3] as is indicated not only by figures[4] but also by numerous applications to the Board for additions and rewards, by the extortion of fees, occupation in supplementary employment, and connivance in smuggling. An instance in 1710 shows the harmful effects of such payments upon the character of personnel and the revenue alike. The Customs Board informed Godolphin in a letter "That the Salary of the Two Mates to the Boatmen at New Castle is so small being but £20 P. ann. that sev^{ll} of them have Quitted that service as not being Able to Subsist thereon and the Comm^{rs} being Apprehensive, that the many frauds that have been Comitted in that Port have arose from the meaness of the Officers Salarys, and therefore they doe humbly pray that the Salarys of the said Mates as also the Salarys of the four Boatmen at Shields which is but £15 P. ann. Each may be Advanced to £25 Each."[5] It would appear that the increased cost of living in some of the newly flourishing outports caused salaries once sufficient to become inadequate. The Hull tide-waiters in 1756 represented to the Treasury that "House Rent and all sorts of Provisions is as Dear at this place as in London and having Little more than Nineteen Pence Pr Day to Defray all necessary Expences attending thereto, having our Families to maintain on shore and our Selves (for the most part) on board that your Lordships Hble Petit^{rs} are re-

---

[1] Cust. Ho. Lib., Sel. from Cust. Outport Recds., South Coast, 1922, p. 115, Weymouth, Collector to Board, 1745–1750, 1745, Mar. 1. In the outport correspondence are to be found other references to delays in payment of salaries.
[2] *Ibid.*, p. 215, Penzance, Collector to Board, 1774–1776, and note.
[3] See for example *Repts. of Comrs.*, 1787, III, 865, App. No. 59, "Fifteenth Rept.," 1786.
[4] See the volumes of Customs Registers: Series I, Customs Quarterly Establishments, in the P.R.O.
[5] P.R.O., Treas. Out-letters, Cust., XV, 277–278, Cust. Comrs. to Lord High Treasurer; Treasury warrant, 1710, Apr. 25.

duced to the greatest Distress."[1] The Commissioners were undoubtedly slow to appreciate such conditions, but they believed in adequate remuneration, and there are numerous instances of the increase of salaries, particularly where the growth of business added to the work of the officer.

The remuneration of some officers by incident tended to be pernicious. Under such a scheme, certain inferior grades were allowed a small salary on the establishment and so much in addition as incidents, usually for their work by the day. This form of remuneration frequently cost the institution more than a straight salary,[2] and as far as the officers were concerned it offered only irregular encouragement.[3] Though it would appear in some instances that the men themselves preferred such a plan of payment[4] and that it was feasible to leave some wages on that basis,[5] the administration was well aware of the advantages on the whole of established salaries. Throughout the period the Board pursued a general policy of paying the officers fixed salaries by placing various incident payments on a salary basis from time to time.[6]

[1] P.R.O., Treasury Papers, Bdl. 367, No. 136, Petition of Hull Tidesmen to Lords of Treas., 1756, Mar. 8. For example in Whitehaven in 1759, see *ibid.*, Bdl. 392, No. 32, Cust. Comrs. to Lords of Treas., 1759, Mar. 3.

[2] Payment of an officer by incident often amounted to more than payment by a fixed sum. For example, remuneration of Plymouth boatmen and watermen by a joint incident and salary arrangement totaled £1,506. 18s. 8d. on an average of four years. The Customs Board, in recommending the establishment of certain of the men by salary, stated that £466. 18s. 8d. would be saved by the alteration. (P.R.O., Treas. Out-letters, Cust., XIII, 260, Treasury warrant, 1696, Apr. 24.) Furthermore, men who originally had been employed on incidents to help out in a glut of shipping were sometimes retained long after they had become unnecessary. See *infra*, n. 6.

[3] Thus, in connection with the Plymouth tide-waiters and boatmen, mentioned above, their remuneration was changed from incidents to an established salary, for the advantage of the revenue and the more "Certain Encouragem^t of Officers and better accomodation of the Service."

[4] P.R.O., Treasury Papers, Bdl. 353, No. 68, 1753, Sept. 22; *ibid.*, Bdl. 367, No. 136, 1756, Mar. 8, Petitions of Hull Tidesmen to Lords of Treas.; cf. Cust. Ho. Lib., Sel. from Cust. Outport Recds., East Coast, 1923, pp. 212–213, Hull, Collector to Board, 1752–1754, 1753, Feb. 24.

[5] Probably such an arrangement was made when there was not enough business to warrant establishing the man as a permanent officer, although his services were frequently required.

[6] There are numerous references in this connection. In the early part of the period, for example, extensive alterations were made "in Order to the Establishing such [outport incidental officers] as Should be thought necessary, and the retrenching those that are useless." (P.R.O., Treas. Out-letters, Cust., XV, 458–460, Cust. Comrs. to Oxford, 1712, Oct. 22; cf. XV, 445; XVI, 112–113, 49–51.) Similar alterations were made from time to time during the entire period. In 1780, the Board

An allowance, though relatively unimportant, must be mentioned as the fourth general form of remuneration. It was very similar to a salary: sometimes it was an annual payment in addition to, or in lieu of a salary; occasionally it was a recognition of some specific service. The separate sums granted for execution of the quarantine business and as commission (a small payment peculiar to two outport officers for superintending the appraisement of goods before prosecution), composed two forms of allowances. The other four allowances were poundages, restricted to relatively few officers, upon the receipt of coal and coinage duties, upon the produce of the sales of enumerated goods, and upon sums returned to the Exchequer arising from seizures.[1]

The emolument which comprised the officers' shares of the produce of seizures gave the strongest impetus to activity against violation of customs laws. By 12 Charles II, c. 4, half the produce of a seizure was to go to the Crown and half to the seizing officer; but the amount varied between one third and nine tenths according to the act of Parliament governing the particular kinds of goods seized, or according to the discretion of the Lords of the Treasury or the Customs Commissioners.[2] If an officer was lucky, a seizure might yield him a neat fortune which would amount to more than he could earn in several years of ordinary labor. The jealousy in search and seizure testifies vividly to the stimulative value of such rewards.

Payment of officers constituted but a part of the expense of operating the system. The maintenance of customs cruisers, which has been examined in Chapter V, formed a considerable item of expenditure; incident payments constituted still another. One division of incidents—incident salaries—has been discussed. The other class comprised those sums that went for the upkeep of the establishment. It

---

ordered that upon an incidental place falling vacant, careful investigation should be made as to whether the incidental allowance should be continued, "it being the Board's intention to put an end to all allowances by Incidents which shall appear to have been granted for reasons which no longer exist or by change of circumstances are become no longer productive of advantage to the Revenue." (Cust. Ho. Lib., Extracts Board Minutes, IV, 192–193, 1780, Nov. 8.) In 1774 and 1782 the Board declared that the wisdom of continuing outport incidental allowances was to be considered with a view to placing on the establishment those which deserved to be retained. *Ibid.*, III, 248, 1774, Sept. 16; V, 149, 1782, July 9, Aug. 14.

[1] *Repts. of Comrs.*, 1787, III, 75–77, "Fourteenth Rept.," 1785; *ibid.*, III, 128, 130, "Fifteenth Rept.," 1786.

[2] *Accounts and Papers*, XXXV, H.C. 366–I, p. 462, App. No. 13 (1868–1869), "Public Income and Expenditure," Part II.

included expenditures for rents and repairs of the buildings, fires and candles, subsistence of witnesses, traveling charges of officers on a survey or on visits to the members and creeks of their ports, charges of tide-waiters for their guard of a ship while en route to a distant port,[1] and other miscellaneous items. These charges of management on an average of five years from 1766 to 1770, inclusive, totaled nearly 6 per cent of the gross produce of the customs; on a similar average for 1774 to 1778 they constituted well over 7 per cent.[2]

Except for disbursements for rent, day-pay, and traveling charges, no collector was permitted to spend more than 40s. on incidents without receiving the orders of the Board [3]; and with what a parsimonious eye the Board watched the account of these expenditures! When the Commissioners could require an explanation of one collector as to why there were two entries amounting to 1s. 6d. each for cleaning in his customhouse on the same day, no doubt may be left as to the frugality of at least one Board.[4] Economy in overhead expenses characterized Board administration throughout the entire period. Well could the Commissioners in 1786 "with Confidence appeal to your L̄dps, that we are not in the Habit of increasing the Charges of the Revenue under our Management, but that on the contrary We have embraced every Opportunity that offered of lessening the same." [5]

---

[1] In 1726 the sum of 6s. 8d. per day to the collector and 5s. per day to the controller was "the constant allowance made to those officers when they travel within the limits of the Port." (Cust. Ho. Lib., Sel. from Cust. Outport Recds., West Coast, 1926, p. 111, Swansea, Board to Collector, 1726, Oct. 27.) In 1743, 3d. a mile was the usual allowance to tide-waiters when they accompanied ships. (*Ibid.,* p. 133, Beaumaris, Board to Collector, 1743, Aug. 16.) In 1779, 15d. per mile was minuted as the standing allowance for portage to all officers who should be ordered on a particular service. Cust. Ho. Lib., Extracts Board Minutes, V, 677, 1779, July 29.

[2] B.M., Add. MSS. 8133 C, f. 133.

[3] Cust. Ho. Lib., Sel. from Cust. Outport Recds., South Coast, 1922, p. 125, Weymouth, Board to Collector, 1708–1719, 1717, Oct. 5. Cf. *ibid.,* South Coast, 1925, p. 159, Portsmouth, Board to Collector, 1741, Nov. 21. Bills, accounts of incidents, the Board's orders for payment, and receipts had to be returned to the Inspector of Outport Collectors' Accounts regularly. See Crouch, *Complete Guide to Officers* (1732), pp. 245–247, on incidents. Cf. P.R.O., Treasury Papers, Bdl. 583, Nos. 374–375, Stiles to Burke, 1783, Oct. 16. See *supra,* Ch. III, p. 111.

[4] Cust. Ho. Lib., Sel. from Cust. Outport Recds., South Coast, 1922, p. 143, Exeter, Collector to Board, 1743–1748, 1747, Mar. 9. There are numerous other instances as well.

[5] It was also a satisfaction to this Board "to acquaint your Lordships, that the Savings made by this Board within the last 14 Years amount to near £8,000 annually in Salaries and Allowances only." (P.R.O., Treas. Out-letters, Cust., XXXIV, 429, Cust. Comrs. to Lords of Treas., 1786, Jan. 20.) In January, 1791, the Commissioners, in a request to the Lords of the Treasury for an increase in their salary,

PERSONNEL

No general estimate of the character of financial policy in the regulation of the customs establishment can disregard the abuses of the fee system and gratuities, the evils of low salaries and incidents, the weaknesses of the contract system of maintaining cruisers, and the effects of an economy at times mistaken in its rigidity. The Board appreciated many of these dangers and took steps to safeguard the revenue accordingly, but no general improvement was effected until the period drew to its close.

If the rules and practices of the customs staff are judged in the belief that the justification of any regulations ends with the efficiency they produce, it will appear that reform along many lines was necessary in the daily operation of the system.

The hours of work for officers, established by the Act of Tonnage and Poundage at a time when colonial trade was in its infancy, remained unaltered during approximately the next hundred and fifty years when British ports became the *entrepôt* of world commerce.[1] Bankers' hours from nine until twelve were the rule for the officers of the Long Room, though the jerquers worked until four. Habitual tardiness, however, meant that many of the Long Room officers were not in their seats much before eleven in the morning.[2] The accounting officers at the outports kept the same morning hours as the London officers, with the addition of two hours from two to four in the after-

---

stated, "That whilst the best judgment and diligence of your Memorialists have been engaged in securing the fair receipt of this Revenue, they have been no less attentive in reducing as much as possible the Charges of Management, and all other items of Expenditure in their department, by discontinuing every Office that appeared to be useless; by disallowing to their Collectors and others every charge however trivial that the Revenue ought not in justice to sustain; by establishing regulations for the more frugal supply as well of Stationary, as of every other Article used or consumed in carrying on the Public Service; and by discontinuing many Annual Allowances by *Incidents* on the death or removal of Officers, to their Successors, in all cases without exception, where it has appeared to your Memorialists, that the Service did not require a continuance thereof, and that the Revenue might be safely exonerated there from." P.R.O., Chatham Papers, Bdl. 283.

[1] With respect to such hours of work, see *Repts. of Comrs.*, 1787, III, 160–161, 166–167, "Fifteenth Rept.," 1786. These hours, established by the thirteenth and eighteenth rules annexed to the Book of Rates, remained the legal hours, though in practice in 1784 the hours of attendance of the Inward Department of the Long Room were from 10:00 A. M. to 1:00 P. M. and for the Outward Department from 10:00 to 2:00. *Ibid.*, III, 850, App. No. 51.

[2] A book of appearances of Long Room officers, required in 1743 to be kept by the Bench Officers and laid before the Board at noon, may have had a salutary effect earlier in the period. Cust. Ho. Lib., Extracts Board Minutes, I, "Bench Officers," 1743, Sept. 22.

noon. For the men out on the quays the working day of course was longer, merchants being permitted to unload in the Port of London during the autumn and winter months between sunrise and sunset, and in the spring and summer between six in the morning and six in the evening. Some of the officers, the searchers in particular, had extremely long mid-day recesses, however, the waterside business being brought completely to a standstill between one and three-thirty, the most precious hours of the day in the winter months. When it is considered that at rush times in the Port of London alone there had been known to be almost 400 entries a day,[1] it is clear that the hours within doors were far from adequate for the transaction of business, and that shipping suffered many inconveniences accordingly. Such hours were permitted to continue throughout the century, despite complaints made against them and the recommendation of their extension by the Commissioners of Accounts. Though the Customs Commissioners agreed that such hours were insufficient, they were of opinion that the subject required much investigation and communication with merchants before adjustment could be made.[2]

Customs holidays—forty-five [3] besides Sundays during the year—were an annoyance. Such holidays were always observed in the Long Room, though the waterside business could be transacted on those days upon special permission of the Board and extra recompense to the officers. Since the searchers refused to work on holidays, however, the export part of the waterside activity could not go on, and all waterside service dependent upon the Long Room was stopped. When one or two holidays happened to come together or near together, the customs business might be tied up for days, and the cargo of the ship or a market affected by the delay,[4] "the loss of one Tide being many times the overthrow of a Voyage." Though it was a rule that merchants should not be over three days in sailing from Gravesend to their place of discharge and entry of goods, "yet by reason of sundays and holydays often intervening, together with many other accidents, it is frequently a week before the same is made," and the water guard officers did not receive the reports until some time later. Thus by permitting the goods to lie in the craft, opportunity for thefts was

[1] *Repts. of Comrs.,* 1787, III, 193, "Fifteenth Rept.," 1786.
[2] *Commons Reports,* 1803, XII, 58, "Fourth Rept. Sel. Com. on Finance," 1797.
[3] Thirty-one of these holidays had been authorized by acts; fourteen were customary. *Repts. of Comrs.,* 1787, III, 161, "Fifteenth Rept.," 1786.
[4] *Ibid.,* III, 167, 850, App. No. 51, "Fifteenth Rept.," 1786.

PERSONNEL

given.¹ When offices were again opened after such holidays, the rush of business resulted in awkward confusion.² In 1724 the Bristol and London merchants represented "the great Detriment they suffer in Trade by the multitude of Custom-House Holidays," and the London merchants complained that the officers did not attend at other times as well. Upon the London merchants' application to the Treasury Board, the Customs Commissioners agreed to the abolition of five specified holidays and promised that one of their number should attend in the Long Room from nine o'clock to despatch business, as was desired by the merchants; but vexedly remarked "that if the Merchants had applied to them, they would have had redress without troubling their Lordships."³ The system of holidays nevertheless continued with no other alteration.⁴ Despite the observations of the Commissioners of Accounts⁵ on the injurious results of such practice, and though the nation's imports had nearly doubled and exports more than doubled between the date of the Commissioners' report (1786) and the "Fourth Report" of the Select Committee on Finance in 1797, no comprehensive measures were taken in reform before the close of the century.⁶

Since there was no system of vacations for officers, absences were frequently indulged in. Excuses for absence were made on the eternal pleas of bad health and need of the waters,⁷ visits to ill or dying rela-

---

¹ *Some Considerations Humbly Offered to the Publick concerning The Revenue of the Customs* (London, 1752), p. 10; cf. Cust. Ho. Lib., Extracts Board Minutes, I, "Holidays," 1698, June 10; *Repts. of Comrs.*, 1787, III, 167, 192, "Fifteenth Rept.," 1786.
² See *ibid.*, III, 193.
³ Cust. Ho. Lib., Extracts Board Minutes, II, "Patent Officers," 1724, July 3; see *Cal. Treas. Papers*, 1720–1728, p. 266, Petition of London merchants to Lords of Treas., 1724, ? about Mar. 13; and *The London Journal*, 1724, Mar. 28, on the Bristol representation.
⁴ In 1783 (June 5) the Customs Commissioners reported to the Lords of the Treasury, in connection with a request by a committee of West India planters and merchants for the abolition of customs holidays, that the present number of holidays had been settled in 1724 and were warranted by law; that the Commissioners gave every possible attention to the despatch of the merchants' business and constantly granted permission to transact business on holidays. P.R.O., Treasury Papers, Bdl. 587, No. 355.
⁵ *Repts. of Comrs.*, 1787, III, 194, "Fifteenth Rept.," 1786.
⁶ *Commons Reports*, 1803, XII, 58, "Fourth Rept. Sel. Com. on Finance," 1797.
⁷ A "paraletical disorder" in the head seems more than once to have wheedled a grant of three months' leave from the Treasury with pay. E. g., P.R.O., Treasury Papers, Bdl. 455, No. 378, Petition of a tidesman in fee to Lords of Treas., [read] 1767, Aug. 13.

tives,[1] necessity of settling debts so that officers should be able to go about their business free from fear of arrest,[2] and that mysterious head, "private affairs," [3] which covered a multitude of sins. Early in the period the importance of officers' strict attendance on duty was recognized; and in 1711 a monthly account of all absentees was required to be laid before the Customs Board,[4] a check which unfortunately seems to have been discontinued at a later date.[5]

The Commissioners soon awoke to the necessity of close supervision over absences, and their policy became one of strict regulation. In 1716 they appear to have made their first important ruling in this connection upon finding that much running took place in parts of South Britain which in a great measure might have been prevented, "if the officers of the Customs in the out Ports gave a due attendance in their respective stations as required by their instructions and repeated orders from this board: notwithstanding which some officers have presum'd to be absent without leave, and others having leave for a certain time, have neglected to return to their ports at the expiration of their time, for which such leave was granted, in manifest contempt of the authority of this board, they pretending to have been indispos'd or otherwise prevented by extraordinary business." The Commissioners, "being sensible how necessary the strict attendance of every officer employed in the customs is to the security of this revenue," ordered that collectors could not be absent without leave from the Board, and that no other officers in the port could be absent without permission from the collector, which permission could not exceed six days; for any greater length of time, application had to be made to the Board. For every day that an officer was absent without permission, he was to forfeit two days' salary, and for the second offense to suffer dismissal. He was further obliged to satisfy his substitute.[6] Two years later a more severe regulation, "the better to pre-

---

[1] E. g., Cust. Ho. Lib., Sel. from Cust. Outport Recds., South Coast, 1922, p. 102, Weymouth, Collector to Board, 1719–1720, 1720, Dec. 21.

[2] *Ibid.*, p. 144, Exeter, Collector to Board, 1743–1748, 1743, Feb. 25.

[3] For example of a petition for six months' leave on private affairs, see P.R.O., Treasury Papers, Bdl. 456, Nos. 391–392, a land-surveyor to Lords of Treas., 1767, May 25. (Leave was granted for three months.)

[4] Cust. Ho. Lib., Extracts Board Minutes, I, "Absence," 1711, Sept. 12. The Lords of the Treasury apparently directed that the account be laid before them as well. (B.M., Add. MSS. 18903, f. 86.) In the case of some classes of officers, lists of absentees were laid before the Board at other intervals also.

[5] B.M., Add. MSS. 18903, f. 86.

[6] Cust. Ho. Lib., Letter Book, Blackney, 1711–1723, pp. 59–60, Carkesse to [Blackney], 1716, July 31.

vent officers asking leave to be absent on frivilous occasions," provided that if an officer, even by permission, was absent longer than a week for private affairs, the Commissioners would deduct two thirds of his salary.[1] With few exceptions the rule was closely adhered to [2] until 1768 when the Commissioners relaxed that policy somewhat and permitted officers to be absent fourteen days on private affairs without loss of salary.[3] In 1779 the time was extended to one month with the provision that the men were to abstain from applying to the Treasury for leave.[4] Officers seeking leave of absence had to see that their work was in an orderly and up-to-date condition: thus land-waiters might not get permission until certain of their books had been turned in to the jerquers,[5] nor, after 1778, could collectors or controllers obtain leave until their accounts and remittances had been made.[6] After 1762, if a man took matters into his own hands and was absent without permission, he was liable to suspension.[7]

The supervision exercised by the Treasury Board in connection with customs absences evinces only too clearly its interference in a matter which should have come under the direct cognizance of the Customs Board alone. A private communication to a Treasury official in 1757 would seem to indicate that the Commissioners could grant leave of absence for eight days only without loss of salary while the Lords of the Treasury permitted, without any deduction, leave for either three or six months for recovery of health or for private affairs. The writer observed that "it's a common thing granted and sev^l of our Office has it Now & obtain'd by any Nobleman speaking to the Secretary of the Treasury." [8] Consequently applications for long absences were made to the Treasury far too often, and many of them were granted generously enough at an unwarranted cost to the revenue and to discipline.[9] Thus the London Warehouse-keeper, for reasons

[1] See Cust. Ho. Lib., Sel. from Cust. Outport Recds., South Coast, 1922, p. 125, Weymouth, Board to Collector, 1708–1719, 1718, July 22; Cust. Ho. Lib., Extracts Board Minutes, I, "Absence," 1718, July 1, 30, Nov. 12.
[2] *Ibid.*, I, "Absence," 1729, Apr. 1; 1733, Apr. 27; 1734, Apr. 27; 1758, June 15.
[3] *Ibid.*, III, 4, 1768, Oct. 4.
[4] *Ibid.*, IV, 2, 1779, Feb. 12.
[5] E. g., *ibid.*, I, "Absence," 1712, Sept. 8.
[6] *Ibid.*, IV, 2, 1778, Feb. 18.
[7] *Ibid.*, III, 339, 1762, June 15.
[8] P.R.O., Treasury Papers, Bdl. 379, Nos. 12–13, J. Manby to My Lord, 1757, Jan. 22.
[9] In the Treasury Out-letters, Customs, are many copies of Treasury warrants authorizing, without deduction, leaves of absence for many months. See a list for the years 1772, 1773, and 1774 in *ibid.*, XXX, 37–40. There was danger that by "re-

of health, secured leave for five consecutive years without deduction of salary,[1] and inferior officers frequently had six months off at full pay. The practice was a continual worry to the Customs Board after the mid-century,[2] but it was not until 1778 that the Commissioners plucked up enough courage to represent the matter in its true light to the Treasury. Their memorial on that occasion well surveys a situation from which the service had suffered for several decades.

> That the Directors of the East India Company, and also various other Considerable Merchants, have laid before Us frequent and very just Complaints of a want of Officers to dispatch their Business, owing principally to the repeated and long continued leaves of Absence granted to so great a Number of them.
> It is therefore Our indispensible duty to represent this Matter, with all due submission, to Your Lordships, leaving it to Your better Judgments whether You will not abstain from the exercise of this power, which has only grown frequent of late Years;—
> Because this Board, which is constantly sitting, and always ready to hear their Officers, never refuses them reasonable Indulgence for Health, or any other proper Occasion, consequently the Applications made to Your Lordships are in truth unnecessary, and as they do not undergo any previous reference or enquiry (contrary to Your practice in most other Matters depending before this Board) Your Lordships are not only surprized too often into granting these requests upon very unjustifiable, and sinister pretences, but they are frequently obtained at times when it is highly prejudicial to the Publick Service, and particularly distressing to the Merchants.[3]

The effort was not in vain. Four years later the Lords surrendered a power which had gone hand in hand with their control of patronage.

---

peated and long continued leaves of Absence," however granted, employments might be converted into sinecures, "which is an Evil that has been long and justly complained of both as Burthensome to the Revenue and prejudicial to the Public Service." P.R.O., Treasury Papers, Bdl. 566, Nos. 131–132, Cust. Comrs. to Lords of Treas., 1781, Sept. 12.

[1] P.R.O., Treas. Out-letters, Cust., XXVIII, 179, Treasury warrant, 1765, June 7, and like warrants for the years 1766–1769.

[2] The following instances indicate the position of the Commissioners in this connection: In 1758 the Treasury "assured" the Customs Board that no officer should have leave without loss of pay, without urgent reason. (Cust. Ho. Lib., Extracts Board Minutes, I, "Absence," 1758, Feb. 7.) In 1776 the Commissioners were on the point of presenting a memorial to the Lords of the Treasury "on the unusual frequency & length of the leaves of absence" that were granted, but were deterred. (*Ibid.*, IV, 1, 1776, June 28.) In a number of cases the Commissioners returned to the Lords of the Treasury their warrants which granted extended leave. Thus, for example, a warrant which authorized six months' absence for a Bristol tide-waiter was sent back to the Treasury and the officer was directed to resume his duties. *Ibid.*, IV, 1, 1777, Feb. 26.

[3] P.R.O., Treasury Papers, Bdl. 542, No. 177, 1778, Dec. 18.

PERSONNEL

In 1782 they resolved not to grant leaves of absence and directed that all applications in the future be made to the Customs Board.[1] From that time on this aspect of administration appears to have been more efficiently regulated. A review of absences over the whole period shows that, while the granting of them was subject to much abuse, the Commissioners were aware of the importance of judicious regulation and struggled accordingly to realize intelligent control.

The efforts of the Board in the management of personnel were supplemented by a system of supervision elsewhere. Discipline of staff and execution of duty were enforced by particular officers designated for that service, and by the provision of various instruments of regulation. In London the Bench Officers superintended personnel; in the outports the collector and controller were the principal supervisors. Below these officials, the superior officials in each class were directly answerable for their subordinates and responsible for the communication of Board orders to them.[2] To the superior officers were delegated such further supervisory duties as the control of daily absence, preparation of certificates of conduct, and examination into complaints.[3] The position of the surveyors-general and of the general-surveyors (after 1771) as personnel officers in the scheme of administration has been indicated in preceding chapters. By their inspection of ports and their examination into cases of delinquency they controlled conduct. The examiners of the books and journals of various officers were another check upon efficiency. Frequently the Board employed "a Trusty Officer in an adjoining Port" to investigate misconduct.[4]

Further means by which duty was regulated were provided in sets of instructions issued to officers and in the system of records. Upon admittance to the service, officers were given detailed instructions which described with great care the several duties belonging to the

[1] Cust. Ho. Lib., Extracts Board Minutes, IV, 4-5, 1782, Aug. 30.
[2] A Board order of 1725, issued when the Commissioners had reason to think that their commands were not duly communicated to the officers, directed that all orders given by the Board to the collector be entered in the collector's order book and given in writing to the superior officers, and that the land- and tide-surveyors (as superintendents of the waterside staff) enter all orders received from the collector and controller in their proper books. Cust. Ho. Lib., Letter Book, Blackney, 1711–1723, p. 112, Carkesse to Blackney, 1725, Nov. 27.
[3] Detailed rules for the guidance of officers in their investigation of such complaints were laid down in 1717 upon the Commissioners "finding that when they have had occasion to appoint an officer to Examine into Complaints made of other officers for Neglect of duty or Misbehaviour, Such Examinations have been very loose." *Ibid.*, pp. 68–69, Carkesse to Blackney, 1717, July 18.
[4] Cust. Ho. Lib., Extracts Board Minutes, I, "Commissioners," 1725, Mar. 2.

office and which, as might appear from one instance, were to be adhered to even to the disparagement of the orders of the superior officers. From time to time such instructions were reviewed and new codes were framed as subsequent Board orders and laws necessitated.[1] The elaborate system of books which the officers were obliged to keep was calculated to check them in their duties and to ensure the revenue against loss. Thus the preventive officers recorded their activities in their journals [2]; the tide-waiters and land-waiters kept their blue books, which contained careful entries of all goods imported at the waterside; and in the outports the land-surveyor was responsible for the jerque book, a record of the comparison of the blue books with the entries inwards. The collector was veritably an accountant: his most important records included accounts of entries in and out and coastwise, his quarterly books, records of bonds, a register of shipping, and a book of seizures. The controller prepared similar accounts as checks. The collector was also obliged to keep a Book of Orders wherein were entered all Board commands and copies of his letters to the Board. A set of the Acts of Parliament and the Book of Rates were also required to be on hand in every port for reference, as were various printed books relating to the customs. Finally, annual accounts of the ages and capacities and abilities of the officers in all the ports had to be returned at Christmas to the customs office by the collectors.[3] These records were probably of direct use in administration, though their utility has not been definitely ascertained.

It is impossible to make any accurate estimate of the efficiency of the personnel system. Certainly it was not as efficient as it might have been. Often there were not enough officers, particularly at the fast-growing ports and at rush times. The situation at Hull is typical of other outports, when at approximately the mid-century the chief officers of that port upon three separate occasions represented the crowded state of the port to the Commissioners and requested extra assistance. In one instance in 1749, thirty-three ships of the plantation trade were lying in the harbor guarded by only thirty-five tide-waiters

[1] Cust. Ho. Lib., Extracts Board Minutes, I, "Instructions," 1722, Dec. 5.
[2] By a Board order of 1716, upon the Commissioners receiving "dayly Complaints that Great Quantities of Goods are run to the Great Detriment of the Revenue & the ruin of the Fair Trade wch coud not possibly be to Such Degree if the Preventive Officers did their duties as they ought." Cust. Ho. Lib., Letters to Dartmouth, 1715–16 to 1731, pp. 25–26, Carkesse to Collector and Comptroller, 1716, Nov. 10.
[3] First required by minute of 1712 and continued annually. Cust. Ho. Lib., Extracts Board Minutes, I, "Ages and Capacities," 1712, Dec. 13.

and boatmen and mariners.[1] Such conditions were costly to revenue and merchants alike. Because there was no age limit or uniform system of examination or promotion, old and unfit men were frequently admitted to the service. Errors in calculation of duties, arrears in accounts, and delays in remittances show only too clearly the employment of unskilled persons in the higher positions of collector and controller. Furthermore, short hours, frequent holidays, and absences were symptoms of laxity in the actual work itself. Sometimes it was to the interest of officers to let business drag, for alluring fees were usually offered for quick clearance of vessels. In many cases there was actual neglect of duty, particularly in the preventive branch. Another element which must have affected business was quarrels among officers,[2] particularly cases of insubordination.

Officers were not of the highest character. Probably many of them would fit the description of a seventy-eight year old Dunbar man who was "Infirm but capable. Likes his cups and a wench."[3] Numerous are the reprimands or penalties for addiction to liquor,[4] though from this it must not be supposed that such irregularity was peculiar to the customs staff. The risk both to revenue and reputation by undue indulgence is well put by a collector [?] in a letter to an inferior officer against whom complaint had been made that he was not sober for two days together when on duty:

> I advise you as a friend to keep yourself composs when you are delivering any coal ships for if you dont you may find the ill consequence thereof for I doubt not but there are people ready waiting for to take all advantages so I think it behoveth you as well as all other officers to be upon their guard as much as they can possibly. One reason I believe there may be something of

---

[1] See Cust. Ho. Lib., Sel. from Cust. Outport Recds., East Coast, 1923, p. 208, Hull, Collector to Board, 1748–1750, 1749, Nov. 15; p. 216, Hull, Collector to Board, 1754–1756, 1755, Apr. 7; p. 227, Collector to Board, 1767–1769, 1767, Dec. 8. See also report of Customs Commissioners to Lords of Treasury, 1765, Nov. 12, on the memorial of merchants trading to and from Liverpool, wherein those merchants complained that because of the deficiency of land-waiters and porters at that port they frequently suffered great delay, losses, and disappointments, and requested the Treasury to consider an additional number of officers. P.R.O., Treasury Papers, Bdl. 441, No. 400. Cf. a report upon a similar petition in 1775. *Ibid.*, Bdl. 516, No. 198.

[2] E. g., Cust. Ho. Lib., Sel. from Cust. Outport Recds., Northern England, 1924, p. 124, Sunderland, Collector to Board, 1750, July 24; p. 176, Stockton on Tees, Board to Collector, 1731, July 1.

[3] Cust. Ho. Lib., Edinburgh Register House, Selections from Records relating to the Customs and Excise Departments, compiled by B. R. Leftwich, 1921, p. 7.

[4] E. g., Cust. Ho. Lib., Sel. from Cust. Outport Recds., Northern England, 1924, p. 42, Whitehaven, Board to Collector, 1704, Oct. 26.

truth in this complaint is because you have certified the cocqt. of Wm. Moorson of one date & the warrant of another date. I want to know wch is the right date. I have heard likewise yt you exposed yourself last Sunday in the same manner by falling off the Squab &c wch. I was sorry to hear—.[1]

A proclamation early issued "for preventing and punishing imorality and prophaneness" was directed in 1726 to be fixed "in some publick and convenient place" in one of the vessels, and the commander was instructed not only to "take care for avoiding all lewdness disorderly practices, prophaneness and other imoralities amongst the Company under your authority but by your own example excite and stir them up to the practice of religion and virtue."[2] A hot temper and a vocabulary which fitted it brought more than one officer into trouble, for abusive language was against the rule. Thus one poor fellow, frightened undoubtedly by the possible consequences, could not humble himself enough: "Gentlemen, I am heartily sorry that I am once more forced to beg you would forgive me once more and I will never again abuse Mr. Wilcock, my Surveyor or give him any abusive language if you will please forgive me this time I shall take particular care to behave as a good and diligent officer always to observe my superior officers' commands and to avoid unbecoming language."[3]

Most serious of all delinquencies was corruption in duty. Records for the period contain instance after instance of connivance in fraud and smuggling. One of the clearest accounts of the methods by which the land-waiters, weighers, watermen, and other officers assisted in such illicit practices at the waterside is given in the report of the parliamentary committee of 1733. And such practices were not confined to the waterside officers; collectors also juggled accounts for their own gain, and preventive officers by intentional negligence permitted smugglers too frequently to land their wares or let the smuggling vessel escape.

It is not difficult to explain whatever inefficiency and corruption may have existed in the customs staff. The very system of duties which had to be enforced and the laws regulating it presented serious problems of administration. Procedure at importation and exportation was complicated; there were difficulties in distinguishing goods; com-

---

[1] Cust. Ho. Lib., Sel. from Cust. Outport Recds., Northern England, 1924, pp. 229–230, Whitby, Collector to Board and General, Letter to Angus MackDonald, 1729, June 16.
[2] *Ibid.*, West Coast, 1926, p. 125, Beaumaris, Board to Collector, 1726, Sept. 1.
[3] *Ibid.*, East Coast, 1923, p. 159, Yarmouth, Collector to Board, 1750-1753, George Winn [to collector and controller ?], 1750-1, Jan. 24.

putation of duties was intricate; the keeping of voluminous accounts required a remarkable skill which few possessed. When such factors combined with abuses in appointment, the presence of incompetent men in the system is not to be wondered at. As will appear in Chapter VII, there were unlimited opportunities for bribery and collusion in the procedure followed at importation and exportation. Only officers of iron will and high integrity could ever have hoped to end their official service as unspotted as when they entered it. Inadequate income and dependence on fees made many officers all the more willing to wink at an irregularity in order to obtain a few extra shillings; and the sin cannot be considered too damning when, as a newspaper of 1728 put it, "Several Officers of the Customs are suspended only for taking Care of their Families, and making the most of their Places." [1]

Irregularities may be partially condoned when it is also realized that officers were confronted by such problems as the highly developed organizations of smugglers. Thus in 1783 it was estimated that 120 large armed vessels and 200 smaller ships were employed in a regular smuggling business and on some parts of the coast were protected in their importations by batteries.[2] The necessity for regiments of soldiers and for men-of-war to deal with gangs of smugglers, numbering sometimes several hundred, indicates the proportions of running during the period and the helplessness of the customs staff in the face of it. Indeed, such was the contempt for customs law that a journal of 1721 observed, "The Insolence of these [French] Smuggling Sloops is so great, that they will insure their Brandy safe from all Officers" [3]; and in 1778 the strength of certain persons assisting the smugglers was declared to be such that the revenue officers "even with all the Assistance the Military can give them [very seldom] dare venture to obstruct or oppose them." [4] The records of the century are full of references to officers being forcibly imprisoned, wounded, and murdered by the smugglers.[5] Sometimes they met with gross torture.

---

[1] *Mist's Weekly Journal*, 1728, June 8.
[2] *Parliamentary Papers*, XXXVI, *Repts.*, VI, H.C. No. 58, p. 5 (1783), "First Rept. on Illicit Practices."
[3] *The London Journal*, 1721, Apr. 8.
[4] P.R.O., Treasury Papers, Bdl. 542, No. 228, Excise Comrs. to Lords of Treas., 1778, Mar. 24.
[5] For an example of the power of the smugglers, see *ibid.*, Bdl. 319, Nos. 102–107, "An Account of what Representations have been made by the Commissioners of the Customs, to the Lords Commissioners of the Treasury for the last Three Years, relating to the Infamous and destructive practice of Smuggling, and what hath been done thereupon," 1743, 1744, 1745.

Thus in 1721 a certain customs officer, captured by brandy smugglers, was obliged to drink brandy as long as he was able. Then when he was "dead drunk" the smugglers poured brandy down him with a funnel to the amount of "two Quarts and a Pint," tied him on a horse and let him go.[1] In another case the smugglers beat several men of a naval cutter, "particularly the Officer, whom they carried to a Pond, stamped on him dragged him through and very near drowned him, after which beat and made him run the Gauntlet from the North to the South end of the Town."[2] Is it any wonder that an officer should be tempted to guarantee his very life and limb?

The smugglers were possessed of amazing ingenuity. So versatile were they in their methods that in 1783 it was believed, "former Boards have observed, as this has done, that the transactions of the Smuglers are constantly, and almost daily varying, and that as fast as exertions are used to stop the evil in one place or mode, it shews itself in some other."[3] These petty criminals were ever constructing boats that were peculiarly adapted to their local shores or that were assured of some distinct advantage over the revenue vessels in respect of size or speed or method of navigation; and as often as the Customs Department hit upon the secret of their success the smugglers would resort to another kind of craft.[4] Smuggling vessels might carry their brandy, rum, or tea in false bulkheads; if discovered, it was an easy thing for the runners to answer the officers that they were bound to foreign parts.[5] Clearances for distant ports and coast despatches protected cargoes intended to be landed,[6] while during time of war letters of marque frequently covered a nefarious trade.[7] Certain wine smugglers were known to "have often baited the Custom-House Officers with a small Cargo, when they have had a much greater to secure."[8] Again, in one port officers were summoned to appear on the jury of the Court Leet and threatened with fine for non-appearance, to which the Swansea collector observed, "it seems to us to looke some-

---

[1] *The London Journal,* 1721, Apr. 22.
[2] P.R.O., Treasury Papers, Bdl. 429, No. 379, Extract of letter of Lieut. Prettie to Stephens, 1764, Aug. 10, enclosure in Stephens to Jenkinson, 1764, Aug. 18.
[3] *Ibid.,* Bdl. 584, No. 56, Stiles to Burke, 1783, Oct. 17.
[4] See *supra,* Ch. V, pp. 177–178.
[5] Cust. Ho. Lib., Sel. from Cust. Outport Recds., West Coast, 1926, p. 80, Swansea, Collector to Board, 1734, Sept. 5.
[6] See *Rept. of Com.,* 1733, pp. 13, 92, App. No. 26.
[7] As was represented to be the practice in 1758. P.R.O., Treasury Papers, Bdl. 380, No. 36, Cust. Comrs. to Lords of Treas., 1758, July 18.
[8] *The London Journal,* 1722, June 30.

PERSONNEL

thing like a design that when they have gott the officers on the Jury they may run vast quantities of goods."[1] Sometimes when apprehensive of a seizure the smugglers would turn informers, whereby they would get a moiety of the produce at a sale.[2] Occasionally they would render an informer against them powerless by having him impressed or imprisoned. In this connection a Yarmouth man suffered sadly by giving intelligence of frauds: the smugglers had him impressed to serve on a man-of-war; his release was effected; the smugglers then resurrected some minor offense of which he had once been guilty and secured his imprisonment, but the customs bailed him out; he was next thrashed by the smugglers—"in a most barbarous & crule manner stamping on his head and body and kicking and beating him with all their might"—in hopes that the pain of wounds might close his mouth.[3]

It was much easier for the customs staff to assist in or at least to be indifferent to frauds than otherwise. The attitude of residents and local officials in a given port was only too often hostile to the officers, as indicated by their assistance in running goods and failure to condemn smugglers. An affray at Deal in 1784, wherein the mayor and the townspeople assisted the smugglers in their depredations against customs and excise officers, dragoons, and His Majesty's ships, took on the aspect of a civil war,[4] which was fairly representative of conditions in many parts of the coast. Two statements of the Sunderland collector to the Board in 1734 and 1734–5 were applicable to other localities as well: "we fear here many gentlemen of the County who are not friends to Officers of Customs,"[5] and "We are humbly of opinion the jurys in this County are not friends to Officers of the Customs nor have they very great encouragement from many Justices of the Peace."[6]

Court prosecutions of guilty offenders sometimes failed miserably through the bribery of royal officials, suborned evidence, false alibis,

---

[1] Cust. Ho. Lib., Sel. from Cust. Outport Recds., West Coast, 1926, p. 79, Swansea, Collector to Board, 1732, Oct. 30.

[2] P.R.O., Treasury Papers, Bdl. 424, No. 243, "Proposal to check the Smuggling of Brandy & Rum by Mr. Broughton."

[3] Cust. Ho. Lib., Sel. from Cust. Outport Recds., East Coast, 1923, p. 153, Yarmouth, Collector to Board, 1742–1744, 1742, Nov. 16.

[4] There are many papers relating to this affair in the Treasury Papers. See, for example, Bdl. 602, No. 96; Bdl. 603, Nos. 234–239; and Bdl. 607, No. 131.

[5] Cust. Ho. Lib., Sel. from Cust. Outport Recds., Northern England, 1924, p. 115, Sunderland, Collector to Board, 1734, Aug. 20.

[6] *Ibid.*, p. 115, Sunderland, Collector to Board, 1734–5, Jan. 28.

and occasionally the mysterious disappearance or change of witnesses to the side of the smugglers. In short, when seizures were made, smugglers were known to "Combine and Unite to prevent the Condemnation, & Recovery of Penalties by Every Cunning Method—In View, if they fail of Success, To Render the Expences of Prosecut^n so Great, as nearly to Exhaust the Amount thereby to discourage the Making such Seizures."[1] A review of the activities of Boyes and Hatch, notorious wine smugglers in the years 1720 to 1730, reveals many examples of the way in which the court was hoodwinked.[2] For instance, when wines were seized, these men would usually take oath that they had purchased the condemned wines from the custom-house or in fair sale. They would then find out the Crown's evidence and bring a greater number of witnesses for themselves from among twenty workers who were in their service and who would swear for them upon any occasion. If the Crown had one or two witnesses only, the smugglers would "trump up some Story to blacken their Characters" or to invalidate their evidence by asserting either that the Crown witnesses had declared that they intended to ruin the defendant, or that they had been promised a gratuity if the verdict went in their favor, or that they had offered the defendants' witnesses sums of money to change to the Crown's side. By these and other methods "they seldom or never failed to obtain a Verdict."[3] Small wonder is it that the officers many a time preferred to cast in their lot with those who seemed sure to win in the end. Officers may further have been cautious in seizures because they might "subject themselves to great Damages on Prosecutions for stopping Ships and Vessels without just Cause." A letter to Boston in 1740 directed that the officers be cautioned "that they may not stop any Ships or Vessels which come on the English Coast with prohibited or uncustomed Goods unless their Proof is very clear, or upon very strong Circumstances."[4]

To increase the efficiency and integrity of its officers, the Board

---

[1] This statement has particular reference to seizures of foreign wrought silks in 1764. P.R.O., Treasury Papers, Bdl. 434, No. 250, Company of Weavers, London, to Lords of Treas., 1764, May 12. For example of alteration of witnesses, see Cust. Ho. Lib., Sel. from Cust. Outport Recds., East Coast, 1923, p. 196, King's Lynn, Board to Collector, 1724–1731, 1729, Aug. 6; for an account of a dangerous society to defeat by perjuries all prosecutions against smugglers, see P.R.O., Treasury Papers, Bdl. 328, No. 91, letter to Thomas Burdens [1747].

[2] *Rept. of Com.*, 1733, pp. 18–19.

[3] *Ibid.*, pp. 92–93, App. 27.

[4] Cust. Ho. Lib., Board's Letters to Boston, Feb. 1732–3 to Mar. 1745–6, Carkesse to [Boston], 1740, Aug. 30.

PERSONNEL

left scarcely anything undone. While the standard of qualifications was not noticeably raised during the period, the Commissioners compelled the strict fulfilment of those already demanded. Thus the necessity of six months' training and various regulations with respect to the residence and extraneous occupations of officers were insisted upon.

The system of payment was also improved in several respects. Efforts were made to regulate fees stringently. Salaries were increased, and those salaries which fell below a certain level (usually £60) were exempted from taxation. In some instances the Board advanced payment to certain officers because of their "very great inconveniences, on Account of their being paid by Quarterly payments, and thereby obliged to borrow Money at an exorbitant rate of Interest, for the support of themselves and Families in the Interval between each Quarter." [1] The change of some incidents to salary basis was calculated to provide a form of steady income. The Board made good use of gratuities for commendable services, and of rewards for apprehending smugglers and as shares of seizures resulting from successful prosecution. In 1769 the Register-General of Tobacco was allowed £150 as a reward for his important services [2]; a solicitor in 1766 received £200 for preparing bills for Parliament [3]; a land-surveyor in 1779 was granted £65 for detecting an error in duty to be paid [4]; a deputy king's-waiter in the same year was awarded £100 for bringing up the arrears in jerquing East India Ships.[5] In the capture of smugglers one officer made a respectable little fortune of £60 at £12 a head [6];

---

[1] Weekly payments to established tide-waiters, weighing porters, and watermen in the Port of London were the practice before 1758 and after 1768. (P.R.O., Treasury Papers, Bdl. 467, No. 219, Cust. Comrs. to Lords of Treas., 1768, Oct. 7. Cf. P.R.O., Treas. Out-letters, Cust., XXIX, 204, Bradshaw to Cust. Comrs., 1768, Oct. 21.) In 1732, the Commissioners, being of opinion "it would be of service to the tidesmen, boatmen and such like inferior officers if they had their sallerys or some part thereof advanced to them from time to time as it becomes due without staying till quarter day," directed an outport collector "to advance them the same without any permission or consideration when they apply for it not exceeding what shall be due to them." Cust. Ho. Lib., Sel. from Cust. Outport Recds., East Coast, 1923, p. 21, Maldon, Collector to Board and Board to Collector, 1732-1738, 1732, June 5.

[2] Cust. Ho. Lib., Extracts Board Minutes, III, 194, 1769, Aug. 25.

[3] *Ibid.*, III, 191, 1766, June 25. This is only one year in many when a solicitor received such allowances.

[4] *Ibid.*, IV, 488, 1779, May 28.

[5] *Ibid.*, IV, 488, 1779, Mar. 16.

[6] Cust. Ho. Lib., Sel. from Cust. Outport Recds., East Coast, 1923, p. 48, Colchester, Board to Collector, 1729-1755, 1734, Aug. 3.

and promise of a good-sized sum to any one who should apprehend smugglers was usual.[1] Rewards in seizures were so profitable that sometimes collusion between officers and smugglers took the form of stage-managed seizures for the sake of the reward, which was often more than the value of the shipment. Tobacco stalks and other rubbish, for example, were even shipped out illegally and a capture prearranged, the crew consequently serving jail sentence, all for the sake of a handsome reward out of the £200 or more received by the officer and his informer.[2]

Another way in which the administration encouraged its officers was in rewarding them for long and faithful service. In the beginning of the period the Commissioners granted retiring officers specific sums in recognition of their work; and in some cases they directed that a part of the successor's salary be turned over as a pension to the outgoing occupant.[3] Such a system was eminently unsatisfactory, and in 1712 the Superannuation Fund was established for tide-waiters, watermen, and weighing porters in London.[4] Funds were created for more and more classes of officers during the period,[5] a number of which funds were consolidated in 1776.[6] In the meantime standards

---

[1] E. g., Cust. Ho. Lib., Sel. from Cust. Outport Recds., East Coast, 1931, p. 48, King's Lynn, Board to Collector, Carkesse to Gentlemen, 1739, Oct. 19.

[2] Alfred Rive, "A Brief History of Regulation and Taxation of Tobacco in England," *William and Mary College Quarterly Historical Magazine,* Second Series, IX, 82.

[3] E. g., *Cal. Treas. Papers,* 1697–1701–2, p. 179, Cust. Comrs. to Lords of Treas., 1698, July 8; P.R.O., Treas. Out-letters, Cust., XV, 106–107, Cust. Comrs. to Lord High Treasurer, 1708, Apr. 22; Treasury warrant, 1708, May 14.

[4] *Ibid.,* XV, 415–416, Cust. Comrs. to Lord High Treasurer, 1712, Apr. 30; Treasury warrant [1712], May 3.

[5] In 1720 the privileges of the Superannuation Fund were granted to practically all London officers having salaries not exceeding £60 on the establishment. (*Ibid.,* XVII, 285–286, Cust. Comrs. to Lords of Treas., 1720, July 20; Treasury warrant, 1720, July 26.) In 1779 the Commissioners declared "That upon many Years experience of the said Regulation We are fully satisfied that the same has been very beneficial to the Public Service as well as to the Officers themselves who have been Partakers of this Charitable Fund," and recommended the extension of the superannuation allowance to officers whose salaries approximated £100 on the establishment. The proposal received the Treasury warrant. (*Ibid.,* XXXII, 181–182, Cust. Comrs. to Lords of Treas., 1779, Jan. 28; Treasury warrant, 1779, Mar. 30.) For earlier extensions of the fund, see *ibid.,* XVI, 34–35, Cust. Comrs. to Lord High Treasurer; Treasury warrant, 1713, June 10; XVII, 18, Cust. Comrs. to Lords of Treas., 1717, Sept. 4; Treasury warrant, 1717, Nov. 6. These earlier warrants are summarized as well in *Cal. Treas. Books and Papers,* 1742–1745, pp. 498–499, Cust. Comrs. to Lords of Treas., 1744, July 12. For a later extension of the fund, see Cust. Ho. Lib., Extracts Board Minutes, V, 553, 1776, July 24.

[6] *Ibid.,* V, 553, 1776, May 14.

PERSONNEL

for admittance were lowered until in 1778 the two main qualifications were that the officer should be less than sixty and that he should have contributed for ten years to the fund.[1] In 1788 the age limit was reduced to fifty-five.[2] Upon the usual payment of 6d. in the pound, the customary allowance to officers at their retirement amounted to one third of their salary, though occasionally it took the form of a lump sum.[3] An even more tender sympathy with officers, on the part of the Board, is shown by the case of a man not entitled to superannuation who nevertheless was granted a sum in consequence of his long services, age, and infirmities.[4] Though there were many undesirable features in connection with the fund, it is notable as the first attempt in the customs service to encourage and protect good officers by pension.

The same principle was applied in the occasional grant of allowances to officers for physical disability incurred by an accident in the service. Thus a tide-waiter, "Lamed while on Duty, so that it is doubtful whether he may ever Return to Duty," was permitted 10s. per week until further order[5]; a waterman who had received the same injury was given 18d. a day—apparently while his condition remained serious.[6] A minute for 1731 indicates that London preferable tide-waiters, disabled in the service, were allowed a weekly pension of five shillings[7]; and in 1780 the Board resolved to grant £10 annuity per annum to mariners on cruisers who lost a hand or foot or received such injury by the smugglers' weapons that they were disabled from further service, and also to pay the surgeon's bills for less serious wounds received under such circumstances.[8] Sheer kindliness must have influenced one Board to allow £10 to a dismissed tide-waiter "in consideration of the Loss of the Use of his arm and of the miserable Condition and State of his Family."[9] Medical assistance at all times

---

[1] See Cust. Ho. Lib., Extracts Board Minutes, V, 554–555, 1778, Dec. 30; III, 565, 1773, May 28. Other questions raised in connection with the admittance of an officer to the fund were whether he had behaved himself well while in the service, whether he had any other means of subsistence or was capable of securing subsistence in any other way, and, if he was retiring before he had paid the full number of years into the fund, whether he had been disabled by accident.
[2] Ibid., V, 559, 1788, Dec. 10.
[3] E. g., see ibid., III, 561, 1761, Nov. 27.
[4] Ibid., III, 192, 1768, Oct. 6.
[5] Ibid., II, "Subsistence," 1722, Nov. 6.
[6] Ibid., II, "Subsistence," 1722, Feb. 21.
[7] Ibid., II, "Tidesmen," 1731, June 16.
[8] Ibid., IV, 267, 1780, Dec. 9.
[9] Ibid., III, 190, 1765, Mar. 7.

was provided to officers injured in the service. Bills of such unfortunates were paid,[1] and in London a surgeon was appointed to the house for specific care of the men.[2]

The Commissioners displayed genuine compassion with the poor widows and children of officers who met death by an accident in the service or were killed by smugglers. Under the former of these circumstances the usual sum allowed was £7. 10s. annually to the widow, 30s. for each child until it was grown, and an additional 30s. if the wife was expecting a child.[3] Upon a tragic accident in 1704 when twenty-two tide-waiters and watermen were drowned at Bristol, the widows were each paid one fourth of their husbands' salaries, 30s. for each child living, and the same rate for each posthumous child.[4] The families of those men who lost their lives by violence were even better provided for. In 1776 the Commissioners recommended to the Treasury that a widow whose husband had been murdered by the smugglers be allowed £15 per annum for herself and an additional £10 per annum to enable her to bring up her four children until they came of age, "in like manner as was allowed to the Widows of Chater and Galley in the year 1748 William Odgers in the year 1768 and John Franick in the year 1771 whose Husbands were Murdered in the Service of this Revenue."[5] One orphan whose father was killed by smugglers was given £50 which "may likewise prove an encouragement to the officers in exerting themselves in the execution of their

---

[1] E. g., Cust. Ho. Lib., Sel. from Cust. Outport Recds., South Coast, 1925, p. 175, Portsmouth, Board to Collector, 1758, May 18, granting permission to pay the surgeon's bill of £15. 13s. for the care of a mariner whose skull was fractured in the execution of his duty. Possibly with the hope of securing an additional sum from the Board, the Exeter collector, in transmitting bills for the care of an unfortunate boatman who had been ill used by the smugglers, thought "it our duty to observe to your Honours that Hunt hath undergone great pain and misery during his confinement from the shocking treatment he met with from the smuglers, his shoulder being dislocated but not discovered by the surgeon from the terrible condition his arm and body was in till three weeks afterwards insomuch that he was obliged to be carried to an apple engine and being fastened round the body to a stake in the ground it was by the meer force of that screw brought in again." Ibid., South Coast, 1922, p. 158, Exeter, Collector to Board, 1766–1771, 1766, July 12.

[2] See Cust. Ho. Lib., Extracts Board Minutes, II, III, V, entries under "Surgeon."

[3] E. g., Cust. Ho. Lib., Sel. from Cust. Outport Recds., East Coast, 1923, p. 50, Colchester, Board to Collector, 1729–1755, 1738, June 6.

[4] P.R.O., Treas. Out-letters, Cust., XIV, 345, Cust. Comrs. to Lord High Treasurer, 1704, Mar. 7; Treasury warrant, 1704, Mar. 9.

[5] Ibid., XXXI, 302, Cust. Comrs. to Lords of Treas., 1776, Aug. 6; Treasury warrant, 1776, Aug. 9.

duty and may intimidate the smugglers." [1] Another daughter, left by a boatman drowned in duty, received but 30s., "the usual allowance in such cases." [2] Occasionally funeral expenses of officers killed in the service were partly defrayed by an allowance from the Board.[3] Perhaps the best instance of the very human character of one Board is that of their allowance of £3 to one poor fellow who had lost his clothes when a ship on which he was boarded was cast away.[4]

Besides attention to the qualifications of some officers, and improvement in the system of remuneration and its employment for the encouragement of good service, the welfare of the revenue was protected in still other ways. A plan of occasionally "rolling" or removing officers from place to place was designed to prevent too great an intimacy between officers and merchants in a port. Exchange of positions was not unusual. Though such procedure seems to have been applied only in particular cases, its adoption as a general policy was strongly recommended by several persons during the period.[5] One writer even went so far as to propose a definite rolling of the entire water guard and the preventive land officers, for "An officer, by residing long in any of the Out Ports, contracts a friendsp with the Traders in that Place, some of them, which tis' to be apprehended does very often engage him to connive at the running of Goods, or may give the Smuglers better opportunities of corrupting the officer by Bribes, in case nothing else can prevail on him. . . . for t'is a work of time to beget such a confid^{ce} between the Smugler and the officer as will be necess^{ry} to a mutual trust of each other in a matter of this nature." [6]

---

[1] Cust. Ho. Lib., Sel. from Cust. Outport Recds., East Coast, 1923, p. 52, Colchester, Board to Collector, 1729–1755, 1742–3, Jan. 5.

[2] *Ibid.*, South Coast, 1925, pp. 170–171, Portsmouth, Board to Collector, 1753, July 17.

[3] E. g., Cust. Ho. Lib., Extracts Board Minutes, V, 747, 1778, Feb. 18.

[4] Cust. Ho. Lib., Sel. from Cust. Outport Recds., South Coast, 1922, p. 121, Weymouth, Board to Collector, 1694–1709, 1700, Nov. 7.

[5] In 1698 appears the first instance of "rolling" as a form of more effective administration. On October 25th the Lords of the Treasury issued their warrant for the appointment of the Lynn surveyor to be surveyor of Harwich, the Customs Commissioners having represented the vacancy at Harwich and indicated that they were "willing to take this opportunity to put in practice that kind of management which has been approved by us [the Lords], viz. The Rolling or removing of Officers from place to place." (P.R.O., Treas. Out-letters. Cust., XIII, 470.) There are several cases of this kind at approximately this time. For an instance at a later date, see Cust. Ho. Lib., Sel. from Cust. Outport Recds., East Coast, 1923, p. 23, Maldon, Collector to Board and Board to Collector, 1732–1738, 1733, July 10.

[6] B.M., Add. MSS. 18903, f. 89. In connection with the prevention of frauds in the tobacco trade, one writer states, "The Limitation of the Ports for the Tobacco

Also, to secure efficiency in personnel, good work was recognized. Often encouragement took the form of promotion,[1] and it is not infrequent that one finds a petition for a new position submitted by an officer who has been unusually successful in seizures.[2] Approval was sometimes bestowed publicly in the custom-house. Officers were protected whenever possible by numerous laws passed in punishment of smugglers and of those persons who obstructed or abused them in execution of their duty.[3] If a customs officer was prosecuted for a seizure made, he was defended by the Board, provided the cause and circumstances of the seizure were according to those prescribed by the Commissioners.[4] The assistance of soldiers and Admiralty cruisers was generously afforded.

In addition to these measures, the Board made numerous miscellaneous regulations to ensure the efficiency and integrity of its men. Certain officers were desired to live near the custom-house,[5] a requirement that may have laid a hardship on the men in some cases in view of higher rents; apparently women could not visit ships or watch-houses [6]; and officers could have no other business. The waterside staff were strictly forbidden to accept treats from merchants,[7] for at least in the early part of the period "The long Practice of Tide-survey[rs] in taking Presents of bottles of wine & Brandy, Hams of Bacon, small parcells of Tea Sugar, & the like from masters of Ships, & merch[ts] at the clearing of Ships (which is likewise practised by the Tydewaiters) has introduced a notion amongst those officers that such Presents, which they call triffles, cannot be reckon'd bribes." [8] Even an innocent dinner at the expense of a merchant whose ship the offi-

---

Trade in England and Scotland is a very material point to be considered, and it is believed a part of Mr. Dinwiddies' Scheme, as also the Rotation of the Officers of the Customs at those Ports which is humbly submitted." (P.R.O., Treasury Papers, Bdl. 326, No. 75.) Another person suggests, "If there be Doubt that there be any Fraud in the officers of the Customs in the Importation or Exportation, Make a Rotation of officers Thro England & Scotland." *Ibid.*, Bdl. 326, No. 54.

[1] See *supra*, p. 211.
[2] E. g., *Cal. Treas. Papers,* 1720–1728, p. 191, John Elliott to Lords of Treas., 1722, Aug. 17.
[3] See *infra*, Ch. VIII, pp. 288–289.
[4] See *infra*, Ch. VIII, p. 286.
[5] See *Cal. Treas. Books and Papers,* 1731–1734, p. 376, 1733, Apr. 19; Cust. Ho. Lib., Extracts Board Minutes, II, "Officers," 1733, Apr. 21.
[6] E. g., Cust. Ho. Lib., Sel. from Cust. Outport Recds., East Coast, 1923, p. 165, Yarmouth, Collector to Board, 1763–1769, 1763, Nov. 19.
[7] E. g., Cust. Ho. Lib., Extracts Board Minutes, I, "Inspectors of the River," 1717, Apr. 4; II, "Tide Surveyors," 1718, Sept. 17; cf. III, 260, 1767, Oct. 1.
[8] B.M., Add. MSS. 18903, f. 87.

PERSONNEL

cers were unloading was eyed suspiciously, and in some cases forbidden,[1] though one collector, in defending his officers to the Board, believed them of such integrity "as not to be influenced by Breakfasts of Tea or otherwise."[2] The danger of such a connection was amply appreciated by the Board: "It having been found a practice of officers in some ports for a trifling consideration to permit goods to be run on shore or delivered duty free, The Commissioners are resolved to observe as a standing rule for the future that in any instance it shall appear that any sum of money or present tho' ever so trivial shall be received by any officer in order to permit or suffer any goods to be run on shore or delivered free of duty, they will in every such instance dismiss the officer concerned."[3] There were further strict rules against making erasures in shipping documents and books of the waterside staff,[4] designed obviously to protect the service against fraudulent practices by masters and officers. These together with many other directions of similar nature regulated the conduct of officers.

The Board, however, was not loth to wield the "big stick" for violation of officers' trust. Penalties inflicted took many forms. Reprimand in the public custom-house for lesser offenses was not infrequent. Mulcts, which were fines often proportioned according to salary, were the most common form of punishment for negligence in duty, disregard of instructions, and the like. Such deductions were not light, as is revealed by the various references under "Mulcts" in the Extracts of the Board Minutes—a fine of £300 imposed on the collector of Hull in 1766 being perhaps the heaviest of these.[5] Suspension for the above reasons was not uncommon, either with or without loss of pay.[6] Officers were dismissed for marked inefficiency, insubordination, and corruption (it being "the uniform practice of this Board to dismiss every Officer who is found guilty of any fraud or Collusion what-

[1] Cust. Ho. Lib., Extracts Board Minutes, III, 293, 1771, Jan. 16.
[2] Cust. Ho. Lib., Correspondence. London and Whitehaven, 1744–1748, p. 82, Collector to Board, 1746, May 20.
[3] Cust. Ho. Lib., Sel. from Cust. Outport Recds., South Coast, 1925, p. 121, Southampton, Board to Collector, 1753, Mar. 13.
[4] For minutes on the subject, see Cust. Ho. Lib., Extracts Board Minutes, III, IV, entries under "Erazures." The Attorney-General in a case in 1774 described the conduct of the Bench Officers in issuing an erased cocket as "perfectly scandalous." In this case, suit had been brought against a Newfoundland officer for seizing an innocent ship which he had thought to be engaged in illicit practices because of the erasure on the cocket issued by the London officers. P.R.O., Treasury Papers, Bdl. 507, No. 237, Cust. Comrs. to Lords of Treas., 1774, Aug. 25.
[5] Cust. Ho. Lib., Extracts Board Minutes, III, 325, 1766, May 28.
[6] See entries under "Suspension" in *ibid.*, II.

soever" [1]), or for a second offense, though in 1791 the Commissioners resolved that they might relax their severity in this last ruling where the officers had performed any meritorious service or where their good conduct for any length of time warranted a mitigation.[2] In 1716 the Commissioners made it a standing rule that when officers were dismissed for fraud their bonds were to be put in suit.[3] Such also appears to have been the case when they owed a debt to the Crown [4] or when it was a matter of a very serious neglect of duty.[5] In general, however, the attitude of the Board was sympathetic toward its officers, giving encouragement whenever possible, inflicting moderate punishment for the first offense, and relaxing penalties of undue severity. At the same time, the Commissioners exerted stricter supervision in more intelligent measures regulating officers' conduct.

In summing up, several conclusions become evident: there were weaknesses in the control of personnel in the appointment of officers, in the conditions of financial remuneration, and in the regulations governing actual work. That the officers were not of the highest efficiency or morality was often owing to those abuses, to the nature of the system which they had to enforce, and to the power of outside forces with which they had to contend. The Customs Commissioners appreciated these evils and made numerous attempts to remedy many of them. On the other hand, they did not always appreciate the real conditions. And even when they did, many irregularities were permitted probably because of limited powers rather than because of disinclination to deal with them. The Commissioners alone cannot be held responsible for failure to accomplish a sweeping reform which could come only from authority above them, and which had to await a time more favorable than the first three quarters of the eighteenth century.

[1] P.R.O., Treasury Papers, Bdl. 587, No. 352, Cust. Comrs. to Lords of Treas., 1783, June 5.
[2] Cust. Ho. Lib., Extracts Board Minutes, IV, 213, 1791, Nov. 23.
[3] *Ibid.,* I, "Bonds," 1716, July 27.
[4] *Ibid.,* IV, 114, 1784, Aug. 20, Sept. 17.
[5] E. g., *ibid.,* IV, 112, 1778, June 25; 1779, May 11.

CHAPTER VII

Customs Procedure in Import, Export, and Coastwise Shipping

In 1786 the customs produced £3,782,576. 10s. 5d.[1] A comparison of this sum with £285,181. 13s. 2d.,[2] an annual average for the first six and three-quarters years of Charles II's reign when the rudiments of eighteenth-century mercantilism were outlined in the first of the Navigation Acts, and with £1,028,484. 12s. 8d.,[3] the net proceeds of 1696, the year in which the mercantile system was completed in its final form, reveals the increasing importance to the national Treasury of the customs in the era of mercantilism. Such a contrast is of considerable interest in view of the complicated system that had to be enforced. High and discriminating duties on certain foreign goods, restriction of trade by enumeration of specific plantation commodities which had to go to England and had to pay duty, prohibition of the import of other goods into Britain, protection of British manufactures by the restriction of the export of certain articles, encouragement of the importation and exportation of others by bounties—all these regulations and many more were features of that mercantilism calculated to protect British interests and to increase the revenue. Neither the wisdom of such a policy nor the extent to which it was enforced is relevant to this study. That the customs system was able to pay into the Exchequer the sums that it did and that it became an increasingly productive source of revenue throughout the century is enough to justify a survey of the practical methods which the establishment employed to carry on its business, with attention to the way in which the revenue reached the Exchequer.

Tobacco has been selected for the purposes of illustrating procedure through the customs because of its importance as an article of trade.

---

[1] *Accounts and Papers,* XXXV, H.C. 366, p. 194 (1868–1869), "Public Income and Expenditure," Part I.
[2] *Cal. Treas. Books,* 1681–1685, Part I, p. xvi.
[3] *Accounts and Papers,* XXXV, H.C. 366, p. 14 (1868–1869), "Public Income and Expenditure," Part I.

Throughout the eighteenth century, of the hundreds of commodities subject to duty [1] it produced one of the largest proportions of gross returns and furnished one of the greatest single sources of revenue. Thus, the annual average gross account of the customs for the years 1770 to 1775 was £5,144,500, while the annual gross account of tobacco for the same period was £1,445,493, or over one fourth of all the sums that were credited under the head of receipts. This, however, does not give a true picture of the net produce of tobacco to the customs, for the "greatest part of the American Tobacco was usually exported from hence with Drawback," so that the average net annual produce of tobacco for those five years was but £197,933 [2] out of an average net annual produce of customs for the same period of over £2,609,445,[3] or approximately one thirteenth of the net proceeds. This is no insignificant proportion of the net revenue, but the importance of tobacco as an article of trade in the British customs must also be judged by its gross ratio.

Tobacco holds a further significance; as an enumerated commodity of the British plantations it exemplifies procedure under the mercantile system of a cargo of such goods through the customs. Since British ports, by the Navigation Act, became the staples for the American tobacco trade, tobacco, as has been noted, was peculiarly subject to reëxportation and thus illustrates that feature of trade so common to enumerated commodities. Tobacco figured prominently in Anglo-Colonial commercial relations. During the colonial period it was the one staple commodity of Virginia and Maryland; hence its value to the planters was dependent upon the prices it would bring upon shipment to Britain and furnished the key to the economic situation in those colonies. From time to time spirited protests were made by the planters against the frauds and abuses in the British customs service, particularly with regard to the treat-

[1] *First Rept. of Comrs. of Cust. on Cust.* [Cd. 2186], p. 21, H.C. (1857), iii, includes a table showing the number of articles subject to duty at various times: in 1660 there were 490 principal dutiable articles and 1,140 sub-divisions, a total of 1,630; in 1787 there were 290 principal articles, and 1,135 sub-divisions, a total of 1,425.

[2] B.M., Add. MSS. 8133 B., f. 350, "Observations on the apparent diminution of the gross Rect. of Customs in 1776," Musgrave's paper to Cooper, 1777, Nov. 20.

[3] B.M., Add. MSS. 8133 C., f. 124. This figure is calculated from an account of the payments by the Receiver-General into the Exchequer, 1760–1784, as contained in Sir William Musgrave's papers, "Revenue of Customs." These statistics are used rather than those given in *Accounts and Papers* (from which they differ little) in comparison with the tobacco returns, since they are all part of the accounts in Musgrave's papers, and I believe they are logically more comparable.

CUSTOMS PROCEDURE IN SHIPPING 245

ment of their tobacco when it was landed at a British port.[1] It is not within the scope of this survey to consider those irregularities, but rather to see what the machinery was like through which those shipments had to pass. Finally, the procedure of tobacco through the customs is typical, for the most part, of the general procedure of almost any commodity and is of particular importance since it represents features of both the drawback and warehousing systems of the eighteenth century.

1. *Procedure at Importation*

It is of interest, then, to look back upon a few typical days in the life of London at approximately the middle of the period and to watch the customs mechanism at work in superintending a cargo of imported tobacco. From the time that the ship appeared in the Channel off Rye she was guarded by sloops and boats appointed at proper stations for that purpose, from Rye through the Downs to Deal and Margate and on to Gravesend. At the Gravesend stations tide-surveyors boarded and rummaged her and placed several tide-waiters on her to guard her in the passage up the river to the Pool of London. From the time that these officers were first stationed on board until the vessel was cleared, she was never left without guard. Tide-waiters had to watch on board day and night to prevent the running of goods before they had been entered and had paid duty and to discover any tobacco concealed in the dark recesses of the hold or hidden deftly behind false bulkheads.[2] Better for a tide-waiter if he had never been born than that he should be found on shore at a tavern without leave or caught napping at an unexpected visit of his tide-surveyor on board.

Every ship coming into the port had to observe certain regulations. The master could not be over three days in sailing from Gravesend to the place of discharge in the Thames, nor could he touch at any quay or wharf between Gravesend and Chester's Quay, unless hindered by contrary winds or an accident to the ship. But he might unload his goods at any of the lawful quays between the

---
[1] Perhaps the most significant of these remonstrances was *The Case of the Planters of Tobacco in Virginia, As represented by Themselves; signed by the President of the Council, and Speaker of the House of Burgesses. To which is added, A Vindication of the said Representation* (London, 1733).
[2] In connection with the guard of ships, see *Rept. of Com.*, 1733, p. 4; Cust. Ho. Lib., Extracts Board Minutes, I, "Inspectors of the River," 1724, Sept. 17; Crouch, *Complete Guide to Officers* (1732), pp. 126-128; see *supra*, Ch. IV, pp. 157-162.

Tower of London and London Bridge, at any time from sunrise to sunset from September 10th to March 10th, and between six o'clock in the morning and six in the evening from March 10th to September 10th, provided he gave notice to the proper officials.[1]

When the ship moored (usually at a distance from the quay "on Account of the great Burthen of a Tobacco Ship"), it was necessary for the master to hie himself to the Custom House and there make an official report of his vessel. To two of the Bench Officers in the Long Room, one of whom was the deputy to the Collector-Inwards, he had to certify the particulars of his entry: the burden of his ship, its cargo and the marks and contents of each hogshead, the port of loading, from whence the vessel came, the country of her build, her owners, and how she was manned. At the same time, he had to produce a certificate that he had given bond in the plantations to carry his enumerated tobacco only to Britain or to some other colony. Both the entry and the evidence of the plantation bond had to be made on oath, administered by the Bench Officers, theoretically with the greatest solemnity. These oaths, however, were futile as a means of guaranteeing honest entries. "For," as Brett put it in speaking of custom-house oaths in general, "the Officers of the Revenue having Power in many Cases to Administer Oaths, to detect the Fraudulent Contrivances of Traders, 'tis to be feared, than when a Rich Cargoe is at stake, many are tempted to Perjure themselves, either out of Affection or Compassion to the Merchant, or Greediness of Gain to themselves. And to this End 'tis observable, that in Places of Trade, a Poysonous sort of Doctrine is slily and artificially insinuated among Masters of Ships, Common Saylors and Porters, (Men by the way, so guilty of Common Swearing, in their ordinary Conversation, that Perjury is the more easily imposed upon them) that a *Custom-House*-Oath is nothing but Matter of Form."[2] Crouch, that oracle on customs procedure for the greater part of the century, was also of opinion that perjuries in general

---

[1] See Hatton, *Comes Commercii* (1723), pp. 263, 264. The author of *Ductor Mercatorius*, p. 49, states that from September 30th to March 1st all goods were to be shipped or landed in the outports between seven in the morning and four in the afternoon, and from March 1st to September 30th between sunrise and sunset. Thomas Daniel, *Ductor Mercatorius: or the Young Merchants' Instructor with respect to the Customs: Being a minute and particular Detail of the Regular Method of Proceeding at Out-Port Custom-Houses, In the several Branches of Marine Commerce* (Newcastle upon Tyne, 1750).

[2] Jasper Brett, *The Sin of With-holding Tribute by Running of Goods, Concealing Excise etc.* (Dublin 1721), p. 16.

were "but too frequently committed at the Custom-House, viz. That it is but a Custom-House Oath; as if God who is omnipresent, did not see, and was not equally offended at profaning his Name there, as at any other Place whatsoever: But let these Offenders remember the Punishment which is denounced against them in the third Commandment."[1] The oaths of the masters, however, were but a few of the many oaths required in the procedure at importation and exportation; and "as the Multiplicity of Oaths in the Business of the Customs, does, it is to be feared, in a great measure, lessen that Awe and just Regard that ought to be paid to such solemn and sacred Ties; it is much to be wished, that fewer Oaths were necessary."[2]

Two entries by the master were necessary, one of which had to be recorded in a book to be left in the Long Room, and the other on a loose sheet of paper which was to be sent to the Register-General of Trading Ships that he might see that all was duly sworn and the ship manned according to the Navigation Act. Upon the master's report inwards, the vessel was listed in the register of all ships reporting into London during the day, which was placed before the Commissioner for the appointment of the land-waiters to discharge the cargo.[3]

When the London merchant had been notified that his ship had arrived from the plantations, he either went down to the Custom House or sent his servant or agent to make the entry of his cargo, the latter being the more usual practice—"many Entrys made by Brokers & Servants in the name of the merch^{ts} traders & private psons not merch^{ts} who come not themselves in pson to be Exam-

[1] Crouch, *Complete Guide to Officers* (1732), p. 143.
[2] *Ibid.*, p. 143; Forster, *Digest of Customs Laws* (1727), p. 366, also observes that the frequency of oaths at the collection of duties and the granting of certificates and drawbacks "has taken off that Solemnity and infinite Regard that should be paid to such sacred Acts." Oaths were subject to strict regulation: thus, they had to be administered by at least two of the Bench Officers or principal officers of the port (e. g., Cust. Ho. Lib., Extracts Board Minutes, III, 35, 1770, Mar. 23); a written form of oath was necessary (Cust. Ho. Lib., Letters to Dartmouth, 1675–6 to 1715, p. 331, Carkesse to Dartmouth, 1715, Oct. 17); in 1703 the Attorney-General gave his opinion that the *ad valorem* oath should be performed by the merchant himself and not by his servant, a decision confirmed by Board minute of 1778. *Ibid.*, p. 189, Board to Dartmouth, 1703, Apr. 22; and Extracts Board Minutes, V, 136, 1778, June 2.
[3] For reference to the master's report inwards, see Crouch, *Complete Guide to Officers* (1732), pp. 134, 136–138, 143 (pp. 134–143 contain detailed information); Daniel, *Ductor Mercatorius* (1750), p. 1; *Repts. of Comrs.*, 1787, III, 16, "Thirteenth Rept.," 1785.

248 ORGANIZATION OF THE ENGLISH CUSTOMS

in'd."[1] For particulars with regard to his shipment, the merchant was obliged to search the Ships' Entry Book which lay publicly in the Long Room, and in which was listed the names of the ship and the captain, the land-waiters appointed to attend the unloading, and at what quay the goods would be landed. If the merchant found his vessel recorded, he might immediately enter his cargo,[2] and he was obliged to declare every tobacco shipment sometime within thirty days after the report of the master.

From the invoice of his cargo[3] which the merchant had received, an officer in the Long Room made out a warrant on which he specified the ship, the master's name, the importer's name, the place from whence the tobacco was being imported, the kind and quantity of it, and the marks, numbers, and weights of the hogsheads. This warrant, which the merchant signed, was the instrument which would authorize the landing of the cargo after payment of duties. Of this record the clerk then made out as many transcripts, called Bills of Entry, as there were principal officers who were employed in the computation and control of the duties: namely, the Collector, the Computer, the Surveyor-General, the Controller, the Surveyor of the Port of London, and the Examiner.[4] After the entry had been completed, the importer took his warrant and Bills of Entry to the Computer or Clerk of the Rates, who calculated the duties and, on the bill designed for the Receiver, specified them in numbers which amounted to twenty times their sum in order to avoid errors in computation of minute fractions. In former times the merchant had employed his own clerks in his Long Room business, but the multiplicity of duties made accuracy and dispatch so difficult that by

---

[1] B.M., Stowe MSS. 324, f. 238, a paper which appears to have been written by a Commissioner to the Lords of the Treasury, in "Revenue Collections, 1396-1764" of Sir Richard Temple.

[2] For a description of the merchant's entry inwards, see B.M., Add. MSS. 32864, f. 387, enclosure in letter of Hooper to Newcastle, 1756, Apr. 23; *Repts. of Comrs.*, 1787, III, 16, "Thirteenth Rept.," 1785; Crouch, *Complete Guide to Officers* (1732), p. 144; Daniel, *Ductor Mercatorius* (1750), pp. 1-2; *Rept. of Com.*, 1733, p. 5; Hatton, *Comes Commercii* (1723), pp. 258-259.

[3] If the merchant had not received his invoice, he might be permitted to make out a Bill of Sight which, upon his deposit of a sufficient sum to cover the duties, would permit the tobacco to be landed and the duties computed from the weights of the hogsheads. Crouch, *Complete Guide to Officers* (1732), pp. 174-175; Daniel, *Ductor Mercatorius* (1750), pp. 2-3.

[4] The records vary as to the number of Bills of Entry that had to be prepared; but it is certain that there was at least one bill for each of the chief officers in the several divisions.

the middle of the century the merchants had long since stopped using their own men, and made use instead of some Long Room officer or his clerk to whom they gave appropriate fees for his trouble. This practice had become so common an irregularity by 1756 that Commissioner Hooper wrote to Newcastle:

these Officers of the Revenue get more by these *Clients* (for That is the Long-room phrase) than by the Crown. This is notorious; and tis believed that when by a promotion to the rank of a Bench-Officer one of these Agents is disabled from acting as such (openly & directly) He retains a large share of the Profits by recommending & turning over his Clients to one of his Clerks. That some bargain must be settled on such Turnings over there seems no room to doubt, since otherwise the officer so promoted must be a considerable Sufferer in point of Income. The Profits of some of these Agents are supposed to amount to £700, or £800 a year, . . . [Though the system by no means was considered a wrong thing in the Long Room] But still this general & accustom'd practice cannot Change the Nature of the thing itself, nor confute what both Reason & Scripture say about serving two Masters. The Board of Customs therefore regret this practice, and keep a jealous Eye upon it, tho' tis out of their reach to suppress; and will no doubt continue as long as the various Duties on the same Goods remain unconsolidated. Such consolidation has been for some time talk'd of as a desirable thing. It would certainly increase the Revenue, & be at the same time an ease to Trade.[1]

When the duties on his tobacco had been cast, the merchant last of all carried the warrant and bills to a deputy of the Collector-Inwards, probably the Receiver of the Plantation Duties,[2] who, upon finding that the calculation had been approved by the Clerk of the Rates or had been made by some officer known to himself, either received the duties, as was the usual case, or desired that they be paid to the Receiver-General.[3] Of the total tobacco duties, the mer-

[1] B.M., Add. MSS. 32864, f. 388, enclosure in Hooper's letter to Newcastle, 1756, Apr. 23. At the earlier period, if a merchant did not make out his entry bills himself, he had to pay 1s. to an officer for the service. This was usually the safest way in the case of unusual entries because of severe penalties for mistakes, but a merchant by practice might make out his bills himself. Hatton in *Comes Commercii*, p. 259, observes, however, that "some of the Clerks of the Custom-house are very cautious lest any one should understand their way of passing an Entry; but, by due care, any one that is minded may (after two or three times seeing the Clerks write the Bills, and pass the Entrys) do the same himself."
[2] It has been indicated in Chapter IV that there were two other collectors of duties under the Collector-Inwards: the Receivers of the Grand Receipt and Wine Duties.
[3] This statement is given in *Repts. of Comrs.*, 1787, III, 17, "Thirteenth Rept.," 1785. It appears that it was not irregular both at this time and early in the period for payments of duties to have been made to the Receiver-General. A Board minute for 1726 states, however, that money to be applied to the duties was for the

chant paid immediately that part known as the Old Subsidy; for the rest of the duties he was permitted to give bond, upon sufficient securities, for payment within eighteen months.[1] Duties were settled in cash, a circumstance that often involved considerable risk, particularly in the nineteenth century when money was habitually entrusted to young clerks who had to carry it through the crowded streets. Apparently it was not until 1855 that in London checks were permitted to be received in place of cash.[2]

Meanwhile, to prevent mistakes in the assessment of the duties, the extra copies of the merchant's Bill of Entry were delivered by the Clerk of the Warrants to the several checks: the Computer, the Controller-Inwards and Outwards, the Surveyor-General, the Surveyor of the Port of London, and the Examiner of the Computations. These officers examined the calculations to see that they were correct and that each Bill agreed with the warrant. Upon their satisfaction, the warrant was delivered to the land-surveyor and land-waiters who had been appointed by the Commissioner to attend the discharge of the ship.[3] As often as they could, these checks met together to compare their accounts with those of duties actually received kept by the Receiver.

The duties having thus been collected and checked, they were

---

future to be paid to the Collector-Inwards, that it might be more "expeditiously" brought to account than when it was paid to the Receiver-General in the first instance. Cust. Ho. Lib., Extracts Board Minutes, I, "Bench Officers," 1726, Mar. 14.

[1] By 9 Geo. I, c. 21, s. 3. This act also provided for a discount of 25 per cent on all duties paid down and a discount of 15 per cent on those duties that were bonded. The Old Subsidy amounted to one shilling per pound value. The other tobacco duties as they stood in 1777, when the Customs Commissioners recommended consolidation to the Treasury, comprised the Additional Duty (1d. per pound weight), New Subsidy (raised from the rate of the Old Subsidy but under the regulations of the Additional Duty—namely, 1d. per pound weight), Additional Subsidy (one-third part of the New Subsidy), Impost (3d. per pound weight), and the two Subsidies of 1747 and 1759 (raised as the New Subsidy). P.R.O., Treasury Papers, Bdl. 530, No. 267, enclosure in memorial of Cust. Comrs. to Lords of Treas., 1777, Apr. 29. For further information on duties, see *ibid.*, Bdl. 334, Nos. 15–19, "State of the Tobacco Duties. . . ." On bonds, see Crouch, *Complete Guide to Officers* (1732), pp. 167, 170–172; and B.M., Add. MSS. 18903, f. 29, "The Method of taking Bonds for the Duties of goods imported," 1714, Oct. 26.

[2] *First Rept. of Comrs. of Cust. on Cust.* [Cd. 2186], p. 31, H.C. (1857), iii.

[3] For a description of procedure in the computation, check, and payment of duties to the Receiver-General, see *Repts. of Comrs.*, 1787, III, 16–17, 26–29, 31, 32–33, "Thirteenth Rept.," 1785; B.M., Add. MSS. 32864, f. 387, Hooper's enclosure to Newcastle in a letter of 1756, Apr. 23.

CUSTOMS PROCEDURE IN SHIPPING

paid by the Receiver of the Plantation Duties into the office of the Receiver-General during the day,[1] while the bonds which had been given were returned to that same office monthly. Of all his receipts and payments the Collector sent weekly accounts, examined and signed by his Controller or some other check, to the Controller-General and the Supervisor of the Receiver-General's Receipts and Payments. Every week the Receiver-General made out four accounts, three of which were sent to the Treasury, the Customs Board, and the Supervisor of his Receipts respectively, for check. He delivered the fourth account to the Exchequer and paid with it his week's balance in cash at the Teller's Office. There an entry of the sum paid was recorded. A copy of the entry was then made out on a slip of parchment known as a "Bill" or "Teller's Bill" and thrown down a pipe into the Tally Court where a tally was struck as receipt of the payment and delivered to the customs officer. This method of payment into the Exchequer continued until 1823 and perhaps later, though indented checks were substituted for tallies by 23 George III, c. 82.[2] An account of all such payments and other disbursements, together with the vouchers, was returned annually by the Receiver-General to the Auditor of the Imprest for final check.

The collection of duties in the outports was like that at London, though not so complicated. In the receipt of the duties by the collectors, the customers and controllers acted as checks. The collectors remitted their bills of exchange to the Receiver-General at any time when they had received money on duties, and returned to the Board monthly, quarterly, and annual accounts of their receipts and payments, of which the quarterly accounts were compared with the books of the controllers and customers sent to the Controller-General. From these records and those of the collector, the Controller-General made up his annual account and sent it to the Auditor of the Imprest, while the Receiver-General paid in the outport receipts to the Exchequer and returned his annual account to the same

[1] All of the Collectors (with the exception of the Collector-Outwards) and Receivers of the Collector-Inwards in the Port of London paid their receipts and debentures daily into the office of the Receiver-General.

[2] *First Rept. of Comrs. of Cust. on Cust.* [Cd. 2186], p. 83, App. B, H.C. (1857), iii. A further check in the Exchequer was provided by the Clerk of the Pells' entry of the bill with the teller's name in order to charge that officer with it. This was known as the Pell of Receipt. In connection with the accounts of the Receiver-General and his payments into the Exchequer, see *Repts. of Comrs.*, 1787, III, 29–31, "Thirteenth Rept.," 1785.

officer.[1] Thus did the proceeds of duties reach the Exchequer, and their accounts the Auditor.

And now what of the tobacco ship lying at anchor in the Pool? After the tobacco had been entered and the duties settled by the merchant, the land-waiters at the waterside received the warrant which permitted the cargo to be unloaded and delivered to the importer. Such goods had always to be brought to the quay for examination at the charge of the merchant,[2] and the head tide-waiter on the ship had to be notified officially of the entry by the land-waiter before he permitted the goods to be unshipped.

When the vessel was ready to be unloaded and the weighers and land-waiters appointed to supervise the discharge were on hand, the tobacco was stowed into a lighter under the superintendence of the head tide-waiter, who took an account of each hogshead. When the lighter was filled, one of the other tide-waiters watched it to the quay, carrying with him to the land-waiter a note containing the account of all the hogsheads on the lighter, as recorded by the head tide-waiter.

The two land-waiters employed at the quay where the tobacco

---

[1] On the adjustment of cash in the outports, the remittances of outport duties, and the preparation and return of outport accounts, see Crouch, *Complete Guide to Officers* (1732), pp. 253–278; *Repts. of Comrs.*, 1787, III, 34–37, "Thirteenth Rept.," 1785.

[2] The expenses of delivery in general consisted of lighterage (charges for the transport of the tobacco from the ship to the quay), primage (payments to the ship captain for the use of cables and ropes in the landing of goods, and to the mariners for their service in unloading the tobacco), cooperage (the sum for opening, closing, and repairing of tobacco hogsheads on the quays), porterage (fees for carrying the tobacco to the warehouses or carts), wharfage (fees for landing the goods on a wharf or shipping them off), warehouse rent, and payments to the husband and officers for unloading the ship and watching the tobacco. It was in reality, however, the colonial planter who defrayed these charges, to which were added as well the freight, the duties, and the commission which the merchant exacted for his trouble in passing the tobacco through the customs and selling it in either a foreign or a home market. The total of these expenses was deducted from the value of the tobacco and the balance was placed to the credit of the planter. It must be feared that in these rates an unscrupulous factor frequently found opportunity to overcharge the distant and uniformed planter. (See *Case of the Virginia Planters* [1733], pp. 11, 37–53.) Hugh Jones stated, with particular reference to customs duties, that some of the planters, instead of clearing anything by their shipments, had actually been brought into debt, "the Charges and Duties far over-balancing the Price of the Tobacco . . . of late Years they sometimes get little or nothing by it, but Trouble and Loss; because of the great Expence in making and sending it *Home* to Market, and the great Duties which are paid out of it, and the small Price that it usually bears." Hugh Jones, *The Present State of Virginia* (London, 1724; *Sabin's Reprints,* No. 5, New York, 1865), p. 144.

CUSTOMS PROCEDURE IN SHIPPING

was landed checked the cargo by comparing the marks and numbers of the hogsheads sent on the lighter with those contained in the report of the tide-waiter, in order to see that none of the tobacco had been run. When the shipment was landed, each hogshead was stripped and the tobacco put upon scales in order to be weighed by sworn weighers, who would call out the weights to the land-waiters, to be entered in the land-waiters' books. Frequently the tobacco was badly damaged, and though the merchant received no allowance in duties for such damage, he was permitted to separate the damaged part from the good, and given an allowance of ½d. per pound on the rejected lot.[1] It was customary to grant the merchant two pounds duty free in each hogshead for his trouble and expense in stripping and making up the hogsheads,[2] and eight pounds for draught[3] on hogsheads of 350 pounds or more.[4] The merchant was supposed to draw any samples after the tobacco was weighed. If on the last unloading there happened to be a small excess of weight over and above the usual allowance made for samples, the importer was permitted to make what was called a post-entry and pay duties for it. If the quantity was small, the land-surveyor, who closely watched the unshipping of the cargo, permitted it to be carried away before the merchant made his post-entry; but if large, it theoretically lay on the quay until a deposit had been made for the duties or they were paid. The land-waiters, however, were often very generous with the merchants with respect to these post-entries, frequently giving them credit for some length of time in open disregard of strict Board orders on the subject.[5] In the case of an over-entry, if the merchant

[1] By 9 Geo. I, c. 21, s. 13.
[2] From 1716 on. See Cust. Ho. Lib., Letter Book, Blackney, 1711–1723, pp. 62–63, Carkesse to Blackney, 1716, Nov. 10.
[3] "Draught" was an allowance made in the weighing of commodities. Richard Rolt, *A New Dictionary of Trade and Commerce* (London, 1756).
[4] By 9 Geo. I, c. 21, s. 15. In connection with such allowances, see Cust. Ho. Lib., Letters to Dartmouth, 1715–16 to 1731, p. 173, Carkesse to Dartmouth, 1723, Nov. 23; p. 258, Board to Dartmouth, 1727, Jan. 13.
[5] Such credit was induced by fat fees—"indeed," wrote Preston to Pitt in 1782, "their [the land-waiters'] situation differs from all other Revenue appointments, there being none else, where an Officer is accountable, for a Merchant or Traders non payment of Dutys, his business being but to charge them." If a merchant failed, the officer came in as a creditor "of which there hath been many, very many instances." True, the land-waiter might stop the goods, but then he would receive no fees, and without them he could not live—"from this his thorny situation, springs much of that hurry, bustle distrust and delay, which all who have anything to do at the Custom house experience." P.R.O., Chatham Papers, Bdl. 284, Preston to Pitt, 1782, Feb. 18.

had paid more duties than there were goods unloaded, his money was refunded upon a proper application or certificate of such over-entry.[1] After the tobacco had finally been unladed and weighed, a porter known as the "Book" (book-keeper), who had taken an account of it for the merchant, saw that it was safely stored in the warehouses along the waterside and loaded out for the particular merchant to whom it belonged.[2]

When the last hogshead had been sent to shore, the tide-surveyor went on board the ship, made a final rummage, and discharged the tide-waiters. The tide-waiters then delivered their books to the jerquers in order that they might be compared with those of the land-waiters and the master's report. Finally, within three days after the ship had been cleared, the land-waiters made up their accounts and delivered them with their warrants to the jerquer. In the jerquer's office the books were carefully examined to see that the allowances for sample, damages, and the like were correct and the total amounts accurately computed. These accounts were then compared with the books of the tide-waiters to make sure that all the goods unloaded had been accounted for and to detect any fraudulent landing. Last of all, they were compared with the report of the master, and, if the master's entry of his cargo was found correct, he was entitled to his portage. After the ship had been jerqued and the Collector's record was known to agree with the warrants for the delivery of goods, those documents were canceled by being cut through and were filed away.[3] Such, according to official theory, was the procedure at importation, though in actual practice there were many minor deviations.

It is apparent that the method was complex in the many entries that had to be made out and in the computation of duties and allowances and their examination by the several checks. The merchant's vexations were many: delays, penalties for wrong entry if he entered the goods himself, burdensome fees for having such entries made and

---

[1] For a description of procedure in the delivery of a ship see Crouch, *Complete Guide to Officers* (1732), pp. 179–183, 185–186; Daniel, *Ductor Mercatorius* (1750), pp. 2, 4, 28–29; *Rept. of Com.*, 1733, p. 5; Cust. Ho. Lib., Letters to Dartmouth, 1715–16 to 1731, p. 269, Board to Dartmouth, 1728, Sept. 28. See also B.M., Add. MSS. 18903, f. 32, "The Method of making out and passing Certif^{tes} of Damage & Over-Entries."

[2] Hatton, *Comes Commercii* (1723), p. 275.

[3] On jerquing, see Crouch, *Complete Guide to Officers* (1732), pp. 194, 198.

CUSTOMS PROCEDURE IN SHIPPING

securing the discharge of a cargo, inconvenient hours (confined principally to the morning) for settling duties, and the necessity of paying the duties in cash. Opportunities for imposition in the delivery of goods abounded. One of the principal frauds in tobacco importation consisted in under-estimating the weight of the hogsheads in the land-waiters' books (by which the duty was computed and paid). This fraud, of course, could be effected only with the connivance of the officer, the offer of remuneration to the land-waiters sometimes taking the form of a gratuity or a certain proportion of the duty saved, even to the extent of one third or one half. The fraudulent lowering of weights could be carried out in various ways. Sometimes when the land-surveyors caused the hogsheads to be reweighed, the land-waiters would take down the real figures on loose sheets of paper to show to the surveyors, and enter the short weight in their books. Again the weigher might be in collusion with the merchants, in which case he would call out short weights to the land-waiters. When the tobacco was being weighed, the merchant's agent usually attended and kept a book similar to that of the land-waiters. One of these officers and he might then meet together to make their books correspond; when any two accounts tallied, the third was altered to agree with them.[1] Forging papers to facilitate the smuggling of goods was a common abuse. Fraudulent landing of tobacco was also practised by bribing one or more of the tide-waiters, who were supposed to be on board the ship from the time of its anchorage until it was cleared, to desert their posts or wink at a sly unloading. "Socking" tobacco, that is, stealing it from the boats before it was landed and running it to warehouses along the quays, was a notorious fraud.[2] In the outports, smuggling on the open coast was perhaps the most common evasion of duties.

While rates remained as burdensome as they did, however, it was not possible to effect any real improvement in the system at importation. Complexity in making entries and computing duties and the requirement of numerous checks in the examination of accounts all resulted from a confused scheme of duties; frauds were inevitable in view of the great temptation offered by the evasion of excessive taxes. On the other hand, there was one important facility afforded to trade which was a marked advance over the import pro-

[1] See *Rept. of Com.*, 1733, pp. 6, 8–9.
[2] E. g., *ibid.*, p. 14. See *supra*, Ch. IV, pp. 124 (esp. n. 2)–125.

cedure of a century earlier, namely, the privilege of bonding in the payment of tobacco duties.[1] Since only a part of the duties had to be paid down at importation and the rest could be secured, the merchant was relieved from having to advance huge sums of capital and thus could employ his money in furthering his commercial interests. Such an arrangement foreshadowed that greatest contribution to the ease of commerce, the warehousing system of the nineteenth century.

2. *Procedure at Exportation*

Exportation comprised two principal forms: the shipping-out of British goods—particularly manufactured articles—for foreign markets or the plantations, and the reëxportation of colonial or foreign goods which had previously been imported into British ports. The Navigation Acts, which forced certain enumerated plantation commodities to a British port before they could be shipped to a foreign market, and which required that articles from a foreign country destined for the British plantations had first to be unloaded and pay duty at a British port, gave this second type of procedure at exportation a significance during the eighteenth century which it has, perhaps, held never before nor since. Not only was the practical application of a part of the mercantile system involved but a considerable portion of the gross revenue was at stake.

During the seventeenth and eighteenth centuries, the drawback system governed the reëxportation of goods.[2] The underlying princi-

[1] The system of bonding, however, was not without its abuses. An injustice to the public lay in a merchant's ability to discharge old bonds by new importations and thus to trade for some time upon the money that he really owed the Crown. Hence it not infrequently happened that when his money was lost in unsuccessful adventures, the Crown, as well as the merchant and surety, suffered. Another evil in bonding arose from the temptation some merchants were under to sell for exportation the tobacco entrusted to their care, without regard to price and merely to discharge their bonds, thereby clogging the market to the detriment of the planter and the fair trader. Finally, the merchant was enabled to keep the tobacco in his warehouse under his lock and that of the Crown; it must be feared that under this arrangement he sometimes could take from his storage a large part of the whole, and yet by the connivance of a corrupt officer, when it came to be weighed for exportation, could obtain a debenture for the full quantity, thereby not only defrauding the Crown of the duty which ought to have been paid, but even receiving a drawback for what was never paid. See *Rept. of Com.*, 1733, p. 15; and *Case of the Virginia Planters* (1733), pp. 8–9.

[2] For this general survey of the drawback and warehousing systems I am indebted principally to F. S. Parry, "The Drawback System," 1920, an unpublished study in the Custom House Library.

ple of the drawback arrangement was that practically all goods should pay duty upon importation into Britain, but that if such goods were reëxported, the duty or some part of it might be repaid the exporter or "drawn back." The drawback allowed by 12 Charles II, c. 4, was only half the subsidy paid, though in the case of several commodities, of which tobacco was one, the additional duty also might be returned at exportation. An act of 1722 further provided that in the case of tobacco all the duty might be refunded.[1] Subsequent tariffs, however, removed these distinctions.

Since procedure in the exportation of tobacco was based on the drawback scheme and also included several features of the warehousing plan, it will serve to illustrate the general outlines of eighteenth-century exportation. The same general procedure was followed in the reëxportation of other imported commodities and in the shipment of British manufactures, except that in this last case no proof of the identity of the product and the payment of import duties was necessary.

When the tobacco to be exported had been made up in firm hogsheads properly labeled (the ship having been decided upon by the merchant and agreement made with the captain for freight) before the goods could be taken on board the master had to go to the Custom House and there before the Collector-Outwards declare his intention of loading and register his ship as outward-bound in the Ships' Entry Book Outwards in the Long Room.[2]

All the merchants who were shipping any goods on that vessel then had to make out their Bills of Entries outwards. Before the entries were executed, however, if a merchant wished a drawback of the duties that had been paid on importation, there were certain forms that had to be observed.[3] To obtain the drawback of his money, which was permitted if the tobacco were reëxported within three years from its importation,[4] the merchant had to take from the importer's books a record of the day when the duty inwards was paid, and by whom, together with other particulars, and deliver it with an account of the quantity to be exported to the Clerk to the Controller Inwards and

---

[1] 9 Geo. I, c. 21, s. 6. See also *First Rept. of Comrs. of Cust. on Cust.* [Cd. 2186], p. 25, H.C. (1857), iii.
[2] Crouch, *Complete Guide to Officers* (1732), p. 40.
[3] See *ibid.*, pp. 66–68; Daniel, *Ductor Mercatorius* (1750), p. 39; P.R.O., Treasury Papers, Bdl. 326, No. 28, "Relating to the Exportation of Foreign Goods etc."
[4] The three years for reëxportation and the eighteen months for bonds were dated from the time of the master's report inwards.

Outwards in the Long Room. Upon searching his books and finding that the duty had been paid or secured on the day declared by the merchant, this officer made out a certificate, on the basis of which was granted the cocket for shipping the tobacco and the drawback of the duties which had been paid. After the certificate had been made out, the original importer had to confirm the truth of it by making oath that he had paid or secured the duties. If the exporter had not purchased his goods directly from the importer, then all other buyers through whose hands the goods had passed had to make a like oath to the truth of the transactions. After the exporter had proved the payment of the duties and the sale of the goods, he then had to state on oath that they were the same which he had purchased from the importer or the first buyer. If, however, the merchant had imported and was exporting the tobacco himself, he had only to make oath that he had paid the duties and that the goods were being shipped on his account.

After all these requirements had been observed, the merchant drew up his entries outwards,[1] containing the ship's name, the master's name, the port of consignment, the exporting merchant's name, and the kinds and quantities of goods. As in the case of goods imported, he took care to make out as many bills as there were checks on the Collector-Outwards. When the bills had been completed, the merchant presented them with his certificate to the Collector-Outwards, who granted him a cocket and warrant for shipping.[2] On the back of the cocket the merchant endorsed the marks, numbers, contents, and weight of each hogshead intended to be reëxported, and this cocket became an authority to the searchers to permit the loading. It was at this stage of the procedure that any export duties were settled with the Collector-Outwards if the commodity happened to be one liable to such taxes. The Collector-Outwards paid such duties weekly to the Receiver-General; and the checks on the Collector-Outwards—the Controller Inwards and Outwards, the Surveyor-General, the Surveyor of the Port of London, and the Copying Clerk Outwards—

[1] In connection with merchants' entries outwards, see Crouch, *Complete Guide to Officers* (1732), pp. 70–74; Daniel, *Ductor Mercatorius* (1750), p. 31; Hatton, *Comes Commercii* (1723), pp. 255, 256.

[2] When cut tobacco was exported, since no drawback was permitted for stalks or stems, the merchant was obliged to make oath on the back of the cocket that the shipment contained no more stalks than what originally grew with the tobacco. Crouch, *Complete Guide to Officers* (1732), p. 74.

CUSTOMS PROCEDURE IN SHIPPING

examined the Bills of Entry with the warrant and checked the computations and accounts of the Collector-Outwards.[1]

After the merchant had received his warrant and cocket and the tobacco was ready to be loaded, he delivered those documents to the searchers who had to see that the endorsements on the cocket corresponded with the marks and weights of each hogshead as it was examined on the quay and loaded on to the vessel. Assisting the searcher and acting as a check on him was a controlling searcher, for it was important that the goods should be carefully examined so that no less a quantity should be shipped out to secure a drawback than was indicated by the merchant's endorsements on his cocket. Usually in order to despatch business quickly, however, only a few hogsheads of each exportation were weighed, and if the weight of those appeared right, the remainder was passed according to the endorsement. If all was found correct, the searcher certified it on the back of the merchant's cocket, which he delivered to the Collector-Outwards as an authority for the ship to sail at any time that the master might choose.[2]

Meanwhile, before the ship could clear, the master was obliged to observe special regulations if he was bound to Newfoundland, Greenland, Portugal, Spain, Italy, Ireland, or the colonies.[3] In any case he had to take out victualing bills,[4] and, finally, he had to deliver to the Collector upon oath a content or report of every person shipping goods on his vessel, together with the marks and numbers of all the goods.[5] This report having previously been compared by the searchers with the merchant's endorsements on his cocket, and agreement certified, the master was permitted to clear with the Collector-Outwards.

---

[1] See *Repts. of Comrs.*, 1787, III, 19, 24, "Thirteenth Rept.," 1785.

[2] For procedure in the examination of goods at the waterside, see Crouch, *Complete Guide to Officers* (1732), pp. 75–76; Daniel, *Ductor Mercatorius* (1750), p. 31; *Rept. of Com.*, 1733, p. 9; Cust. Ho. Lib., Letters to Dartmouth, 1715–16 to 1731, pp. 210–211, Board to Dartmouth, 1726, July 26.

[3] Crouch, *Complete Guide to Officers* (1732), pp. 88–96. All ships engaged in the plantation trade had to be registered as of British build and give bond with security to go only to the plantations or to return to Britain if they carried enumerated commodities. If the vessel were less than a hundred tons, the value of the bond was £1,000; if over a hundred tons, the amount was £2,000. Such bonds could be canceled only by a certificate of the collector of the port of landing, produced within eighteen months.

[4] Victualing bills were granted to exempt dutiable provisions, which had been taken on board for the voyage, from payment of the duty.

[5] Crouch, *Complete Guide to Officers* (1732), pp. 97–99; Daniel, *Ductor Mercatorius* (1750), pp. 31–32.

260 ORGANIZATION OF THE ENGLISH CUSTOMS

The cocket was then delivered to the searcher for final check with the goods on board, entered by the searcher in his book, and despatched by land to Gravesend. The controlling searcher made a like examination and entered the warrant in his book in the same manner, in order that the ship might be properly jerqued. The tide-waiters, who had been stationed on board to guard the cargo from relanding before the ship sailed, were last of all taken off. The master was then permitted to sail, though he had to stop at Gravesend, where a searcher boarded the vessel, checked her contents with the cocket which he had received from the London searcher, and, upon finding the cargo intact, delivered the cocket to the master for the voyage.

After the vessel had cleared, the Debenture Clerk in the searchers' office verified the amount of the tobacco shipped and gave the merchant his debenture, the instrument by which the repayment of the import duties was allowed.[1] The debenture was then examined by the proper checks and the drawback computed according to the former certificate for such a quantity as the searcher certified to have been put on board. Upon the oath of the merchant that the tobacco had actually been shipped to foreign lands and had "not been relanded in any Port or Creek in England or Wales since last shipped," the Register of Cockets received the debenture, made out an order for the payment of the drawback, signed it, and received the Board's directions upon it. The exporter was then entitled to the payment of his duties within a month. Such was the procedure at exportation as in general it existed in the Port of London between 1696 and 1786.

The evils of the drawback system as they affected the customs administration, the revenue, and the merchant are at once apparent. As more branches of duties came to be added, calculation of drawbacks became more complicated, and the numerous customs laws passed from time to time defining the drawback policy with respect to particular goods[2] brought about increasing difficulties. The customs offi-

---

[1] For references in connection with tobacco debentures, see Crouch, *Complete Guide to Officers* (1732), pp. 99–100, 113–118; Hatton, *Comes Commercii* (1723), p. 257. See also P.R.O., Treasury Papers, Bdl. 507, No. 266, Cust. Comrs. to Lords of Treas., 1774, Nov. 22; cf. B.M., Add. MSS. 18903, f. 29, "An Acc[tt] of the method of passing Debentures in the Port of London," 1714, Oct. 26 [prepared by?] the Patent Officers.

[2] As for example, in the case of tobacco by 9 Geo. I, c. 21, s. 14, exportation in any package but cases of 300 pounds' weight or more was not allowed a drawback except in cut or rolled tobacco; stalks or stems when torn from the rest of the leaf, and exported separately, were refused a drawback by 9 Geo. I, c. 21, s. 20; and leaves of walnut trees, hops, and sycamore could not be exported under pretense

cers were put to much trouble in the necessary identification of the exported tobacco as being the same as originally imported, and in sampling it when it was weighed and loaded to see that it was good throughout and that the weights were not made heavier by any foreign material.

Opportunities for defrauding the Crown in order to obtain a drawback and discharge of bonds were afforded at almost every stage. First of all, it was easy for the exporter, when endorsing his cocket, to add to the weight of every light hogshead as much as would make it amount to the ordinary weight of the other hogsheads. It was not customary to weigh more than two or three hogsheads, picked at random from out of the total number to be exported, and if those agreed with the weight entered in the cocket, it was taken for granted that the others were correct. A merchant planning fraud might first send down accounts of a large number of hogsheads which had been fairly weighed. After these had passed the searchers, he would take back his cocket and endorse the rest at higher weights, for which he would obtain the drawback after they had been shipped. To prevent discovery of the altered weights, the searchers were often bribed to see that those particular hogsheads were not weighed. A second common fraud at exportation was to ship bad or damaged tobacco—"good for nothing either to smoak or chaw"—tobacco mixed with dirt, rubbish, and sand, or stalks alone, stripped from the leaf, which by act of Parliament received no drawback. Frequently stones, lead, and heavy articles were put into hogsheads to make them weigh more. Such frauds could be effected by filling the hogsheads with rubbish lightly covered over with tobacco at either end to pass a possible examination. The master of the vessel would then put to sea, where he would throw the whole overboard or sell it at a low price to complacent Flemish or Dutch buyers.

Drawback and running went hand in hand. After debentures had been obtained for tobacco exported, it was often relanded and sold for home consumption at the market price. Taking clearances for Norway, Spain, or some Continental port, the master protected himself if questioned on the seas, for he could declare that he was shipping to foreign lands. After getting out of port it was an easy thing for him to transfer his tobacco to small smuggling sloops, or run it

---

of being tobacco in order to obtain the drawback, upon forfeiture of 5s. per pound weight, by 1 Geo. I, c. 46, s. 2. See Samuel Baldwin, *A Survey of the British Customs; containing the Rates of Merchandize* (London, 1770), pp. 268, 269, 273.

from Dunkirk, Ostend, or the Channel Islands free of duty to some point along the British or Irish coast. As an alternative, he might run the tobacco himself to a point out of ken of the port of debenture —Ireland or North Britain.[1]

Finally, the trader himself suffered under the drawback system. For him it meant a temporary lock-up of capital. There was wastage of material on which duty had been paid, endless red tape in accounting for goods, and much bother in the examination of them by the officers.[2] Such were the prejudices of this form of reëxportation.

In the eighteenth century, however, an alternative had its beginnings in what was known as the warehousing system. Under this plan, the commodity upon importation was stored in warehouses under the joint locks of the Crown and the merchant, and paid duty only when it was delivered out for home consumption. The drawback system postulated the actual payment of duty; the warehousing system postponed or waived payment of duty. The advantages of warehousing are at once apparent: it did away with many of the opportunities for fraudulent practices that drawbacks afforded, and it relieved the merchant and the customs staff of considerable inconveniences which the drawback arrangement entailed.

The first approach to a perfected system of warehousing in the customs is traceable in 1700, when Indian and Persian wrought silks, which were prohibited from use in Britain, were permitted to be warehoused and reëxported without payment of duty.[3] In 1709 pepper came under a form of warehousing whereby half the "subsidy" had to be paid down and the other half was required only when the pepper was delivered out for home consumption; if it was duly exported, no duty whatsoever was asked.[4] Certain features of the warehousing system were incorporated in the case of still other commodities during the period, notably rum, coffee, cocoanuts, rice, and tobacco.[5] In none of these

[1] The best account of these various methods is contained in *Rept. of Com.*, 1773; and *Case of the Virginia Planters* (1733). The Treasury records for the entire period provide a vivid picture of such abuses, as do several other Parliamentary reports.

[2] See Parry, "The Drawback System," pp. 4–5, for a good brief account of the evils of the system.

[3] *First Rept. of Comrs. of Cust. on Cust.* [Cd. 2186], p. 25, H.C. (1857), iii.

[4] *Ibid.*, p. 25.

[5] In 1714 tobacco was allowed to be warehoused with a payment of part of the duty and a drawback at exportation. This arrangement was continued until 1789, when, for the first time, tobacco might be reëxported without such payment. In 1742 rum was permitted to be warehoused for a limited time without payment of excise duty, and rice in 1765 received like privileges in some ports upon payment

cases, however, were all the privileges of warehousing granted, for some part of the duty usually had to be paid at importation even though the commodity might be warehoused and part of the duty bonded. But the evils of the drawback system were becoming apparent, while the advantages of the warehousing system were being recognized in some instances.[1] Walpole's Excise Bill, for instance, provided for the compulsory storage of tobacco and wine in excise warehouses, and a form of warehousing was suggested by many merchants and others at the time of the Tobacco Act of 1751, which was designed to prevent frauds.[2]

The deplorable effects of the drawback system on the revenue, and the obstacles which probably prevented the adoption of a warehousing scheme earlier in the century and which certainly deterred the too-conservative Customs Commissioners from recommending it at the time of the Consolidation Act, are indicated in the report of the Customs Board to the Lords of the Treasury in 1777: "The payment of large Drawbacks upon Exportation of foreign Goods affording great room for frauds, We have been led on this occasion to consider whether any method more Effectual than the present to secure the Revenue from the loss it sustains by those frauds may be suggested to Your Lordships, but We are not so happy as to discover any such method as may be fit to be recommended to Your Lordships for this desirable purpose,—We make no doubt that the Revenue is defrauded (tho' no exact Estimate be possible) to the Amount of Ten P Cent or nearly £200,000 P Annum at least in the Drawbacks, on an Average of the last Ten Years." The Commissioners stated that they had considered two methods of remedying these abuses: one, the abolition of all drawbacks which they felt "would probably prevent the Importation of any more foreign Goods than what might be used here, and consequently put a stop to all Exportation of them from this Country to the very great detriment of its Trade and Naviga-

---

of a part of the duty. An act of 1766, which was repealed, provided for a form of warehousing of sugar similar to that of tobacco, while in 1767, cocoanuts and coffee were allowed to be warehoused upon payment of a small part of the duty to be drawn back at exportation if the goods were of the British plantations. *Repts. of Comrs. Appointed to Inquire into Customs and Excise.* H.C. 46, pp. 9–10 (1820), "Second Rept.," 1818, vi.

[1] See Parry, "The Drawback System," p. 5.
[2] See, for example, P.R.O., Treasury Papers, Bdl. 326, Nos. 77–80, "A Scheme For better Securing and Improving the King's Revenue on Tobacco, and encouraging the Merchants"; Bdl. 332, Nos. 32–33, Thomas Hyam's communication of 1747, Dec. 14, "A State of the Tobacco Trade of Great Britain with some Proposals for Preventing Frauds & Augmenting the Customs."

tion," and the other, a scheme of warehousing which "must be unavoidably attended with a very heavy expence of Management and many great abuses might be therein nevertheless committed thro want of Vigilance and care in some Officers, and of fidelity in others; and if these objections should not be supposed, still Warehousing could afford no Security, while high Duties remain, against that mischevious mode of Smugling, the relanding of Exported Goods, so that there does not appear at present to Us to be any method (within the nature of Our Management at least) preferable to the continuance of Drawbacks."[1] In the face of such a confessedly hopeless situation, the drawback system remained predominant to the end of the century. It was not until the Warehousing Act of 1803 that the "simplicity and security" of the warehousing system was adopted in contrast to the "complexities and frauds" of the drawback system.

3. *The Coastwise Trade*

The coastwise trade was a flourishing one, partly owing to the fact that Britain is an island, partly to the position of British ports as staples in the mercantile system, and partly because of the importance of London as the distributing and commercial center of the nation. While the actual receipt of revenue from the coast trade was negligible when compared with the returns from foreign commerce, coastwise shipping was of considerable importance in its indirect effects upon the ends of revenue and trade policy. Its position in this connection becomes apparent with respect to the various kinds of goods involved. There were free goods—mainly local products or foreign goods formerly imported—sent from port to port for local consumption without having to pay duty; a few commodities such as coal paying coast duties; articles such as foreign wrought silks which used British ports as staples only and were prohibited from importation into Britain because of their discouragement to the productive activities of the state; goods prohibited to be exported, such as wool or fuller's earth, or subject to payment of duty at exportation, in order to encourage English manufactures and deprive foreign manufacturers of raw materials; foreign or plantation commodities, formerly imported at high duties, which were to be reëxported with a drawback,

---

[1] P.R.O., Treasury Papers, Bdl. 530, Nos. 254–255, Cust. Comrs. to Lords of Treas., 1777, Apr. 29.

CUSTOMS PROCEDURE IN SHIPPING 265

such as tobacco or sugar; and merchandise, such as manufactured silks and linen, exported with the grant of a bounty. It was the responsibility of the customs establishment in connection with such goods sent coastwise to enforce the payment of coast duties or to prevent illicit importation or exportation as the case might be.

The coastwise trade took two forms over which the customs had supervision: port-to-port traffic by water and land-carriage. Of these, the first was the more important. Coastwise procedure outwards corresponded very closely with the general outlines of the methods employed at exportation. For instance, if a merchant wished to send his imported tobacco from London to some port on the north coast, the master in whose vessel he was shipping his tobacco was obliged to make an entry of his ship with the Collector-Outwards. The proposed voyage having been recorded, the merchant then applied for a sufferance to permit the clearance of his goods coastwise, specifying the marks, contents, and qualities of his shipment and making statement on oath that the import duties for his tobacco had been paid. If, however, he was planning to export his tobacco on drawback from the port to which he was sending it, he was not obliged to give such oaths because an official certificate, testifying that the duties had been paid, had to be transmitted to the port instead. After the necessary regulations had been observed, the merchant was granted his sufferance. On it he endorsed his hogsheads with their marks and weights and then gave it to the coast-waiter as an authority to permit his goods to be loaded. The coast-waiters executed the sufferance by examining the tobacco, seeing it safely stowed on board, and certifying the same on the instrument. They then returned the sufferance to the merchant, who in turn submitted it to the Collector-Outwards. Upon the basis of it, that officer granted the master a coast cocket or despatch permitting the shipping of the cargo, upon his taking out bond to land its contents at the port designated. Security in connection with such bonds was given to the amount of the value of most goods, and unless such a bond was discharged by a certificate of due landing within six months, it was sent to the Exchequer in London and listed in a schedule of forfeited bonds returned to the Solicitor of Coast Bonds in the Central Office. Coast cockets, involving such bonds, had to be taken for all goods prohibited from exportation or subject to duty on exportation (unless the duties did not exceed twenty shillings, and apparently later, forty shillings), and for sundry imported goods when carried in the same packages or which exceeded a certain quantity. In the case of other articles, a *transire* or let-pass was issued for their despatch coastwise.¹

When the master arrived at the intended port, he immediately presented to the collector his sufferances, despatch (or coast cocket), and the certificate of the original payment of import duties. If the cocket was regular, he was granted a sufferance for landing the goods, which he delivered to the coast-waiter who permitted the hogsheads to be unloaded—examining them with care and comparing them with the quantities listed in the sufferance. When all the tobacco was delivered, the coast-waiter recorded a description of the goods in his book, canceled the sufferance, and returned it to the collector, who certified on the despatch the quantity discharged. It was then returned to the master and he was granted a certificate of landing, which enabled him to cancel his bond in London.²

This procedure in general governed practically all the coastwise commerce, with the exception of coal, which, as one of the principal articles of the trade and practically the only article of importance

---

¹ Applications were frequently made to be freed from the legal despatches required for goods of inconsiderable value carried coastwise; but the Customs Commissioners steadfastly opposed any alterations in the coast laws. In a report in 1769, upon an application to ship lime on the York and Durham coasts without sufferance, the Commissioners stated that, apart from a few exceptions authorized by Parliament, "Yet We do not know of any instance where the Sufferance and Transire which is all that is required in the present Case have been dispensed with—[and therefore they could not recommend] the making a dangerous precedent [by granting the request]." (P.R.O., Treasury Papers, Bdl. 470, No. 202, Cust. Comrs. to Lords of Treas., 1769, Mar. 22.) Upon further investigation of this application, however, the Commissioners did suggest that sufferances, but not cockets, be required. (*Ibid.*, Bdl. 470, No. 227, Cust. Comrs. to Lords of Treas., 1769, June 22.) In 1785, upon a similar application, the Commissioners could not recommend a relaxation in the coast laws "which have subsisted ever since the Reign of Charles the 2ᵈ, and seem well calculated for the security of this Revenue, and the improvement of the Maritime Strength of the Kingdom, though, like all other general regulations, they may sometimes occasion inconveniences to particular persons or districts. But this Board being always desirous to afford every possible relief, consistent with Law, that can be granted to remove such local complaints [resolved to order blank sufferances or warrants and transires to be used in certain places]." *Ibid.*, Bdl. 621, No. 134, Cust. Comrs. to Lords of Treas., 1785, June 18.

² This account of coastwise procedure is taken from Crouch, *Complete Guide to Officers* (1732), pp. 11–17, 21–25, 28; and Daniel, *Ductor Mercatorius* (1750), pp. 41–42, 44. In connection with bonds, see also Cust. Ho. Lib., Letters to Dartmouth, 1715–16 to 1731, p. 332, Carkesse to Dartmouth, 1731, Dec. 11; *ibid.*, 1675–6 to 1715, p. 301, Carkesse to Collector and Controller at Dartmouth, 1714, Aug. 3.

CUSTOMS PROCEDURE IN SHIPPING

subject to coast duties,[1] had a procedure all of its own. In the shipping out of coal coastwise the method was similar to that used for any other commodity; but upon arrival at the intended port, before the coal could be unloaded, some security for payment of the duties had to be given. Since the master did not know his exact quantity of coal, he could not pay the correct amount of duties before his cargo was landed; thus, as an alternative, he was required either to give bond for such payment or to make a deposit sufficient to cover the duty. The latter method was the more usual, such a sum generally amounting to twice the duties for the number of chalders which he estimated his shipment to contain. Upon the guarantee of the duties, the master was granted a warrant which permitted the coal meters to unload and weigh the coal. During the process these officers kept a careful account on the back of the warrant of the number of chalders landed, and when the coal ship had been discharged they returned the warrant to the collector, who compared it with the meters' account, computed the final duties, and repaid the merchant any sum left over.[2] In London the Collector of the Coal Duties paid his receipts into the office of the Receiver-General daily and weekly and kept his weekly accounts as did the Collectors Inwards and Outwards. The Controller and Examiner acted as his checks.

If the merchant wished to send his tobacco by land-carriage, as was frequently the case in times of war because of the danger to goods carried by water, he usually secured from the deputy to the Collector-Outwards a certificate or "let-pass" which was a kind of safe-passage or direction to any customs officer not to stop the carriage. This pass, in the case of foreign goods, was mainly for convenience in transport, since it did not need to be shown at the custom-house unless the shipment was destined for exportation with a drawback of the duties or unless it consisted of prohibited articles sent from London to be shipped. In those cases, if the merchant desired to export his goods, he was obliged to give security that they would be duly cleared,

---

[1] In 1791 the Customs Commissioners stated that the net receipt of coal duties amounted on an average of the last twenty years to £377,224, and that "there is not an object in their extensive department which creates greater trouble, or requires more particular attention." P.R.O., Chatham Papers, Bdl. 283, Cust. Comrs. to Lords of Treas., 1791, Jan.

[2] The account of coal procedure is based on Crouch, *Complete Guide to Officers* (1732), pp. 28–31; Daniel, *Ductor Mercatorius* (1750), pp. 44–45; *Repts. of Comrs.*, 1787, III, 19–20, 24–25, 26, 27, "Thirteenth Rept.," 1785.

upon which a cocket was sent by post by the Customs Commissioners to the collector of the port for which they were intended. Upon the arrival of the goods, the cocket was compared with their quantities, and if they were found to agree such goods were permitted to be shipped. The debenture was sent to the port where the duties had originally been paid, and the merchant received his drawback from the Collector.[1]

Coastwise procedure for free goods was fairly simple. With respect to other kinds of goods it was complicated by the varying regulations governing them. Plentiful opportunities for frauds were provided in false *transires* or coast cockets; in the fraudulent clearance out of small coasters with no goods on board under cover of which clearance goods were run[2]; in the weighing of coal in chalders that were larger than the official measure, whereby greater quantities of coal were landed at the same rate of duties[3]; in the transport of coal abroad (the masters pretending to have been forced overseas) without payment of the export duty[4]; and in the land-carriage, without official permit, of certain exportable commodities. The coastwise system can-

[1] For coastwise procedure by land-carriage, see Crouch, *Complete Guide to Officers* (1732), pp. 18–19, 38–39.

[2] E. g., P.R.O., Treasury Papers, Bdl. 434, No. 346, "Memorial concerning Smuggling from Isle of Man. . . ."

[3] E. g., Cust. Ho. Lib., Sel. from Cust. Outport Recds., West Coast, 1926, p. 123, Beaumaris, Board to Collector, 1724–5, Feb. 18.

[4] Upon his return, the master had to pay the overseas duty, but in the meantime he was enabled to keep considerable sums of the King's money in his hands and he paid duties on a smaller number of chalders than if he had shipped abroad voluntarily. Upon swearing before Exchequer officials, instead of customs officers, that he had been forced overseas, he frequently did not have to forfeit his bond. Perhaps the most amazing instance of this kind was the case of a master who entered coastwise from Sunderland, 1769, Sept. 27, and gave bond to land his coals at Falmouth. Instead he carried them overseas to Marseilles, where he sold them, yet he did not pay the overseas duty for them until 1770, June 16—which appeared "to be a most flagrant Instance of Perjury in the Master, for it seems next to an Impossibility, that being bound to Falmouth, he should contrary to his Will and Intentions be drove by contrary Winds up the Mediterranean so far as Marseilles." (P.R.O., Treasury Papers, Bdl. 476, No. 411, Lutwidge and Frewin's report to Cust. Comrs., 1770, Aug. 12.) These frauds were notorious at Sunderland and Newcastle—a trade which had existed from 1680 but did not appear to have been general until about 1742 and 1743 "from which time [to 1778] almost the whole oversea Coal Trade from hence has been carried on by one continued Scene of Wilful Perjury of the Masters." (*Ibid.*, Bdl. 560, No. 274, Lutwidge to Cust. Comrs., 1778, Nov. 17.) Numerous investigations were made during the period, but the frauds continued unabated until after the act of 1785. *Ibid.*, Bdl. 632, No. 148, Cust. Comrs. to Lords of Treas., 1786, May 24. See also *ibid.*, Bdl. 332, Nos. 174–175; Bdl. 484, Nos. 192–193; P.R.O., Treas. Out-letters, Cust., XXIX, 241; XXXII, 60–61.

not be explained apart from the procedure at importation and exportation, however, nor could its general outlines be altered very much as long as the various regulations of the mercantile system remained in force.

CHAPTER VIII

PROCEDURE IN SEIZURE CASES

The magnitude of illicit trade throughout the eighteenth century made the contrivance of preventive measures against it and procedure against the offenders a matter of particular importance in customs administration. The character of the preventive measures has been indicated in preceding pages in connection with the organization established for enforcement of customs laws. The punitive, or negative aspect, is treated in this chapter.[1] Since the customs was powerless to alter the system of high duties, it was only by inflicting severe penalties for their evasion that it could hope to draw customs revenue through the channels of fair trade. Violation of law was met with seizure of the goods and prosecution of the offender, a branch of customs procedure which frequently aroused greater enthusiasm on the part of the staff than did the daily round and common task.[2]

Further, the revenue yielded by fines and forfeitures was a consider-

---

[1] It has been considered advisable to exclude from this discussion a technical analysis of procedure in personal prosecutions for offenses against the customs laws; and rather to confine it to a general survey of procedure in seizure cases as it was carried on at approximately the mid-century.

[2] Such eagerness may at times have affected the trade of certain ports. Thus, a firm of London merchants, in protest against an unwarranted seizure, represented to the Treasury in 1728 "that the Conduct of the officers of the Revenue is become very detrimental to the commerce and trade of London in general by their frequent making vexatious seizures upon every frivolous occasion, which ought not to be countenanced, especially in cases where there is no concealment, and it evidently appears that there is no intention of doing wrong by the Merchant Importer, as such Proceedings in a great measure defeat the salutary views of the legislature, discouraging the Navigation of this Nation." (P.R.O., Treasury Papers, Bdl. 575, Nos. 167–168, Grote Harksen and Company to Lords of Treas., 1782, May.) Seizure of ships for violation of the Navigation Act likewise appears to have been a favorite expedient of the customs officers. In 1697, a Spanish-built and Spanish-manned vessel, importing wines from the Canaries, was seized for infringement of the Navigation Act. The customs officers, in justification of their action, asserted that the ship was French-built. When Spanish origin was proved, they then insisted that the Canaries were a part of Africa! P.R.O., Treas. Outletters, Cust., XIII, 338, Treasury warrant, 1697, Apr. 9.

ation, and became increasingly more so during the period.¹ The significance of seizure in this connection, however, cannot be judged by the remittances under that head into the Exchequer, for out of the proceeds of seizures were paid various expenses incurred by the establishment. Thus between the years 1760 and 1785, fines and forfeitures varied between roughly 5½ per cent and less than 1 per cent of the Receiver-General's payments into the Exchequer,² but the gross receipts were considerably greater. The shares appropriated to the officers who carried out and prosecuted the seizure generally constituted one third or one half of its value, while the expenses of prosecution and sale to the customs, and, after 1781, the payment of certain charges of management, increased the discrepancy between gross and net receipts.

Goods were liable to seizure upon suspicion of fraud or running. Hovering or breaking bulk in port without entry, false oath by masters and failure to declare the whole cargo, mistakes in entry of goods and endorsements of greater or less amounts than were shipped, fraud in weighing, substitution, adulteration, running, and importation of prohibited articles were some of the most common causes of seizures. Early in the period, boats, horses, and carriages used for conveying smuggled goods were made subject to seizure and condemnation as well; and persons assisting in fraudulent practices either by receiving or concealing such goods or aiding in their running could be prosecuted.

Because the powers of the customs officers were very great, strict regulations governed the circumstances of search and seizure. In 1773 the Customs Commissioners asserted that since an act of 13 and 14 Charles II, which provided that no person other than officers of the revenue duly authorized could seize, there had been no instance of granting such power to any other persons except by an act of 3 George III which had been altered two years later.³ Only those who in some measure were under the control of the Board were given authority to seize. Apart from the deputed officers, the Board issued

---

¹ Compare the sum of £28,565. 0s. 3¼d., the annual average of the King's share of the produce of seizures and penalties on personal prosecutions for five years, 1751 to 1755, with annual averages for succeeding five-year periods, and finally with £88,787. 8s. 2¾d., the annual average from 1776 to 1780. B.M., Add. MSS. 8133 B, f. 214.
² B.M., Add. MSS. 8133 C, f. 124.
³ P.R.O., Treasury Papers, Bdl. 499, No. 276, Cust. Comrs. to Lords of Treas., 1773, Apr. 2.

commissions only to excise and salt officers, as empowered by the Treasury in 1718 and at subsequent dates, to officers of the Navy, and to extra tide-waiters and boatmen in order that their authority in a seizure should not be disputed and the seizure lost.[1] The Commissioners had learned that to grant the right of seizure to persons outside their jurisdiction could make for abuse. In 1752 they reported to the Treasury that, though in the past frequent applications had been made to them by various persons for such deputations, in such cases the applications had been rejected and no commissions issued except to the excise, salt, and naval officers upon the request of their respective boards.[2]

Regulations defining procedure in stopping goods upon suspicion or information of fraud, and in searching upon information, were based on the principles of protection to the revenue and observance of the rights of private property. If an officer met with goods passing near the waterside in the absence of any customs officer, and he suspected them of having been run, or was informed that they were run, he could stop them and take them to the warehouse to be kept under the King's locks until they were either released upon proof being made that no fraud was intended, or else prosecuted and condemned.[3] The officer, however, was strictly cautioned against abuse of this power in making unwarranted arrests and was permitted to stop goods only upon information or strong suspicion.[4] The regulations governing searching of houses or ships for run goods were far more severe. No officer could search a house without a particular information of concealed goods, which information was supposed to be in writing and from persons of "repute," unless on a "fresh pursuit" which did not allow time for an information. Neither could he search without a writ of assistance [5] and a peace officer, and then only in the

[1] See P.R.O., Treas. Out-letters, Cust., XVII, 263–264, Cust. Comrs. to Lords of Treas., 1720, May 4; Treasury warrant, 1720, May 12; cf. XXVI, 336, Treasury warrant, 1761, May 19.

[2] P.R.O., Treasury Papers, Bdl. 349, No. 39, Cust. Comrs. to Lords of Treas., 1752, Dec. 19. Though this general principle was followed, there were some instances in which it was not adhered to. For example, in 1760 the Commissioners reported that in the last war they had granted deputations to seize to several commanders of privateers, but finding that such commissions were open to ill use, the Board had recalled them and had not granted any since that time. *Ibid.*, Bdl. 403, No. 103, Cust. Comrs. to Lords of Treas., 1760, May 9.

[3] Crouch, *Complete Guide to Officers* (1732), pp. 279–280.

[4] E. g., Cust. Ho. Lib., Letters to Dartmouth, 1715–16 to 1731, p. 110, Carkesse to Dartmouth, 1720, July 16.

[5] Attorney-General Thurlow in a report in 1771, touching compulsion of the

PROCEDURE IN SEIZURE CASES 273

day-time, while it appears that the London officer was also required to secure permission from the Board to search a house, or else to acquaint the Secretary or Chief Clerks of his intention. Inferior men were not permitted to search a ship or a house without informing their superiors, or, if the latter were absent, the collector of the port.[1] In the outports, the collector or surveyor probably gave the writ of assistance to a searching officer as occasion demanded, a port customarily being allowed one or more writs to be used when necessary.[2] In London, writs were granted to particular officers, though in 1770 several of such writs were called in to be deposited with the solicitors for use as occasion demanded, and in that same year writs were directed to be furnished to certain of the superior men—the River Inspectors, land-surveyors, and tide-surveyors—to whose offices the inferior men might apply.[3]

Well might the Board control search and seizure by severe restrictions, for only too often unwarranted seizures could provoke suits of considerable embarrassment to the service, while unjustified use might be made by outsiders of commissions for seizing, under cover of which gross frauds could be perpetrated. For disregard of searching rules by officers, penalties were inflicted, and the Board refused to defend the officer in any prosecution incurred.

There was a slight variation in procedure in seizure cases according to whether goods were stopped upon suspicion or whether they were actually caught in the act of running or found in search. If goods were taken up near the waterside upon suspicion or information, they were carried to the warehouse, where the seizing officer left an account of them with the warehouse-keeper to be forwarded to the Board. The person from whom the goods were taken then had to ap-

---

American supreme courts to grant writs of assistance to the customs officers in America, agreeable to the practice in England, stated that the present writ of assistance [for use of customs officers] in England was founded on 13 Charles II, c. 11, which head of authority "has been in constant use above a century; has often been recognized, and confirmed by judicial decisions." P.R.O., Treasury Papers, Bdl. 485, No. 307.

[1] For general regulations in searching, see Cust. Ho. Lib., Letter Book, Blackney, 1711–1723, pp. 96–97, Carkesse to Gentlemen [Blackney], 1721, Apr. 24; Crouch, *Complete Guide to Officers* (1732), p. 280. For more specific references to the necessity of the Board's permission for searching, see Cust. Ho. Lib., Extracts Board Minutes, I, "Informations and Informers," 1710, June 9; II, "Officers," 1733, Nov. 23; 1737, Dec. 24; 1742, Oct. 2; II, "Seizures," 1749, Nov. 2.

[2] As would appear from an indication of such an arrangement in Cust. Ho. Lib., Letters from Whitby, 1721–1724, Collector and Controller to Board, 1722, Dec. 2.

[3] Cust. Ho. Lib., Extracts Board Minutes, III, 352–353, 1770, Aug. 30.

pear at the custom-house within ten days and claim them if he hoped to keep them from prosecution. To effect a delivery of his property, it was necessary for him to make proof on oath before some law officer to the satisfaction of the collector that the duties had been paid or secured by himself, or, according to his best belief, by the original importer; or that the articles had been compounded for or condemned in the Court of Exchequer or lawfully delivered from a warehouse; or had not been relanded after the drawback had been paid—in short, that no fraud of any kind was intended. This application was then transmitted to the Board by the collector with an account of the seizure and the officer's statement as to whether he was willing to prosecute at his own charge. If the Commissioners were satisfied with the application they ordered the immediate discharge of the goods without any cost to the merchant. If, on the other hand, no proof of fair removal of property was made by the person from whom the goods were stopped, they were ordered to be seized and prosecuted.[1]

In cases of actual evidence of fraud (such as running at importation or the detection of false weights in shipments for the drawback) or discovery of uncustomed or prohibited articles on search, the goods were seizable; and the officer made his seizure by laying his hand on the packages and declaring that he seized them for His Majesty and himself. Such proclamation had to be made before one or more persons, and if the officer was alone at the time of taking up the goods, he was obliged to declare the seizure again before witnesses. As soon as the seizure had been made, the goods had to be taken to the warehouse of the nearest port, an account of them left with the warehouse-keeper, and the articles weighed or gauged under the direction of the warehouse-keeper and a controller in the presence of the seizing officer.[2] Upon the packages being properly warehoused, the officer then had to acquaint the collector and controller with the seizure, at which time the collector took a detailed account of it: the quantity and quality of the goods, when and where seized, the cause of seizure and under what law (if the seizure was a particular one), the officer's name, the name of the place or ship from whence seized, and whether the officer was willing to prosecute at his own charge. This report was immediately submitted to the Customs Commissioners for their deci-

---

[1] Crouch, *Complete Guide to Officers* (1732), pp. 279–280.
[2] *Ibid.*, pp. 280–281. If the article was liable to excise duties, an excise officer had to be notified as well, in order to take a like account. *Ibid.*, p. 283.

PROCEDURE IN SEIZURE CASES

sion on the seizure, and additional accounts at the same time were sent to the Register of Seizures.[1]

Upon receipt of all the papers relative to the particular case, the Commissioners referred them to that solicitor within whose province the seizure came, for advice as to what action should be taken upon it.[2] There were three possibilities: the Board might order discharge, composition, or prosecution. If the officer had made an unwarranted seizure, or the evidence was not strong enough to risk a suit, or if the principals were particularly deserving, delivery of the seizure was directed, in which case the merchant was obliged to pay a fine to the seizing officer for his trouble.[3]

If discharge were not ordered and the merchant wished to compound rather than to suffer prosecution, the Customs and Treasury Boards might permit such composition upon the advice of the solicitor. In such an event, the seizing officer was obliged to see that the sums due for his share and that of the Crown, together with any charges incurred, were deposited by the defendant where the Board directed; he then executed the license out of the Court of Exchequer which permitted the composition.[4]

Third, the Board might order prosecution of the seizure [5] either at the officer's charge, if he was willing so to prosecute it, or at the charge of the Crown. If the case was tried at the officer's expense, he received a certain share of the produce of the seizure, usually a third or a moiety; but if he desired that the Crown bear the costs, he relinquished his claim to a part of the proceeds of condemnation.[6] In cases

[1] See Crouch, *Complete Guide to Officers* (1732), pp. 283-286; Cust. Ho. Lib., Board's Letters to Boston, Feb. 1732-3 to Mar. 1745-6, Manley to Boston, 1741, Feb. 23. If there were seizures of coffee, tea, chocolate, cocoanuts, brandy, other foreign spirits, mum, and spruce-beer, a quarterly account had to be sent to the Commissioners of Excise. Crouch, *Complete Guide to Officers* (1732), p. 287.
[2] For one reference out of many, see Cust. Ho. Lib., Extracts Board Minutes, III, 504-505, 1761, May 19.
[3] For instances of regulations in settlement of such satisfactions, see *ibid.*, II, "Seizures," 1726, Dec. 7; "LandWaiters," 1743, June 21.
[4] See Crouch, *Complete Guide to Officers* (1732), pp. 287-288. On compositions, see also entries under "Compositions" in Cust. Ho. Lib., Extracts Board Minutes, I, III, particularly I, 1726, Feb. 9, and numerous communications regarding compositions in P.R.O., Treasury Out-letters, Customs.
[5] Numerous reports of the Customs Commissioners to the Treasury, respecting prosecutions for smuggling, show that the Commissioners, fearful that leniency might encourage such offenses, frequently recommended prosecution "as an Example to deter others from being guilty of the like Offences." E. g., P.R.O., Treasury Papers, Bdl. 485, No. 161, Cust. Comrs. to Lords of Treas., 1771, May 16.
[6] See Crouch, *Complete Guide to Officers* (1732), p. 287; Cust. Ho. Lib., London to Harwich, 1699-1788, p. 57, Manley to Harwich, 1741, Feb. 23. It will be

of prosecution for penalties, this arrangement was found to be a great discouragement to the men, for law costs were so heavy that officers frequently were unable to bring action at their own charge, and their zeal in discovery of frauds was undoubtedly affected accordingly. To improve this situation, the Lords of the Treasury in 1736 ordered that when a customs officer could not pay all the charges of a prosecution for an offense against the customs laws, but was willing to pay the costs of making the arrest, the Treasury would bear the other expenses of the prosecution and the officer should have one third of whatever might be recovered.[1]

If prosecution was ordered, the case was taken to a court of common law. The opinion of the Attorney and Solicitor-General in 1750 in connection with a dispute as to whether a certain case in Ireland was of Admiralty or customs jurisdiction clearly defines the place of prosecution of customs cases: "That as clearly all forfeitures by the Laws relating to the Customs are of Common Law Cognizance only and if Goods are claimed upon that foot, the only remedy is in the Courts of Common Law and especially the Exchequer as a Court of Revenue." [2] The Exchequer was the traditional court for prosecution of seizure cases, the method of proceeding in that court being "the most ancient as well as usual," [3] and the sales of condemned goods in the Exchequer dating back to the time of Henry VI.[4]

---

noted here that in the case of certain specified commodities, though the officer undertook to prosecute at his own expense, he was repaid his charges if the goods were condemned.

[1] Cust. Ho. Lib., Sel. from Cust. Outport Recds., Northern England, 1924, p. 178, Stockton on Tees, Board to Collector, 1736, Sept. 1; cf. *Cal. Treas. Books and Papers,* 1742–1745, p. 11, Cust. Comrs. to Lords of Treas., appended to the Treasury warrant of 1741–2, Feb. 10.

[2] The position of the Admiralty Court further is stated in this opinion:

"That where Suits are in both Courts as to the same Goods and dispute is between the Common Law and Admiralty whether the Goods are Flotsam etc. the Common Law Court & particularly the Excheq^r has the preference and must finally determine it.

"That the manner in which that Superiority is exercised is either by prohibition or Order of the Exchequer Court not to proceed in the Admiralty, and if they do notwithstanding, Attachment will be granted against the Contemners of such prohibition or Order.

"That consequently when the Court of Exchequer have once determined the Question in favour of the forfeiture by the Laws of the Customs the Court of Admiralty must submit and can never bring that matter in Question again." P.R.O., Treasury Papers, Bdl. 342, No. 101, opinion of Ryder and Murray, 1750, July 12, as enclosed by Cust. Comrs. to Lords of Treas., 1750, July 20.

[3] Crouch, *Complete Guide to Officers* (1732), p. 288.

[4] P.R.O., Treasury Papers, Bdl. 426, No. 252, "Memorandum of what the

PROCEDURE IN SEIZURE CASES 277

In the early eighteenth century, however, several acts of Parliament provided for the prosecution of particular customs cases before the justices of the peace.[1] Though these magistrates had been able to commit to jail certain offenders against the customs by 13–14 Charles II,[2] to condemn seizures of coastwise wines and spirits by 3 George I,[3] and to decide upon certain personal prosecutions by 1 George I,[4] the earliest eighteenth-century act which permitted the determination of important customs seizures before them was apparently that of 6 George I, c. 21, s. 21, when brandy, arrack, rum, and other spirits could in certain circumstances be prosecuted before two or more justices.[5] Shortly after that, additional commodities, namely, tea, coffee, cocoanuts, chocolate, and tobacco, under particular conditions, were also permitted to be prosecuted before them.[6] Besides such goods, boats of less than fifteen tons, horses, cattle, and carriages used to convey run goods might be condemned before the justices[7]; and persons receiving, buying, or carrying goods which they knew to have been run,[8] or masters importing fresh fish caught by foreigners, came within their jurisdiction.[9]

Because of the importance of customs cases tried both in the Exchequer and before the justices, a survey of procedure in each court is appropriate. If, upon decision of the Board, the case was to be prosecuted in the Exchequer, the collector of the port had to write to the solicitor for a Writ of Appraisement, without which the prosecution could not be carried on in that court. Upon receipt of the writ, certain commissioners in the port, designated in the writ, appointed two or more persons of the county to make a careful examination of the goods and to judge their true value. When the appraisers had completed their estimate they returned an account thereof to the com-

---

Barons of the Court of Exchequer were pleased to say, upon the Draught of a Bill, 'For the further Improvement of His Majesty's Revenue of Customs, And for the Encouragement of Officers making Seizures,'" enclosed by Cust. Comrs. to Lords of Treas., 1763, Mar. 8.

[1] For a survey of cases that could be tried before the justices, see Crouch, *Complete Guide to Officers* (1732), pp. 293–294.
[2] 13–14 Chas II. c. 11, s. 7.
[3] 3 Geo. I, c. 4, s. 17.
[4] 1 Geo. I, c. 18, s. 2.
[5] Two acts of Anne had to do more particularly with excise cases.
[6] 10 Geo. I, c. 10, s. 41–42; see Crouch, *Complete Guide to Officers* (1732), p. 299.
[7] 8 Geo. I, c. 18, s. 16–17.
[8] See 8 Geo. I, c. 18, s. 10; 11 Geo. I, c. 30, s. 16, 39; 9 Geo. II, c. 35, s. 21.
[9] 1 Geo. I, c. 18, s. 1, 2.

missioners, who saw that an indenture of appraisement was drawn up and sent with the writ to the customs solicitor in time for the Register of Seizures to enter it in his books before term opened. The indenture of appraisement was then proclaimed in the Exchequer to the effect "That if any Person can shew any Cause to the Court, why the said Goods shall not remain forfeited, he may come forth, and he shall be heard," and "That if anyone will give any more for the said Goods, than what they are appraised at, he has now liberty to offer the same, or else the said Goods to be recovered for the Use of his Majesty, and of the Person seizing the same."[1] Upon this proclamation of the indenture of appraisement, the goods might be disposed of in one of three different ways: (1) if they were unclaimed or condemned, they were sold; (2) if, upon their being put up to sale, offers were not made, they became the property of the seizing officer who paid the Crown's share; (3) if they were claimed, the case could be brought to trial.

Goods put up for sale and remaining unclaimed for fourteen days, or goods claimed but condemned, were forfeited and sold to the person who had made the highest bid over the appraised value. After the purchaser had paid into the Exchequer the King's share of the seizure (and he was expected at approximately the same time to pay the seizing officer his part as well), a Writ of Delivery was issued which permitted him to take his property out of the warehouse.[2] There were some seizures, however—horses, cattle, vessels, carriages, and other articles condemned before the justices, and certain "enumerated goods" as thy were called—brandy, excisable liquors, tea, coffee, tobacco—which by 12 George I, c. 28, were to be disposed of at the direction of the Customs Board.[3] Practically all other things continued to be sold in the Exchequer until 1763, when the Customs Commissioners recommended to the Lords of the Treasury that the sales there should be discontinued and that all merchandise should be sold at the direction of the Customs Board according to the practice established for the "enumerated" articles. The Commissioners represented that, in the Exchequer sales, goods were often mixed together in such

[1] Crouch, *Complete Guide to Officers* (1732), p. 292.
[2] For this survey of procedure in connection with the Court of Exchequer, see *ibid.*, pp. 288–292. Cf. orders relating to the general practice of the Court of Exchequer, 9 Geo. I, as included in Cust. Ho. Lib., Letters to Dartmouth, 1715-16 to 1731, pp. 167–169.
[3] See Crouch, *Complete Guide to Officers* (1732), p. 299.

large lots (as returned in the indenture of appraisement) that dealers in particular commodities were discouraged from buying; and that, further, because goods could be bid upon before condemnation while they were up for claim, it frequently happened that after a man had gone to the trouble of bidding and making his purchase, he could not have his property until the claim was determined, or he might lose his purchase completely if the goods were not condemned. Because of such uncertainties, genuine buyers had been discouraged from attending the sales, and had left them to certain persons who for some years had combined together to keep down the prices by agreeing not to bid against each other, or to let any one else bid unless they were properly paid. As a result, the sales had been sadly unproductive, goods realizing little more than the appraised value. Finally, the money that a sale did bring was often not paid to the Exchequer and officers for many months after it was due.[1] As a result of the Commissioners' recommendation and in spite of some opposition by the Barons of the Exchequer, an act was passed in 3 George III (c. 22) which provided that seized goods were no longer to be sold in the Court of Exchequer, but in such a place as the Customs Commissioners should appoint. Thereafter, sales of seizures were entirely under the direction of the customs.

With regard to the second possibility in the disposal of the seizure —namely, that upon proclamation of the sale in the Exchequer there might be no offers—the articles might not be bid for because they had been appraised at too high a value. If such was the case a new Writ of Appraisement was granted and a new estimate of value returned. If upon the proclamation of a second indenture in the Exchequer, still no offers were made, the goods were awarded to the seizing officer, upon his payment of the King's share of the appraised value to the solicitor.

As frequently happened, however, claim to the merchandise might be made by the defendant within the time allowed by law. Upon such a claim being preferred, an information or complaint could then be filed by the seizing officer within a month, and the case brought to prosecution upon proper notice being given to the Board and to the

[1] P.R.O., Treasury Papers, Bdl. 426, No. 250, "Observations of the Commissioners of the Customs on what the Barons of the Court of Exchequer were pleased to say upon the Draught of a Bill 'For the further Improvement of His Majesty's Revenue of Customs, and for the Encouragement of Officers making Seizures,'" enclosed by Cust. Comrs. to Lords of Treas., 1763, Mar. 8.

Inspector of Prosecutions. If, however, no information was entered by the officer, a Writ of Delivery for the goods was granted, and the officer was obliged to show cause why he had seized them.[1]

Procedure before the justices of the peace corresponded fairly closely to that in the Exchequer. When the seizure was brought before the justices, if the seizing officer knew the person whose goods had been taken, or if that person applied to him for their discharge, the officer might immediately enter his information before the justices to bring the case to trial, and the individual was accordingly summoned. If, on the other hand, the person was unknown or the proprietor did not lay claim to the goods, and the seizure happened to be brandy, arrack, rum, spirits or strong waters, boats, horses or cattle, or carriages, the officer could not file his information for twenty days. In the meantime he was obliged to apply to the justices for a date of trial and then to see that the common crier proclaimed and posted a notice of the process on the market cross of the nearest market town on the next market day. On the date appointed, after the justices had received a return of the appraised value of the goods, made on oath by two persons commissioned for the purpose, they proceeded to examine into the circumstances of the seizure, and declared it forfeited or discharged.[2]

Goods condemned by the justices could be sold only at the direction of the Customs Board; and, as has been indicated above, after 3 George III that arrangement of sale included Exchequer goods as well. When such disposal was under the administration of the Customs Department, an account of the condemned merchandise, together with a list of any articles that had been in the warehouse longer than six months, had to be sent to the Board monthly by the collector of the port to await the Commissioners' order of sale.[3] Besides forfeited goods such an account might include articles that had been awaiting payment of duties, merchandise that had been imported and was

---

[1] Crouch, *Complete Guide to Officers* (1732), pp. 292–293.

[2] *Ibid.*, pp. 294, 296–298. See *Cases Relating to the Duties of Excise, and to the Jurisdiction of Justices of the Peace, Upon Informations laid before them for Offenses against the Laws of Excise: And to the Jurisdiction of the Justices at the Quarter-Sessions, relating to Appeals in Cases of the Duty upon Malt* (London, 1715), "Forms for Proceedings on Such Seizures, As by the late Act for Preventing Frauds, etc., in the Publick Revenues, Are to be Heard and Determined by Justice of the Peace," 1720.

[3] See Crouch, *Complete Guide to Officers* (1732), p. 299.

PROCEDURE IN SEIZURE CASES

never claimed, and finally goods that had been over-valued and had remained unsold at a preceding sale.

Because London markets frequently assured more productive sales and were freer from combinations against bidding which prevailed in the outports, certain commodities were sent up to the London officers for disposal. If the seizures happened to be coffee or stripped tobacco, and frequently if they were tea, the Commissioners were obliged to order them to be sold in London; and they might direct that certain other goods—rum, foreign brandy, other foreign excisable liquors, and tobacco—be sent up as well for sale.[1] In order to prevent embezzlements in transportation to London, the commodities had to be carefully weighed, packed, marked, and numbered, and an account of them taken at the outport and sent to the London warehouse-keeper. A duplicate of the report and the particulars of the conveyance were sent to the Board at the same time. Upon arrival in London, the quantity and quality of the goods had to be carefully checked with the account received from the outports; any serious deficiencies were represented to the Board immediately, small deficiencies quarterly.[2] The outport collector drew upon the London warehouse-keeper for the proceeds of the sale of outport seizures in London and paid his officers their share.[3]

Sales of condemned goods were usually held quarterly, in January, April, July, and October, though they could be held more often[4] as occasion demanded. In the latter part of the period they numbered about five a year in London.[5] In order to make them as profitable as possible, they were advertised extensively by proper notices,[6] the goods were permitted to be viewed or "tasted" some days before the

---

[1] See Crouch, *Complete Guide to Officers* (1732), p. 302. It appears that lustrings, alamodes, and several other East Indian commodities might also be sent to London.

[2] Cust. Ho. Lib., Extracts Board Minutes, II, "Warehouse Officers," 1743, Feb. 10; cf. Crouch, *Complete Guide to Officers* (1732), p. 302. See specific case in Cust. Ho. Lib., Board's Letters to Boston, Feb. 1732-3 to Mar. 1745-6, Nos. 128-129, Board to Boston, 1733, Dec. 11.

[3] Such would appear to have been customary from a case in *ibid.*, Board to Boston, 1733, Mar. 2.

[4] Cust. Ho. Lib., Extracts Board Minutes, III, 458, 1763, Apr. 28.

[5] See B. M., Add. MSS. 8133 B, f. 210, enclosure of Needham and Pritchard to Cust. Comrs., 1778, Oct. 8; P.R.O., Chatham Papers, Bdl. 284, "Kings Ware House Custom House."

[6] See Crouch, *Complete Guide to Officers* (1732), p. 302; e. g., Cust. Ho. Lib., Letter Book, Blackney, 1711-1723, p. 138, Carkesse to Gentlemen [Blackney], 1736, Oct. 4.

sale,[1] and the articles were carefully lotted [2] and catalogued.[3] The goods being put up for sale, bidding opened, and the public had to make an advance on the price or they were returned to the warehouse until the next sale.[4] The London sales took place in the Long Room,[5] and goods were generally sold by inch of candle. That purchaser secured the goods whose bid stood "at the snuff of the candle," after it had burned a certain length during the time that they were bid upon, or, in some cases, "upon the last stroke of the hammer." If at the sale there was any tea, brandy, spirits, or tobacco which did not sell at the price specified by the customs, or if the seizure happened to be worthless tobacco stalks and stems, the Commissioners had to be notified, that they might give directions for the burning or destruction of such goods.[6] By 24 George II,[7] however, it was enacted that all tobacco should be burned after condemnation, and that an allowance per pound should be made to the seizing officer. As in

---

[1] See Cust. Ho. Lib., Extracts Board Minutes, II, "Warehouse," 1728, June 20. For an example of an advertisement to this effect, see Cust. Ho. Lib., Sel. from Cust. Outport Recds., East Coast, 1923, p. 145, Yarmouth, Collector to Board, 1728–1730, 1730, July 31.

[2] P.R.O., Treasury Papers, Bdl. 459, No. 138, Cust. Comrs. to Lords of Treas., 1767, Aug. 7. See also Crouch, *Complete Guide to Officers* (1732), p. 302.

[3] B.M., Add. MSS. 8133 B, f. 210, enclosure of Needham and Pritchard to Cust. Comrs., 1778, Oct. 8. See also Cust. Ho. Lib., Extracts Board Minutes, II, "Warehouse Officers," 1734, Aug. 20.

[4] In a report to the Treasury in 1767 (Aug. 7), the Customs Commissioners stated that "When Goods are not advanced upon by the Buyers, it is a proof, that they are overvalued by the appraisers, and put up too high, which is frequently the Case, Nevertheless this is no Injury to the Crown, or Officers, as the Goods are put up at the next sale on another Valuation, And the Books of the Sales, are a proof that the Goods are very seldom put up without considerable advances, frequently to upwards of Fifty Biddings. It must be allowed, that Goods have sometimes sold under prime cost, but that is accounted for when it is considered that Smugled Goods, passing through variety of hands, and being frequently hid in Very improper places to evade the Search of Officers, acquire a quite different Face, from what they had when turned out of the Manufacturers hands, and the Purchasers must frequently be at the expence of cleaning the same to render them fit for Exportation." P.R.O., Treasury Papers, Bdl. 459, No. 138.

[5] P.R.O., Treas. Out-letters, Cust., XIX, 323, 324, Cust. Comrs. to Lords of Treas., 1728, Mar. 2.

[6] Crouch, *Complete Guide to Officers* (1732), p. 302.

[7] 24 Geo. II, c. 41, s. 27. During the greater part of the period, certain ships and boats, engaged in smuggling, were required by law to be burned after condemnation if not wanted for use in the customs service. (E. g., see Cust. Ho. Lib., Sel. from Cust. Outport Recds., South Coast, 1925, p. 58, Dartmouth, Board to Collector, 1767, Feb. 28.) By 19 Geo. III, c. 69, s. 6, however, it was provided that in lieu of such disposal it might be lawful for the Customs Commissioners to direct the hull to be broken up and the materials sold.

PROCEDURE IN SEIZURE CASES

Exchequer sales, at the time of his purchase the buyer had to make a deposit to guarantee that he would take away his property and pay for it within a specified time. When the articles were finally delivered out of the warehouse, either on Writ of Delivery, composition, or order of the Board, they were properly examined and stamped,[1] and any necessary payment was made to the warehouse-keeper.

Throughout the century, the Commissioners carefully regulated warehousing and sales in order that they should be made as productive as possible. The warehouse-keeper was required to keep careful account of goods while they were in the warehouse in order to prevent variations in quantity between the time of seizure and appraisement, and between the time of appraisement and sale, he being answerable for deficiencies if suspected to be negligent in that respect.[2] The officers were responsible for seeing that the commodities were appraised at a high enough value; that when sales were held they were well advertised and managed publicly and openly; and that the goods were lotted carefully into small single lots according to species or quality when possible and never sold for less than the appraised value unless they had been injured or damaged. In deciding where merchandise should be sold, the Commissioners chose the best markets and evaded combinations by removing sales to another outport or to London. Though there were some complaints against sales, in general they appear to have been well conducted [3] and reasonably productive,[4] unless the disposal of condemned old horses be ex-

[1] See Crouch, *Complete Guide to Officers* (1732), pp. 318–319, for directions on the delivery of goods from the warehouse. With respect to the order for stamping articles, see Cust. Ho. Lib., Letters to Dartmouth, 1715–16 to 1731, p. 79, Carkesse to Dartmouth, 1718, Feb. 20.

[2] See Cust. Ho. Lib., Letter Book, Blackney, 1711–1723, p. 137, Carkesse to Gentlemen [Blackney], 1727, July 18.

[3] In 1767 (Aug. 7) the Customs Commissioners, in review of the London sales, reported to the Treasury: "On the whole it does not appear to Us, that there is any necessity for altering the present method pursued in respect to the Sales of Condemned Goods, as the Conduct of the Sales, and appraisement of the Goods is invested in Trusty, and Experienced Officers, who after many Years practice have acquired a Competent knowledge in the Value of most sorts of Goods, and when any disagreement arises between them relative to any particular Articles they call in to their Assistance Merchants, and Traders of Integrity, and Eminence in those particular Branches." P.R.O., Treasury Papers, Bdl. 459, Nos. 138-139.

[4] In 1778 the London sales were said to produce from £38,000 to £50,000 per annum (B.M., Add. MSS. 8133 B, f. 210, enclosure of Needham and Pritchard to Cust. Comrs., 1778, Oct. 8); while in 1783 they were stated to have yielded nearly £100,000 a year. (P.R.O., Chatham Papers, Bdl. 284, "Kings Ware House Custom House.") With respect to the outport sales, the Customs Commissioners reported to the Treasury in 1778 (June 30) that it had been necessary for them to establish

cepted. In one instance two such creatures, "so poor and so full of mange that no one would take them to grass or give them stable-room being quit of service," fetched but 6s. 9d.¹; and in another case the upkeep of three mares from the time of seizure until sale cost the service £2. 4s. more than they fetched.²

From the proceeds of the auction the condemnation and sale charges were deducted, and the remainder was divided between the Crown and the seizing officer according to the regulation of the particular act under which the seizure was made. The Deputy Receiver of Fines and Forfeitures for London, who, it will be remembered, also acted as warehouse-keeper until approximately the close of the period, received the proceeds of the London sales. After the deductions had been made and the resulting amount divided into the Crown's and officer's shares, the Crown's portion, after 1781, was still liable to disbursements for various expenses of management. After those charges had been covered, the sum left over was paid by the Receiver of Fines and Forfeitures into the Exchequer. The outport proceeds, however, already represented the net returns when they reached the Receiver of Fines and Forfeitures for the Outports. From the produce of an outport sale, the collector paid the sale and condemnation charges and the officer's share of the proceeds, and drew upon the Crown's share for certain additional payments. After these disbursements had been made, the remaining sum was remitted by the collector to the Receiver of Fines and Forfeitures for the Outports, to be paid by that officer into the Exchequer. The Warehouse-keeper of the Crown acted as a check on the accounts of the Warehouse-keeper in London, while in the outports the controller checked the collector's books. Accounts of both the Receivers and of the outport collectors, as far as they related to the produce of seizures, were passed by the Accountant of Petty Receipts.³ Payments into the Exchequer by the two Receivers of Fines and Forfeitures did not, however, include all the sums from seizures which

---

at a fixed sum the salary of the Controller on the Receiver of Fines and Forfeitures, otherwise by the increase of seizures "and the advanced prices at which they have sold since the Sales have been under Our Management" the Controller's salary would have exceeded that of the Receiver. P.R.O., Treasury Papers, Bdl. 542, No. 139.

¹ Cust. Ho. Lib., Sel. from Cust. Outport Recds., West Coast, 1926, p. 99, Swansea, Collector to Board, 1766, May 31.

² *Ibid.*, Northern England, 1924, p. 67, Newcastle on Tyne, Collector to Board, 1731-2, Jan. 21.

³ See *supra*, Ch. III, pp. 102-105.

were remitted to that Treasury. When a seizure was compounded or a fine was exacted, the money was handed over to the solicitors in London, who, after deducting charges, paid the Crown's share into the Exchequer and gave the officers their parts. The solicitors' accounts were passed by their Auditor.[1] Through this machinery, then, did the revenue of fines and forfeitures reach the Exchequer.

The administration responsible for all this procedure was carrying out a seizure policy based on a dual principle: the discouragement of illicit trade by means of seizures and severe penalties, and strict regulation of procedure in seizure cases in order that they might be made to yield the greatest possible revenue to the customs treasury.

Efforts to realize the first of these objectives took the form of encouragement to officers and their assistants for seizures, and heavy penalties on the principals when goods were taken up. As might be expected, the most effective incentive to officers was a share in the seizures, and many were the regulations laid down to secure a fair distribution of proceeds among the men concerned.[2] Furthermore, there were rules to ensure early payment to officers by setting limits to the time during which purchasers might settle for their goods [3] and by making provision for despatch in the customs offices.[4] Then there were poundages on seizures for several of the higher officers (the collectors, controllers, appraisers, and a number of men in the Central Office [5]), while huge rewards might be the good luck of any one who could make himself proficient in the matter of seizures. As has been indicated above, in 1736 the administration lightened the burden of condemnation charges in suits for the greater convenience of officers. The prosecution of enumerated goods before the justices was an added encouragement to officers, for it provided for more speedy disposal of seizures at lower costs than when sent

---

[1] See *supra*, Ch. III, pp. 94–95.

[2] For instance, inferior officers were not obliged to give their superiors any part of a seizure unless the superior officer was present or the seizure had been made upon information furnished by him; and superior officers were obliged to make allowances to subordinates who assisted them in a seizure. See Crouch, *Complete Guide to Officers* (1732), pp. 319–320; Cust. Ho. Lib., Extracts Board Minutes, II, "Officers," 1739, Feb. 1; 1745, Apr. 24. See also *ibid.*, I, "LandWaiters," 1743, June 21.

[3] E. g., Cust. Ho. Lib., Board's Letters to Boston, Feb. 1732–3 to Mar. 1745–6, Board to Boston, 1735, Jan. 3

[4] E. g., Cust. Ho. Lib., Letter Book, Blackney, 1711–1723, p. 138, Carkesse to Gentlemen, 1736, Oct. 4.

[5] See Cust. Ho. Lib., Extracts Board Minutes, I, "Condemned Goods," 1728, May 9.

to the Exchequer. The more profitable sales of condemned goods by direction of the Customs Board further yielded the officer a larger sum than if the sales were carried on in the Exchequer. Moreover, officers were encouraged to make seizures by the knowledge that they would be defended in an action brought against them if the seizure was made in accordance with prescribed rules and was correctly represented by them to the Board.[1] Finally, Board action against collusive seizures,[2] strict directions to seize boats and carriages as well as run goods, and regulations against secreting the persons concerned in running [3] were designed to break the strength of fraudulent traders.

Despite the best of these efforts, effective procedure against illicit trade was not assured, for there were many discouragements to officers: they were often intimidated by the power and organizations of the smugglers; there was sometimes uncertainty of customs backing in a seizure, and danger of counter-suits by the runners; charges of prosecution were costly; the process of the law was slow; prejudiced juries and justices [4] frequently failed to convict; sales of goods often enough brought little, owing to low appraisements, large lots, combinations in bidding, and delays in payments of shares of seizures.[5] Still, the administration never faltered in a defense which from the beginning was helpless against the opposition which confronted it.

Every possible assistance was afforded to the officers. By an Order in Council soldiers were directed to assist in customs enforce-

[1] Cust. Ho. Lib., Extracts Board Minutes, V, 144-145, 1780, Dec. 15.
[2] See several entries under "Seizures" in *ibid.*, II.
[3] Strict regulations in connection with the accounts of seizures taken by the collectors were designed to prevent this; see for example Cust. Ho. Lib., London to Harwich, 1699-1788, p. 47, Carkesse to Harwich, 1737, Mar. 26.
[4] Justices sometimes discharged goods upon the application of the defendant. In such cases, customs officers were cautioned to retain the goods for the Commissioners' direction. E. g., Cust. Ho. Lib., Letters to Dartmouth, 1715-16 to 1731, p. 222, Carkesse to Dartmouth, 1726 [Nov. 1?]; *ibid.*, pp. 305-306, Carkesse to Dartmouth, 1730, Oct. 27.
[5] An anonymous petition to the Lords of the Treasury, 1767, Feb. 2, probably exaggerates conditions. The writer remarks: "but when the Goods are Sold at the Excise the money is paid in Six weeks or Two Months at most but not at Customs is almost Two Years Which hurts the inferior Officers who has no more Salery from the Government then will just maintain their Families" and "so long as this is the case that the officers of the Lowest Class cannot have their Business done with the Solicitors nor to have there money from the Warehouse keepers The Revenue is prejudiced several hundred a year as none of these men can get their money without some discount." P.R.O., Treasury Papers, Bdl. 456, Nos. 264-265.

PROCEDURE IN SEIZURE CASES

ment; and their stations, their instructions, and miscellaneous regulations to assure their most effective support were subjects of constant rulings. Such was likewise true of Admiralty vessels, which cooperated throughout the period. Soldiers who assisted in a seizure received from a sixth to a half of the Crown's share and two thirds of the officer's part, according to the numbers of soldiers engaged and the nature of their participation.[1] When dragoons personally helped to effect a seizure, they were allowed half of the King's share and half of the officer's part, those sums being divided among them according to the pay of the military officers and soldiers respectively.[2] Admiralty commanders were also well rewarded for their trouble. In 1723 the Treasury directed that they should receive half of the officer's share of any seizure which they might make, while the principal officers of the port should have the other half for supervising the prosecution and condemnation of the goods.[3] In 1757, however, this was considered an unfair division, and the navy commanders were given two thirds and the customs officers one third.[4]

Informers, too, were encouraged. Thus the Board considered that a particular increase in running might in some measure be prevented if the officers strictly executed their duties and "If due Encouragement were given to Such persons who Shall be willing to discover the Runing of Goods as well with regard to the benefit they Shall receive by Such discovery, as to their being well assured that their Names Shall be Concealed."[5] Informers were paid by the officers

[1] B.M., Add. MSS. 8133 B, f. 267, a paper on soldiers' rewards allowed in consequence of an Order in Council, 1716, Dec. 17, and of subsequent orders [signed by John Bastin, 1783, Dec. 6].

[2] This distribution was settled by Order in Council of 1716, Dec. 17. (P.R.O., Treasury Papers, Bdl. 602, No. 280, Stiles to Steele, 1784, May 6. Cf. Cust. Ho. Lib., Extracts Board Minutes, III, 506, 1763, July 20.) There was frequently difficulty in enforcing payment to the soldiers by the customs officers whom they had assisted. In 1783, Feb. 15, the Board ordered that in view of such difficulty the outport collectors be directed to retain in their hands so much out of the customs officers' share as was due to the soldiers, to be paid the soldiers as soon as the Board's order for it was received. (*Ibid.*, V, 492.) This measure was not wholly effective, however, for in 1786 Yonge of the War Office twice requested the Treasury to direct payment of soldiers' accounts which had remained unsettled for several years (P.R.O., Treasury Papers, Bdl. 627, No. 248, 1786, Feb. 13; Bdl. 639, No. 27, 1786, Dec. 13); upon the first request the Treasury gave its order accordingly. P.R.O., Treas. Out-letters, Cust., XXXIV, 345, Steele to Cust. Comrs., 1786, Feb. 25.

[3] *Ibid.*, XVIII, 231, Treasury warrant, 1723, June 6.

[4] *Ibid.*, XXV, 257, Treasury warrant, 1757, May 12; see pp. 255–257, Cust. Comrs. to Lords of Treas., 1757, Apr. 19.

[5] Cust. Ho. Lib., Letter Book, Blackney, 1711–1723, p. 71, Board to [Blackney], 1717, Nov. 20.

from their shares—the sum of one third being considered by the Board to be a suitable recognition of their services,[1] and for failure so to compensate their assistants the officers were liable to stoppage of salary, suspension, and dismissal by the Commissioners.[2] Now and then informers were subsisted by the Customs Department for a certain length of time; those who gave evidence at trials received the usual rate of 10s. a week [3] or occasionally were given temporary employment.[4] Sometimes they were granted positions in the service.[5] Such encouragement seems to have been a general practice despite the observation of the Attorney-General in 1712 that such subsistence, promise of preferment, and a share of what was recovered were contrary to law, to which the Board in defense answered that "when labouring Men or of poor Circumstances give any Informaĉion of Frauds . . . during the time such Persons are attending as Evidences and are kept from their Usuall way of Subsistence they are allowed 10^{sh} P week which We think is of Service to the Revenue and not contrary to the Intent of the Law. But We know of no Promises made of Preferm^t or of Part of what is recovered to any Witnesses." [6]

Further efforts were made to check smuggling by the infliction of severe penalties on the principals if the goods were seized; thus punishment might take the form of enforced satisfaction to the officer for discharge of the goods, composition to the amount of a considerable proportion of the value of the seizure plus charges, forfeiture of the goods and of the boats, vehicles, or horses by which they were conveyed, fines amounting perhaps to several times their worth, the imprisonment of persons engaged in running, or transportation [7]

---

[1] See P.R.O., Treasury Papers, Bdl. 602, No. 280, Stiles to Steele, 1784, May 6. See also Cust. Ho. Lib., Extracts Board Minutes, I, "Informations and Informers," 1721, Nov. 8.

[2] E. g., *ibid.*, I, "Informations and Informers," 1725, Jan. 11; 1721, Jan. 29; 1727, Aug. 9.

[3] See *infra*. There are several instances of the grant of a lump sum for services as a witness. For example, one person was allowed as much as £50 for his evidence in a trial involving a personal prosecution. Cust. Ho. Lib., Extracts Board Minutes, IV, 487, 1776, June 12.

[4] *Ibid.*, I, "Informations and Informers," 1721, Mar. 31.

[5] As in the case of an evidence against persons concerned in the murder of a customs officer. *Ibid.*, IV, 372, 1776, Sept. 26.

[6] P.R.O., Treas. Out-letters, Cust., XVI, 16, Cust. Comrs. to Lord High Treasurer, 1712, Mar. 16.

[7] By 9 Geo. II, c. 35, s. 28.

or death [1] for those guilty of obstructing or wounding an officer within the limits of a port.

After every means had thus been employed to effect seizures in discouragement of illicit trade, strict regulations governed procedure in seizure cases in an effort to realize the second objective of seizure policy: the greatest possible returns to the customs treasury. The Commissioners evidently based their defensive program on the principle that the nefarious trade should be prevented if possible, but that if it could not be controlled, it was to be made to pay heavily into the customs treasury. The proceedings in connection with seizure and prosecution, surveyed in the first part of this chapter, were the chief method of achieving such an objective. The elaborate records that had to be kept in connection with seizures were further directed toward that end: collectors' accounts of seizures, condemned articles in the warehouse, sales of goods and those sent to London for sale, and quarterly records of proceedings on enumerated commodities all had to be carefully kept and transmitted to the Customs Commissioners and the proper officers in the Central Office for examination and check. A strong body of law officers, consisting of the Attorney and Solicitor-General and the solicitors of the customs, assisted by the Inspector of Prosecutions and the Register of Seizures, directed prosecutions and saw that penalties were inflicted. Thus close control was kept over the quantities of goods seized and their produce. The customs receipts were swelled by the proceeds of fines and forfeitures, but that very fact levels an indictment against the system of high duties, the detected evasion of which furnished such a revenue. That illicit trade suffered so little by seizure [2] is an even stronger comment on the policy of duties.

[1] By 19 Geo. II, c. 34, s. 1. This law at first suppressed smuggling to a great extent; but after a while it fell into disuse, and smuggling by aid of arms increased. Doubt as to the legality of enforcing parts of the statute prevented it at several times from being effectively invoked. (Cross, *Eighteenth Century Documents* [*Univ. of Mich. Publ.: Hist. and Pol. Science,* VII], pp. 319-321.) By several acts and proclamations during the period, pardon for offenses against the customs was granted, frequently with the provision that the offender enter into the Army or Navy or secure a substitute.

[2] For example, with respect to only one of the many forms of frauds, namely, drawbacks, see *supra,* Ch. VII, p. 263.

Conclusion

The main outlines of customs organization, as regards offices and the method of carrying on the business, had been well established by the beginning of the period covered by this study. The eighteenth century saw marked development and expansion to meet the tremendous increase in British trade. The system was an exceedingly complex one owing to the persistence of medieval outport patent offices in the eighteenth-century organization, and to the existence of various other sinecures and redundant offices in the Central Office and London establishments. Customs administration was further encumbered by the intricate system of high duties which confused accounts, necessitated many additional offices as checks, and encouraged illicit trade. Procedure at importation and exportation, complicated by this scheme of duties and the drawback system, invited frauds. The virulence of the smuggling which resulted from all of these causes required constant concentration of ingenuity on preventive measures, the negative side of customs administration. Abuses in regulation of the customs staff, touching the patronage, fee system, low salaries, short hours, and frequent holidays, led to an indifferent quality of personnel, the effect of which was undoubtedly reflected in the operation of the system.

Administration by the bodies of executive control was for the most part sound. A carefully constructed organization for the collection of the revenue, together with a system of supervision and check on every department, was provided, and endless efforts were made to secure its most effective working. Regulation of the customs staff took the form of encouragement of every kind to deserving officers for good service and just infliction of penalties for violation of trust. In many cases the Board was aware of abuses, such as those of useless offices, heavy fees, and unwarranted absences, and by numerous regulations sought to abolish or control them. The Commissioners were conscientious in duty and intelligent and fair in their decisions on customs cases. They made continuous attempts to improve the service along many lines.

There were some evils in the system, however, for which the administration must be held in part responsible: the persistence of many holidays and short hours of work, the lack of a plan of examination, classification, and promotion in appointments to the customs staff, and a certain informality in outport administration. On the other hand, the worst evils of all in the system—the scheme of duties to be enforced, sinecures, and the fee system—were largely beyond the power of the Customs and Treasury Boards to alter. That the service functioned as well as it did is evidence of a certain kind of judicious administration.

TABLE OF ABBREVIATIONS USED IN FOOT-NOTE CITATIONS

Acad.	—Academy
Add.	—Additional
Admin.	—Administration
Bdl.	—Bundle
B.M.	—British Museum, London
Cd.	—Command
Cal.	—Calendar
Com.	—Committee; Commission (rarely)
Comr(s).	—Commissioner(s)
Conn.	—Connecticut
Cust.	—Custom; Customs
Desc.	—Descriptive
Dom.	—Domestic
Eng.	—England
Estab.	—Establishment
F(f).	—Folio(s)
Hist.	—Historical
Harl.	—Harleian
Ho.	—House
Journ.	—Journal
Lib.	—Library
Mem.	—Membrane
Mich.	—Michigan
MS(S).	—Manuscript(s)
No.	—Number
Plant.	—Plantations
Pol.	—Political
P.R.O.	—Public Record Office, London
Publ.	—Publications
Quart.	—Quarterly
Recd(s).	—Record(s)
Rept(s).	—Report(s)
Sel.	—Select; Selections
Stud.	—Studies
Trans.	—Transactions
Treas.	—Treasury
Univ.	—University
Vol.	—Volume

BIBLIOGRAPHY

It is inadvisable to extend a bibliography of this kind to include the many works that have been consulted. Only the most important of those sources that have served as direct references in the foot-notes of the preceding pages are here recorded. The materials which have been used in the preparation of this study of customs organization are classified under three headings: Manuscripts, Printed Sources, and Secondary Works. Manuscripts are cited according to location; Printed Sources are divided into three classes according to the nature of the items: Official Sources (as for example, calendars); Parliamentary Papers; and Contemporary Writings on the customs, London, trade, and commerce.

I. *MANUSCRIPTS*

London Custom House Library

The most important material in the London Custom House Library for the purposes of this investigation is the Notes and Extracts from the Minutes and Orders issued by the Commissioners of the Customs for the Instruction and Government of their Officers, 1696–1792, Presented to the Board of Customs by Sir William Musgrave, 5 vols. Without this source, which consists of detailed entries on nearly every aspect of customs business, it is doubtful if a study of customs organization could have been attempted. Since practically all of the official Board and London customs records were destroyed in the London Custom House fire of 1814, these extracts, which were probably compiled originally for the private use of Sir William Musgrave, a Commissioner from 1763 to 1786, are the only complete chronological record of Board administration throughout the period.

Of the several books which list the personnel of the Customs Department at specific dates, two were indispensable: A list of the Commissioners and Officers of His Majesty's Customs in England, Wales, and in the Plantations with their Respective Salaries, to 1782; and An Establishment of the Officers of the Customs belonging to the Outports, 1671. The first of these books contains the eighteenth-century customs establishment and indicates the dates of the warrants or minutes by which the various offices were created or their nature affected. The second constitutes the earliest establishment book of the customs after its administration had been placed in the hands of the Board of Customs Commissioners; for this reason it is of primary value in a comparison of the establishment at the end of the eighteenth century with the first one under the commission.

The correspondence between the Board of Customs Commissioners and the outports was of great service in obtaining a knowledge of outport administration and Board policy. The following outport books were the most useful, and, of these, the Letters to Dartmouth were the best single source of information: Letter Book. Blackney. 1711–23; Board's Letters to the Port of Boston, Lincolnshire, February $\frac{1732}{3}$ to March $\frac{1745}{6}$; Letters to Dartmouth. 1675–6 To 1715; 1715–16 To 1731; London to Harwich, 1699–1788; Letter Book. Wells, 1712 To 1730; Letters From Whitby, 1721–1724; and Correspondence. London and Whitehaven, 1744–1748. The Selections from Customs OutPort Records, (South Coast) 1922; (East Coast) 1923; Northern England, 1924; South Coast, 1925; West Coast, 1926; East Coast, 1931, compiled by Mr. B. R. Leftwich, Librarian of the London Custom House Library, have been of excellent assistance in supplementation of the outport books to be found in the Custom House Library. These collections include transcripts of letters both from the Board to the outport and from the outport to the Commissioners—incorporating, with few exceptions, portions of the correspondence of every important port in England and Wales.

The following miscellaneous items contributed material relating to specialized departments of the customs: 4½ P C Minute Book, 1776–1829 (including entries of orders to the Husband of the Four-and-a-Half Per Cent and a record of his action in conformity therewith); Surveyor's Reports (London) Board's Orders Thereon (of the twenty-eight volumes, the one for 1768–1770 is of particular interest in connection with the tobacco business); and Opinions of Counsel (England) 1727–1781, 4 vols. (consisting of the Attorney-General's opinions on customs cases).

Public Record Office

The Treasury In-Letters, Treasury Board Papers [T. 1], Bundles 319–640, were examined in detail for the years 1746 to 1786 inclusive. Many of the papers preceding 1746 were consulted in amplification or verification of the *Calendars of Treasury Papers*. The Treasury Papers were of particular service in a study of the position of the Treasury in the scheme of customs administration, the relationship between that Board and the Board of Customs Commissioners, and conditions obtaining in various parts of the service. Consisting of in-letters to the Treasury, these papers include all kinds of petitions, reports, and representations relating to customs matters, submitted to the Lords of the Treasury by merchants, private individuals, state departments, customs officers, and the Customs Board, as the case may be.

The Treasury Out-letters, Customs [T. 11], of which volumes 13–19, 23–34 were studied for the years 1692–1729, 1745–1787, inclusive, contain copies of Treasury warrants, directions, and other communications relating to the customs business, most of which are addressed to the Customs Commissioners. Since each Treasury warrant almost always bears with it a copy of the original report or representation of the Customs Commissioners in connection with some particular aspect of the service, these records were invaluable in their information on nearly every phase of administration.

BIBLIOGRAPHY

Important customs documents are to be found among the Chatham Papers [G.D. 8]. The following bundles yielded the richest material: 231 includes a manuscript booklet which describes the business done in various branches of the Treasury at approximately 1782; 283 contains letters and reports of the Customs Commissioners to the Treasury and customs accounts for the latter part of the eighteenth century; 284 comprises miscellaneous papers relating for the most part to customs offices and fees; 285 consists in general of papers connected with the Bills of 1783 and 1792 for the abolition of certain useless offices in the customs and the reform of the fee system.

The State Papers Domestic, George II [S.P. 36], Bundles 35–119 for the years 1735 to 1752 and Volume 6 for 1728, furnished material that bears primarily upon the relationship between the Secretaries of State and customs administration, and to a lesser extent upon customs patronage and smuggling. For other years of the period the following catalogues were consulted: Descriptive List of State Papers Domestic, George I, four books of references to volumes 1–76 of the State Papers of George I for the years 1714–1727; and Manuscript Calendar of State Papers Domestic, George II, I, 1727–1729, II, 1727–1744.

For a knowledge of the dates of the creation and abolition of customs offices, numbers of officials on the establishment, and the salaries received, the Customs Registers: Series I, Customs Quarterly Establishments [Cust. 18], Volumes 36–430 for the years 1696–1786, were of service.

Patents of especial interest in connection with the constitution of the several boards of Customs Commissioners are the following: 23 Charles II, Part 2, No. 1, dorse, [1671], Sept. 27; 2 James II, Part 9, dorse, No. 6, [1686], June 25; 13 William III, Part 3, No. 1, [1701], Dec. 18; 6 Anne, Part 6, No. 16, [1707], June 5; 9 George I, Part 2, No. 12, [1723], June 27; 15 [incorrectly dated; should be 16] George II, Part 5, Nos. 3–4, [1742], Sept. 9; 7 George III, Part 5, No. 11, [1767], Sept. 8.

The Treasury Minute Book, 1696–1786 [T. 29], was occasionally used to supplement or verify other sources.

The various volumes of the Ledger of Imports and Exports [Cust. 3] constitute part of the records of the Inspector-General of Imports and Exports and illustrate the way in which the accounts of trade were kept.

British Museum

It is impossible to cite all of the British Museum manuscripts which have been consulted in the course of this study. Only those of significance which have been used in foot-note references are included here:

Additional Manuscripts 8133, "An Account of the Officers employed in the Revenue of the Customs in England with the Value of their Places, arising from Salaries Fees and other Perquisites," in five parts.

Additional Manuscripts 8133 B, papers of Sir William Musgrave, "Revenue of Customs," ff. 91, 93, "Observations on the Laws for Regulating the Importation and Exportation of Corn," William Arnold, Cowes collector [to

Musgrave?; probably after 1783]; ff. 110–113, a report of Samuel Brown [to Musgrave?] on the water guard of the customs service in 1773 and 1775; f. 210, enclosure—relating to sales in the Long Room—in a letter from T. Needham and John Pritchard to the Customs Commissioners, 1778, October 8; f. 214, an account of the King's share of the produce of seizures and penalties from prosecutions, 1751–1780; f. 267, a paper on the rewards of soldiers assisting in customs seizures [signed by John Bastin, 1783, Dec. 6]; ff. 350–351, "Observations on the apparent diminution of the gross Rect. of Customs in 1776," Sir William Musgrave's paper to Sir Grey Cooper, 1777, Nov. 20.

Additional Manuscripts 8133 C, papers of Sir William Musgrave, "Revenue of Customs," ff. 1–4, a small printed booklet headed "Commissions of the Customs and Succession of the Commissioners"; f. 116, a list of certain ports and their gross receipt for ten years, 1771–1780; f. 124, an account of payments into the exchequer by the Receiver-General, 1760–1784; f. 133, an account of the gross produce of the customs and of the charges of management, 1766–1778; f. 149, a list of goods entitled to bounty on importation into Britain, dated 1781, Nov. 6.

Additional Manuscripts 18903, "Papers Relating to the Customs, Trade and Plantations. 1703–1721," ff. 8–9, "Abs^t of the Rep^t ab^t the Office of Rec^r Gen^{ll}"; f. 29, "An Acc^{tt} of the method of passing Debentures in the Port of London," 1714, Oct. 26; f. 29, "The Method of taking Bonds for the Duties of goods imported"; f. 30, "Methods of passing Debentures in the Port of London, [1714]"; f. 32, "The Method of making out and passing Certif^{tes} of Damage & Over Entries"; ff. 78–82, "The Com^{rs} Attend^{ce}"; ff. 85–93, a rough paper on customs personnel: its state and suggestions for reforming it; f. 166, "Copy of the Patent Officers Report on the referred Mem^l [?] of the East India Comp^a."

Additional Manuscripts 32523, f. 252, "A Digest of the Book of Rates, & some other laws Relating to the Customes."

Additional Manuscripts 32864, f. 385, a communication of Edward Hooper to Newcastle, 1756, April 23, in which is enclosed a paper relating to the business of the Long Room and the office of the Secretary of the Customs, ff. 387–390.

Additional Manuscripts 32900, f. 452, "Mr Page's Paper concerning The Office of Receiver General of the Customs [to Newcastle; dated 1759 by the index]."

Additional Manuscripts 35906, ff. 205–206, 207, 209, 211, 213, 219–221, 227, papers on the business of the London quays, 1762–1763.

Harleian Manuscripts 2263, f. 206, docket of a customs commission of 1708, May, signed by Godolphin.

Harleian Manuscripts 4309, f. 3, "Vectigalium Systema or A Compleat View of that Part of the Revenue of Great Britain commonly called Customs . . . ," by William Edgar [1713?]. This manuscript was published in 1714.

Stowe Manuscripts 324, "Revenue Collections, 1396–1764," of Sir Richard Temple, f. 238, a report [of a Customs Commissioner to the Lords of the the Treasury?] of interest in connection with entries in the Long Room.

BIBLIOGRAPHY

II. PRINTED SOURCES

Official Sources

The Act of Tonnage & Poundage and Rates of Merchandise (London, 1702).
Acts and Ordinances of the Interregnum, 1642–1660, 3 vols., edited by Sir Charles Harding Firth and R. S. Rait (London, 1911), I.
Calendar of Treasury Books, 1660–1667; 1669–1672, Part II; 1681–1685, Part I; Oct. 1697–Aug. 1698.
Calendar of Treasury Papers, 1556-7–1696; 1697–1701-2; 1702–1707; 1708–1714; 1714–1719; 1720–1728.
Calendar of Treasury Books and Papers, 1729–1730; 1731–1734; 1735–1738; 1739–1741; 1742–1745.
The Case of the Planters of Tobacco in Virginia, As represented by Themselves; signed by the President of the Council, and Speaker of the House of Burgesses. To which is added, A Vindication of the said Representation (London, 1733).
Cobbett's Complete Collection of State Trials and Proceedings for High Treason and Other Crimes and Misdemeanors from the Earliest Period to the Present Time, 33 vols. (London, 1809–1828), VI.
Eighteenth Century Documents Relating to the Royal Forests, the Sheriffs, and Smuggling, Selected from the Shelburne Manuscripts in the William L. Clements Library by Arthur Lyon Cross [*University of Michigan Publications: History and Political Science*, VII], (New York, 1928).
Historical Manuscripts Commission, *The Manuscripts of the House of Lords* (New Series), V, *1702–1704*; VIII, 1708–1710.

————, *Fourteenth Report*, App. Part IV, *The Manuscripts of Lord Kenyon* [Cd. 7571] (1894).

————, *Fourteenth Report*, App. Part I, *The Manuscripts of His Grace The Duke of Rutland, K. G. preserved at Belvoir Castle*, III, [Cd. 7476] (1894).

————, *Fifteenth Report, Report on the Manuscripts of His Grace The Duke of Portland, K. G., preserved at Welbeck Abbey*, VIII, [Cd. 3475] (1907).

————, *Eighteenth Report, Report on the Manuscripts of the Marquess of Downshire, Preserved at Easthampstead Park, Berks*, I, Part II (1924).

Journal of Commissioners for Trade and Plantations, 1718–1722; 1722-3–1728; 1728-9–1734; 1734-5–1741.
Instructions to Officers in the Out Ports, 1781 [in the British Museum].
Instructions to be Observed by Supervisors; Instructions to be Observ'd by Riding Officers (London, 1734) [in the Custom House Library].
The Statutes at Large.

Parliamentary Papers

(Arranged in chronological order)

The Report, with the Appendix, from the Committee of the House of Commons appointed to enquire into the Frauds and Abuses in the Customs, to the Prejudice of Trade, and Diminution of the Revenue (London, 1733).

Parliamentary Papers, XXXVI, *Reports,* VI, H.C. No. 58 (1783), "First Report from the Committee appointed to Enquire into the Illicit Practices used in Defrauding the Revenue"; H.C. No. 59 (1784), "Second Report from the Committee appointed to Enquire into the Illicit Practices used in Defrauding the Revenue"; H.C. No. 60 (1784), "Third Report from the Committee appointed to Enquire into the Illicit Practices used in Defrauding the Revenue."

The Reports of the Commissioners Appointed to Examine, Take, and State The Public Accounts of the Kingdom, Presented to His Majesty and to Both Houses of Parliament; with the Appendixes Complete: by John Lane, Secretary to the Commissioners (London, 1787), III, "Thirteenth Report, Relative to the Manner of Passing the Accounts of the Customs, in the Office of the Auditors of the Imprest," 1785; "Fourteenth Report, Relative to the Charges of Management of the Custom Duties in the Port of London for the Year 1784," 1785; "Fifteenth Report, Relative to the Payments to the Officers of the Customs at the Out Ports, and to other Charges of Management incurred on Account of the Custom Revenue for the Year 1784," 1786. These three reports constitute the findings of the group of commissioners who made the first exhaustive survey of the customs system. Of the printed sources consulted, these reports were by far the most valuable in their information on nearly every aspect of customs organization in the eighteenth century.

Ten Reports of the Commissioners Appointed by Act 25 Geo. III, cap. 19, to enquire into the Fees, Gratuities, Perquisites, and Emoluments which are or have been lately received in the several Public Offices therein mentioned, H.C. 309 (1806), "Second Report," 1786, vii.

Parliamentary Papers, XLVII, *Reports,* XVII, H.C. No. 129 (1796), "Report from the Committee appointed to enquire into the best Mode of providing sufficient Accommodation for the increased Trade and Shipping of the Port of London."

Commons Reports, 1803, XII, "Fourth Report from the Select Committee on Finance, Collection of the Public Revenue, Customs," 1797.

Parliamentary Papers, LIII, *Reports,* XXIII, H.C. No. 153 (1799), "Report from the Select Committee Appointed to consider Evidence taken on Bills for the Improvement of the Port of London"; H.C. No. 154 (1799), "Second Report from the Select Committee upon the Improvement of the Port of London."

First, Second, Third, Fourth, Fifth, and Sixth Reports of the Commissioners appointed to inquire into the departments of the Customs and Excise; and Of the Proceedings of the Lords Commissioners of the Treasury

BIBLIOGRAPHY

thereupon (*Customs*), H.C. 46 (1820), VI, "First Report, Board of Customs," 1818; "Second Report, The Warehousing System," 1818; "Fourth Report, Long Room," 1819.

First Report from the Select Committee appointed to inquire into the Constitution and Management of the Customs; together with the Minutes of Evidence and Appendix, H.C. 209 (1851), xi.

Second Report from the Select Committee appointed to inquire into the Constitution and Management of the Customs; together with the Minutes of Evidence and Appendix, H.C. 604 (1851), xi, in four parts.

Report from the Select Committee on Customs; together with the Proceedings of the Committee, Minutes of Evidence, Appendix, and Index, H.C. 498 (1852), viii, in two parts.

First Report of the Commissioners of Her Majesty's Customs on the Customs [Cd. 2186], H.C. (1857), iii.

Accounts and Papers, XXXV, H.C. 366, 366–I (1868–1869), "Public Income and Expenditure."

Contemporary Writings

1. *Customs*

Baldwin, Samuel, *A Survey of the British Customs; containing the Rates of Merchandize* (London, 1770).

Cases Relating to the Duties of Excise, and to the Jurisdiction of Justices of the Peace, Upon Informations laid before them for Offenses against the Laws of Excise: And to the Jurisdiction of the Justices at the Quarter-Sessions, relating to Appeals in Cases of the Duty upon Malt (London, 1715), "Forms for Proceedings on Such Seizures, As by the late Act for Preventing Frauds, etc., in the Publick Revenues, Are to be Heard and Determined by Justice of the Peace," 1720.

Crouch, Henry, *A Complete Guide to the Officers of His Majesty's Customs in the Out-ports. Being Forms, Precedents, and Instructions for the Execution of every Branch of the Business of that Revenue* (London, 1732). This book served as the official guide of customs officers throughout the greater part of the eighteenth century. The survey of procedure through the customs and of fines and forfeitures has been of especial value in connection with the last two chapters of this study.

————, *A Complete View of the British Customs* (London, 1727?).

Daniel, Thomas, *Ductor Mercatorius: or the Young Merchants' Instructor with respect to the Customs: Being a minute and particular Detail of the Regular Method of Proceeding at Out-Port Custom-Houses, In the several Branches of Marine Commerce* (Newcastle upon Tyne, 1750).

Forster, Samuel, *A Digest of all the Laws Relating to the Customs, to Trade, and Navigation; with a short Historical Dissertation Concerning the Nature, Extent, and Method of Collection of the Ancient Revenue of the Crown* (London, 1727).

A General Law-Treatise of Naval Trade and Commerce, I.

Hatton, Edward, *Comes Commercii or The Trader's Companion* (London, 1723).
Jacob, Giles, *Lex Mercatoria: or, the Merchant's Companion* (London, 1729).
The Rules of the Water-side; or The General Practice of the Customs, Being A Collection of the most proper and useful Examples practis'd in the Customs; alphabetically digested into a very concise and easy Method, necessary for the Use of Custom-house Officers, Husbands of Ships, Merchants, Merchants Apprentices, or such who design to qualify themselves in that Kind (London, 1715).
Some Considerations Humbly Offered to the Publick concerning The Revenue of the Customs (London, 1752).

2. *London and Miscellaneous*

Brett, Jasper, *The Sin of With-holding Tribute by Running of Goods, Concealing Excise, etc.* (Dublin, 1721).
Chamberlain, Henry, *A New and Compleat History and Survey of the Cities of London and Westminster . . . The Borough of Southwark, and Parts adjacent: from the Earliest Accounts to the Year 1770* (London, 1771).
Defoe, Daniel, *A Tour Thro' the whole Island of Great Britain,* 2 vols., edited by G. D. H. Cole (London, 1927), I.
Entick, John, *A New and Accurate History and Survey of London, Westminster, Southwark and Places Adjacent,* 4 vols. (London, 1766), IV.
Gwynn, John, *London and Westminster Improved* (London, 1766).
The History of our National Debts and Taxes from 1688 to 1751, in four parts (London, 1753).
Jones, Hugh, *The Present State of Virginia* (London, 1724) [*Sabin's Reprints,* No. 5, New York, reprinted for Joseph Sabin, 1865].
The London Journal, 1721, 1722, 1724.
Maitland, William, *History and Survey of London From its Foundation to the Present Time,* 2 vols. (London, 1756), II.
Mist's Weekly Journal, 1728.
Rolt, Richard, *A New Dictionary of Trade and Commerce* (London, 1756).

III. SECONDARY WORKS

There are no secondary works confined to customs organization in the eighteenth century. Several writings on the customs service in general were of aid, however, and various institutional and economic studies have assisted in interpretation.

Andrews, Charles M., *Guide to the Materials for American History, to 1783, in the Public Record Office of Great Britain,* 2 vols. (Washington, D. C., 1912–1914).
———, "The Acts of Trade," *Cambridge History of the British Empire,* I, Ch. IX, pp. 268–299.
Atton, Henry, "Commissioners of Customs, Excise, Hearth Money, and

BIBLIOGRAPHY 301

Inland Revenue," 1912, an unpublished study in the Custom House Library.
———, and Holland, Henry Hurst, *The King's Customs*, 2 vols. (London, 1908, 1910).

Basye, Arthur Herbert, *The Lords Commissioners of Trade and Plantations commonly known as the Board of Trade 1748–1782* (New Haven, Connecticut, 1925).

Beatson, Robert, *A Political Index to the Histories of Great Britain & Ireland: or, A Complete Register of the Hereditary Honours, Public Offices, and Persons in Office, from the Earliest Periods to the Present Time*, 3 vols. (London, 1806), II.

Broodbank, Sir Joseph Guinness, *History of the Port of London*, 2 vols. (London, 1921), I.

Capper, Charles, *The Port and Trade of London* (London, 1862).

Cunningham, William, *The Growth of English Industry and Commerce in Modern Times: The Mercantile System* (Cambridge, 1921).

Dietz, Frederick C., *English Public Finance, 1558–1641* (New York, 1932).

Dowell, Stephen, *A History of Taxation and Taxes in England from the Earliest Times to the Year 1885*, 4 vols. (London, 1888), II.

Egerton, Hugh Edward, *A Short History of British Colonial Policy* (London, 1910).

Firth, Sir Charles Harding, *The Last Years of The Protectorate, 1656–1658*, 2 vols. (London, 1909), II.

George, M. Dorothy, *London Life in the Eighteenth Century* (London, 1925).

Heath, Sir Thomas L., *The Treasury* (London, 1927).

Hughes, Edward, *Studies in Administration and Finance, 1558–1825, with Special Reference to the History of Salt Taxation in England* (Manchester, 1934).

Hughson, David, *London; Being an accurate History and Description of the British Metropolis and its Neighbourhood, To Thirty Miles Extent*, 6 vols. (London, 1805?–1813), II.

Keith, Arthur Berriedale, *Constitutional History of the First British Empire* (Oxford, 1930).

Kennedy, William C., *English Taxation 1640–1799, An Essay on Policy and Opinion* (London, 1913).

Knight, Charles, ed., *London*, 6 vols. (London, 1841–1848), II.

Levi, Leone, *The History of British Commerce* (London, 1880).

Newton, Arthur Percival, "The Establishment of the Great Farm of the English Customs," *Transactions of the Royal Historical Society*, Fourth Series, I (1918), 129–156.

Parry, F. S., "The Drawback System," 1920, an unpublished study in the Custom House Library.

Rees, J. F., "Mercantilism and the Colonies," *Cambridge History of the British Empire*, I, Ch. XX, pp. 561–602.

Rive, Alfred, "A Brief History of Regulation and Taxation of Tobacco in England," *William and Mary College Quarterly Historical Magazine*, Second Series, IX, 73–86.

Suviranta, Br., *The Theory of the Balance of Trade in England, A Study in Mercantilism* (Helsingfors, 1923).

Thomson, Mark A., *The Secretaries of State, 1681–1782* (Oxford, 1932).

Westerfield, Ray Bert, "Middlemen in English Business Particularly between 1660 and 1760," *Transactions of the Connecticut Academy of Arts and Sciences,* 1915, May, XIX, 111–445.

INDEX

A

Abbreviations, table of, 292
Absence, leaves of, 225, 226, 227
Abuses, customs, 4, 228ff., 244, 290
    see also Frauds
Accountant of Petty Receipts, 102, 103, 104, 105, 106, 107, 119, 284
Accounts, 92, 101, 103-104, 105, 106, 107ff., 133ff., 144, 147, 184, 189, 190, 231, 251, 259
    arrears in, 110
    examination of, 255
    outport, 107, 117, 176
    special, 50
    system of, 63
Act of Tonnage and Poundage, 25, 30, 221
Act of Union, 117
Acts of Parliament, 228
Acts of Trade, 1, 94
Administration, customs, 1ff., 6, 24, 36, 37, 49, 50, 51n, 55, 56, 57, 61, 63, 66, 69, 78, 90n, 91, 92, 94, 96, 124, 128, 186, 190, 214, 218, 227, 228, 236, 270, 290, 291
    colonial, 3
    outport, 170, 174, 192, 291
    problems of, 4–5ff., 25
Admiralty, the, 41, 43, 64, 87, 88, 178, 181, 186, 240, 287
    jurisdiction of, 276
    Lords of the, 47n, 88
Adulteration, 271
Ad valorem duties, 29, 30, 31, 36
    see also Duties
African trade, 122
Aggregate Fund, 27
Agriculture, 1
Aldeburgh, 169n
Allowances, 34, 138, 141, 142, 173, 219
America, 40n, 43n, 67n
    see also, Colonies, American
American Plantations, *see* Colonies, Plantations
American Revolution, the, 43n
Anne, Queen, 2, 26, 34, 110
Annuities, 27n
Appointer of the Watchmen, 144
Appointers of the Weighers, 143, 144
Appointment, 195ff., 231
    see also Customs officers, Patronage
Appraisement, Indenture of, 98, 278, 279
    Writ of, 94, 277, 278, 279
Appraisements, 283, 286
Appraisers, 151, 198, 277, 285
Arrack, 280
Arundel, 169n
Assessment, methods of, *see* Duties, calculation of
Assistance, Writs of, 63, 272, 273
Assistant Clerk, 108
    see also Clerks
Athol, Duke of, 170
Attorney-General, the, 14, 19, 20, 23, 30, 53, 60, 61n, 90, 91, 95, 97, 247n, 276, 288, 289
Auctions, 102, 156, 281ff.
Auditor, 95, 285
Auditor of the Imprest, 27, 101, 109, 251-252

B

"Back Doors," 192
Balance of trade, *see* Trade, balance of
Ballot, use of, 196
Baltic, the, 42
Bank, national, 122
Bank notes, 174
Barbadoes, 156
Barnstaple, 168n, 206n
Barons of the Exchequer, 5, 168, 279
    see also Exchequer, the
Beaumaris, Port of, 15, 169n
Bench, the, 131, 195

303

INDEX

Bench officers, 19n, 20, 23n, 47n, 75, 76, 129, 130, 132, 133, 136, 142, 227, 246
Bibliography, 293ff.
Bidding, 281, 282, 286
Bideford, 169n, 206n
Billingsgate, 124, 150
Bill of 1783, 166n
Bills, 62, 100, 116, 251
Bills of Entry, 248, 250, 257, 259
    see Entries
Bills of exchange, 122, 174, 175, 176, 251
Blathwayt, 58
Blue Book, the, 141, 228
Boarding Station, 157
Board of Customs, see Customs Board
Board of Customs Commissioners, see Customs Commissioners
Board of Trade, 16, 47n, 57, 68, 79, 85, 86, 116, 117
Boatmen, 161, 173, 205, 206, 218n, 229, 238, 272
Boats, 162, 177, 193, 245, 254, 280
    construction of, 178
    inspection of, 163
Bonding, 256
Bond Office, 70
Bonds, 10, 38, 63, 65, 69, 70, 90, 95, 99, 101, 135, 136, 205, 251, 265, 266, 267
    coast, 149
    delivery of, 51
    discharge of, 261
    payments on, 101
    prosecutions of, 93
    receipts of, 134
    records of, 228
    security by, 62
    tobacco, 100
    uncertified, 149
Book of Orders, 228
Book of Rates, 25, 27, 29, 30, 221n, 228
Boston, 168, 169n, 234
Bounties, 33, 62, 65, 92, 111, 145, 147n, 243, 265
    calculation of, 135, 136
    payment of, 136
Boyes, 234
Brandy, 32, 33, 49n, 86, 170, 231, 232, 278, 280, 281, 282
Bribery, 203, 231, 240, 255, 261
    see also Frauds, Smuggling, Trade, illicit
Bridlington, 169n

Bristol, 12n, 13, 54n, 162, 168, 169n, 170, 192, 193, 206n, 217, 223, 238
Britain, 38, 118, 122, 153, 170, 243, 244, 246, 257, 262, 264
British Museum, 295f.
British Plantations, 117
    see also Colonies, Plantations
Brokerage business, 122
Brokers, 247
Brookes, John, 124n
Bugles, 143
Burgoyne, Sir John, 15
Burke, 2, 47, 48n, 65n
Butlerage, 40
Buyers, 261

C

Calculation, of duties, see Duties, calculation of
Calicoes, duties on, 67n, 147n
Cambrics, 143
Candles, 93, 160
Cape of Good Hope, 165n
Capital, 122
Cardiffe, 169n
Cardiff officers, 172
Cardigan, 169n
Cargoes, 117, 123, 125, 132, 138, 152, 157, 158, 163, 164, 180, 213, 232, 246, 247, 252, 260, 267
    admittance of, 51
    clearance of, 62, 124, 145ff., 265
    see Entries
    entry of, see Entries
    treatment of, 65, 159
    see Frauds
Carkesse, Charles, 30, 68, 82n, 83, 85
Carlisle, 16n, 169n
Carmarthew, Lord, 91
Carmen, 165
Carolinas, 67n
Carriages, 280
Carter, John, 204
Carts, 127, 128
Cash, custody of, 188
Cashiers, 92, 95, 99, 100, 118, 119
Cattle, 280
Central Office, the, 13n, 61, 63, 92ff., 99, 101, 116, 135, 136, 166n, 168, 176, 186, 189, 190, 265, 285, 289, 290
    law staff of, 92ff.

INDEX

Central Office (*continued*)
    organization of, 92, 119ff.
    revenue branch of, 99ff.
Certificates, 38, 62, 69, 100, 135, 146
    Landing, 266
Chalders, 268
Chancellor, the, 5
Chancellor of the Exchequer, 198
Chancery, 5
Channel, the, 140, 245
Channel Islands, 170, 262
Charing Cross, 210
Charles II, 8n, 12, 25, 26, 29, 126, 146n, 148, 168, 219, 243, 257, 271, 277
Chester, 15, 206n
Chester's Quay, 245
Chief Clerks, 75, 108, 273
    see also Clerks
Chief Cocket-writer, 135
    see also Cockets
Chief Packer to the Searchers, 147n
Chief Patent Searcher, 147, 166
China, 152
Chinamen, 130
Chocolate, seizure of, 277
Cinders, 149, 150
Clark, William, 124n
Clay, 169n
Clearance, 124, 261, 268
    see also Cargoes, Entries
Clearing Station, 157–158
Clerk of the Certificates, 134
Clerk of the Coast Business, 149
Clerk of the Rates, 134, 248, 249
Clerk of the Ships' Entries, 133
Clerk of the Warrants, 134, 250
Clerk to the Controller Inwards and Outwards, 257
Clerks, 70, 71, 74, 93, 101, 129, 132, 136, 147, 148, 149, 153, 154, 198, 248
    junior, 70, 71
    petty, 163
    staff of, 118
Cloth, woolen, 193
    duty on, 26, 137
Coal, 77, 93, 149, 150, 160, 193, 264, 266, 267, 268
    duties on, 49, 167, 168
    frauds, 208, 268
Coal Collector, 150
Coal Department, 149
Coal-meters, 150, 198, 206, 267
Coal offices, personnel of, 148ff.
Coal ships, 150, 229n
Coast, the, 65n, 83, 115, 169, 177, 183, 185, 186, 262
    guarding of, 36, 37, 43, 64, 81, 182
    nature of, 170
    traffic on, 58
Coast bonds, 7, 10, 63n, 93, 149
Coast business, 7, 136, 140, 152, 167
Coast laws, 266n
Coast officers, 136–137, 148–149, 150
Coast offices, personnel of, 148ff.
Coast-waiter, 12n, 149, 196, 199n, 206, 265, 266
Coastwise duties, *see* Duties
Coastwise trade, 7, 173, 264ff.
Cocket Office, 123, 135
Cockets, 63n, 135, 146, 147, 148, 258, 259, 260, 261, 268
    coast, 265, 266, 268
Cocoanuts, 38n, 152, 262, 263n, 277
Codes of instructions, 228
Coffee, 38n, 86, 152, 262, 263n, 277, 278, 281
Coinage branch, 216
Coinage duties, 108, 219
Collection of customs, 3, 4, 5, 6, 25ff., 28, 33, 36, 37, 44, 86, 191
Collector and Controller of the Coast Duties, 149
Collector-Coastwise, 99, 150
Collector:
    Exeter, 89
    Harwich, 83
    Hull, 171
    Sunderland, 233
    Swansea, 232
    Weymouth, 184
Collector-Inwards, 14n, 99, 104, 123, 131, 133, 134, 136, 139, 150, 151, 152, 246, 249, 267
Collector of Coal Duties, 149, 267
Collector of Great Customs on Wool and Leather Exported, 136, 140
Collector of Petty Customs Inwards, 134, 140, 166
Collector-Outwards, 100, 120n, 131, 135, 136, 137, 139, 148, 149, 250, 257, 258, 259, 265, 267
Collectors, 6, 7, 8, 10, 12, 13n, 16, 35, 40, 41, 49n, 60, 63, 75, 88, 98, 102, 104, 108, 110, 112, 132n, 134, 140, 149, 150, 151, 153, 154, 156, 167, 171, 172, 173, 175, 176, 180, 181, 183, 184, 188, 189,

Collectors (*continued*)
  203, 205, 206, 207, 209, 215, 216, 217, 220, 224, 225, 227, 228, 229, 230, 241, 248, 251, 259, 266, 267, 268, 273, 274, 277, 280, 284, 285, 289
  accounts of, 109, 111
  London, 74, 100, 101, 109
  outport, 100, 103, 173, 179, 184, 281
  plantation, 100
  reports of, 64
  vouchers of, 111, 154
Collusion, *see* Bribery, Frauds, Smuggling
Colonial officers, appointment of, 57
Colonial policy, 57
Colonial trade, 67, 85
Colonies, American, 4, 38, 43n, 70, 86, 130, 240, 244, 259
  see also Plantations
Commanders, 179, 180, 181
Commerce, 1, 2, 3, 67, 85, 167, 172, 194, 256
  coastwise, 264ff.
  expansion of, 18, 165, 243
  restrictions on, 3, 33–34, 243
Commission business, 122
Commissioners' Clerk in the Searchers' Office, 147n
Commissioners for Trade and Plantations, *see* Board of Trade
Commissioners of Accounts, 3, 4, 14, 15n, 19, 23, 25, 32, 98, 99, 102, 106, 112, 116, 118, 119, 179, 204–205, 212, 214, 222, 223
Commissioners of the Revenue, 185
Commissioners of the Revenue in Ireland, 57
Committee on Finance, 120
Common crier, the, 280
Common law, court of, 276
Commons, House of, 59n, 212
  see also, Parliament
"Common Warehouse," 170
Compositions, 64, 93, 95, 275, 283
Comptroller of the Issues and Payments of the Receiver-General, 102
Computers, 134, 139, 248, 250, 259
Condemnation of goods, 169, 271, 275, 279, 284
Conduct:
  certificates of, 227
  of officers, 118; *see also* Customs officers

Consolidation Act, 3, 4, 31, 35, 263
Constables, 142
Consuls, 91
Contractor, 178, 179
Control Department, 139, 140
Controller, 5, 6, 7, 8, 10, 11, 12, 13, 14, 15, 16, 18, 22n, 24, 75, 77, 92, 105, 106, 108, 109, 111, 112, 118, 119, 131, 136, 137, 140, 150, 152, 154, 156, 167, 171, 173, 179, 180, 183, 187, 188, 189, 195, 205, 206, 215, 225, 227, 228, 229, 248, 251, 267, 274, 284, 285
Controller-General, 27, 74, 101, 106, 107, 108, 109, 110, 111, 112, 118, 120, 167, 187, 251
Controller-Inwards, 139, 153, 154, 165, 250, 258
Controller of the Customer of Cloth and Petty Customs Inwards and Outwards, 166
Controller of the Customs in the Port of London, 136, 149
Controller of the Receiver of Fines and Forfeitures for the Outports, 104, 106, 107
Controller-Outwards, 139, 165, 258
Controllers and Examiners of the General Accounts, 107
Controlling searchers, 147, 148, 259, 260
Coopers, 147, 151, 156, 252n
Copying Clerk of the Entries Inwards, 134
Copying Clerk Outwards, 135, 258
Copying Clerks, 74
Corn, 29, 193
Corporation of London, 150
Corruption, 19, 195, 203
  see also Bribery, Frauds, Smuggling
Cotton, 67n
Cotton-wool, 38n
Counties, boundaries of, 169
Court Leet, 232
Court of the Exchequer, 59, 94, 151, 169, 274, 275, 279
Court of King's Bench, 126n
Credit, 122
Creek, 12, 167, 168, 169, 212, 220, 260
Crews, 39, 40, 42, 180, 181
Crown, the, 2, 5, 13, 22, 59, 78, 83, 91, 94, 95, 96, 103, 109, 148, 150, 151, 163, 178, 179, 209, 219, 234, 242, 249, 256n, 261, 262, 275, 278, 284, 285, 287

INDEX

Crown offices, 24, 93
Cruiser contracts, 179, 180
Cruisers, 64, 66n, 88, 167, 177, 178, 179, 181, 182, 183, 237, 240
    maintenance of, 178, 219, 221
    regulation of, 180
Culm, 149, 150
Custodes custumae, 5
Customer, 5, 6, 7, 10, 11, 12, 13, 16, 18, 22n, 24, 25, 108, 167, 195, 251
    duties of, 8, 10
Customer of Cloth and Petty Customs, 137, 140, 166
Customer of the Great Customs Outwards, 166
Customs, the, 4, 5, 9, 10, 11, 13, 17, 18, 26, 27, 34, 36, 37, 40, 45, 46, 53, 59, 64, 65, 67, 79, 80, 82, 84, 85, 88, 89, 91, 93, 95, 97, 99, 101n, 111, 112, 131, 148, 149, 152, 153, 157, 160, 164, 177, 178, 185, 186, 191, 198, 204, 208, 212, 224, 228, 232, 233, 243, 244, 245, 265, 270, 271, 279, 280, 282, 285, 288, 289
    accounts of, 28, 31, 37, 92, 101, 107, 110
    Acts, 33
    administration, *see* Administration, customs
    appointments, *see* Appointment, Patronage.
    Central Office of, *see* Central Office
    collection of, *see* Collection
    collectors of, *see* Collectors
    colonial, 57
    eighteenth-century, 5ff., 123
    enforcement of, 64, 91, 170, 185, 287
    imposition of, 1
    Irish, 57
    jurisdiction of, 276
    knowledge, 32
    machinery of, 61, 63, 245
    offenders against, 277
    organization of, 2, 4, 5ff., 24, 34, 37, 45, 57, 290
    personnel of, *see* Personnel
    plantation, 57, 69
    policy of, 4, 48, 51, 62, 64, 66, 67, 76
    practice of, 76
    produce of, 244
    records of, 111
    reforms in, 3, 4, 24, 120, 166

Customs (*continued*)
    regulations of, 64
    revenue, *see* Revenue, customs
    routine of, 50
    Secretary of the, 67
    seizures by, 270ff.
    service of, 37, 44, 120, 237
Customs Board, 4, 5, 9, 10, 12n, 19, 20, 21, 22, 23, 24, 28, 30, 31n, 34, 39, 41, 42, 43n, 45, 46, 48, 49n, 50, 51, 52, 53, 54, 55n, 56, 57, 58, 59, 60, 61, 63, 64, 65, 66, 67, 68, 69, 70, 71, 72n, 73, 74, 75, 76, 77, 78, 79, 82, 83, 84, 85, 86, 89, 90, 91, 92, 93, 94, 95, 96, 97, 98, 100, 102, 103, 105, 107, 108, 109, 111, 112, 113, 114, 115n, 117, 126n, 128, 131, 132, 133, 138, 142, 143, 152, 154, 155, 158, 160, 161, 162, 171, 172, 174, 176, 178, 179, 181, 182, 186, 187, 188, 189, 190, 191, 196, 197, 198, 199, 200, 201, 202, 203, 204, 205, 206, 207, 208, 209, 210, 211, 215, 217, 218, 220, 221, 222, 224, 225, 226, 227, 228, 232, 233, 234, 235, 237, 238, 239, 240, 241, 242, 251, 253, 260, 263, 271, 272, 274, 275, 277, 278, 279, 280, 281, 286, 287, 288, 290, 291
    authority of, 132
    chairman of, 52, 73, 74, 115
    duties of, 62ff.
    efficiency of, 78
    minutes of, 129
    supervision of, 187
    see also Customs Commissioners
Customs boats, 161, 177
    inspection of, 163
Customs business, 68, 70, 90, 170
    accounting of, *see* Accounts
Customs cases, 91
    importance of, 277
    prosecution of, *see* Prosecutions
Customs Commissioners, 3, 4, 7, 14, 15, 16, 17, 18, 19, 20, 21, 22, 24, 28n, 30, 32, 33, 35, 36, 39, 41, 42, 45, 46, 47, 48, 49, 50, 51, 52, 53, 54, 55, 56, 57, 58, 59, 60, 61, 62, 63, 64, 65, 66, 67, 68, 69, 71, 72n, 73, 74, 75, 76, 77, 78, 79, 80, 83, 84, 85, 86, 87, 88, 89, 90, 91, 92, 94, 96, 97, 101, 103n, 107, 109, 110, 113, 115, 116, 117, 120, 126n, 127, 128, 129, 130, 131, 133, 136, 139, 140, 141, 146, 147n, 156, 157, 159, 160, 162, 167, 168, 170, 175, 177, 180, 181n, 189, 190, 191, 193,

INDEX

Customs Commissioners (*continued*)
196, 197, 198, 199, 200, 201, 202, 203, 204, 205, 208, 210, 211, 212, 214, 215, 216, 218, 219, 220, 222, 223, 224, 225, 226, 227, 228, 229n, 235, 236, 238, 240, 241, 242, 247, 250, 263, 266n, 268, 271, 272, 274, 275, 278, 279, 280, 282, 283, 288, 289, 290
   activities of, 61ff.
   politics and, 58
   powers of, 59ff.
   privileges of, 59f.
   salaries of, 59
   succession of, 57–58
   see also Customs Board
   farming of, 6–7, 99, 126, 148
Custom House, 20, 35, 65, 68, 71, 72, 77, 96, 124, 127, 128, 131, 144, 154, 171, 172, 181, 212, 213, 234, 240, 241, 246, 247, 257, 267, 274
   conditions in, 171–172
   first, 128
   housekeeper of, 132, 133
   locations of, 171
   London, 73, 76, 92, 99
   officers at, 157
   outports, 170, 171–173
Customs laws, 25, 26, 34, 36, 48, 49, 63, 65, 66, 75, 78, 81, 84, 90, 91, 93, 94, 99, 132, 231, 260, 276
   colonial, 57
   evasion of, 62
   execution of, 79
   enforcement of, 50, 61, 192, 270; *see* Customs, enforcement of
   guard of, 177
   infringement of, 92, 99, 185, 219, 270
Customs officers, 29, 31, 32, 33, 34, 38, 40, 42, 43n, 47, 51, 53, 54n, 65, 66, 71, 75, 76, 77, 81, 83, 84, 85, 86, 87, 88, 89, 91, 92, 94, 95, 97, 100, 101, 106, 108, 112, 113, 116, 126, 127, 129, 132, 133, 134, 135, 136, 138, 139, 140, 149, 155, 160, 162, 167, 168, 171, 179, 189, 191, 193, 195, 198, 202, 207, 208, 209, 212, 213, 214, 215, 216, 218, 222, 224, 225, 227, 228, 229, 230, 231, 233, 234, 235, 236, 237, 238, 239, 240, 241, 242, 251, 255, 260, 262, 267, 272, 273, 276, 278, 283, 285, 286, 287, 288, 289
   appointment of, 47n, 50, 60, 195ff.
   dismissal of, 64, 210, 288

Customs officers (*continued*)
   efficiency of, 228ff.
   extraneous duties of, 37ff.
   penalties of, 64, 241–242
   powers of, 271
   promotion of, 64, 211
   qualification of, 64, 204ff.
   regulation of, 49, 50–51, 64–65, 114, 186ff., 227–228, 234ff.
   remuneration of, 50, 64, 211ff., 235ff.
   "rolling" of, 239
   see also Personnel
Customs offices, 7, 8, 40, 70, 113, 119, 136, 137, 156, 161, 195, 285, 290
   creation of, 64
   increase in, 119, 165
   patronage of, 198ff.; *see* Patronage
   purchase of, 209–210
   reduction of, 119ff., 166ff.
   reform of, 120, 166
Customs procedure, 61, 76, 270
   in shipping, 243ff.
   regulation of, 62
Customs receipts, 50, 58, 99, 243, 244
   payment of, 106, 244
Customs staff, 113, 201, 221, 230, 290, 291
   see also Customs officers, Personnel
Customs system, 2, 3, 4, 25, 67, 164, 243
   abuse of, 242, 244
   administration of, 6, 46, 56, 59
   corruption in, 195
   eighteenth-century, 4, 5
   frauds in, 244
   inefficiency in, 195
   organization of, 3
   personnel of, 195ff.
   purposes of, 1ff.
   reform of, 78, 195
   warehousing in, 262
   writing on, 299
   see also Customs
Customs treasury, 107
   see also Central Office
Cutters, 88, 177, 178

D

Damages, 33, 116, 138, 141, 142
   allowances for, 155

INDEX

Day pay, 145, 220
Deal, 123, 157, 169n, 233, 245
Debenture clerk, 147, 148, 260
Debenture goods, 158
Debentures, 62, 65, 92, 99, 102, 134, 135, 138, 139n, 145, 146, 147, 260, 261, 262, 268
Debts, 65, 95, 224
 imprisonment for, 64
 national, 1, 3
Delafaye, 83
Delivery:
 expenses of, 252n
 writ of, 98
Deposits, 136
Deptford, 127
Deputies, 12, 13, 14, 16, 16n, 17, 18, 19, 20, 21, 22, 24, 41, 50, 76, 136, 200
 outport, 21
 payment of, 17–19
Deputy Collector, 149
Deputy Controller-Coastwise, 136–137
Deputy Controller-Inwards, 136
Deputy Controller-Outwards, 136
Deputy Receiver, 104
Deputy Receiver of Fines and Forfeitures for London, 284
Deputy searcher, 173
Desertions, 39n
Despatch, 266
Disbursements, 101, 103, 109n, 176
Discharge, 64, 280
 of seizures, 275
Discounts, 34, 35, 62, 111
Dismissal, *see* Customs officers, dismissal of
Distribution, 122
Doctors' Commons, 93
Door-keeper, 77n
Dorchester, 15n
Dover, 49n, 83, 169n
Downs, 245
Draught, 62, 141, 253
Dredging of Thames, 124
Drawbacks, 31, 33, 34, 35, 38, 111, 145, 147n, 170, 233, 245, 247n, 257, 259, 260, 261, 265, 267, 268, 274
 abolition of, 263
 calculation of, 136, 138, 139n, 260
 on tobacco, 244
 payment of, 136
 policy of, 260

Drawback system, 256, 260, 262, 263, 264, 290
 evils of, 263
Drugs, 32n, 33
Dunbar, 229
Dunkirk, 169, 262
Durham coast, 266n
Duties, 1, 2, 3, 5, 6, 7, 11, 25, 26, 27, 28, 29, 30, 31, 34, 36, 39, 40, 43, 57, 59, 62, 63, 86, 92, 95, 99, 100, 107, 111, 122, 130, 133, 136, 152, 156, 158, 167, 216, 249, 253, 254, 255, 257, 267, 290, 291
 abuses of, 29
 ad valorem, 29, 30, 31
 alterations in, 31
 appropriation of, 28, 37
 benefits of, 34–35
 branches of, 2, 4, 26, 27, 32, 37
 calculation of, 28, 29, 30, 31, 32, 35, 36, 62, 134, 135, 136, 137, 154, 229, 231, 248, 249, 250, 254, 255
 checking of, 250
 classes of, 26
 coal, 149, 167, 168, 267
 coast, 149, 264, 265, 267
 collection of, 6, 10, 33, 110, 115, 134, 136, 137, 191, 247, 250, 251
 computers of, 134
 consolidation of, 30, 35
 control of, 248
 drawback of, *see* Drawbacks
 entry of, 141
 evasion of, 255; *see* Frauds, Smuggling
 excise, 40
 export, 115, 135, 137, 140, 258, 268
 high, 3, 36, 37, 290
 import, 2, 31, 115, 133, 136, 140, 257, 260, 265, 266
 increases in, 2, 34
 levying of, 33
 payment of, 51, 102, 136, 141, 167, 173, 248, 250, 255, 256, 258, 267, 268, 274, 280, 289
 proceeds of, 243; *see* Revenue
 receipt of, 135, 137, 149
 salt, 57
 security for, 150
 specific, 30
 specialized, 147
 system of, 110, 230, 270, 289
 tea, 36
 tobacco, 36, 155, 249

INDEX

Duties (*continued*)
  variations in, 32, 191
  wool cloth, 26
Duty, 4½ per cent, 186
Dye-woods, 38n

E

East India, 29, 235
  see also East Indies
  commodities of, 29, 30, 61, 143, 152
East India Company, 145, 150, 152, 226
East Indiamen, 160
East India service, 161
East India staff, 151
East India system, 150
East India trade, 122
East India warehouses, 152
East Indies, 32, 157
Edgar, William, 32
Edinburgh, 57
Edward I, 5, 11
Elizabeth, Queen, 8, 9n, 11, 125, 168
Embargo, 37, 42, 80, 81
Embargo warrants, 42
Emigration, 40n
Emoluments, 153, 164, 219
  see Fees, Salaries
Employment, 2, 47n
  purchase of, 209
England, 49n, 57, 81, 93, 108, 116, 117, 122, 170, 194, 243, 260
  commercial policy of, 2
  Northern, 182
  ports of, 69, 169n
  revenue of, 192
  Western, 93, 193
Entries, 134, 246ff., 257ff., 265
"Enumerated goods," 278
Established offices, 199–200
Examiner in the Coast Business, 150
Examiner of the Computations, 250
Examiner of the Inferior Officers' Day Pay Bills, 108, 112
Examiner of Outport Accounts, 119
Examiner of the Outport Books, 107, 111
Examiner of Riding Officers' Journals, 115
Examiner of the Sufficiency of Officers' Securities, 108, 111
Examiner of the Water Guard Officers' Journals, 163

Examiners, 92, 108, 120, 134, 150, 152, 155, 156, 183, 248, 267
Exchequer, the, 2, 6, 7, 8, 10, 12, 23–24, 27, 28, 62, 92, 94, 95, 97, 98n, 99, 101, 102, 103, 105, 106, 109, 123, 135, 149, 151, 198, 219, 243, 251, 252, 265, 271, 276, 277, 278, 279, 280, 283, 284, 285, 286
  Barons of, 168
  Chancellor of, 9, 46
  Court of, 9, 59, 94
  procedure in, 277
Excise, 156, 208
Excise Commissioners, 40, 53, 86, 170n
Excise Department, 186
Excise duties, 80, 86
Excise officers, 86, 87, 97, 233, 272
Executive control, 45ff.
Exeter, 18, 169n
  controller, 177
Exportation, 62, 63, 135, 136, 170, 193, 230, 231, 243, 247, 257, 261, 263, 264, 267
  duties of, 137
  eighteenth-century, 257
  forms of, 256
  illicit, 146, 265
  of tobacco, 257ff.
  procedure at, 256ff., 260, 269, 290
Export business, 6, 133, 134, 135, 136, 137, 140, 143, 147, 148, 152, 173
Export Department, 135–140, 145–148, 165–166, 173
Exporters, 137, 146, 258, 261
Exports, 1, 5, 7, 8, 11, 25, 38, 63, 70, 85, 116, 123, 125, 135, 136, 193, 223
  accounting of, 133
  Britain's, 122
  check on, 135, 136–139
  regulation of, 33
Export shipping, customs procedure in, 256ff.
Export trade, 147, 173

F

Falmouth, 170
Farming, system of, 3, 7
Fees, 11, 13, 14, 17, 18, 24, 27n, 78, 93, 98, 99, 108, 118, 127, 137, 140, 141, 145, 148, 150, 151, 153, 163, 212, 214, 215, 229, 249, 253n, 290

INDEX 311

Fees (continued)
  abolition of, 214
  dependence on, 231
  extortion of, 217
  legal, 209
  reform of, 214
  system of, 195, 211, 213, 221, 290, 291
  tables of, 212
Fiants, 14
Fiat, Treasury, 195
Finance, 122
  committee on, 120
Fines, 64, 92, 97, 102, 103, 105, 106, 107, 119, 241, 270, 271, 275, 285, 288, 289
First Copying Clerk, 70, 71
Fish, 149
Foot-notes, key to, 292
Forfeitures, 48, 92, 97, 102, 103, 105, 106, 107, 119, 180, 270, 271, 276, 285, 289
"Fountain," the, 160
France, 32, 84, 165n, 170
  Court of, 82
  trade with, 1
  war with, 178, 182
Frauds, 35, 36, 37, 51, 64, 65, 78, 86n, 90, 90n, 93, 124n, 157, 159, 179, 185, 190, 192, 207, 213, 230–234, 241, 242, 244, 255, 261, 263, 265, 268, 271, 273, 274, 290
  coal, 208
  discovery of, 276
  evidence of, 274
  prevention of, 167, 263, 285–289
  suspicion of, 272
  tobacco, 154, 192, 239–240n, 255, 261–262
  see also Bribery, Smuggling, Trade, illicit
Freight, 116
French goods, duties on, 27
French Plantations, 32
French Royal Paper, 27
Fuller's earth, 264

G

Gaugers, 142, 144, 145
General Fund, the, 27
General-surveyors, 75, 76, 96, 113–115, 120, 132, 189–190, 191, 227

George I, 29, 97, 277, 278
George II, 43n, 282
George III, 33, 251, 271, 279, 280
Georgia, 67n
Germany, 83, 165n
Ginger, 38n
Glutmen, 128, 160, 165, 198
Godolphin, Commissioner, 12n, 14n, 58, 77n, 117, 217
Goods, 36, 38, 43, 62, 71, 84, 95, 116, 125, 127, 128, 133, 140, 145, 146, 148, 149, 150, 157, 158, 164, 165, 173, 219, 256, 257, 264, 268, 272, 274, 278, 281, 287
  carrying of, 143, 164
  condemned, 37, 63, 95, 102, 151, 274, 276, 278, 280, 281, 286, 287
  East India, 29, 30, 143
  examination of, 140, 147
  exported, 135, 147
  foreign, 38, 147n, 170, 256, 264
  forfeited, 102, 278, 280, 288
  imported, 32, 38, 86, 94, 136, 228, 258, 265, 280
  landing of, 62, 91, 126, 135, 138, 140, 141, 149, 191, 266
  reëxportation of, 134, 256
  sale of, 258, 278, 282, 286
  seizure of, 94, 270, 274, 279
  shipping of, 126, 135, 145, 147, 149, 191, 256
  smuggled, 83, 86, 97, 115, 183, 255, 271
  storing of, 143, 151, 164
  unclaimed, 278, 281
  unladed, 138, 140, 143, 164, 254
  unrated, 29, 30, 152
  warehousing of, 62, 140
  weighing of, 62, 138, 140, 141, 143, 144, 164
Grand Receipt, 134
Gratuities, 99, 108, 140, 145, 148, 150, 151, 153, 161, 163, 215, 221, 235, 255
Gravesend, 124, 146, 148, 157, 158, 160, 166, 245, 260
  Station, 160
Great Britain, 117, 119, 153
Great Statute of Charles II, 26
Greenland, 122, 259
Greenland Fishery Trade, 163
Greenwich Hospital, 41
Grindstone, 193
Grocers, 124n

Guernsey, 93, 170
Guilford, Earl of, 131
Gun powder, 147n
Guns, 178
Gweek, 169n

H

Hambro' Boats, 160
Harbors, 169
Harnage, 71n
Harwich, 21, 22, 169n
Hatch, 234
Hauling, 165
Head-ports, 167, 168, 212
 definition of, 167
 jurisdiction of, 169
Henry IV, 11, 212
Henry VI, 5, 45, 276
Henry VIII, 122
Herring, 193
Hinterland, the, 122
Holidays, Customs, 126, 222–223
Homeward Bound Stations, 157, 160
Hooper, Commissioner, 68n, 201
Horses, 160, 280
 condemned, 283
House-keeper, 76–78, 132, 133
Hull, 15n, 169n, 192, 193, 200, 206n, 217, 228
 collector of, 241
Husband of the Four-and-a-half Per Cent in London, 156

I

Importation, 62, 63, 135, 230, 231, 243, 247, 256, 262, 263, 264, 274
 procedure at, 245ff., 269, 290
Importations, fraudulent, *see* Frauds, Smuggling, Trade, illicit
Importation, tobacco, 245ff.
Import business, offices for, 132, 133–134, 136, 137–145, 157–166, 173
Import duties, 2, 133, 136, 140, 150, 257
Import trade, 173
Importers, 141, 248, 252, 274
Imports, 2, 5, 7, 8, 11, 25, 32, 34, 36, 63, 85, 116, 123, 125, 133, 135, 136, 137
 regulation of, 33
 value of, 123, 192

Imposts, 27, 36
 see Duties
Impressment, 43, 44, 181, 233
Imprest, Auditor of the, 101
Imprests, 100n, 103, 134, 217
Incidental officers, 198
Incidents, 145, 219, 235
Indenture of Appraisement, 98, 278, 279
 see Writ of Appraisement
Index Vectigalium, 26
Industry, 1, 67, 194
Inspector-General of Imports and Exports, 3, 116, 117, 118, 119, 122, 135, 192
 accounts of, 123
Inspector of the Delivery of Unrated East Indian Goods, 152
Inspector of Exchequer Books in the Outports, 107, 108, 111, 112, 119
Inspector of Manufactured Tobacco for Exportation, 154
Inspector of Officers' Conduct, 116
Inspector of the Outport Collectors' Accounts and Vouchers, 107, 108, 111, 112, 119, 216
Inspector of Prosecutions, 97, 98, 119, 280, 289
Inspector of Ships in the Whale and Herring Fisheries, 163
Inspector of the Tobacco Ground, 155
Inspector of the River, 161, 162, 163
Insurance, 122
Inverness, survey of, 190n
Ipswich, 21, 123
Ireland, 259, 262, 276
 coast of, 262
 trade of, 195
Iron, 38n
Isle of Dogs, 124
Isle of Man, 170
Isle of Thanet, 123
Italy, 165n, 259
 trade of, 122

J

Jackson, Edward, 9
James I, 6
Jerque book, 228
Jerquers, 137, 138, 139, 141, 142, 152, 159, 206, 221, 225, 254, 260
Jerquing, 235
Jersey, 93, 170

INDEX 313

Journals, 185, 189, 190, 228
  examination of, 227
  officers', 181, 182, 183, 184
Jury service, 59
Justices of the peace, 91, 186, 233, 277, 280

K

Kelly, Mrs. Bridget, 77–78
Kent, 93, 169
Key, John, 202
King, the, 5, 7
King's Chamberlain, 5
King's Lynn, 208
King's Remembrancer, 168
"King's Tobacco Pipe," 127
King's-waiters, 12n, 13, 15, 16n, 17, 21, 141, 145, 166, 235
King's warehouse, 143, 150, 151, 152, 198
King's warrants, 156

L

Labor, 1
Labrador Whale Fisheries, 163
Lading, ships', 147, 148, 259ff.
Lancashire, 193
Lancaster, 170, 206n
Land-carriage, 265, 267, 268
  men, 164
Land-guards, 140, 176, 178, 182, 183, 185, 186, 239
Landing, 132, 140, 156
  fraudulent, 158, 254
  see Bribery, Frauds, Smuggling, Trade, illicit
Land-surveyors, 141, 142, 143, 144, 145, 173, 196, 206n, 207, 227n, 228, 235, 250, 255, 273
Land-waiters, 11, 12, 138, 140, 141, 142, 143, 144, 145, 152, 153, 154, 158, 159, 173, 189, 196, 202, 205n, 206, 209, 210, 225, 228, 229n, 230, 247, 248, 250, 252, 253, 254, 255
Law business, 64, 90–91, 92–99, 118, 119, 120
Lawns, 33
Laws, 53, 90, 91
  customs, 34, 65
  new, 188
  trade, 60, 85
Leases, 170–171

Leather, exported, 136
Leeward Islands, 156
Leghorn Vessels, 160
Legislation, 51, 84, 132
Leigh, 16n, 168n
Letters of Marque, 232
Letters patent, 195
Lighterage, 252n
Lightermen, 164, 198
Lighters, 125, 126n, 128, 144, 158, 164, 252, 253
Lighthouses, 40
Lime, 266n
Linen, 67n, 265
Liquors, 86, 126
  excisable, 278, 281
Lisle, 202
Liverpool, 15, 38n, 67n, 170, 171, 192, 193, 206n, 229n
  First Earl of, 131
  population of, 193
  shipping of, 193
Loans, war, 1
Lockers, 152, 153, 154, 156, 157
London, 13n, 14n, 15, 16n, 17, 20, 21, 22n, 23, 31, 33, 40, 41n, 57, 61, 62, 63, 65, 66n, 71, 74, 75, 76, 83, 99, 100, 102, 104, 106, 107, 109, 112, 113, 114, 115, 116, 117, 122, 123, 129, 133, 147n, 148, 149, 150, 151, 153, 155, 156, 157, 160, 161, 162, 163, 164, 167, 168, 173, 174, 175, 176, 186, 187, 189, 191, 193, 195, 198, 201, 204, 206, 216, 221, 223, 227, 236, 238, 245, 247, 251, 264, 265, 266, 267, 273, 281, 283, 285, 289, 290
London Bridge, 123, 124, 125, 142, 246
London Custom House Library, 293f.
Long Parliament, 6
Long Room, the, 23, 68n, 75, 76, 128–130, 131, 132ff., 145, 151, 221, 222, 223, 246, 247, 248, 249, 257, 258, 282
Lower Stations, 142
Lowndes, 201
Lug-sail, 177
Lumber, 38n, 67n
"Lumpers," 124n
Lyme Regis, 202
Lynn, 192, 206n

M

Magistrates, 42, 61, 168, 186
Mahogany, 67n

Mails, the, 90
Malago, 91
Maldon, Jonas, 16n, 169n
Malt, 149, 193
Man, 93
Manchester, Duke of, 23, 120n, 131
Mann, Sir Horatio, 14n, 131n
Manufactures, 1, 2, 3, 47n, 193, 243, 257, 264
    foreign, 264
    Lancashire, 193
    Yorkshire, 193
Manuscripts, 293ff.
Margate, 123, 157, 245
Margerum, John, 21, 22
Markets, foreign, 256
Marque, letters of, 232
Maryland, 244
Masters, 62, 130, 133
    see Ships, Vessels
Mates, 179
Member-port, 167, 168, 212
Memorials, 54, 71, 75
Men-of-war, 88
Mercantile policy, 2
Mercantile system, 3, 4, 4n, 243, 244, 256, 264, 269
Merchantmen, 157
Merchants, 3, 5, 10, 17, 27, 29, 30, 31, 32, 33, 34, 35, 38n, 39, 45, 47n, 51, 53, 61, 65, 66, 75, 90, 100, 114, 126, 127, 129, 130, 132, 134, 135, 139, 141, 145, 146, 147, 154, 164, 165, 168, 171, 176, 191, 193, 194, 205, 209, 212, 213, 214, 222, 223, 226, 229, 240, 246, 248, 249, 250, 252, 253, 254, 255, 256, 257, 258, 259, 260, 261, 262, 265, 267, 268, 274, 275
    allowances to, 62
    complaints of, 125
    deposits of, 101
    exporting, 258
    Liverpool, 67n
    London, 67n, 122, 126n, 192n, 214n, 247
    notes of, 174
    petitions of, 62
    securities of, 136
Money, 160, 189
Middle Station, 142
Ministers, foreign, 51
Minute Clerk, 70, 102
Mulcts, 105, 106, 142, 241

Musgrave, Sir William, 14n, 15, 17, 18n, 24n, 29n, 205
Muslins, 147n
    duties on, 67n

N

National bank, the, 122
Navigation Acts, the, 3, 4, 38n, 39, 91, 117, 163, 243, 244, 247, 256
    enforcement of, 37, 40, 91
Navigation Laws, 58
Navy, the, 205, 272
Navy Board, 43n
Naze, the, 123
"New," the, 160
Newcastle, 193, 206n, 208
Newcastle, Duke of, 68n, 131
Newfoundland, 259
Noli prosequi, 51, 64
North Britain, 100, 153
Northern Clerk, 69, 70, 71, 73, 74
Northern ports, 115, 116
North Europe, ports of, 138
North Foreland, 123
North, Lord, 49n
Norway, 271
Notes, 10c

O

Officers, customs, *see* Customs officers
Offices, customs, *see* Customs offices
Office Station, 158
Old Customs, 216
    see Duties
Old Subsidy, 250
    see Duties
Order in Council, 42, 79, 286
Orders, Book of, 228
Orientals, 130
Ostend, 169, 262
Outport plantation bonds, 63
Outport Receiver of Fines and Forfeitures, 103, 104
Outports, the, 8n, 9, 12, 13, 14, 21, 31, 36, 41, 42n, 57, 59n, 61, 63, 65, 74, 99, 104, 107, 108, 109, 112, 116, 117, 122, 123, 149, 153, 155, 161, 162, 163, 164, 167ff., 171, 173, 174, 176, 180n, 183, 185, 186, 191, 192, 193, 194, 195, 201,

INDEX

Outports (*continued*)
  210, 214n, 217, 221, 227, 228, 239, 246n, 251, 273, 281, 283
  accounts of, 107, 111, 112, 117
  administration of, 170, 174, 176, 192
  controller of, 40, 44, 106, 107, 110, 153, 173, 180, 209n, 235n
  corruption in, 192
  definition of, 167
  officers of, 32, 75, 98, 113, 219
  offices of, 24, 25
  personnel of, 173f.
  problems of, 174
  proceeds of, 107, 174, 284
  smuggling in, *see* Smuggling
  surveys of, 114, 173, 187
Outward Bound Station, 157, 160
Oxford, 30
Oysters, 33

P

Packet-boats, 43, 81, 90
Paper, duties on, 27, 28n
Parliament, 1, 7, 24, 28, 35n, 46, 47n, 52, 59n, 61, 66, 67, 81n, 84, 85, 92, 96, 107, 110, 117, 132, 168, 203, 212, 219, 235, 261, 266, 277
  acts of, 228
Parliamentary Papers, 298–299
Patent, 50n, 120, 131, 156
Patent controller, 11, 21, 200n
  see also Controller
Patent customer, 11
  see also Customer
Patentees, 6, 11, 13n, 14, 15n, 16, 17, 18, 20, 22, 23n, 24, 40, 76, 131, 195, 200
  deputies to, 50; *see* Deputies
Patent King's-waiters, 145
  see also King's-waiters
Patent officers, 8, 12, 13, 14, 15, 16, 19, 20, 21, 22, 23, 24, 25, 30, 108, 133, 135, 137, 139n, 148, 167, 211, 212
  see also Customs officers, Patentees
Patent offices, 11, 12n, 19, 24n, 25, 78, 97, 134, 140, 195, 203, 204, 212, 290
  see also Customs offices
Patent searcher, 11, 17, 146, 148, 166
  see also Searcher
Patronage, 50, 120, 195–204, 225–226, 290

Pay-master of Incidents, 102, 103, 216
Paymasters, 92
Peace of Ryswick, 130
Peerage, British, 131
Pelham, 9, 131n
Penalties, 48, 276, 290
  smuggling, 288
Pensions, 27n, 106, 156, 236, 237
Penzance, 170, 184
Pepper, 152, 262
Perjury, 246
Personnel, 51, 61, 65, 66, 68, 69, 78, 81, 119, 195ff.
  administration of, 62, 64–65, 92, 112–116, 120, 227–228
  inefficiency in, 211, 228ff., 242, 290
  outport, 173f.
  see Customs officers
Petitions, 51, 52, 53, 61, 62, 65n, 71, 73, 78, 83
Petition clerk, 70
Petty Customs, duties under, 134
Piazza Men, 160
Pictures, duty on, 26n
Pilferage, 124, 127, 144, 148, 155, 159
  see Frauds
Pimento, 38n
Pitt, 2, 3, 31, 209
Plague, the, 41
Plantation and Wine Duties, 134
Plantation business, 40, 69–70
Plantation Clerk, 69
Plantation duties, 27
Plantation letters, 73, 74n
Plantations, the, 57, 65n, 66n, 85, 86n, 93, 138, 247, 256
  bond in, 246
  commodities of, 256
  tobacco of, 244–245
  see Tobacco
Plantation trade, 194, 228
Planters, 244
Plunderage, 124, 125
Plymouth, 12n, 49n, 168, 170, 206, 218
  controller of, 22
Pool of London, 140, 245, 252
Portage, 41, 62, 65, 138, 159, 252n, 254
Portage bills, 63n, 100
Porters, 165, 198
Port-gauger, 40
Port of London, 99, 107, 115, 120, 122ff., 173, 190, 222, 235n, 260
  see London

INDEX

Ports, 2, 3, 5, 6, 7, 8, 10, 11, 12n, 15n, 16, 17, 18, 19, 35, 38, 41, 42, 43, 49n, 63, 64, 66, 69n, 75, 83, 89, 92, 98, 100, 102, 108, 111, 113, 114, 116, 118, 123, 138, 168, 170, 173, 174, 179, 186, 190, 192, 196, 206, 207, 212, 221, 224, 244, 245, 256, 258, 260, 264, 268, 277
  added, 169
  Baltic, 165n
  books of, 7, 8, 9
  collector of, 117, 151, 174
  condition of, 78
  Continental, 169, 261
  Eastern, 193
  Flemish, 169
  French, 169
  head-, 12, 167–168
  inspection of, 227
  island, 169
  jurisdiction of, 170
  limits of, 169
  list of, 168n–169n
  member-, 12, 167–168
  Northern, 93, 96
  Plantation, 38
  quays of, 124, 125
  receipts from, 92
  Southern, 194
  survey of, 49, 63, 114, 190
  Western, 69, 170, 194
Portugal, 259
Post-entries, 253
Postmaster-General, 90
Poulton, 169n
Poundage, 25, 26, 98, 99, 104, 105, 108, 150, 151, 285
Preferable Men, 144, 145
Preston, Thomas, 169n, 209
Primage, 252n
Prisage, 40
Privateers, 43n, 89
Privy Council, the, 5, 36, 42, 46, 52, 56n, 66, 68, 73, 74, 79, 80, 82, 86, 93, 95, 117
  orders of, 59, 63, 81
Privy seal, 156
Prizes, 89, 143n
Promotions, 51, 64, 65, 211, 240
Property, private, rights of, 272
Prosecutions, 90–91, 92ff., 118, 119–120, 275ff., 285–286, 288
Public Record Office, 294f.
Pulham, Francis, 21

Q

Quarantine, 37, 42, 59n, 65, 81, 219
  enforcement of, 41, 80
Quays, 126, 127, 140, 142, 143, 144, 149, 150, 154, 157, 161, 162, 164, 168, 172, 193, 215, 222, 245, 246, 248, 252, 253, 255, 259
  extension of, 126n
  inspection of, 132
  lawful, 145, 245
  legal, 125, 126, 127
  London, 126
  patrolling of, 158
  port, 124, 125
  reforms of, 127
Quay Station, 158
Queen's Bench, 24
Queen's Remembrancer, 8

R

Rates, Book of, 25, 26
Raw materials, 1, 2, 38
Receipts, customs, 111, 176, 243, 244, 289
  outport, 174
  remittance of, 176
Receiver-General, 60, 74, 95, 99, 100, 101, 102, 106, 107, 109, 112, 119, 120, 133, 150, 156, 167, 175, 187, 216, 249, 251, 258, 267, 271
  Scottish, 100
  Supervisor of, 101ff.
Receiver of Fines and Forfeitures for London, 102, 103, 104, 105, 106, 107, 119, 151, 197n, 284
Receiver of Fines and Forfeitures for the Outports, 102, 103, 104, 105, 284
Receiver of the Money for the Superannuation Fund, 102, 105, 106, 120
Receiver of the Plantation Duties, 249, 251
Receivers, 102, 105, 106, 134, 135, 136, 248, 250
Reëxportation, 31, 38, 244, 256, 257, 262
Reference, order of, 76
Reform, customs system, 3, 145, 195
  see also Customs, Customs System
Register-General of Tobacco, 153, 154, 235

INDEX

Register-General of Trading Ships, 117, 118, 119, 247
Register of Certificate Cockets, 137, 138, 139
Register of Cockets, 260
  see also Cockets
Register of Seizures, 98, 119, 275, 278, 289
Register of Ships, 118
Register of the Tide-waiters, 158
Register of Watermen, 158, 163
Register of Warrants, 135, 139, 165
Remittances, 176
  delays in, 229
  outport, 174, 175
Rents, 170–171, 220
Restoration, the, 8n, 196n, 212
Revenue, the, 4, 9, 14, 16, 23, 24, 26, 31, 32, 34, 35, 37, 49, 50, 51, 54, 61, 65, 66, 78, 80n, 85, 99, 139n, 141, 146, 173, 178, 179, 186, 202, 204, 205, 207, 209, 210, 211, 213, 217, 221, 224, 228, 229, 243, 244, 246, 256, 260, 270, 285, 289
  collection of, 6, 25, 37, 40, 44, 57, 173, 186, 202, 290
  customs, 5, 27n, 67n, 107, 157
  drawback system and, 263
  duties for, 3
  England's, 192
  increases in, 243
  laws, 25, 86n, 132
  loss to, 30, 37, 192
  national, 45
  need for, 26
  officers of, 41, 249, 271
  outport, 174
  protection of, 142, 239, 272
  receipt of, 92, 264
  records of, 63
  remittance of, 186
  security of, 17
  sources of, 2
  system, 25
Revolution, American, 43n
Rewards, 51, 65, 235, 236
Rice, 272
Riding officers, 88, 115, 164, 169, 177, 180, 182, 183, 185, 206
  duties of, 182-183
  stations of, 190
Riding supervisors:
  duties of, 182-183
  stations of, 190

Riding surveyors, 182, 183
River Inspectors, 144, 158, 273
Robbers, 124
"Rolling," 239
Royal letters patent, 195
Rum, 232, 262, 280, 281
Rummage, 254
Rummage, see Smugglers
Running, see Smuggling
Rye, 245

S

St. Ives, 49n, 169n
Salaries, 13, 14, 17, 23, 24, 48, 50–51, 64–65, 66n, 93, 98, 99, 100, 103, 105, 106, 108, 111, 115n, 140, 145, 148, 150, 151, 153, 156, 157, 163, 164, 178, 179, 213, 215, 216, 217, 218, 219, 221, 226, 235, 288, 290
Sales, 104, 105, 283, 284, 286
  London, 282, 284
  produce of, 106
Salt, 149, 193
  duties on, 57, 86n
Salt office, the, 199n, 272
Salvage, 43
Sandwich, 12n, 123, 157
Saxby, 31n
Scotland, 15n, 32, 56, 57, 149, 168n, 182
  Customs Board of, 56
  ships of, 117
Sea-damage, to cargoes, 125
Seamen, 41, 43–44, see also Impressment
Search, 271-273
Searchers, 5, 6, 11, 12, 13, 14, 16, 18, 21, 22n, 24, 143, 145, 146, 147, 148, 153, 154, 167, 173, 183, 195, 206, 212, 222, 258, 259, 260, 261
Secondary works, 300ff.
Secretaries, 70, 71, 74, 81, 82, 83, 84
  business of, 69
Secretaries of State, 81–84
Secretary, Customs Commissions, 67–69, 70, 273
Securities, 112, 216
  of merchants, 136
Seizures, 37, 51, 60, 81, 87n, 88, 90, 92, 93, 94, 95, 96, 97, 98, 102n, 105, 153, 157, 169, 178, 180, 182n, 183, 186, 189, 219, 233, 234, 235, 240, 270, 271, 272, 274, 275, 277, 278, 280, 281, 282, 283, 284, 285, 286, 287, 288

318 INDEX

Seizures (*continued*)
  accounts of, 104, 274
  book of, 228
  causes of, 271
  circumstances of, 280
  collusive, 286
  delivery of, 275
  outport, 281
  procedure with respect to, 233, 270ff.
  proceeds of, 179, 271, 275, 284
  prosecution of, 63, 275ff.; see Prosecutions
  regulation of, 271ff.
  rewards in, 236
  sales of, 278–279, 281–284, 286
  shares of, 64, 182, 287–288
  significance of, 271
  unwarranted, 273, 275
Severn, the, 193
Shelburne, 14n, 15, 17, 24n
Sheriffs, 91
Shipping, 1, 2, 11, 36, 40, 50, 58, 70, 122, 123, 213, 222, 261
  account of, 116, 120
  coastwise, 264
  colonial, 85
  customs procedure in, 243ff.
  delayed, 124, 127
  foreign, 116, 167
  management of, 62–63
  outport, 173
  register of, 228
  warrant for, 258
Ships, 38, 40, 42, 43, 62, 69, 70, 80, 81, 88, 123, 133, 138, 140, 145, 157, 161
  accounts of, 118
  British, 32, 38, 118
  burden of, 246
  burned, 127
  clearing of, 158, 254
  coastwise, 117
  crews of, 39
  delivery of, 141
  entries of, 132, 135
  foreign, 118
  French, 82
  incoming, 124
  lading of, 146, 147; see Lading
  number of, 190
  prize, 43n
  registration of, 117

Ships (*continued*)
  searching of, 60, 271ff.
  trading, 117
  unlading of, 124; see Unlading
  voyages of, 118
  see also Vessels
Ship's Entry Book, 248
Ship's Entry Book Outwards, 257
Short-Traders, 160
Silk, 38n, 262, 264, 265
Sinecures, 4, 7ff., 78, 98, 102, 108, 112, 115, 118, 119, 120, 139–140, 148, 165, 166, 226n, 290, 291
Sinking Fund, 27
Skins, 38n
Skippers, 128, 130
Sloop-masters, 183
Sloops, 65, 157, 162, 176, 177, 178, 182n, 190, 245
Smacks, 177
Smith, Adam, 2
Smugglers, 82, 83, 89n, 90, 161, 164, 169, 177, 178, 180, 181, 182, 183, 185, 230, 232, 233, 234, 235, 236, 238, 240, 286
  brandy, 231, 232
  French, 231
  organizations of, 186, 231
  Scottish, 182
  tobacco, *see* Smuggling
  wine, 232, 234
Smuggling, 36, 37, 51, 56n, 65, 78, 80n, 81, 82, 86, 88, 90, 91, 97, 170, 174, 182, 183, 185, 188, 190, 191, 213, 217, 224, 230, 231, 255, 264, 271, 273, 289n, 290
  prevention of, 49, 64, 176ff., 182ff., 285ff.
  tobacco, 152–153, 169–170, 255, 261–262
  see also Frauds, Trade, illicit
Soap-making, 155
Soldiers, 89, 90, 105, 287
Solicitor-General, 91, 276, 289
Solicitor of Bonds, 96n
Solicitor of Coast Bonds, 10, 265
Solicitors, 74, 75, 76, 93, 95, 96, 97, 98, 99, 100, 102n, 106, 120, 132, 149, 168, 235, 273, 275, 277, 278, 279, 285, 289
  duties of, 94ff.
Sources, 297ff.
South Carolina, 67n, 126n
South Sea Fund, 27

INDEX

Southwark, 164
Spain, 165n, 259, 261
Spices, 26n, 145
Spirits, 277, 282
Stanley, 71n
Stanwell, Lord, 131n
Staples, 264
State Papers Domestic, 81, 295
Stations, 143, 149, 157, 245, 287
Statistics, 122
Stevens, Robert, 21, 22
Stiles, 48n, 65n
Stock-jobbers, 129n
Stockton on Tees, 17
Stone, 154
Stowell, Lord, 131
Subsidies, 27, 35, 257
Substitution, 271
Sufferances, 149, 265, 266
Sufferance wharf, 124, 125, 126n, 127, 145, 215
Sugar, 38n, 124n, 143, 156, 265
   sales of, 156
   warehousing of, 263n
Sunderland, 208
   officers, 172
Superannuation Fund, 64, 102, 105, 106, 119, 196n, 216, 236, 237
Supervisor of the Receiver-General's Receipts and Payments, 101, 102, 107, 109n, 119, 120, 251
Surveyor-General, 115, 119, 131, 137, 139, 165, 248, 250, 258
Surveyors-General, 113–114, 183, 187, 189–190, 227
Surveyor of the Act of Navigation, 163
Surveyor for the Building and Repairing of Sloops and Boats, 162, 163
Surveyor of the Coast-waiters, 149
Surveyor of the Controlling Searchers, 147
Surveyor of Baggage, 143n
Surveyor of the Outport Accounts, 107, 108, 111, 112, 119
Surveyor of Paper, 143n
Surveyor of the Port of London, 131, 137, 139, 248, 250, 258
Surveyor of the Quays, 143
Surveyor of the Searchers, 146, 148
Surveyor of Sloops, 163
Surveyor of Subsidies and Petty Customs in the Port of London, 131, 165

Surveyor of the Warehouse, 151
Surveyors, 13n, 33, 108, 137, 152, 162, 173, 188, 190, 191, 205n, 206, 255, 273
   special, 143, 155
Surveys:
   of ports, 114, 190, 191
   Scottish, 190n
Suspension, 241, 288
Sussex, 93, 169

T

Tallard, Count, 130
Tally Court, 251
Tar, 33
Tare, 33, 138, 141, 142
Taxes, *see* Duties
Tea, 86, 152, 170n, 232, 278, 282
   duty on, 36
   seizure of, 277, 281
"Teller's Bill," 251
Teller's Office, 251
Tenure, 7, 171
Thames, the, 124, 125, 127, 128, 157, 161, 245
Ticket Porters, 165n
Tidesmen, 203, 205
Tide-surveyor, 16, 144, 157, 158, 159, 160, 161, 173, 206n, 227n, 245, 254, 273
Tide-waiters, 138, 148, 157, 158, 159, 160, 161, 173, 198, 199n, 201, 204, 206, 218n, 220, 228, 235n, 236, 237, 238, 245, 252, 253, 254, 255, 260, 272
Tobacco, 38n, 127, 143, 152, 153, 155, 160, 199n, 216n, 243, 244ff., 252, 253, 254, 255, 257, 260, 262, 265, 266, 278, 282
   accounts of, 154
   ash of, 155
   Bill of 1751, 52, 153, 263
   bonds, 100
   Burning Ground, 127, 154, 155, 162, 163
   burning of, 155
   customs history of, 155f.
   condemned, 282
   cut, 258n
   damaged, 155, 261
   drawbacks on, 244
   duties on, 36, 155, 156, 244, 249, 256

Tobacco (*continued*)
  enumerated, 246
  excise on, 156
  exported, 153, 257ff.
  importance of, 244–245
  imported, 153, 155, 192, 245ff.
  land-carriage of, 267
  landing of, 154, 255
  loaded, 259
  manufactured, 154
  office, 152, 153–155
  produce of, 244
  reëxportation of, 257, 265
  seizure of, 154, 277, 281; *see* Seizures
  storage of, 263
  trade, 152–156, 243–245; *see* Frauds, Smuggling
  warehousing of, 263n
Tonnage, 25, 26, 40, 117, 118, 123, 163, 178, 190
Tonnage and Poundage Act, 25, 30, 221
Tower Bridge, 125, 142, 150, 246
Trade, 3, 35, 39, 53, 58, 61, 85, 86n, 92, 116, 117, 122, 126, 132, 171, 190, 192, 208, 243, 244, 246, 255, 263, 266, 270
  accounts of, 116, 118, 120
  Acts of, 94
  African, 122
  American, 193
  balance of, 1, 3, 116, 117
  Board of, *see* Board of Trade
  Bristol, 193
  carrying, 40, 118
  coast, 190, 194, 264ff.
  colonial, 3, 64, 85, 221
  Continental, 194
  decentralization of, 122, 191
  East India, 122
  French, 194
  Greenland, 122
  illicit, 36, 64, 82, 83, 88, 90, 113n, 153, 169, 170n, 174, 183, 191, 192, 207, 270, 285, 286, 289, 290
  see also Bribery, Frauds, Smuggling
  increase in, 146n, 290
  Irish, 193, 194
  laws on, 26, 37, 60, 85
  outport, 192, 193
  plantation, 117, 194, 228
  policy, 1, 2, 45, 61, 67n, 264
  Scandinavian, 194

Trade (*continued*)
  tendencies in, 122–123
  West Indian, 193
  tobacco, *see* Tobacco
Trade and Plantations, Committee of Council on, 79, 80n
Traders, 239, 262
Trading companies, foreign, 122
Transires, 268
Transportation, 288
Treasurer, Lord High, 5, 45, 46, 195, 202
Treasury, the, 1, 2, 7, 9, 14, 22n, 23, 24, 25, 31n, 46, 47, 48, 49n, 50, 51, 52, 53, 56, 57, 61, 65, 66, 67, 68, 71, 72n, 73, 74, 79, 81n, 84, 87, 90, 91, 92, 95, 101, 109, 114, 117, 132, 147n, 175, 176, 192, 197, 198, 199, 200, 201, 202, 204, 205, 210, 211, 212, 214n, 217, 225, 226, 238, 243, 251, 270n, 272, 276, 285, 287, 289
  authority of, 45, 56
  Central, 106, 120
  see also Treasury, Treasury Board
  orders of, 54, 59, 63, 79
  papers of, 54
  policy of, 55
  Secretary of, 82
  solicitor of, 94
  warrants of, 42, 48, 50n, 51, 54, 60, 64, 79n, 102, 110, 140, 143, 157, 196, 197, 202
  see also Treasury Board, Treasury, Lords of the
Treasury Board, 22, 45, 46, 48, 50, 51, 52, 54, 55, 64, 68, 79, 80n, 89, 196, 207, 209, 223, 291
  power of, 49
  supervision of, 225
  see also Treasury, Treasury, Lords of the
Treasury Books and Papers, 90, 294
Treasury, Lords of the, 5, 6, 9, 15, 16, 18, 20, 21, 28, 34, 35, 36, 37, 38n, 39, 41, 43n, 45, 46, 47, 48, 49, 50, 51, 52, 54, 55, 60, 61, 64, 65, 66, 79, 81, 84, 85, 86, 89, 90n, 91, 101, 113, 116, 124n, 126n, 139n, 168, 170, 195, 196, 197, 199, 200, 201, 202, 211, 215, 219, 225, 226, 229, 239n, 263, 276, 278
Trinity House, 40
Tripoli, 28n
Troneur, 5
Turkey, 157, 160, 165n

INDEX

U

Under-Patent Searcher, 166
United Branches, 216
Unlading, 124, 140, 141, 173, 252ff.
Upper Station, 142
Usher of the Long Room, 132, 133, 135, 139, 165, 166

V

Vessels, 133, 138, 157, 162, 163, 229, 230, 246, 257, 259, 261
  armed, 231
  building of, 163
  contract for, 179
  danger to, 124
  discharged, 159
  entries of, 135
  increase in, 123
  inward, 124
  maintenance of, 178
  register of, 141
  revenue from, 232
  smuggling, 190; see Smuggling
  tonnage of, 163
  unloading of, 252ff.
  see also Ships
Victualing, 148, 178, 179
Viewer, 155
Vinegar, 216n
Virginia, 244

W

Wagons, 165
Wales, 93, 162, 260
Walpole, 1
Walpole's Excise Bill, 263
War, 3, 37, 81, 89, 267
War Department, 90n, 186
  see Secretary at War, Soldiers
Warehouse-keeper, 102, 104, 106, 151, 152, 156, 157, 173, 225, 273, 274, 281, 283, 284
Warehouse rent, 252n
Warehouses, 43, 124, 127, 128, 144, 150, 157, 158, 164, 254, 255, 262, 273, 274, 278, 282, 283, 289

Warehouses (continued)
  East India, 152
  excise, 263
  personnel of, 140
  sugar in, 156
  system of, 127, 256
  tobacco, 154
Warehousing, 152, 156, 283
  Act of 1803, 127, 264
  system of, 245, 256, 257, 262–264
Warrant Chairmen, 52, 73
Warrants:
  clerk of the, 134
  dormant, 27n, 28n, 215
  merchants', 27, 140–141, 248, 249, 259, 260, 267
  Register of, 135
  special, 198
  system of, 48
Warrington, 38n
War, Secretary at, 82, 89
  see War Department, Soldiers
Wastage, 262
Watch-houses, 240
Watchmen, 136, 144, 145, 158, 161
Water-carriage, 265
Water-guard, 42, 140, 148, 161, 162, 163, 176, 177, 178, 182, 186, 206, 239
Watermen, 129n, 158, 161, 206, 218n, 230, 235n, 236, 237, 238
Waterside officers, 145, 230
Wealth, 3, 122
Weigher, 5, 143, 144, 145, 147, 151, 154, 206, 230, 235n, 236, 252, 253, 255
Weighers in Fee, 143–144, 145
Weighing, 156, 165, 173, 253–254, 255, 271
Wells, 169n
Western Clerk, 69, 70, 73, 74
Western ports, 115, 116
  see also Ports
West Indies, 15, 67n
Westminster, 164
Weymouth, 162, 217
Whalebone, 34n
Whalefins, 38n
Wharfage, 252n
Wharfingers, 127, 129n, 164
Wharves, 140, 245
Wheat, 33
Whitehaven, 170, 192, 206n
William III, 2, 3, 26, 58, 59n, 84n, 215
Wilson, John, 17

Wine Branch, 137
Wines, 33, 40n, 49n, 149, 160, 216n
    duty on, 25, 192n
    French, 32, 170, 188n
    officer of, 138
    seizure of, 277
    smuggling of, 169, 234
    storage of, 263
Wine Taster, 33
Wisbech, 169n
Wood, William, 9, 68
Woodbridge, 169n
Wool, 264
    export of, 1, 136, 182

Wren, Christopher, 128
Writ of Appraisement, 94, 277, 278, 279
    see also Indenture of Appraisement
Writ of Delivery, 278, 280, 283
Wye, the, 193

Y

Yarmouth, 169n, 174, 193, 206n, 216, 233
York coast, 266n
Yorkshire, 193

(1)